THE RETRIEVAL OF ETHICS

The Retrieval of Ethics

TALBOT BREWER

OXFORD
UNIVERSITY PRESS

OXFORD
UNIVERSITY PRESS

Great Clarendon Street, Oxford OX2 6DP

Oxford University Press is a department of the University of Oxford.
It furthers the University's objective of excellence in research, scholarship,
and education by publishing worldwide in

Oxford New York

Auckland Cape Town Dar es Salaam Hong Kong Karachi
Kuala Lumpur Madrid Melbourne Mexico City Nairobi
New Delhi Shanghai Taipei Toronto

With offices in

Argentina Austria Brazil Chile Czech Republic France Greece
Guatemala Hungary Italy Japan Poland Portugal Singapore
South Korea Switzerland Thailand Turkey Ukraine Vietnam

Oxford is a registered trade mark of Oxford University Press
in the UK and in certain other countries

Published in the United States
by Oxford University Press Inc., New York

© Talbot Brewer 2009

The moral rights of the author have been asserted
Database right Oxford University Press (maker)

First published 2009

British Library Cataloguing in Publication Data

Data available

Library of Congress Cataloging-in-Publication Data
Brewer, Talbot.
The retrieval of ethics / Talbot Brewer.
p. cm.
Many ideas presented at graduate seminars, audiences at various
universities and colleges, and various conferences.
Includes bibliographical references and index.
ISBN 978-0-19-955788-2 (alk. paper)
1. Ethics. I. Title.
BJ1012.B675 2009
170—dc22
2009013840

Typeset by Laserwords Private Limited, Chennai, India
Printed in Great Britain
on acid-free paper by the
MPG Books Group, Bodmin and King's Lynn

ISBN 978-0-19-955788-2

1 3 5 7 9 10 8 6 4 2

Acknowledgments

While I wrote the bulk of this book in 2006 and 2007, the main ideas took form quite slowly. The first seeds were planted more than a decade ago, during my last years as a graduate student at Harvard. Those years would not have been nearly as fruitful if it were not for the help and guidance of Tim Scanlon, whom I regard as the Platonic ideal of a philosophy teacher: someone who combines enormous philosophical gifts with the solicitude and self-restraint to help others give birth to their own ideas. I also learned a great deal during my years at Harvard from Stanley Cavell, Christine Korsgaard, Dick Moran, Fred Neuhouser, and Gisela Striker.

Professors have relatively little control over where they are employed, so I view it as a great piece of luck that I ended up in the University of Virginia Department of Philosophy, where I have received support, encouragement, and very helpful philosophical input from a number of colleagues, including especially Jim Cargile, Dan Devereux, Loren Lomasky (probably the only person in the world who has read everything I've written, and certainly the only one who has done so and is still asking for more), John Marshall, Trenton Merricks, Jorge Secada, Becky Stangl (who wrote a thorough and extremely insightful set of comments on the entire manuscript), and the late and sorely missed Bill Diggs. I have also enjoyed and benefited from frequent conversations with other thinkers in the U.Va. community, including Colin Bird, Matt Crawford, Kevin Hart, Claire Lyu, and Chuck Mathewes (who incited my interest in Gregory of Nyssa, and helped me to deepen my understanding of Augustine). I am thankful, too, for the support and intellectual stimulation that I have found at U.Va.'s Institute for Advanced Studies in Culture, where I have been a Faculty Fellow for the past six years.

I have presented many of the ideas in this book in graduate seminars, and my graduate students have prodded me to refine and deepen them. It would take several pages to list all of the students from whose suggestions and comments I have benefited, but I am especially grateful to Ayca Boylu, Chris Collins, Adam Kadlac, and Ty Landrum for the extraordinary philosophical insight they have brought to our discussions. Similar thanks are due to Professor Nancy Schauber of the University of Richmond Philosophy Department, who has attended several of my seminars over the years and has taught me a great deal.

The rise of modern communications technology has created a global philo-sophical village, and I have benefited from repeated virtual conversations with many of its residents. Among these, I am especially indebted to Timothy Chap-pell of the Open University, UK, whose thorough and insightful commentary on the manuscript has made this book far better than it otherwise would have been. But I have received invaluable help and encouragement from many others, including Barbara Herman, Steve Darwall, Carlos Pereda, Brad Hooker, Martha Nussbaum, Maggie Little, Nancy Sherman, Henry Richardson, Tamar Schapiro, Bennett Helm, Sergio Tenenbaum, Justin D'Arms, Dan Jacobsen, Ruth Chang, Elijah Millgram, Gene Mills, Tobias Hoffman, and George Rudebusch. Still others have helped me without knowing who I was or that they were helping me. Among these I count Alasdair MacIntyre and Raimond Gaita.

Certain key ideas and arguments from this book have been presented to audiences at Johns Hopkins University, Georgetown University, McGill University, the Center for Social Philosophy and Policy at Bowling Green State University, Virginia Commonwealth University, Franklin and Marshall College, Virginia Tech, the National Autonomous University of Mexico, the American University in Beirut, the British Society for Ethical Theory, the Values and Virtues Conference at the University of Dundee in Scotland, the Bled Conference on Rationality, the annual meetings of the American Philosophy Association and the Virginia Philosophy Association, and two Kant Conferences at the University of San Diego and the University of Navarra in Pamplona. I thank the audiences at these events for their helpful comments and criticisms.

Precursors of several portions of this book have been published elsewhere. Chapters 1 and 2 grew out of a shorter piece called "Three Dogmas of Desire" that appeared in a volume entitled *Values and Virtues*, edited by Timothy Chappell and published by Oxford University Press in 2007. Portions of Chapter 4 grew out of a much shorter essay on pleasure entitled "Savoring Time: Desire, Pleasure, and Wholehearted Activity" that appeared in the June 2003 issue of the journal *Ethical Theory and Moral Practice*. Some of the material in Chapter 6 was included in an essay entitled "Is Welfare an Independent Good?" that appeared in the Winter 2009 edition of *Social Philosophy and Policy*. The arguments in the last section of Chapter 6 descend from an essay entitled "The Real Problem with Internalism about Reasons," published by the *Canadian Journal of Philosophy* in December of 2002. An earlier version of Chapter 7 was published in the July 2005 edition of *Ethics* under the title "Virtues We Can Share: A Reading of Aristotle's Ethics." I thank the original publishers for having granted permission to include descendants of these essays in this book.

Finally I thank my children, Ben and Ethan, and my wife Saphira Baker, for the constant encouragement and good humor they have shown me even during those times when I was too thoroughly absorbed in the ideas of this book to be good company.

Contents

Introduction

...it is not profitable for us at present to do moral philosophy; that should be laid aside at any rate until we have an adequate philosophy of psychology, in which we are conspicuously lacking.

(Elizabeth Anscombe)[1]

...in so far as modern ethics tends to constitute a sort of Newspeak which makes certain values non-expressible, the reasons for this are to be sought in current philosophy of mind and in the fascinating power of a certain picture of the soul. One suspects that philosophy of mind has not in fact been performing the task... of sorting and classifying fundamental moral issues; it has rather been imposing upon us a particular value judgment in the guise of a theory of human nature. Whether philosophy can ever do anything else is a question we shall have to consider. But in so far as modern philosophers profess to be analytic and neutral any failure to be so deserves comment. And an attempt to produce, if not a comprehensive analysis, at least a rival soul-picture which covers a greater or a different territory should make new places for philosophical reflection.

(Iris Murdoch)[2]

THE SHORT HAPPY LIFE OF RADICAL VIRTUE ETHICS

Philosophy could be characterized with only a bit of irony as what is left if you begin with the sum total of human thought and subtract those areas in which clear progress has been made. Matters are even less encouraging when it comes to philosophical ethics. The history of ethics looks like a story of progress only if its main texts are read in reverse chronological order. In some respects the past half-century of ethical theorizing counts as an exception, but it is the sort of exception that proves the rule. During this time the dominant trend has been to seek deeper

[1] Elizabeth Anscombe, "Modern Moral Philosophy," first published in the journal *Philosophy* in 1958, can be found in *The Collected Philosophical Papers of G.E.M. Anscombe, Volume Three: Ethics, Religion and Politics* (Oxford: Basil Blackwell, 1981), 26–42; quote from 26.

[2] Iris Murdoch, "The Idea of Perfection," in *The Sovereignty of Good* (London: Routledge and Kegan Paul, 1970), 1–44. The quote is found in the essay's third paragraph.

understanding by retreating further and further into the history of Western thought. A field that at mid-century had all but renounced any pretension to speak substantively about matters of value proceeded to reclaim nineteenth-century Millian utilitarianism in the 1960s, eighteenth-century Kantianism in the 1970s, Aristotelian virtue ethics beginning in the 1980s, and a decidedly Platonist brand of realism in the 1990s. We might expect Heraclitus next if his thinking were the sort that could conceivably be revisited.

The deepest philosophical ethics is written with one eye on the past and the other on the contemporary world. Yet as practitioners have delved into a past that is increasingly remote, both chronologically and culturally, large questions have opened concerning the degree of consonance between our contemporary philosophical preoccupations and those of the figures from whom inspiration is sought. Enthusiasts of the movement that has come to be called "virtue ethics" can usefully be divided in accordance with their implicit stance on this matter. While most virtue ethicists trace their views to the Ancients (usually to Aristotle, less commonly to Plato), some regard Ancient texts as a source of fresh answers to established questions in philosophical ethics, while others find in them a vantage point from which these questions themselves can be put in question.

The pioneers of contemporary virtue ethics fall decisively into the latter camp. The two texts that are most widely cited as the starting points and the inspiration for the movement are Elizabeth Anscombe's "Modern Moral Philosophy" and Alasdair MacIntyre's *After Virtue*.[3] Both Anscombe and MacIntyre emphasize the fundamental *strangeness*, to modern ears, of the basic concepts through which Aristotle and other Ancient and Medieval thinkers framed their inquiries into the virtues and the human good. With characteristic wit and precision, Anscombe writes that someone who draws the ideas of Aristotle directly into contemporary philosophical discussions about morality "must be very imperceptible if he doesn't constantly feel like someone whose jaws have somehow got out of alignment."[4]

This conceptual misalignment is not, in Anscombe's view, a benign marker of cultural change. She regards it as the form taken within a not-so-isolated "Ivory Tower" of a quiet calamity in Western Culture—one that has torn our ethical concepts adrift from the surrounding beliefs and practices which once gave them their point, thereby preparing the way for arbitrary and corrupting uses of the vestigial ethical concepts remaining to us. In Anscombe's view, we have no hope of clearing away our confusions until we have done a great deal of preparatory work in philosophical psychology—work that contests and refigures contemporary notions of practical deliberation, intention, desire, choice, and

---

[3] Alasdair MacIntyre, *After Virtue: A Study in Moral Theory* (Notre Dame: University of Notre Dame Press, 1981).

[4] Anscombe, "Modern Moral Philosophy," 26.

action.[5] In the meantime, she avers, "it is not profitable for us . . . to do moral philosophy."[6]

MacIntyre picks up these themes right at the outset of *After Virtue*, where he asks his readers to imagine a group of people who live in the wake of a near apocalyptic, civilization-destroying disaster and who spend their time tinkering with scientific lab equipment whose proper use has been forgotten, or puzzling over fragments of obscure science texts. MacIntyre forwards the "disquieting suggestion" that our relation to the language of the virtues is just like the relation of these would-be scientists to the language of modern physics.[7] While we go on speaking of the virtues as if we understood their nature and significance, "those contexts which would be needed to make sense of what [we] are doing have been lost, perhaps irretrievably."[8] Yet our ethical inarticulacy and disorientation cut closer to the bone than would the loss of the modern sciences. We are inarticulate in the face of questions that cannot be left to specialists, questions that are basic and unshirkable markers of the human condition, questions such as how we ought to live our lives and what we ought ideally to be like. MacIntyre's view—both announced and enacted in *After Virtue*—is that if we are to recover depth and coherence in our thought about the human good, we must first strive to recover a sense of the cultural and intellectual history whose fragmentary conceptual remains provide us with our only resources for framing a livable conception of the good life. This is largely a matter of recovering a richer sense of practical thought and the activities springing from it. More particularly, it is a matter of retrieving a lost framework of practical thinking that permits us to engage in unimpeded activity, that unifies our lives rather than scattering our passing moments into discrete fragments, and that reinvigorates rather than shrivels our inherited stock of practices and traditions.

MacIntyre's book was published in 1981. Since its publication, and to a great degree because of its publication, there has been a flood of new work on the ethical virtues and an almost equally voluminous surge of virtue-theoretic work in epistemology. However, as it has climbed to a position of prominence within Anglo-American philosophy departments, virtue ethics has retreated to an increasingly conventional conception of its central message. If one re-reads the works of Anscombe and MacIntyre today then turns directly to one of the many new readers in virtue ethics, one cannot help but notice the virtual disappearance of the movement's *despair* over the fallen state of our culture, its *distress* over the

---

[5] Anscombe makes this claim in "Modern Moral Philosophy," 26, and manifests her commitment to this philosophical project in many other works—perhaps most obviously in her short, elegantly argued, and deservedly influential book *Intention* (Cambridge: Harvard University Press, 2000; first published by Basil Blackwell in 1957).

[6] Anscombe, "Modern Moral Philosophy," 26.　　[7] MacIntyre, *After Virtue*, chapter 1.

[8] MacIntyre, *After Virtue*, 1.

inarticulacy of contemporary moral philosophy and the inaptness of the field's guiding questions, and its call for *radical* reform in modes of ethical thinking in the academy and beyond. Virtue ethics is now commonly portrayed as one of a number of competing theoretical accounts of our moral concerns rather than as a frontal assault on the coherence, articulacy, or vitality of those concerns. This "normalization" of virtue ethics manifests itself in a particularly bald form in the first pages of Rosalind Hursthouse's *On Virtue Ethics*, one of the most prominent virtue-theoretic works of the past decade. Here is Hursthouse's brief history of contemporary virtue ethics:

> Up until about thirty years ago, normative ethics was dominated by just two theories: deontology, which took its inspiration from the eighteenth-century philosopher Immanuel Kant, and utilitarianism, which derives, in its modern incarnations, from the eighteenth and nineteenth-century philosophers Jeremy Bentham and J. S. Mill . . . Gradually, a change was observable. In some books designed as undergraduate texts in normative ethics, various articles critical of the prevailing orthodoxy were cited as calling for a recognition of the importance of the virtues, and a few paragraphs on 'what a virtue ethicist would say' inserted. At first, the mentions tended to be short and dismissive. Virtue ethics was regarded not as a third approach in its own right, but as emphasizing a few interesting points—such as the motives and character of moral agents—that deontologists and utilitarians could usefully incorporate into their approaches. Then, as more articles were written in its defence, it acquired the status of 'the new kid on the block'—yet to establish its right to run with the big boys, but not to be dismissed out of hand. And now in the latest collections (as I write, in 1998), it has acquired full status, recognized as a rival to deontological and utilitarian approaches, as interestingly and challengingly different from either as they are from each other.[9]

Contemporary ethical theory is here pictured as a well-defined discipline of thought—one whose central questions and problems are agreed upon by all parties to what can be called, in virtue of this very agreement, "*the* debate." The virtue ethics movement has succeeded in the sense that it has now joined this debate as a fully enfranchised participant whose theoretical account of morality deserves a good hearing, alongside the rival accounts offered by the deontologist and the consequentialist.

Whatever may have been incorporated as a full-fledged participant in ongoing debates about ethics, it can't have been the fundamental dissatisfactions with contemporary moral thought voiced by Anscombe and MacIntyre. MacIntyre's disquieting suggestion was not that there might be another interestingly different approach to the central questions of moral philosophy. Like Anscombe before him, MacIntyre put forward the rather more stunning suggestion that a great deal of what our culture and its philosophers have been saying about how humans ought to live has the status of arbitrary venting of untutored feelings, and that this is not a timeless fact about value-talk but an idiosyncratic fact about the

---

[9] Rosalind Hursthouse, *On Virtue Ethics* (Oxford: Oxford University Press, 1999), 1–2.

cultural condition of the post-Enlightenment Western World. MacIntyre went so far as to claim that contemporary non-cognitivism—which diagnoses talk of value, or at least of moral value, as mere expression of subjective sentiment—is true if taken as a piece of empirical anthropology. As MacIntyre sees it, our talk of morality and of the good life has degenerated into the mere venting of feelings of approval and disapproval. Such talk does not rise even to the level of opinion-mongering, since one must have a definite grip on the meanings of one's words in order to express anything as definite as an opinion. Yet MacIntyre sees this as a contingent fate to be lamented and combated, and not as the timeless insight into the nature of value talk that non-cognitivists take it to be.

The selected passage from Hursthouse's book is not an isolated case. It epitomizes a widely accepted understanding of the place of virtue ethics in contemporary philosophy. It is the view affirmed by Gregory Trianosky in an anthologized article entitled "What Is Virtue Ethics All About?" where he portrays virtue ethics both as emerging from Anscombe's "Modern Moral Philosophy" and as offering a theory of right action that differs from the other main contenders—utilitarianism and deontology—in that it explicates right action in terms of more basic claims about virtuous character traits.[10] Trianosky does not take up the question of how a movement offering a distinctive theory of morally right action could possibly have been inaugurated by an essay calling for a moratorium on moral philosophy and urging the elimination rather than the analysis of talk about moral rightness and wrongness.[11] Gary Watson at least notices this tension in his own anthologized essay on the rise of virtue ethics, but he proceeds to sketch the field of play in moral philosophy as a confrontation between those who explicate the right without invoking a more basic notion of the good (deontologists), those who explicate the right in terms of good consequences (consequentialists) and those who explicate the right in terms of good character (virtue ethicists). He places Anscombe in this last category while admitting that this is "a stretch."[12] Offhand this seems somewhat worse than what would ordinarily be called a "stretch," since it categorizes Anscombe's view by making ineliminable use of a term whose elimination she urges, thereby effectively placing her view on a conceptual map that in her view ought to be discarded. Yet this curious refusal to take Anscombe at her word is repeated quite self-consciously by Robert Louden in his own widely anthologized reflections on the nature and shortcomings of virtue ethics. Louden argues that we ought not

[10] Gregory Trianosky, "What Is Virtue Ethics All About?" *American Philosophical Quarterly* 27 (October 1990), 335–44, see especially 336–8; anthologized in Daniel Statman, ed., *Virtue Ethics: A Critical Reader* (Washington DC: Georgetown University Press, 1997 and Edinburgh: University of Edinburgh Press, 1997).

[11] Anscombe, "Modern Moral Philosophy," 33.

[12] Gary Watson, "On the Primacy of Character," in *Identity, Character and Morality*, Owen Flanagan and Amelie Rorty, eds. (Cambridge: The MIT Press, 1990), 449–69, see especially 450–2; anthologized in Statman, ed., *Virtue Ethics: A Critical Reader*.

to read Anscombe literally because we could not sensibly "attempt to do moral theory" if we jettisoned the concept of moral duty. Somehow it escapes Louden's attention that Anscombe explicitly tells her readers that the inquiry currently unfolding under the name of moral theory rests upon infirm foundations and that they should cease and desist from it.[13]

It is worth pausing over the fact that so many prominent philosophers feel compelled to place Anscombe's view within the field of inquiry whose basic terms and conditions she plainly rejects. Why should this way of construing Ancient discussions of ethics have so relentless an appeal? Part of the answer is that the reigning understanding of the field's proper subject matter is stabilized by its coherence with broader cultural convictions concerning moral rightness and wrongness. Philosophical ethics is widely thought to consist in an inquiry into the nature, source, and content of moral reasons for action, including those overriding reasons we call duties or obligations. This putative class of reasons is often distinguished by contrast with reasons of self-interest. Moral reasons are thought to apply to us whether or not acting on them would serve our interests or further our own good. Indeed, they are thought to place an authoritative limit on the pursuit of our own good—a limit that serves at least in part to guarantee that others will have the elbow room, and perhaps the resources, to advance their own good. If we demarcate the subject in this rather common way, we will have made it very nearly impossible to retrieve the characteristic Greek notion that virtuous actions are essential constituents of the life that is best for those who perform them, and that the value of the virtues can be traced to this fact. At the same time, we will have prepared the way for the contemporary liberal dogma that a full array of standards of rightness can be articulated and defended without reference to any concrete or controversial conception of the human good, and indeed that it must be articulated in this way since otherwise its content and authority could not be appreciated by adherents to a wide array of conflicting religious or philosophical conceptions of the human good.

This liberal ethos makes itself felt in the contemporary academy under the guise of a prevailing sense of academic decorum. It is regarded as mildly embarrassing to forward substantive conceptions of the human good under the

---

[13] Louden writes: "On the Anscombe model, strong, irreducible duty and obligation notions drop out of the picture, and are to be replaced by vices such as unchasteness and untruthfulness. But are we to take the assertion literally, and actually attempt to do moral theory without any concept of duty whatsoever? On my reading, Anscombe is not really proposing that we entirely disposed of moral oughts." The retrievable core of her proposal, Louden goes on to say, is that "the concept of the moral ought" should be "explicated in terms of what the good person would do." This prepares the way, in by-now-familiar terms, for slotting virtue ethics into the field of competing conceptions of morality, each distinguished by which of the field's main concepts it takes to be fundamental. See Robert Louden, "On Some Vices of Virtue Ethics," first published in *American Philosophical Quarterly* 21 (1984), 227–36. Reprinted in Statman, ed., *Virtue Ethics: A Critical Reader* (quote from 181 of that volume) and in Roger Crisp and Michael Slote, eds., *Virtue Ethics* (Oxford: Oxford University Press, 1997), 201–16.

banner of philosophy—embarrassing not merely to the philosopher forwarding the conception but to the field as a whole. Good taste, along with a sound grip on what could and what could not possibly form the subject of a genuine academic expertise, requires that one stay clear of the topic of the good life, or restrict oneself to one-size-fits-all theories that do not disqualify any particular cultural tradition as a possible avenue to the good life. This is the model followed, for instance, by those utilitarian theorists who reduce the human good to pleasures no matter what their source, or to the satisfaction of preferences or desires no matter what their content. Yet on full reflection, these "one-size-fits-all" conceptions of the good life cannot be affirmed as sources of meaningful guidance for our life choices and activities. Few would agree that pleasure would make their lives go better if it were taken in the gratuitous torturing of small children, or that such malevolent activities conduce to the good of those who desire to engage in them. These conceptions of the good life are preludes to nihilism, not proper guides for the enhancement of some purely personal form of human flourishing—or so it will be argued in the pages ahead.

Aristotelian ethics is an affront to this prevailing understanding of the proper ambitions and limits of philosophical ethics. It offers a sweeping and controversial conception of the human good, and presents answers to questions about justice as an inseparable element of this conception of the good. This is one aspect of the conceptual misalignment that Anscombe observed in those who attempt to present Aristotelianism as one among the contending theoretical stances on "*the* debate" about ethics, and it is one explanation for the hydraulic pressure to "normalize" Aristotelianism by construing it in this way. This pressure takes a specific, institutionally mediated form within the colleges and universities where most contemporary philosophers make their living. It is confusing in the extreme to introduce undergraduates to philosophical thought in ethics by exposing them to a set of fundamentally conflicting views concerning how best to understand the main questions and concerns of the field itself. It is confusing, in other words, to teach a fundamentally reflexive subject matter—one that is perpetually concerned with the proper specification of its own focal preoccupations. It is far easier to present normative ethics to undergraduates in the form of a survey course—one that begins with a characterization of a well-defined field of questions and proceeds to set out and assess a series of competing answers to these questions. It helps if the field's basic concerns can readily be recognized by newcomers as concerns that are already familiar, already theirs. This self-presentation staves off questions of legitimacy and relevance that would undoubtedly arise if professors were to call in question the conceptual framework of the background culture's conversation about morality. It is far easier to convince students of the relevance of a course that engages with, and attempts to answer, questions that already have a powerful grip on their imagination and that already structure their daily deliberations. These institutional pressures conduce to the normalization of virtue ethics.

PHILOSOPHICAL PSYCHOLOGY AS ETHICS
AND AS CULTURAL CRITICISM

The main concern of this book is not to explain the normalization of the initially radical philosophical movement launched by the works of Anscombe and MacIntyre, but to develop and extend some of the more radical themes sounded in these works. One such theme, central to Anscombe's work, is that we ought to lay aside direct engagement with ethics until we have seen our way to a more coherent "philosophical psychology." This is where the current volume begins: with a far-reaching reconsideration of the notions of the nature and sources of human agency, and particularly of the way in which practical thinking gives shape to activities, relationships, and lives. This reconsideration is meant to raise fundamental doubts about the adequacy and/or the coherence of familiar ways of thinking about philosophical ethics, and to put in place, one by one, the elements of a more tenable conceptual framework for the field.

This extended discussion of the nature and sources of human agency is also meant to contest the usual understanding of the relationship between philosophical psychology and ethics. It is relatively standard practice in contemporary philosophy for basic ideas about agency and action to be presented as an ethically innocent prelude to ethical theory—that is, as a philosophical psychology or action theory that can serve as a value-neutral framework for adjudicating philosophical disputes about ethics. However, a close inspection of these views often reveals that they are by no means ethically neutral. The views that are most prominent in contemporary philosophy are a case in point. On inspection, they turn out to be integral elements of a substantive vision of the point or value of human action—a vision that is both results-oriented and anti-contemplative. I hope to convince the reader that unless we contest this vision, and begin to put another one in place, we will remain unable to make optimal sense of our efforts to unify our lives around a tenable conception of how best to live them, or of the yearnings that draw us to our ideals and to each other.

On reflection, it is hard to see how our attempts to understand the nature of action and agency could possibly be disentangled from our attempt to understand what might make an action choiceworthy or what it might mean to say that an agent acted sensibly. After all, when we try to make sense of a bit of behavior as an action, what we are trying to do is to uncover what the agent saw in the performance such that it made sense for him to engage in it. This interpretive task cannot so much as begin unless we presuppose some picture or another of what might sensibly be thought to confer value upon our doings. It seems, then, that Anscombe went subtly astray in suggesting that we can *postpone* ethical theory while doing philosophical psychology. We are already engaged in substantive ethical theory when we attempt to get clear on the nature of agency and action. Murdoch shows a more incisive feel for the conceptual terrain when she suggests that the "soul-pictures" on offer in the philosophy of mind and philosophy of action are already ethical, and that this might be an inescapable feature of any philosophical picture of the self (to use a word that I find a bit more comfortable, if a bit less evocative, than Murdoch's 'soul'). One way to describe the aim of this book is to sculpt an alternative picture of the self—a picture with recognizably MacIntyrean and Murdochian (which is to say, Aristotelian and Platonic) overtones—and to put that picture to work in elaborating a somewhat unfamiliar yet appealing conception of human flourishing and of the place of ethical concern for others in a life well-lived. The hope is to open what Murdoch calls "new places for philosophical reflection" and to show how our lives and our proper aspirations begin to make more sense when we reflect about them within these newly opened vantage points.

The critical bite of this book is directed, from the outset, at various elements of a picture of agency, practical thought, and action that is prevalent among contemporary Anglo-American philosophers. This, however, does not mean that the book's scope is limited to the critique of a small circle of philosophers. There is reason to think that the ascendant philosophical conception of agency is a marker of our place and time, and that it brings to articulacy a conception of the self that plays a fundamental though usually unarticulated role in shaping contemporary Western Culture. This is precisely what one would expect from a philosophical world that is still more than a bit embarrassed by those who forward substantive philosophical conceptions of the good life (rather than, for example, of the bounds of justice or morality within which competing conceptions of the good life can justly be pursued), and that feels fully certain of its authority only when attempting to restrict itself to the ethically neutral analysis and regimentation of received evaluative concepts. Such a method is well-suited to bringing out internal paradoxes and contradictions in a given domain of discourse. Yet it tends to generate theories of agency and allied ethical theories that systematize and entrench—rather than, say, identify and contest—the background culture's reigning prejudices. If the fixed ideas of contemporary philosophy are indeed the clearer and more articulate mirrors of some of the most basic fixed ideas of contemporary Western Culture, this greatly magnifies the excitement of subjecting them to critical examination. Such an examination might help us to discern and to put in question some of the most fundamental elements of the conceptual framework through which we attempt to make sense of our lives. The hope of this work, then, is not merely to open up new places for reflection by professional philosophers, but to open up new vistas for reflection about certain fixed ideas and grounding prejudices of the post-Enlightenment West.

The book returns repeatedly to the history of Western Philosophy because this history provides a treasure trove of rival conceptions of the self and its tasks in life, each set out with exemplary articulacy. The hope is that by drawing from these works, it might be possible to retrieve the conceptual scaffolding of a compelling alternative picture of the human self, its distinctive capacities, and its proper aspirations and concerns. To the extent that this book realizes this hope, it might be called a work in self-retrieval and not merely in the retrieval of a certain half-lost framework for thinking about ethics. I speak here of self-retrieval and not merely of re-description because the self is not the sort of entity that can be expected to remain still while the philosopher redraws its portrait. It is itself its own portrayer and its portrait of itself plays a consequential role in giving shape to its mode of thinking and acting. In this domain, one cannot easily distinguish between self-description and self-formation. One of the proper activities of the self is to arrive at a conception of its defining capacity for agency in light of which it can impart a sensible shape to its own deeds, and with respect to which it can understand how those deeds add up over time to a properly human life. What a given self can be, what it can make of itself and its life, is acutely dependent upon its conception of its nature as an agent—on its sense, for instance, of what might conceivably serve it as an end capable of guiding its actions, or how its thoughts can make themselves practical by surging forth in deeds. This formative activity need not involve anything that would commonly be called philosophy; it is the sort of thing that occurs in the course of a normal upbringing, and it can occur without focused and explicit reflection. Yet it can be done philosophically. Insofar as philosophical ethics seeks to extend and refine this everyday task, it ceases to be mere armchair inquiry and becomes a self-formative activity in its own right. Put another way, it ceases to be "mere theory"—where theory is misleadingly understood via an implicit contrast with practice—and becomes an intensified form of a vital life activity.

If we think of ethical philosophy in this way, we gain further insight into the significance of the fact that as a field it makes so little progress. It is not the sort of activity that could yield findings that could be learned by future generations so as to spare them the trouble of engaging in the activity for themselves. The reason is that ethical philosophy consists in a focused effort to examine one's own concerns, bring them to articulacy, and see whether they stand up to reflective scrutiny. This is not the sort of thing that one can do for another, any more than one can do another's thinking or loving or living. Of course, a growing stock of philosophical theses and arguments could be and indeed has been accumulated, and these might help future generations by bequeathing to them a wide range of thoughts that they might fruitfully consider and by giving them a sense of what it is to engage actively and fruitfully in philosophical ethics. Yet an arm's-length relation to these theses and arguments would not yet be a philosophical engagement with them. Until one rolls up one's sleeves and begins writing critical responses in the margins, or arguing with oneself as one falls to sleep and continuing the argument when one wakes up in the morning, one is not yet philosophizing. If philosophy is an intrinsically valuable and potentially focal activity rather than a communicable expertise, then perhaps we should not be greatly troubled by the field's lack of progress, just as we are not greatly troubled by lack of progress in friendship or sex or art. Preoccupations for the health of the field might fruitfully be directed to the question whether the practice is surviving in a vital and uncorrupted form rather than to the question whether our mode of engagement is adding to a stock of settled findings or insights that can be handed to the next generation.

1

Contesting the World-Making Prejudice

I hear from afar the clamors of that false wisdom which incessantly projects us outside of ourselves, which always counts the present for nothing, and which, pursuing without respite a future that retreats in proportion as we advance, by dint of transporting us where we are not, transports us where we shall never be.

(Jean-Jacques Rousseau)[1]

ANCIENT AND MODERN CONCEPTIONS OF AGENCY

Contemporary philosophers have for the most part come to agree on a particular, historically distinctive conception of the nature and point of human action. On the ascendant view, all actions borrow their intelligibility as actions, and their meaning or point in the eyes of their agents, from the states of affairs that they are calculated to bring about. Actions that are chosen for their own sake are not viewed as exceptions but as limiting cases: they are motivated by the desire or intention to bring it about that they occur. On this view, action is at heart a technique for remaking the world so that it answers to the agent's intentions or desires. It is a species of production. To make sense of someone's bodily motions as agency rather than mere thrashings about, it suffices to identify a possible state of affairs that these bodily motions can intelligibly be interpreted as an attempt to bring about.

This world-making conception of agency represents a fundamental break with an earlier tradition of thought about human activity, its motivational sources, and its point. This earlier conception can be traced back to Plato and Aristotle, and variations of it are affirmed by a long series of late Hellenistic and Medieval philosophers and theologians in both the Platonist and Aristotelian traditions of thought. On this conception, to view a bodily motion as intentional activity is to trace it to some intelligible conception of what it is good or fitting for human beings to do or to be. To complete this interpretive task, it is neither necessary nor sufficient to identify a state of affairs that the bodily motions in

---

[1] Jean-Jacques Rousseau, *Emile: Or, On Education*, translated and introduced by Allan Bloom (New York: Basic Books, 1979), 79.

question can be seen as calculated to produce. It is not sufficient, since we must also catch at least a glimmer of the evaluative outlook through which that state of affairs could show up for the agent as in some way good or worthwhile. Nor is it always necessary, since some actions are valuable in themselves rather than in virtue of their expected products, and these cannot be shoe-horned into the production-centered paradigm without serious distortion.

The ascendant production-oriented conception of human agency is deeply flawed, and the path to a more adequate conception of the source and point of human action lies in the retrieval of certain key elements of the tradition of thought that it has replaced. What is central to this tradition of thought is that apprehensions of the good can motivate us even when we are not able to identify an achievable state of affairs that would represent the full realization of the good by which we are guided. We must appreciate the conception of motivation that informs this tradition of thought if we are to appreciate Aristotle's insights into the value of unimpeded activity and the role of the virtues in sustaining and completing such activities.

The question at hand is a large one: Why do human beings do what they do? The philosopher cannot hope to make headway with this question if it is understood as a request for a generic causal explanation of the events that we call human actions. If the question is understood in this way, there is no guarantee that the answer will provide us with an understanding of what agents see in their actions such that they regard them as worth performing. A plausible answer might be cast entirely in terms of neuron firings and consequent muscle movements, without any mention of appearances of reasons or value. Such an explanation might not itself make clear what distinguishes actions from garden-variety events. Actions, after all, seem to be events with a special sort of provenance—events produced by a conscious being out of a sense that they are in some way worth performing.

In this book, the question at hand will be understood in a second, quite different way. It will be understood as a request for insight into what human beings must see in their doings if these doings are to be intelligible as actions. The "why" question in play here does not concern causation but justification. This is the sort of question that one encounters, for instance, when one does something injurious to a loved one and is asked by that loved one, "Why in the world did you do that?" It would be an evasion of this "why" question to provide a comprehensive account of the neuron firings and muscle contractions that sent one's body into the objectionable motion. The question at hand is what possessed one to think that the injurious action was an acceptable thing to do. When we ask the "why" question in this spirit, we are in search of the sort of explanation that uncovers how the action showed up for the agent as worth performing.

This second sort of explanation is sometimes called a "rationalizing explanation," not because its availability guarantees that the action was the most rational thing to do, but simply because it uncovers the agent's rationale for the action. That is, it displays the action as the product of the agent's (possibly quite bad) practical thinking. If we find such an explanation, we will have thereby succeeded in making the behavior intelligible as the agent's doing rather than merely as an event that set his body into motion, on all fours with a twitch or a sneeze. Hence, views about what counts as a rationalizing explanation are, at the same time, views about the nature of agency and action.

In contemporary Anglo-American philosophy, the world-making conception of agency has been captured and perpetuated by three interwoven and mutually supporting theses about desires—where the term 'desire' is used in a broad sense to encompass the various motivational sources of human actions. The first of these rather technical theses is that desires are attitudes towards propositions. The second is that desires are distinguished from other propositional attitudes by the typical or proper direction of fit between the world and the desirer's mind (or, more exactly, the propositional object of the desire). The third is that we can formulate a rationalizing explanation of any action by tracing it to a belief/desire pair consisting in a belief that the action will bring the world into conformity with some proposition and a desire that takes the same proposition as its object. I call these three theses the *dogmas of desire*. It is no accident that many contemporary philosophers have come to see these three theses as obvious. They are the philosophically tidy version of the above-mentioned idea that there is a point in acting only insofar as this promises to remake the world in accordance with our desires. Since this world-centric and pragmatic conception of the point of action has a firm grip on contemporary Western culture, it is no surprise that it surfaces both in popular beliefs about desire and in the philosophical analyses of desire that take their bearings from these popular beliefs.

The dogmas of desire are often presented as elements of an ethically innocent philosophical psychology that can serve as a neutral framework for philosophical debates about ethics. On close inspection, however, it turns out that the dogmas of desire are integral elements of a substantive vision of ethics—a vision at once worldly, progressive, and anti-contemplative. Moreover, this substantive vision of ethics is one that cannot make optimal sense of our depth, of the intelligibility of our life quests, or of the yearnings that draw us to our ideals, and to each other. To the extent that this vision has a hold not only on contemporary philosophy but on contemporary culture, this ought to be regarded not as a mere idiosyncrasy of our times but as a cultural calamity.

It is a truism that desires figure in the explanation of much if not all of what we do. However, this is not yet a very informative thesis, for there are daunting philosophical puzzles concerning what desires could possibly be such that they are suited to play a central role in explaining the rise of that curious class of events we call actions. If the ascendant philosophical conception of desire were true, then attributions of desires would be wholly unsuited to play the central role that they are commonly believed to play in explaining what people do. We could not bring bodily motions into view as the doings of agents merely by citing a desire.

In framing an alternative to this conception of agency and action, we do well to take guidance from an alternative tradition of thought about desire and its role in the genesis of action. This tradition, which is discussed explicitly in Chapter 2, has roots in the works of Plato and Aristotle, and can be traced through the writings of Plotinus, Gregory of Nyssa, Augustine, and Aquinas. According to this tradition of thought, a desire is an intimation of a concrete instance (or possible or apparent instance) of some kind of goodness or value. Such intimations incite efforts both to gain a clearer understanding of the goodness in question and to respond in some appropriate way to that goodness. What counts as an appropriate response will turn out to be a complicated matter, but it will not always be an action calculated to bring about the goodness in question. According to this tradition of thought, the object of a desire need not be a propositionally specifiable state of affairs, nor is it essential to desire that one be inclined to bring the world into correspondence with the representation that gives the desire its specific content. On the contrary, it might well make sense to adjust the desire's representational content—insofar as one can—so as to bring it into line with whatever evaluative facts there might be. Nor is it true that all actions will have their genesis in desire.

Both of the above-sketched conceptions of human agency are teleological in the sense that they put forward a standard of rational intelligibility that bodily motions must display if they are to count as human activities. One way to characterize the difference between them is that the contemporary conception attempts to limit itself to a formal standard of rationality—one that could be displayed no matter what one's ends happen to be. By contrast, we cannot wield the more traditional conception without presupposing some notion of what can and cannot intelligibly be seen as good. If we think of the difference in this way, we might be inclined to welcome the modern view as a marker of increasing toleration. By the same token, if we are driven on reflection to conclude that the view cannot make good sense of our actions or our lives, we might come to view it as a misguided over-extension of the modern ideal of toleration.

Another way to characterize the difference is that the contemporary conception attempts to make sense of agents without assigning evaluative representations to them, while the more traditional conception requires that we assign such representations to others as a condition of understanding them as agents, hence as a condition for viewing them as leading recognizably human lives. If we think of the difference in this way, we can think of the modern view as an accommodation to the narrowly naturalistic, value-denuded ontology encouraged by the rise of the modern sciences. From the perspective of this ontology, the traditional view can appear to imply that we can count as agents only if we have and act on strictly illusory representations. Again, if the contemporary view fails to hold water, then this will appear not as a proper accommodation of the insights of natural science but as a misguided over-extension of them.

THREE DOGMAS OF DESIRE

The first dogma of desire, again, is that desires are propositional attitudes. On this view, the real intentional object of any desire is a proposition, and the desire itself is a particular kind of attitude towards that proposition.[2] What might be called the "representational content" of the desire—that is, the mental representation of the object of the desire that makes the desire the particular desire that it is—is exhaustively constituted by the proposition towards which one takes the desiring attitude. Some desires wear their propositional structure on their sleeves. For instance, my current desire that you find this essay illuminating relates me, the desirer, to the proposition "You find this essay illuminating." To claim that desires are propositional attitudes is to commit oneself to the claim that any desire can be expressed fully, without distortion or loss, as a desire that thus-and-such. Here is a representative affirmation of this first dogma, drawn from Wayne Sumner's influential book on welfare:

That desires have objects is, of course, scarcely news; this much is ensured by the fact that *every desire is for something or other.* In the surface grammar of desire, these objects are often literally things, as when I want this book or that car. Sometimes, however, they are activities (I want to go to France) or states of affairs (I want the weather to be good for our wedding). It is a simple trick to homogenize all these ostensibly different kinds of objects into states of affairs: to want the book is to want to own it or read it, and to want to do something is to want the state of affairs which consists of your doing it. It is then a further simple trick to turn these states of affairs into propositions: to want the state of affairs which consists of my owning the book is to want the proposition 'I own this book' to be true. By this process of transformation, every desire comes to take some proposition as its intentional object.[3]

If we accept the first dogma of desire and agree that desires are always attitudes towards propositions, we must ask what the relevant attitude might be. The second dogma is supposed to answer this question. It tells us that one has the

---

 [2] See for example Michael Smith, *The Moral Problem* (Oxford: Blackwell Publishing Company, 1994), 107; Mark Platts, "Moral Reality and the End of Desire," in *Reference, Truth and Reality* (New York: Routledge and Kegan Paul, 1981), 74–7; L. W. Sumner, *Welfare, Happiness and Ethics* (Oxford: Oxford University Press, 1996), 124; Robert Brandom, *Making It Explicit* (Cambridge, MA: Harvard University Press, 1994), 5; and David Velleman, *The Possibility of Practical Reason* (Oxford: Oxford University Press, 2000), 24 and 182. A more tentative endorsement is found in G. F. Schueler, *Desire: Its Role in Practical Reason and the Explanation of Action* (Cambridge, MA: MIT Press, 1995), 12.

 [3] Sumner, *Welfare, Happiness and Ethics*, 124.

relevant attitude towards a proposition when one is disposed to act on the world in ways calculated to make the proposition true.[4]

This second dogma has implications for how we are to understand the first dogma. It implies that one can take a desiring attitude only towards those propositions that specify a future state of affairs that one might conceivably seek to promote through one's actions. This provides us with a way of distinguishing the attitude of desire from mere wishes: if we cannot imagine acting in a way that would help to bring about some state of affairs, then we might perhaps wish that the state of affairs obtained but we cannot be said to desire it. For instance, many people wish for a different past, but it is hard to make sense of a desire for a different past.

This conception of desires fits neatly together with a corollary picture of another important kind of propositional attitude: belief. A belief is an attitude towards a proposition that typically is adjusted, and at any rate ought to be adjusted, in the face of evidence that the world does not correspond to the proposition. It is true, of course, that such adjustments are not always made. However, if one lacked any disposition whatever to alter the content of a set of propositional attitudes in the presence of clear evidence that they do not correspond to the world, then these attitudes cannot be beliefs. This is an application of the more general Davidsonian dictum that rationality is the constitutive ideal of the mental. The norm of rationality governing the representations we call beliefs is that they should maintain a mind-to-world direction of fit, and actual representations must at least roughly approximate this norm in order so much as to count as beliefs. Desires, by contrast, are said to be propositional attitudes with a world-to-mind direction of fit. A desire is an attitude towards a proposition that typically prompts one to adjust the world in ways calculated to make it correspond to the proposition. If one lacked any disposition whatever to bring the world into correspondence with a proposition towards which one has a certain attitude, then—on this second dogma—the attitude cannot be desire.

This pleasingly unified and symmetrical view of desires and beliefs leads to the third dogma of desire: beliefs and desires can be paired to yield a rationalizing explanation of any action.[5] To put the point in terms of the two preceding

---

[4] The general idea that mental states can be classified in terms of their direction of fit with the world can be traced back at least to G. E. M. Anscombe's *Intention* (Oxford: Basil Blackwell, 1957), 56 ff. It has been affirmed in one form or another by a wide array of subsequent philosophers, including Smith, *The Moral Problem*, 111–19; Sumner, *Welfare, Happiness and Ethics*, 124–5; Velleman, *The Possibility of Practical Reason*, 24 and 182; Robert Audi, "Moral Judgments and Reasons for Action," in Garrett Cullitty and Berys Gaut, eds., *Ethics and Practical Reason* (Oxford: Oxford University Press, 1997), 129; and David Brink, "Kantian Rationalism: Inescapability, Authority and Supremacy," in Cullitty and Gaut, *Ethics and Practical Reason*, 264.

[5] The most prominent exponent of this view is Donald Davidson. See chapters 1, 2, 4, 5, 12 and 14 of Davidson's *Essays on Actions and Events* (Oxford: Oxford University Press, 1980). Smith embraces this notion of action-explanation in *The Moral Problem*, 115–16, as does Robert Brandom

dogmas, any action can be explained as the product of an agent's belief that the action will bring the world into correspondence with some proposition towards which the agent is related by the attitude of desire. More simply, agents act only in ways calculated to fulfill their desires. Belief–desire explanations of this sort are regarded as illuminating because they make clear what in the world agents think they are doing when they engage in intentional action. In other words, such explanations are regarded as rationalizing explanations, and that's the kind of explanation that must be produced when we want to explain that peculiar class of events known as actions. Behavior can be made intelligible as action, on this view, only to the extent that it can be brought into view as an attempt by the agent to remake the world in the image of his desires. This explanatory paradigm, in turn, provides us with a way of identifying desires. People desire that *p* if and only if they are disposed to act in ways calculated to make it true that *p*.

The three dogmas of desire fit together into a natural package, each illuminating and lending plausibility to the others. Consider, to begin with, how the propositional account of desires supports the other two dogmas. Without a propositional account of desires, it is not clear that one could speak sensibly of a "direction of fit" between desires and the world. For instance, if desires could have people as their objects, it's not clear what it would mean to speak of the object as fitting or failing to fit with the world. How could a person do *that*? Nor could we move directly from the attribution of a desire to the explanation of an action, since the desire for a person has a very unclear bearing on what it makes sense to do—whether for instance to bed or befriend or build a life with the person. To explain a particular action, it seems, one must trace it to a desire with a propositional or infinitival object (i.e. a desire to φ).[6] Even if one takes the latter alternative, the thought goes, one can use Sumner's "simple trick" to restate any desire to φ as a desire that one φ. This seems to imply that any desire suited to explain an action can be captured fully in standard propositional form.

The second dogma also tends to support both of the other dogmas. It does not so much bolster as complete the propositional account of desires, since it purports to tell us what *sort* of propositional attitude a desire is. And because it accounts for desires as dispositions to act in ways calculated to bring about certain envisioned states of affairs, it seems perfectly suited to play a pivotal role in the explanation of action. When a dispositional desire of this sort is conjoined with the belief that a certain action would bring about the desired state of affairs, the disposition can express itself directly in action. Citing a belief–desire pair,

---

in *Making It Explicit*, 56. Other influential expositions of this conception of agency can be found in: Daniel C. Dennett, *Kinds of Minds: Toward an Understanding of Consciousness* (New York: Basic Books, 1996), chapter 2; and Alvin Goldman, *A Theory of Human Action* (Princeton: Princeton University Press, 1970), chapter 3.

   [6] Davidson makes this point in "Actions, Reasons and Causes," *Essays on Actions and Events*, 6.

then, is widely thought to provide an exhaustive rationalizing explanation of an action.

The third dogma can be regarded as a kind of confirmation of the prior two dogmas, because it provides a compelling answer to the question *why* our conception of desire takes the shape specified by the first two dogmas. Our conception takes this shape, and ought to take this shape, because such a conception is optimally suited to provide illuminating explanations of what people do. Belief–desire explanations help us to understand people's aims and purposes, and to see why they choose the actions that they do. We speak of desires because we want to understand and anticipate the actions of others. The first two dogmas permit us to do this effectively.

It would be an exaggeration to say that these three dogmas stand or fall together. Still, given the way that they cohere with and draw support from each other, a telling objection to any of them will tend to undermine the grounds for affirming the other two. Given this, I will sometimes take the liberty of evaluating them as a package, under the name of *the propositional account of desire* (or *propositionalism*, for short), though I realize that some readers might be tempted to accept my criticisms of some elements of the package while continuing to affirm other elements.[7] I hope to show that we should reject all three dogmas. More specifically, I hope to show: (1) that few desires really have propositions as their intentional objects; (2) that while the objects of many desires can be captured in propositional form, the objects of certain desires cannot be; (3) that some of the ideational content of desires has a mind-to-world rather than a world-to-mind direction of fit; and (4) that some actions are best explained as issuing forth from desires whose objects are neither propositions nor propositionally specifiable states of affairs (the main argument for this last claim is set out in Chapter 2).

DOUBTS ABOUT THE PROPOSITIONAL ACCOUNT OF DESIRE

The word 'desire' is slipping from ordinary speech. We often ask others what they want or would like, but it sounds just a bit servile to ask what they desire, and it sounds correspondingly presumptuous to announce to others what we desire. The word has a great deal more currency in philosophy than in ordinary speech, and this makes it difficult to hold the feet of philosophers to the fire of ordinary usage. It is worth noting, however, that when non-philosophers do make use of the word 'desire,' they tend to use it in one of two ways, both

---

[7] For instance, Velleman embraces the first two dogmas but holds that belief/desire combinations can provide suitable explanations only of goal-directed activity, and not of autonomous action. See Velleman, *The Possibility of Practical Reason*, 5–11, 24, 182.

of which philosophers tend either to misinterpret or to ignore entirely. In its most common use, the verb 'desire' carries a direct object, as when I say that I desire a Harley Davidson, or the sylvan fields of my youth, or (and this is probably the verb's most common use) some person. In its next most common use, 'desire' is followed by an infinitive, as when I say that I desire to kindle a friendship, to travel, or to read some author's latest book. There are intuitive reasons for doubting that all such desires can really be translated without loss into the supposedly standard propositional form.

Suppose that Dorothy says that she desires this Harley Davidson or that man. Must we agree that she has thus far provided a less than fully informative statement of her desire because she has not said what proposition she is disposed to make true? In the case of Dorothy's desire for this Harley Davidson, it might seem straightforward to bring a proposition onto the scene in order to specify Dorothy's aim. What Dorothy desires, it might be presumed, is that she possess this Harley. But when we turn from desiring things to desiring people, the propositional account seems more clearly procrustean. What proposition might specify the object of Dorothy's desire for this man she loves? Well, we don't know much about Dorothy, so we can only guess. Maybe what she wants is that he clutch her hips while roaring full-throttle down Highway One. Maybe she desires that he marry her at a drive-thru chapel on the outskirts of Las Vegas. Maybe she desires that they make love after a night of blackjack. Some cases of desiring people might be exhaustively characterized by propositions of this sort. But Dorothy might find (she might *hope* to find) that her desire for this man is not satisfied, but continues to draw her to him, even when she is roaring down Highway One with him, and even when they are saying their vows in Vegas, and even when they make love after a night of blackjack. Being with him, dwelling on his words, and touching and kissing him might all figure as propitious conditions for the intensification of her desire for him rather than as satisfactions of that desire. Her desire might well spawn a wide array of actionable desires that things be thus and such, but it is far from clear that the desire itself must be analyzable as a conjunction of such propositional desires.

Let us consider, finally, those ordinary uses of the verb 'desire' that take infinitival phrases as their objects. Should we agree with Sumner that the true intentional object of such a desire is a proposition, and that it is always a "simple trick" to translate this sort of desire-talk into propositional form? It seems that an apt propositional translation can always be formulated, and this marks a difference from cases of desiring persons. Yet the translations could also be run in the other direction, and intuitively these latter translations seem to yield a more perspicuous representation of the true objects of desires than do the translations favored by Sumner. In general, when we desire some determinate state of affairs (including those states of affairs in which we do something or other), the object of the desire is the state of affairs itself and not the truth of the proposition picking it out. As Stephen Darwall points out, it is possible to want it to be true of one's life that its narrative includes engagement in an activity, without wanting to engage in the activity.[8] But this is not what we normally want when we want to engage in some activity or another. We normally want the truthmaker and not the proposition's truth. Nor can the two be equated, since we would thereby lose hold of the thought that true propositions are made true by the way the world is.[9]

This last consideration provides a decisive reason to reject *strong propositionalism*, understood as the view that the real intentional object of a desire is always a proposition rather than a state of affairs to which a proposition might relate us, and that the end towards which the desire directs us is the making true of a proposition rather than the production of some state of affairs that might be represented by a proposition. It might seem tempting to retreat to *weak propositionalism*, understood as the view that the object of any desire is *capturable* in propositional terms, in the sense that the truth of the relevant proposition is a necessary and sufficient condition for the attainment of the desire's end.[10] Yet if my brief reflections about Dorothy's desire for her lover are on target, there are difficulties with this view as well.

It might be thought that we cannot account for the semantics of desire-talk unless we regard desires as relations to propositions. Consider, for example, the following sentence: Dorothy will desire her lover tomorrow. The adverb 'tomorrow' in this sentence might be understood as modifying 'desire,' in which case the sentence means that tomorrow Dorothy will desire her lover. But 'tomorrow' might also be heard as modifying a "silent" verb in the object of the desire. In that case, the sentence means that sometime before tomorrow, Dorothy will develop a desire to "have" her lover tomorrow. Some semantic theorists have portrayed such ambiguity as evidence that the verb 'desire' always has a propositional object.[11] But this seems too hasty. The ambiguity shows up only if we have already discounted the sense of desire under which it denotes the sort of fundamental attraction that draws many lovers to each other, and that makes sense of their more tractable world-making projects. It disappears if we assume that the desire in question is a fundamental attraction of this sort. It would be a category mistake to think of such a desire as wholly

---

[8] Stephen Darwall, *Welfare and Rational Care* (Princeton: Princeton University Press, 2002), 93.

[9] I owe this point, and the distinction between strong and weak propositionalism to which it leads, to my colleague Trenton Merricks.

[10] While Sumner and other propositionalists have not generally distinguished between strong and weak propositionalism, it seems most charitable to attribute to them the weaker and more plausible view rather than the stronger and far less plausible view.

[11] See, for instance, Richard K. Larson, "The Grammar of Intensionality," in G. Preyer and G. Peter, eds., *Logical Form and Language* (Oxford: Clarendon Press, 2000). A similar argument is put forward by Larson, Peter Ludlow, and Marcel den Dikken in an unpublished manuscript entitled "Intentional Transitive Verbs and Abstract Clausal Complementation." Thanks to Steve Gross for directing me to these texts.

satisfiable by anything that could fit within the confines of tomorrow or any other day.[12]

We can bring out the difficulties of propositionalism more clearly by noting that even if the propositionalist translation of infinitival desires can succeed in capturing a necessary and sufficient condition for attainment of the desire's end, it seems unable to capture the entire representational content of all such desires. If I want to go fishing, and my wife wants me to go fishing, then the most straightforward version of the propositional account would assign our desires the same content—that TB go fishing. But our desires might well differ markedly in their representational content. My desire might involve a tendency to dwell on the prospect of fishing, not neutrally but such that fishing is lit up for me as a good or attractive activity. My wife's desire need not involve a tendency to see anything good about the activity of fishing, but only a tendency to see something good about *my* going fishing. These desires might be directed towards the same state of affairs yet represent the appeal of that state of affairs in very different ways.

It might be thought that the problem here can be resolved by distinguishing between the proposition 'I go fishing' and the proposition 'TB goes fishing,' and holding that my desire takes the first proposition as its object, while my wife's desire takes the second. But we can run into a version of the problem at hand even if we stick with first-person cases. My own desire to go fishing can itself vary in its way of representing fishing as good or choiceworthy. For instance, fishing might be lit up for me as good or choiceworthy because of the prospect of catching a tasty trout, or because it would take me up into a beautiful mountain range, or because it would involve wading in the cool rushing waters of mountain streams. These all seem to be different ways to represent going fishing as good or worthwhile—different ways of apprehending fishing's desirability—and it seems possible for a desire to go fishing to consist partly in one or another of these representations. Indeed, Elizabeth Anscombe has argued that desires must

---

[12] Much of the literature on the semantics of desire-talk is built on the mistaken assumption that the object-place of the verb 'desire' is always an "opaque" or "intensional" context—that is, a context within which the substitution of one co-extensive expression for another can alter the truth value of the whole. This assumption would be sound if desires were relations to propositions or parts of propositions (e.g. noun phrases), and only in a mediate sense to the states of affairs, activities, or people picked out by those propositions or phrases. There are desires whose object-places do seem to be opaque. For instance, it could be true that Dorothy desires to marry the richest man in the world, true (unbeknownst to Dorothy) that the richest man in the world is the least intelligent man in the world, but false that Dorothy desires to marry the least intelligent man in the world. This is evidence that Dorothy's relation to this desire's object is mediated by a proposition. But there are other cases in which we are torn about whether to regard the object-place of a desire clause as opaque. Suppose, for instance, that Dorothy desires her lover in the fundamental way that we have been considering, and that she does not know that he is the one who sent her a certain anonymous letter. There is a considerable temptation to say, in this case, that Dorothy desires the man who sent her the letter, though she doesn't realize this. This unclarity about whether desire-talk induces an opaque context is just what we should expect if some desires are attitudes towards the things themselves, unmediated by linguistic representations.

involve grasping as desirable—e.g. that one could not want a saucer of mud unless one saw *something* good or worthwhile about getting it.[13] And this point seems right: one cannot offer a rationalizing explanation of an otherwise entirely senseless action, such as getting oneself a saucer of mud, simply by noting that one desired to do so. The explanatory question is how such a thing could appear to be good or worthwhile. Yet the propositionalist must limit the content of the desire to the description of some state of affairs that one could sensibly seek to bring about, such as 'I go (or TB goes) fishing and catches a tasty trout,' or 'I go (TB goes) fishing while wading in the cool rushing waters of mountain streams.' Those who accept the second dogma must deny that the propositional content of a desire is that some possible line of action or state of affairs would be good or valuable. Such content is not the sort of thing that one could sensibly seek to bring about; on the contrary, it would seem to demand a mind-to-world direction of fit (even if we conclude, at the endpoint of ontological reflection, that there is nothing in the world to which it can be fitted).

Perhaps there is some other way, consistent with the dogmas of propositionalism, that a reference to goodness or value can be incorporated into the supposedly propositional content of a desire. I will consider this possibility below. If (as I believe) it can't be done, propositionalism faces a serious difficulty. The view cannot affirm the truism that desires function as the core of rationalizing explanations of the actions arising from them. That is to say, the third dogma will have to be jettisoned. But to jettison this dogma is to lose hold of the most compelling reason for affirming the first two dogmas—i.e. that they provide us with a conception of desires capable of offering illuminating explanations of exercises of agency.

The problem is particularly obvious if we hold that to have a propositional attitude with a world-to-mind direction of fit is merely to be disposed, other things equal, to act in ways calculated to make the relevant proposition true. If I perform an action, one can hardly provide a rationalizing explanation of my performance by tracing it to my disposition to behave in ways calculated to make it true that I perform actions of a kind to which the action belongs. Even if we grant that this dispositional claim escapes "dormitive powers" problems and hence counts as a genuine explanation, still it cannot be regarded as a *rationalizing* explanation, since it cannot plausibly be thought to lay bare a pattern of deliberation to which I have reason to adhere. This form of explanation might help to make clear what exactly others are up to—e.g. whether the parent reading the paper at breakfast is aiming to stay abreast of tumultuous world events or insulated from tumultuous household events. But such explanations rationalize actions only given the background supposition that the person sees something good or worthwhile about the behavior he is inclined to go for, and

[13] Anscombe, *Intention*, 70 ff.

this is not guaranteed by the mere existence of a disposition to engage in such behavior.

This point is best seen in the first-person case. If I myself am deliberating about whether I have reason to φ and I realize that I am disposed occasionally to φ, this does not advance my deliberation at all. It only leads to the question whether I have any reason here and now to manifest the disposition in question—which is to say, whether I have any reason to φ—but that's exactly the question that I am trying to answer. It is consistent with having a disposition to φ that I φ-ing strikes me as wholly without value and my tendency to engage in it as a pointless obsession. But the same point holds in the third person case. We cannot provide a rationalizing explanation of an episode of agency simply by tracing it to some class of performances that the agent is disposed to produce, since the agent might see no more point in these performances than in obsessions or nervous tics. This is what lies behind Anscombe's claim that desiring requires that the desirer see something desirable in that which is desired. Ordinary usage of the term 'desire' is perhaps ample enough to encompass merely obsessive urges. However, tracing behavior to such a bare urge does not help us to see how the behavior could show up as good or worthwhile for the person displaying it, hence does not suffice to make the behavior intelligible as something the person saw fit to choose. No conception of desire can play a central role in rationalizing explanations of action—that is, in making behavior intelligible as action—unless it takes desiring to consist at least partly in appearances of desirability.

At this point, one might remain a propositionalist yet give up on the idea that desires can rationalize actions—i.e. that tracing an action to a desire can exhibit the point of the action. Put another way, one might either reject dogma three or tone it down by holding that belief/desire explanations permit us only to predict behavior and not to rationalize it (not, that is, to exhibit it as something an agent saw fit to do). Some have taken this route.[14] The problem with this alternative is that it loses sight of the place that the notion of desire has in our attempts to understand each other and to make ourselves understood. We talk about desires not just to predict each other's bodily motions but to understand each other by grasping the point or value that we see in what we do. If propositionalism cannot make sense of this ordinary function of desire-talk, we should cast about for an alternative account that can.

THE "EVALUATIVE OUTLOOK" CONCEPTION OF DESIRE

Propositionalism runs into problems because it banishes all evaluative content from desires. If this is the problem, the solution must lie in insisting that

---

[14] This is the route taken by Velleman in *The Possibility of Practical Reason*, 5–11, 24, 182.

desires do have evaluative content—that is, that desires consist at least partly in representations of reasons or values. This does not mean that desires are to be conflated with *beliefs* about reasons or values. That would be a clear mistake. While it can be perfectly sensible to call a desire misguided or debased, it makes little sense to say that a desire is false. Likewise, it sometimes happens that we come to believe that one of our desires inclines us towards actions that are in no way good, yet we continue to have the desire. Such cases would be deeply paradoxical if they involved believing that some one of our persisting beliefs is false.

A more plausible position, associated with the work of T. M. Scanlon and Dennis Stampe, is to hold that desires are *seemings* of goodness or of reasons for action.[15] Call this the "evaluative outlook" conception of desire. On Stampe's view, the relevant patterns of evaluative attention bring possible actions or states of affairs into view as good, while in Scanlon's view they bring certain features of our circumstances into view as counting in favor of (i.e. as reasons for) some sort of action. On this approach, desires are suited to play a role in practical reasoning akin to the role played by perceptions in theoretical reasoning. Perceptions provide us with conceptually structured "takes" on our circumstances that focus and inform our ongoing efforts to formulate true beliefs about these circumstances. Similarly, desires provide us with conceptually structured takes on our changing circumstances that focus and inform our ongoing efforts to discern and pursue the possibilities for fruitful activity afforded by these circumstances. To have an occurrent desire is to find oneself attending to (or imagining) certain possible activities or courses of action as good. To have a dispositional desire is to have a tendency to experience such patterns of attention when circumstances afford an opportunity to embark upon the relevant line of action.

This "evaluative outlook" account of desire is often developed in ways that obscure the tension between it and propositionalism. Stampe, for instance, claims that the *object* of a desire—that is, what it is a desire *for*—is given by a proposition picking out the state of affairs that one desires to bring about, but that this proposition does not exhaust the *representational content* of a desire, since the desirer must also represent the desired state of affairs as one that would be good.[16] Scanlon has argued, in a similar vein, that in one very common sense of the term 'desire' (the "directed attention sense"), a person has a desire that P "if the thought of P keeps occurring to him or her in a favorable light, that is to say, if the person's attention is directed insistently toward considerations that present themselves as counting in favor of P."[17] Here again, the object of desire is portrayed as a propositionally specifiable state of affairs, but the representational

---

[15] Thomas M. Scanlon, *What We Owe to Each Other* (Cambridge: Harvard University Press, 1998), 33–55; Dennis Stampe, "The Authority of Desire," *Philosophical Review* 96/2 (1987), 335–82.

[16] *Ibid.*, 355–7, 368.   [17] Scanlon, *What We Owe to Each Other*, 39.

content of desire is more ample, and includes a picture of what counts in favor of the desire's object. I will argue in the next chapter that the evaluative content of desires must be incorporated into their objects rather than into the way we see these objects when we desire them. Still, the views of Scanlon and Stampe both lead naturally to the thought that other things equal, desires ought to be altered so as to track any genuine goods or reasons with which the world presents us. Hence, while it might still be a constitutive requirement of having a desire that one is inclined to bring it about that the world corresponds with the proposition that specifies the desire's object, still full rationality might also require that one adjust one's desires so as to track genuine reasons or goods. Desires would then stand at the crossroads between two rational demands, each addressing itself to a different element of the desire's representational content and each demanding a different direction of fit between representation and reality (assuming for a moment that there are real reasons or goods).

The "evaluative outlook" conception of desire is perhaps most persuasive when applied to those desires that accompany and partly constitute a variety of common emotions. For instance, fear often involves a desire to flee. When one is in the grip of fear, the desire to flee is inseparably fused with a certain way of understanding why it would be good to flee. Fleeing shows up as good because it provides a way of evading some perceived or imagined threat. Provided that the fear does not devolve into an extreme and indiscriminate terror, the shape of the desire will ordinarily change over time in ways that make sense given one's changing conception of the reason to flee. For instance, the desire will tend to grow more urgent as the appearance of danger grows, and the desired path of flight will typically change with changes in the imagined location of the threat. The desire, then, takes its evolving shape from a specific notion of the point of fleeing.

If we carefully examine the phenomenology of many other desires not annexed to emotions, we find that they too reflect a subjective picture of the point or value of doing that which they incline us to do. For instance, the desire I now have to hike with my children up to a swimming hole in the mountains involves a tendency to recollect the sudden welcome coldness of a plunge into mountain stream-waters after a sweaty hike, and the restorative calm that descends afterwards when one stretches out on a sun-warmed boulder with eyes closed and ears filled with the sound of waterfalls. The desire also involves a tendency to dwell on the joyful energy that wells up in children when they go off in search of the perfect diving perch and discover their body's innate sense, inherited from a distant animal past, of how to stay in balance while scrambling up rocks. The role of this desire in lighting up the trip to Blue Hole as good would be entirely lost if the desire were viewed merely as a functional state that produces behavior calculated to make true the proposition: 'the children and I go for a swim at Blue Hole.'

This is not to deny that invocation of a propositionally specified desire can provide an important clue to the rationalizing explanation of an action. If someone is wandering through the woods, it helps a great deal to know that he is doing so because he wants to go for a swim at Blue Hole rather than, say, because he desires to stay in shape, or to avoid his wife, or to catch sight of a rare bird. This information helps us to see at least one thing that the man in question sees as good about walking through the woods: it will get him to Blue Hole. What is crucial, though, is that invocation of the desire can put us on to a rationalizing explanation only because most of us have at least an inkling *how* a hike to a swimming hole might show up for someone as appealing. We draw upon this sense to fill in the working elements of a rationalizing explanation. Whenever propositionally specified desires are used successfully to make sense of action, they trade implicitly upon our shared understanding of what human beings are likely to find refreshing, challenging, intriguing, beautiful, exciting, cozy, reassuring, convivial, soothing, or in some other way appealing.

It is only when we run into a propositionally specifiable aim whose subjective appeal we are wholly unable to imagine that we become aware of the background role that this attunement of value plays in our efforts to make sense of each other's actions. We are brought up short in just this way by Anscombe's case of the man who desires to spend his time collecting saucers of mud. We can imagine someone being in the grip of a malady that inclines him to behave in ways calculated to bring it about that he has a collection of mud-filled saucers, but it is passably hard to imagine how such a project might show up in someone's eyes as good or worthwhile. Until we see our way to imagining this, we haven't yet grasped the representational content of a desire capable of rationalizing the collection of saucers of mud. That is, we haven't seen how the collecting of mud-filled saucers could express someone's picture of what it makes sense to do.

When the background attunement of evaluative outlooks breaks down in this way, it simply doesn't help to reiterate that the person in question *desires* the state of affairs in which he is collecting or has collected saucers of mud. That merely reasserts the fact about the agent that we are trying to see otherwise than as a symptom of derangement. Our task is to understand how this behavior counts as action expressive of a conception of the good rather than as mere goal-directed behavior of the sort found throughout the animal and plant kingdoms, and we can only do this if we gain some glimmer of the conception of the good that inspires these actions. This carries the interesting implication that when we attempt to bring agency into view, we must assume a partial community of shared or at least mutually intelligible values. Put another way, we must draw upon a substantive rather than a merely formal conception of practical rationality.

This is not to say that it will always be pointless to reply "I just wanted to" (or some near variant) when asked why one has done something or another. Such a reply might be in order, but its most common function is to make known that one regards the matter as none of the interlocutor's business—as, for instance, when one says "I just felt like it" to an overly intrusive policeman who has asked why one is out walking after dark. What such replies cannot do is to provide a rationalizing explanation of an otherwise wholly senseless bit of behavior such as collecting saucers of mud.

What comes to light here is a very basic insight into what it is to be an agent. One does not count as an agent simply in virtue of consistently behaving in ways that effectively bring about certain describable states of affairs. If this were sufficient for agency, then we would have to include within the ranks of agents such things as heating system thermostats and heliotropic plants. Nor does it suffice to count as an agent that one's bodily motions are *caused* by one's representation of the anticipated effects of these motions, since one might see no point or value in the motions generated by this causal linkage. To be an agent is to set oneself in motion (or to try to do so, or to adopt the intention of doing so) on the strength of one's sense that something counts in favor of doing so. That performing some action would bring about some state of affairs cannot intelligibly be regarded as counting in favor of performing the action unless one sees the state of affairs, or the effort to produce it, as itself good or valuable. Hence if we are to view persistent attempts to bring about some state of affairs as the doing of an agent, we must suppose that the agent sees something good or valuable about attaining or aiming at that state of affairs. Desires can figure centrally in the rationalizing explanation of actions only if they involve a sense of the point or value of acting in the way that they incline us to act, and only if they motivate us by inducing us to act on the strength of this evaluative outlook. If we think of desires in this way, we must recognize that it is hard to attain a full understanding of the desires of others, and almost equally hard to become fully articulate about one's own desires. But this is no surprise: it *is* exceedingly hard to see to the bottom of one's own longings and doings, and even harder to understand the longings and doings of others.

It might be thought that it over-intellectualizes human desires to suppose that they always involve some outlook on goods or reasons. But on reflection it seems that even the simplest human desires carry the phenomenological traces of some inchoate sense of the good that hangs on fulfilling them. Consider, for instance, the varying outlooks on value that can inflect a desire to eat a particular piece of cake. There is a subtle phenomenological difference between: (1) desiring to eat a piece of cake, even though one does not like sweets, because one is very hungry; (2) desiring to eat that same piece of cake because one has had it in the past and one knows it to be delicious; and (3) desiring to eat the same piece of cake because one's elderly uncle has baked it and fawning over his baking is the family's ritual manner of acknowledging him. Each of these desires carries traces of a different picture of the good that might hang on eating the cake.

The "evaluative outlook" conception of desires has an advantage over those phenomenological accounts that attempt to trace the distinctive mark of a desire to some sort of felt urge. It is no small task to isolate some introspective feeling that is shared in common by all those things we call desires, including such disparate psychological states as hunger, sexual desire, the desire to succeed in one's career, the desire for world peace and the desire to wear stylish shoes. The evaluative outlook account can explain what they have in common. Each involves an attentiveness to, or tendency to dwell on, some sort of goodness or value in those things that they incline us to pursue or promote.[18]

This account of desire can also explain how it can be true of desires both that we are to a large degree passive with respect to them and that they can conflict in a rather direct way with our practical judgments. Desires are in obvious tension with judgments when they involve a tendency to see goods or reasons where we judge that there are none.[19] In such cases we might well judge our own desires to be foolish, misguided, or modes of captivity to illusions of goodness (though it is sometimes hard to maintain conviction in such judgments when the desire is in full pitch). Desires are capable of conflicting with judgments, and also of informing our judgments, because they are appearances in the space of practical thinking. They present us with a deliberative problem in the straightforward sense that we must decide, when confronted with them, whether it really makes sense to move our bodies in the way that they incline us to move them. But they also present us with an inchoate sense of how or why it would count as good to act as they incline us to act, and this provides us with the richer and more interesting practical problem of interpreting and assessing our sense of the point of these actions.

If we act on a desire whose evaluative outlook we reflectively judge to be mistaken, we are involved in a kind of irrationality. Desires that we regard as mistaken can still play a role in the rationalizing explanation of any actions to which they give rise, since it is the evaluative outlook encoded in the desire that we act on, not the alternative outlook we affirm on reflection. We have to unearth this desire, and see how things look through its lens, in order to see what the agent saw in the action that gave it so much as a semblance of choice worthiness. Unless we can do this, we can't view the behavior as displaying that minimal degree of purposive intelligibility that behavior must display if it is to qualify as action. This minimal degree of intelligibility is sufficient to provide the working elements of what we call a "rationalizing explanation" of action, but its existence does not itself qualify the action as fully rational, else it would be impossible to act irrationally. Behavior might have sufficient intelligibility to qualify as action

---

[18] Scanlon, *What We Owe to Each Other*, 39.

[19] Scanlon makes this point in *What We Owe to Each Other*, 39–40. It is crucial here that the operative notion of *seeing* is not the one we refer to when we introduce our considered judgments with the phrase "As I see it, . . ." Desires are vivid *seemings* of goodness, not claims or conclusions about goodness.

even when chosen on a conception of the good that is fundamentally at odds with the agent's own long-standing and cherished beliefs about how best to live. In that case it might well make sense to say that the agent was active in the performance—i.e. that it reflected a conception of value in whose grip he found himself and to whose adequacy he assented by voluntarily acting on it—but that he acted against his own considered conception of value.

Another merit of the "evaluative outlook" conception of desires is that it helps to clarify why our desires are generally marked quite profoundly by our evolving convictions about what we have reason to do. By the time we are mature, even primitive desires like hunger and the desire to have children have been pruned and shaped by moral education and reflection, so that even when we strongly desire food we do not ordinarily desire the food on a stranger's plate, and even when we strongly desire to have a child, even by adoption, we do not ordinarily desire the children playing in someone else's yard.[20] If desires are tendencies or temptations to think that some action is worth performing, then this moral pruning and shaping of desire should come as no surprise. Part of what it *means* to reach the settled and wholehearted judgment that stealing and kidnapping are wrong is to cease to be tempted by the idea that a wide range of ordinary considerations could possibly count in favor of such actions. It would be difficult to explain the moral maturation of desire on the hypothesis that desires are blind urges that need to be harnessed by principled moral commitments rather than evaluative outlooks that need to be informed in such a way as to bring reliably to light the practical contours of one's changing circumstances. On such a hypothesis, it would come as an inexplicable surprise that the desires of the morally decent person sometimes exhibit a very nuanced appropriateness in unfamiliar circumstances. This phenomenon is precisely what we would expect if desires are evaluative outlooks structured in part by pre-deliberative deployment of the evaluative concepts we gradually master in the course of a proper upbringing. Hence the "evaluative outlook" conception of desire provides a suitable starting point for vindicating the Aristotelian thesis that those who are truly virtuous, as opposed to merely continent (*enkratic*), rarely find it necessary to overrule desires to act badly.

It would be a mistake, though, to expect too thorough a harmony between the values that we come to accept on reflection and the outlook on value manifest in our desires—and not just because human nature is recalcitrant to ethical learning. Sometimes we must make hard choices between genuinely conflicting goods, and when we do it is not necessarily a defect to find that our desires pull us in different directions. It can instead be a sign of clarity and comprehensiveness in our appreciation of value. Further, it must be admitted that human beings

---

[20] I draw these examples from Barbara Herman's "Making Room for Character," in Stephen Engstrom and Jennifer Whiting, eds., *Aristotle, Kant and the Stoics: Rethinking Happiness and Virtue* (Cambridge: Cambridge University Press: 1996), 36–60; see especially 46.

are so constituted that their desires are substantially resistant even to the clearest and most uncontroversial findings of their own moral reflections. For instance, it is surpassingly rare for people to exhibit a truly fervent and sustained desire for the elimination of famine and genocide, yet in calm moments of reflection most people fervently avow the vital importance of these ends. If a tendency to *see* something *as* one thing or another is sometimes " 'The echo of a thought in sight' " (to borrow Wittgenstein's evocative phrase), we must admit that such echoes are often distorted and faint, and even when faithful to thought they often serve only to betray its inconstancy and equivocality.[21]

It is a perfectly general truth that our immediate apprehension of the world is structured by the concepts we have mastered, and it continues to take on a more refined structure as we master a more complex and ample array of concepts. The untrained eye looking at neurons through an electron microscope will see undifferentiated blobs with no more intelligible form than splattered paint. A trained neurologist will see synapses, axons, dendrites, and growth cones. This conceptual structuring does not seem to emerge as the product of judgments to the effect that certain blotches of color are synapses, axons, dendrites, or growth cones—they are simply seen as such. Indeed, it would be an unstable position to insist that concepts can only structure our experience via implicit judgments to the effect that they are applicable, since some conceptualization would have to precede any such judgment so as to bring into view the putative conditions for the concept's applicability.

There is no obvious reason why the conceptual structuring of our immediate perceptual apprehensions of the world should be expected to stop at the doorstep of practical or action-guiding concepts, and it doesn't. For instance, when a seasoned driver approaches an intersection with a red light, she sees the light immediately as a reason to stop, not as a visual signal that she must then *judge* to be a reason to stop. Similarly, a competent woodworker, entering her workshop with an eye to building a table, does not see undifferentiated objects whose role in her plans awaits to be determined by practical deliberation. She notices the matching colors of a set of cherry planks as lending themselves to being joined in an appealing tabletop, and she sees imperfections on the edges of these boards as a reason to start up the jointer and run them through. To the extent that philosophers have tended to overlook the practical structure of our ordinary perceptions of the world, this is perhaps because they have overlooked or misunderstood the internal conceptual structure and complexity of desires. It is our desires that continuously set the stage for practical reasoning by providing us with a pre-reflective picture of how and why it makes most sense to extend our activities.

---

[21] The phrase and the example are Wittgenstein's. See Ludwig Wittgenstein, *Philosophical Investigations* (3rd edn), translated by G. E. M. Anscombe (New York: Macmillan Publishing Company, Inc., 1958), 212ᵉ.

THE MOTIVATIONAL EFFICACY OF EVALUATIVE OUTLOOKS

Even if it is accepted that desires consist partly in vivid and/or persistent appearances of goods or reasons, it might be thought that they must also have some other essential constituent if they are to be motivational states capable of setting the limbs in motion. The worry here arises from the same picture of the division of mental labor between cognition and conation that animates the three dogmas set out above. On this picture, it is one thing to represent something as the case and a fundamentally different thing to be motivated by the appearance that something is the case. The fundamental difference is taken to remain in place even when the thing doing the appearing is a practical reason or a kind of goodness. This picture implies that desires can't merely be appearances that something is a reason or that something would properly be counted as good, since such appearances are not guaranteed any motivational impetus. Such appearances might perhaps be fit guides to the formation of evaluative beliefs, but this is a task for theoretical reason and not for practical reason. Unless we care about some species of reasons or goods, we might be wholly unmoved by them. And we can recognize their existence yet be unmoved by them if we do not happen to care about being good—as might happen, for instance, if we were feeling depressed or just plain perverse.

This position can be developed in two ways. On the one hand, the propositionalist might admit that things can be represented as good or reason-giving—i.e. that this really is a way things can appear to us to be—yet insist that such representations must engage with a desire to act in the name of the relevant goods or reasons if it is to have any influence on our actions. The charge, in other words, is that the "evaluative outlook" account simply postpones the task of explaining what is essential to desires: their power to motivate actions. This way of formulating the objection is flawed. We impute cares and concerns to agents in virtue of their tendency to act in certain ways on the strength of their awareness of certain kinds of circumstances. That is, cares and concerns are imputable in virtue of patterns in what agents take as good reason for what. The relevant patterns cannot be genuine cares or concerns if they do not involve dispositions to act in particular ways—i.e. to produce behavior out of a sense that there is something good or worthwhile about doing so. To impute a care or concern, then, is to impute a pattern in what one takes to be a reason for what. We fall into conceptual confusion if we suppose that we can explain the individual actions that compose the pattern simply by citing the pattern. Viewing a creature as responsive to what it sees as reasons is a precondition for viewing the creature as having cares and concerns; it is therefore not a status that could coherently be thought to depend upon a prior and independent care or concern. Part of what it is to be a practical reasoner is to be capable of acting, and reliably disposed to act, on what one takes to be reasons. No special desire is needed to explain why agents act on what they take to be reasons. This is one of the basic motivational structures without which one would not so much as qualify as a practical reasoner.

A more plausible way of formulating the objection at hand is to hold that there is no such thing as a representation of reason-giving force, and that the appearance of goods or reasons is nothing more than the subjective gilding cast by the motivational states that incline us to perform certain actions. This was Hume's view. If we side with Hume in thinking that all representations must be localizable in specific elements of perceptions, or in montages of elements copied from past perceptions, it is a very tempting view. The trouble with this restrictive view of what we are capable of representing in thought is that it leads to skepticism not only about practical reasons but also about theoretical reasons, together with such basic elements of common-sense ontology as causes and selves. Hume's interest lies largely in the clarity and tenacity with which he developed these skeptical implications. In my view, his work is best read as an unintentional *reductio* of the restrictive theory of mental content from which these skeptical implications flow, rather than as a set of novel discoveries about human beings and their capacities. In the case at hand, if what we call a grip on reasons is really only the phenomenological shadow cast by *de facto* motivation, then the notion of an action collapses upon itself. There is no such thing as initiating a behavior because one sees something good or worthwhile about it. There are merely impulses that incline us to behave in certain ways and simultaneously cause the prospect of so behaving to take on a pleasant coloration in our eyes. To take this position is not to complete but to foreswear the task of formulating rationalizing explanations of human actions.

It might seem to be a wholly empirical question as to what causes those curious sorts of events we call actions. That is, it might be thought that we get our grip on what an action is by way of paradigmatic examples, reference to which can be secured by ostension without committing ourselves to any picture of their nature or causal provenance. We can then conduct an empirical investigation to determine what causes these events. The trouble with this assumption is that it wholly ignores the internal complexity of the concept of action. To bring an event under the concept of action is to view it as having a special provenance. It is to view it as something produced by a conscious being out of that being's appreciation of reasons for producing it. We commit ourselves to this ontology when we determine ourselves to keep behavior in view as someone's doing, i.e. as action, hence to keep each other in view as agents. Unless we are prepared to abandon this undertaking, we cannot insist that the real explanation of "action" lies in a functional state that produces certain coordinated bodily motions given certain triggering conditions. This explanatory paradigm cannot serve to bring actions into view, only behavior. Nor could we coherently regard some set of findings about ourselves, delivered by the natural sciences, as a good justification for abandoning the aspiration to keep ourselves and others in view as beings who adjust their words, thoughts, and actions in light of justificatory reasons. To do so would constitute a performative contradiction, since it would both insist upon and debunk the call to responsiveness to justificatory reasons.

It is, at any rate, worth noting just how few philosophical naturalists feel compelled to introduce a special motivational system to explain how our awareness of normative reasons for *belief* can influence what we end up believing. It is a constitutive requirement for counting as a theoretical reasoner, and perhaps also for having beliefs, that one's beliefs be at least minimally sensitive to considerations that count for or against regarding their contents as true. But if there is no need to invoke a desire to secure the causal link between the acknowledgment of theoretical reasons for belief and the forming of the belief, why suppose that a special desire is needed to secure the connection between the acknowledgment of practical reasons for action and the forming of a motivationally efficacious intention? It can't be because the awareness of justificatory reasons has no causal efficacy whatsoever in the absence of particular desires. It must be, instead, that they lack whatever sort of causal efficacy is needed to set our limbs in motion. But this would be a very curious lack, since presumably neuron firings and/or cranial chemical reactions must be set "in motion" if we are to come to have a new belief, and presumably there is some set of neuron firings and associated chemical reactions that would be sufficient to launch our limbs into each and every one of the overt motions that it is within our power to choose.

I conclude, then, that desires are best understood as consisting not just partly but wholly in appearances of reasons or values. It must be noted, however, that not just any such appearance will constitute a desire. It is an article of common sense that we sometimes decide that we have good reason to do something, and proceed to do it, even though we have no desire whatsoever to do it. It can hardly be said in such cases that it in no way appears to us that there is reason to do what we've chosen to do. We must have seen and acted on *some* reason for doing it—otherwise there would be no sense in thinking of it as something we've done. Such an appearance, however, need not count as a desire, since it might come into focus only with sustained deliberative effort. Desires are appearances with respect to which we are in some significant measure passive. Their occurrence is not wholly dependent upon our active efforts to bring into view the appearances of goodness in which they consist, and their persistence and vividness does not depend entirely on our deliberate efforts to discern the putative goods they call to our attention.

CONCLUDING REMARKS ON THE EXPLANATION OF ACTION

It was noted above that the provision of a belief–desire pair with matching propositional objects is not itself sufficient to provide a rationalizing explanation of actions, since we might be unable to see how the object could strike anyone as good or worthwhile. This provided us with one reason for rejecting the third dogma, according to which such a matched pair is always sufficient to constitute a rationalizing explanation of any action. We are now in a position to see that not only is the provision of a belief–desire pair not sufficient for rationalizing explanation of actions, it is not necessary either. This finding is wholly in line with common sense, which readily admits the possibility and occasional advisability of doing what one has no desire whatsoever to do. Some actions are best traced not to desires but to other, less vivid and more deliberate appearances of reasons. What is essential to any rationalizing explanation of an action is that it reveal how the action was lit up for the agent as good or worthwhile, and desires are not the only sorts of appearances of goodness, even if they are the most common ones.

We could of course stipulate a sense of 'desire' under which anything capable of motivating someone to act thereby counts as a desire, but this would make it a tautology rather than an informative insight that all actions arise from desires. It seems preferable to restrict the term 'desire' to appearances of goodness that are spontaneously vivid or compelling. This permits us to vindicate the natural thought that, for instance, a depressed person might persevere in everyday activity even in the absence of any desire to do so, while also permitting us to illuminate the difference between those who immediately desire to act virtuously and those who are often without desire to act virtuously but manage to do so through a concentrated effort of will (i.e. *enkratically*, as Aristotle would call it).

Propositionalism, then, is grounded in a mistaken conception of the requirements for rationalizing explanations of action. The view assumes that it is rationally intelligible for someone to bring about some state of affairs if and only if that person has some desire whose propositional object picks out that state of affairs. But citing a desire can contribute to the rationalizing explanation of an action only insofar as it helps us to understand what the agent saw in the action such that it seemed worth choosing. If we can't see how a performance might be traced to some source of subjective appeal, then we have not yet seen why it counts as an action rather than a mere obsession. What this means is that our conception of agency has a hidden teleological structure that is richer than the putatively formal and end-neutral notion of rationality explicitly affirmed by the propositionalist. To bring an agent into view requires that we come to see how the world of value might possibly appear to another, and this interpretive task cannot succeed with just any goal-directed bodily motions. Nor can this interpretive task be incorporated as a mere addendum to the propositionalist picture of agency. Once we do see how a performance showed up for its agent as good or worthwhile, then we already have the core component of a rationalizing explanation of the agent's decision to do it. We don't need to add, for instance, that he desires to do what he regards as good. This would boil down, on inspection, to the unhelpful observation that he tends to see as good that which he sees as good.

2

Fragmented Activities, Fragmented Lives

Perhaps something of the austerity with which the notion of obligation is so frequently imbued may be traced, in the last analysis, to our predicament as fragmentary creatures. For how will we rise to wholehearted action of any final significance when we find ourselves in bits and can view acting only as a round of events, in which each successor displaces its predecessor without fundamental increment of meaning?

(Henry Bugbee)[1]

DIALECTICAL ACTIVITY AS A PROBLEM FOR PROPOSITIONALISM

Sometimes we engage in activities in the name of some intrinsic goodness or value that we see in those activities rather than in the name of conceptually independent goods that the activities might produce or promote. Some such activities have a self-unveiling character, in the sense that each successive engagement yields a further stretch of understanding of the goods internal to the activity, hence of what would count as a proper engagement in it. If the activity's constitutive goods are complex and elusive enough, this dialectical process can be reiterated indefinitely, with each successive engagement yielding a clearer grasp of the activity's proper form and preparing the way for a still more adequate and hence more revealing engagement in it.

Given that propositionalism regards all action as a species of production, one would expect it to have a hard time making sense of any activity chosen for its own sake rather than for its effects. And given that propositionalism regards all action as calculated to produce some state of affairs that the agent has antecedently represented to herself in propositional form, one would expect it to have a particularly hard time making sense of dialectical activities. It does. One throws oneself into dialectical activities on the strength of an as-yet-indistinct intimation of their intrinsic value, hence without the benefit of a clear and definite representation of the mode of engagement that would properly consummate one's desire. It is tempting to say of dialectical activities that as

---

[1] Henry Bugbee, "The Moment of Obligation in Experience," 9.

one engages in them, one sees more clearly what one was really after, or what one really wanted, when one threw oneself into them. Propositionalism cannot accept this tempting thought at face value.

When we try to make sense of dialectical activities through the lens of propositionalism, we find that what appear to be unified and sustained activities are fractured into a succession of different actions, each aimed at the production of a different state of affairs, and each having only the most tenuous relation to its predecessors and successors. When we view these same activities through the lens of the alternative conception of desire that I've begun to set out, we are able to vindicate our intuitive sense of the unity of these temporally extended and outwardly evolving desires. As we do so, we also gain a clearer sense of how best to understand this alternative conception of desire.

The problem with propositionalism emerges in a particularly extreme and telling form when we consider the temporally extended activity which we all undertake at least implicitly, and upon which hangs the possibility of a proper unity in our life stories: the activity of understanding and answering in practice to a tenable conception of a good human life. Through the lens of propositionalism, life quests are fractured into a series of seemingly unmotivated shifts in the direction in which we throw about our causal weight in the world. On the alternative conceptions of desire and agency outlined in the previous chapter, a life quest can be made intelligible as a sustained effort to understand and answer to an adequate conception of the human good. We must adopt this conceptual framework if we are to make optimal sense of the central activities and longings that inform our lives.

DIALECTICAL ACTIVITY, DELIBERATION, AND DESIRE

The notion of a dialectical activity is unfamiliar enough that it will help to begin our exploration of it with an example that readers of this book will presumably find familiar: philosophical thought. Those who throw themselves into the pursuit of philosophy have no choice but to do so without a full understanding of what the activity calls for (that is, what would count as an ideally good mode of engagement in it). There is no other possibility, since a developed sense of what counts as good philosophy (e.g. what counts as a revealing or exciting line of thought, and which ways forward should be avoided as facile or tedious) is itself a high philosophical achievement. Further, it is not the sort of achievement that is ever finally secured or possessed, since there is always room for further clarification or deeper understanding. Under propitious conditions—that is, with the right motivations, the right capacities, the right environment, the right conversational partners, etc.—our first and still halting attempts to philosophize can begin to open our eyes to the goods realizable in philosophy, bringing into progressively clearer focus the initially obscure object of whatever desire might have induced us to give it a try.

I choose the example of philosophy only because readers will find it familiar, and not because activities that are dialectical in the sense at hand are the peculiar province of the philosopher. Dialectical activities are a familiar part of almost any human life. The category includes all those activities whose point lies in an intrinsic goodness that is to some considerable degree opaque to those who lack experience with the activity, but that tends to unveil itself incrementally as one gains first-hand experience with it. Whenever we undertake to kindle a friendship, initiate an intimate love relationship, parent a child, start up a conversation with an intriguing stranger, or deepen our appreciation of an unfamiliar genre of music, we are initiating an activity whose value cannot be grasped with perfect lucidity from the outset, but must be progressively clarified via engagement in the activity itself. All of these kinds of activities, and many more beside them, count as dialectical in the sense at hand.

No activity with merely instrumental value can be dialectical, since one can hardly expect to shed light on the nature or value of the end-state at which such activities aim by engaging in an activity that has a merely causal connection to that goal. While nothing in my argument depends upon it, there is some appeal to the thesis that all intrinsically valuable activities are dialectical. It is, after all, hard to see how one could possibly gain a full appreciation of the intrinsic value of some activity (as opposed to conceptually independent goods such as sensory pleasure that might emerge as a byproduct of some activity) except by engaging in the activity and gaining first-hand experience of that value. The value at stake in these cases is irreducibly the value *of* these activities. It would be exceedingly implausible to suppose that what accounts for the value of all intrinsically value activities is some abstract property that could be seen "from the outside" to belong to them. If we run through the list of human activities that are widely regarded as intrinsically good—for example, contemplative thought, convivial conversation among friends, the creation or appreciation of artwork, athletic competition, mountain climbing, intimate sex—they do not seem to have any common properties whose confirmed presence would convey their value to those who have not experienced them. It might perhaps be said—in the spirit of Rawls' Aristotelian Principle—that they are all complex and nuanced, and that they engage our trained or natural capacities and talents.[2] Yet this seems wholly unhelpful, since we can easily think of activities that are pointlessly complex, require pointlessly nuanced distinctions, and make pointless use of capacities and talents that ought to be actualized in more worthwhile ways. We might for instance devote ourselves to counting the numbers of blades of each of a large number of different kinds of grasses in arbitrarily selected square meters of suburban lawns, then performing complex arithmetic manipulations with the

---

[2] John Rawls, *A Theory of Justice* (Cambridge: Harvard University Press, 1971), 426.

resulting numbers. This would seem to be wholly valueless, yet it would be complex, it would require nuanced distinctions, and it would actualize capacities that are often considered centrally valuable to a good human life.

The concepts through which we grasp intrinsically valuable activities are themselves teleological. We sort out what does and does not count as an instance of such an activity by reference to some picture of what it would be to excel in the activity, or to engage in it ideally well, and we assess particular instances of the activity by reference to this same standard. The activity terms, then, provide us with our working grip on the different kinds of intrinsically valuable activity that might have a place in a good or flourishing life. Consider, for instance, the concept of a conversation. A conversation requires apt attention and responsiveness to what one's interlocutors are saying. One stops conversing and launches into monologue if one's speech does not manifest an attentiveness to what others are saying. One need not be an ideal conversational partner to engage in conversation, but one ceases to converse if one's words drift utterly free from these ideals, hence we must have at least an intimation of the sort of aptness specific to conversations if we are to understand what does and does not count as a conversation. But it is also possible to gain a deeper and more penetrating grasp of the difference between apt and inapt moves in a conversation, and this grasp permits us to do more than distinguish what does and does not count as a conversation. It permits us to see what counts as a good conversation rather than a tepid or superficial conversation, and it can guide us in our efforts to carry forward our conversations well. There seems to be no way to grasp the elusive notion of conversational aptness except by conversing with people whose keen intuitive sense of how to hear and respond to another human being helps us to deepen our own appreciation of the goods that can lie in an exchange of words.

If these observations about conversation can be generalized, then grasping what it is to engage in an intrinsically valuable activity, and how to proceed with it well rather than badly, goes hand-in-hand with grasping the particular kind of intrinsic value that it can have. This does not immediately imply that all intrinsically valuable activities are dialectical, since the intrinsic value of certain activities might be graspable without remainder by those who have some experience with them. But on reflection it seems doubtful that an activity can count as intrinsically valuable for human beings if it is simple and transparent enough that practitioners can arrive at a full and reflectively stable grasp of its highest possibilities and their value. The many and varied human activities that are widely regarded as intrinsically good all seem to admit of indefinitely more ample and discriminating appreciation, and the route to such an appreciation seems to run directly and inescapably through those activities themselves.

To bolster the case that all intrinsically valuable activities have a dialectical structure, it is worth mentioning just how plausible it is to suppose, in a recognizably Aristotelian vein, that we cannot fully understand the intrinsic value of any human activity without grasping the *place* of that activity in a full and flourishing human life.[3] We might fruitfully compare such understanding to an achieved understanding of the value of sensory pleasure. Those who devote so much time to the pursuit of sensory pleasure that they enter into no significant human relationships and engage in no other valuable human activities thereby show that they misunderstand the value of sensory pleasure. A proper understanding of its value seems to require an understanding of its place in a good human life. It won't do to regard the value of an activity as a surd quality that can be fully understood in isolation from any sense of how the activity fits into a good human life. If the value of an activity were such a surd quality, we could fully appreciate the value of an activity yet show the most extreme incompetence in making decisions about when the activity is to be pursued or avoided. Such incompetence, however, would show a shortcoming in our understanding of the activity's value. It would show that we do not yet know how to value it. It is true that one's understanding of what can count as a good human life is broadened and deepened as one gains experience of a variety of intrinsically valuable activities, but the influence seems to run in the other direction as well. We gain a full and proper understanding of the value of different intrinsically valuable activities as we see more clearly what place these activities might have in a good human life, and when their pursuit would cheapen our lives or distract us from the task of living a good life. Given this, there is reason to affirm the thesis that all intrinsically valuable activities are dialectical, though the quarry towards which the relevant dialectic moves may be nothing less than a fully apt conception of what does and what does not count as a good human life. It is the fugitive and perfectionist nature of the concept of the human good that guarantees the endlessness of the dialectic.

Even if we accept only the more modest thesis that a wide array of intrinsically valuable human activities are dialectical in the sense at hand, it would be a serious shortcoming of propositionalism if it could not make good sense of our engagement in dialectical activities. I do not think that it can. The difficulty is easiest to see if we consider the version of propositionalism that limits desired states of affairs to those that can be captured by purely non-evaluative propositions. This is the version of propositionalism favored by those ontologically parsimonious naturalists and Kantian constructivists who deny that value is something we perceive or misperceive, and claim instead that it is a mental projection or construction. This sort of propositionalism might be thought to have an advantage when it comes to the clarity and completeness

---

[3] For a very illuminating Aristotelian discussion of the idea that values can be specified by reference to their *place* in a good human life, see Henry S. Richardson's excellent essay "Thinking about Conflicts of Desire," in Peter Bauman and Monika Betzler, eds., *Practical Conflicts: New Philosophical Essays* (Cambridge: Cambridge University Press, 2004), 92–117, especially 103.

of the action-explanations that it generates. This is because it assigns to desires a content that can direct our will without the intercession of any attempt to interpret the concrete implications of controversial evaluative predicates. When viewed through this conceptual framework, dialectical activities are effectively dissociated into a succession of disconnected spasms of purposive behavior, each consisting in an effort to bring the world into conformity with a new description. Since desires are identified solely by the non-evaluative states of affairs that they take as their objects, there is no obvious way to preserve the possibility that each stretch of activity might be the fruit of a deeper or more satisfying insight into what we were already after when we first threw ourselves into the activity. What might appear as increasing depth shows up as mere change. What might appear as an asymptotic approach to understanding and realizing the activity's proper *telos* (i.e. its constitutive standards and ideals, not some separable goal) shows up as a series of unrelated shifts in what one is trying to bring about.

If we are to display these shifts as the successive moments of a single temporally extended activity, then we must bring to light how each of them shows up for the agent as called for by increasingly more satisfying apprehensions of that activity's constitutive goods or ideals. Propositionalism cannot succeed in capturing this sort of unity. This is a very serious problem, since the intelligibility of each successive moment of such an activity is often wholly dependent upon its place in the longer temporal series, in something like the way that individual phonemes created by the vocal chords are unintelligible as speech when considered in isolation from a longer stream of phonemes. Given this, the isolated motions into which propositionalism fractures temporally extended activities will often lack intelligibility as doings of any sort, temporally extended or not.

One might hope to restore the lost unity, yet remain within the basic propositionalist framework, by supposing that what one typically wants when one engages in dialectical activity is that one engage in the activity well. The typical aim, in other words, is to bring it about that one fully realize whatever goods are internal to the activity. One could have this desire while having only a vague idea what these goods might be or how to specify the world-descriptions that would count as their realization. Yet when this sort of desire is conjoined with a concrete belief concerning what is required in order to perform the activity well, it would be sufficient on the propositionalist model to generate and rationalize action. And when such a desire is conjoined with a succession of changing beliefs about what it takes to excel in an activity, it would be sufficient both to explain and to underwrite the continuity of a series of changes in our mode of engagement in the activity. If the beliefs represent successively deeper insights into the good available through the activity—insights that might well be the product of dialectical interaction with the activity itself—then the framework will display the activity's cross-temporal unity as a progressively deeper and more adequate attempt to satisfy the desire that initially sparked the activity.

What we find, then, is that the propositionalist's most plausible strategy for explaining dialectical activities is to insert into the relevant desire's propositional object the sort of evaluative content that, on my alternative view, must always be present in the representational content of any desire capable of playing a central role in the rationalizing explanation of action. This would be obviously flawed if paired with the sort of non-cognitivism which holds that to call something good just is to express a desire for it. After all, it would shed no light on the special content of the desires that draw us into dialectical activities (henceforth *dialectical desires*) to hold that they are desires to engage in activities in the way that one desires to engage in them. But the position has a serious flaw even if it is not paired with this sort of non-cognitivism. The trouble, in a nutshell, is that goodness cannot plausibly be brought into the picture as one among an undifferentiated array of properties the desire for which can rationalize actions. By the propositionalist's lights, any property could be brought into a rationalizing explanation in this way, yet appearances of goodness have a more direct capacity to rationalize action, a capacity that does not depend upon a special desire to bring about said goodness. Indeed, a capacity to do what one sees as good or worthwhile is a necessary condition of agency, not a contingent capacity traceable to a desire that an agent might permanently lack. Behavior counts as action only if an agent produces it on the strength of a sense that it is in some way good or worthwhile.

This is a crucial point, and it will help to elaborate it by means of a series of examples. We can begin by imagining someone who purports to have a desire to philosophize as badly as possible—for example, in ways that positively impede insight and multiply error and confusion. Such a self-report cannot be accepted at face value. If one were moved to think by a desire to impede insight and multiply confusion, the thinking in question could not properly be counted as philosophy, if indeed it can even be counted as thinking. It is a constitutive requirement of philosophy that it be motivated by certain ideals, and one's thought is not philosophy if one shows no interest in these ideals. Hence there is a sense in which one cannot desire to philosophize badly.

This is not to imply that it is impossible to philosophize badly. This unfortunately remains an all-too-real possibility. Still, if a series of utterances falls disastrously short of the constitutive ideals of philosophy, we will be obliged to say that it counts not as philosophy but as something else—drivel, perhaps, or sophistry, or random musings, or specious simulacra of sagacity. Nor is there any problem in desiring that the world be such as to make true the proposition: I (i.e. the desirer) philosophize badly. We might bring out this possibility by conjuring up an evil demon who will bring it about that one's entire family suffers mightily unless one philosophizes badly. Believing oneself to be in the presence of such a demon, one might strongly desire to alter the world so as to make it true that one philosophizes badly. What is critical here, however, is that bringing about this state of affairs would require coming to have a desire to philosophize passably well—i.e. in ways that approximate philosophy's constitutive norms or standards—since thinking has to arise from some such desire in order to count as philosophy. (Indeed, it might require that one desire to answer as well as possible to these standards, rather than just to whatever minimal degree qualifies an episode of thought as philosophy, since the latter aim would arguably fail to manifest the love of insight that is an essential constituent of the activity we call philosophy.) What one can't desire is that one engage in bad philosophy emerging from and guided by that selfsame desire. If we clarify the real object of any desire that we might be tempted to describe in this way, it would turn out to be not bad philosophy but an imitation or a parody of philosophy.

This is not an isolated case. Consider, for instance, the desire to develop a bad friendship with someone. If one acted from this desire, it would be impossible to satisfy it, because any relationship arising from a desire that we might be tempted to describe in this way would not count as a friendship, good or bad. One could not launch a friendship if one had no inkling whatsoever of the value of the progressively deepening mutual understanding of two human beings bound together by good will, nor of the goodness of the rich forms of shared activity that this deepened understanding makes possible. One need not have a sharply articulated sense of this value in order to launch a friendship, but the first stirrings of anything deserving to be called friendship must necessarily include some degree of apprehension of this kind of goodness.

This presents a serious problem for the propositionalist, who holds that the desire that (it be the case that) one philosophizes badly is the same as the desire to philosophize badly, and that the first way of describing the desire lays bare its real intentional object. This is the first and most central of the above-mentioned dogmas of desire, and it is the central claim of propositionalism. It turns out to be mistaken. To accept the propositionalist translation is to lose hold of the conceptual resources needed to distinguish, in the case at hand, between the desire that (the world be such as to make true the proposition that) one philosophizes badly, and the desire to make a parody of philosophy. The problem, at heart, is that propositionalism thinks of all desires as world-to-mind orientations towards future states of affairs and loses sight of the fact that some desires are essential contemporaneous constituents of the activities arising from them. This turns out to be a serious oversight.

One important lesson here is that performing certain intrinsically valuable activities badly is something that can't successfully be pursued nor even desired as an end in itself, because any such pursuit or desire would disqualify the (actual or projected) performance as an instance, good or bad, of the activity in question. As noted, it is perfectly possible to desire that one engage in some intrinsically valuable activity in ways that depart radically from its constitutive ideals, but in the case of many intrinsically valuable activities, the desire in question will be self-effacing: its consummation will require one to shake loose from its grip and act from some other, quite different desire. Genuinely dialectical desires, by contrast, are self-augmenting: acting on them leads to a deeper and more vivid appreciation of the goods that they are intimations of. Put another way, acting on them deepens and reinforces the selfsame desire to answer to these goods by engaging properly in the activity in question. It is characteristic of dialectical activities that they arise from desires of this kind—desires that involve appreciation of the value of the constitutive standards and ideals of an activity rather than a brute disposition to bring it about that one answers to these standards and ideals. The reason-giving force of these ideals does not await our coming to be inclined to bring anything about.

Just as we must distinguish the incoherent desire to engage badly in an intrinsically valuable activity from the perfectly coherent desire that (it be the case that) one engages badly in such an activity, so too we must distinguish the desire to engage (or engage well) in such an activity from the desire that (it be the case that) one engages (or engages well) in that activity. This is a distinction that propositionalism cannot acknowledge, since it regards these desires as equivalent and takes these expressions to differ only in that the second provides a more transparent specification of the real object of the first. But these two kinds of desires can come apart. For instance, a person could have a desire that (the world be such that) he philosophize (or philosophize well), yet be wholly unmoved by the intrinsic goodness of philosophy. This might happen if he were threatened with severe harm unless he managed to philosophize (or philosophize well), or if he fell into a depression that left him without a direct sense of philosophy's appeal but with a desire that he philosophize (an eventuality that would require the return of his sense of the direct appeal of philosophy). Similar possibilities arise with loving relationships. The desire that (it be the case that) one engage in a loving relationship is different from the simple and direct desire to engage in such a relationship. Here again, the difference can be highlighted by noting that the former, production-oriented desire requires the second and more immediate desire if its world-making enterprise is to succeed.

THE NATURE OF DIALECTICAL ACTIVITIES

The main point here is that there is a little-noticed difference between being drawn to an intrinsically valuable activity out of appreciation for it—that is, being appealed to by the activity, finding it appealing—and being inclined to bring it about that one engages in the activity (or even that one engage in the activity while finding it appealing). There is a phenomenological dimension to finding an activity appealing that need not be present in a desire that one engage in the activity. The propositionalist can capture this phenomenological element only as an additional modification of the propositionally specified state of affairs that one desires to bring about and not as part of the phenomenological character of certain desires themselves. Yet this phenomenological element is often essential to the rationalizing explanation of what might otherwise be a pointless and obsessive effort to alter the world so that it answers to a proposition of the form "I engage in activity X." When an inclination to engage in a particular activity arises from the activity's phenomenological appeal, the inclination is something more than a brute tendency to produce a particular array of coordinated motions; it is a tendency to produce such motions out of a sense of the value of doing so, and this can fundamentally alter what it is that one ends up doing. We glimpse a rationalizing explanation of such motions, hence bring them into view as an agent's doings, when we see how they are lit up in the agent's eyes as sensible responses to some ideal or value.

In the standard case, then, the desire to philosophize is not a desire that (it be the case that) one philosophizes. It is, rather, the state we are in when we feel the appeal, the tug, of philosophy's constitutive ideals. It is hard to shake the sense that this must make it a "world-making" desire after all—i.e. that it is a functional state that inclines one to work on the world so as to make it true that we approximate these ideals in our activities. But this would be yet again to mistake the desire's proper expression for its object. Desires to engage in dialectical activities are quite literally desires for these activities, conceived in light of their constitutive ideals and internal goods. We are drawn to such things as reading or conversing or philosophizing when we have a vivid sense of the appeal of the goods internal to these activities. This way of seeing these activities does typically induce us to bring about the state of affairs in which we are reading or conversing or philosophizing, but it is not reducible to a disposition to bring about these or any other states of affairs. The object of such a desire is that towards which it draws our evaluative focus, not the state of the world that we are inclined to bring about when our evaluative attention is focused in this way.

It is only by accepting this way of conceiving of desires and their objects that we can see how a single enduring desire with a single unchanging object can give rise to a temporally extended and continuously self-deepening activity. Our way of engaging in dialectical activities changes continuously because the engagement itself tends to produce a clearer and more ample appreciation of the goods internal to the activity, hence of what would count as a proper expression of the appeal of these goods. When this happens, we should not say that the desire that drew us into the activity has changed its object. On the contrary, these changes might mean, and in the best of cases they do mean, that we have attained a clearer apprehension of what we wanted all along.

It might be objected that an activity must first be represented in a determinate form if we are to have a determinate representation of it as good. Otherwise there would be no clearly represented subject in which the property of goodness might seem to us to inhere. This would imply that there must after all be a determinate activity, specifiable quite apart from its evaluative properties, that we want to perform. If at some later time we see a second, closely related activity as good and want to perform *it*, we must count this as a different desire with a different object, even if it emerges from reflective revision to the earlier thought that the first activity would be good. What this line of objection overlooks is that the goodness we think we see in the first activity is its desirability characteristic, and we desire it *qua* bearer of this desirability characteristic. Hence if we revise our notion of what concrete form of action would feature this desirability characteristic, we thereby modify our sense of what is called for by the same desire. The revision arises because what we seek is the proper response to the goodness we believe ourselves to have glimpsed—where the proper response will usually be a matter of instantiating that goodness, though it need not be (as will become clear below when we return to the case of loving desire for other human beings). The goodness is seen in the desired activity, and the activity is desired only *qua* realization of the sort of good that we think we see in it. Hence the same desire can direct us to perform very different actions or to pursue very different ends at different times.

Perhaps it will help to develop this rather unfamiliar thought with another example. Imagine a singer who is a masterful interpreter of blues songs and who is searching, just now, for the right phrasing and intonation for a key line in a blues number. Is there desire here? Well, in such cases there is often the sense of being drawn into the song by an intimation of an as-yet-indistinct goodness lying untapped in one of its possible renditions. Given this, it seems perfectly natural to speak here of desire—e.g. to say that the singer *wants* to sing it just right. Can one propositionalize the object of such a desire? It seems not. The singer might say that what she desires is that she sing the song well, but this is hardly concrete enough to be the representation towards which she is stretching her voice. Presumably she knows full well that she wants to sing the song well, yet she is still trying to figure out how she wants to sing it. What induces her to sing is not a concrete propositional representation of a way of singing the song, towards which she has adopted an attitude with a world-to-mind direction of fit. Rather, it is her grasp of a kind of goodness present in an interpretation of the song of which she has an as-yet-indistinct intimation.

There is a benign paradox of inquiry here (and, indeed, in any dialectical activity whose constitutive goods have not been fully mastered): the singer is here imagined as sufficiently aware of what she would count as good to stretch her voice in its direction and to recognize it when she manages to sing it, yet her grasp is not sufficiently clear to permit her to produce it forthwith. She has no way of discerning what counts as the interpretation she wants except by trying to sharpen her grasp of this goodness she indistinctly perceives, and she may be unable to do this except by attempting to approximate it in song, trusting that she will recognize it when she hears herself sing it. She might sing the line many times over before achieving the interpretation towards which she is drawn. She would then have discovered, or uncovered, what was drawing her all along. It is this goodness that stirs her to sing and that her voice strains towards as she sings; it is this goodness that will account for the value of her activity if her straining finds its mark.

To instantiate this goodness in her singing is both to clarify her grasp of said goodness by the only available means and to pay proper tribute to this goodness so clarified. The propriety of the tribute depends upon its being the spontaneous byproduct of a full and clear-headed appreciation of the goodness. The tribute would be hollow if it emerged from an uninspired determination to work on the world in such a way as to make true the proposition that one's lips go through whatever motions happen to manifest that sort of goodness. The difference here is the difference between being moved by a vivid appreciation of a species of goodness and wanting it to be the case that one produces a good performance (i.e. the sort of performance that would emerge spontaneously if one were moved directly and skillfully by vivid apprehension of that goodness). The first sort of motivation is essential to the most unimpeded and rewarding sort of engagement in the activity of singing.

It is perhaps worth remarking that philosophers who talk about action theory tend to speak rather generically about being *motivated* to act, and rarely speak of the more specific and in some ways more curious experience of being *moved* to act. It is possible to be moved—say, by a piece of music—without being motivated to *do* anything beyond listening intently to it. Yet it is also possible to be moved to do something—as when a piece of music moves one to sing or to compose a piece of music of one's own, or as when someone's exemplary selflessness moves one to perform a selfless act of one's own. In general, it seems that we are moved to act when our attention is riveted by some sort of goodness and when our action strikes us as an apt response to the goodness in question.

As suggested above, the doings that emerge from this sort of appreciation of goodness gain their value partly from their role in clarifying and deepening one's intimation of that very goodness. The frustration that would attend a failure to realize the goodness by which one has been stirred is not mere frustration with one's outward performance; the more primary frustration, in many such cases, is that one has not managed to attain a clear appreciation of the obscure goodness whose appeal first stirred one to act. If the blues singer cannot give voice to the sounds she is looking for, she must admit the presence of a zone of obscurity in her apprehension of the practical topography of her most central life pursuit. No doubt part of her reason for wishing to see the contours of this domain is that it will permit her to sing well, but it might just as plausibly be supposed that part of her reason for wishing to strike upon just the right way of singing a particular line is that it will clarify and extend her grasp of this domain. It is a familiar and intuitively plausible thought that innovative musical performances have their value partly as a mode of exploring and illuminating the value of some array of "musical possibilities"—both for the artist and for the audience—and that this owes its value in part to the fact that it is simultaneously a way of opening up and illuminating the value of some unexplored array of human sensibilities and the artistic excellences to which these sensibilities attune us.

When we engage in music or other forms of artistic creation, there is a gap between that to which we aspire and any state of affairs of which we can already form a concrete representation. If the playwright could distinctly imagine a concrete product that would fully answer to the desire by which he is drawn to write plays, the work of artistic creation would be done and only the typing would remain. It seems, then, that the desires that propel artistic creation cannot be "world-to-mind" attitudes towards fully concrete propositional specifications of the desired end. Yet the object of such a desire is not vague, even if the creator's grip on it is hazy. The playwright presumably doesn't want to write just any old play, and he might well be sure in advance that whatever he manages to write will only approximate and not perfectly answer to the end towards which his creative efforts are oriented. So, does he want to write something really good? Well, yes, but at the risk of repetition: one could want *that* without being inspired directly by an intimation of a particular sort of goodness; in that case one would be consigned to writing without the inspiration or guidance of a muse. He is drawn into his writing by his intimation of an indistinctly perceived kind of goodness that might lie in it, if only he can find the words that exemplify it and bring its contours into clearer view.

DIALECTICAL DESIRES AND THE UNITY OF A LIFE

The most comprehensive dialectical activity in which human beings engage is the activity of living a good life. We first become conscious of this bizarre and singular task at a time when we have only the vaguest intimations of how best to rise to it. As we put these intimations into practice, we thereby put ourselves in a position to survey them in the concrete form of doings to which we must own up, whether in pride or embarrassment, mild regret or deep remorse. Sometimes our conception of the good condemns in retrospect an act towards which it inclines us in prospect. If we are to trust such alterations as insights or improvements, then we must credit our evaluative outlook with a recognitional capacity for particular, concrete goods whose content it cannot reliably grasp in the abstract. We must suppose that we have a vision of how it would be good to live that is clear enough to draw upon in order to launch active experiments in living, yet we must also suppose that we can apprehend and critique these experiments in retrospect, with this selfsame vision, in ways that sharpen its resolution.

Because of their shared dialectical character, propositionalism does as badly at making sense of the unity of human lives as of the unity of human activities. Just as the propositionalist conception of desire fractures what are naturally regarded as unified, temporally extended activities into disconnected spasms of motion, so too it fractures what are naturally seen as unified lives into arbitrary alterations in the direction in which one throws about one's causal weight in the world.

Exploring this problem will be much easier if we have before us a concrete and suitably complex case rather than a quickly sketched philosophical example. Let us consider, then, the longing that serves as the unifying thread of Augustine's *Confessions*, and that he eventually comes to regard as the desire for God, in whom "all things find their origin, their impulse, the centre of their being."[4] I turn to Augustine not to suggest that the desire for God is the sole or proper unifier of a human life, but to see what becomes of a life story when it is told under the idea that some desire plays this role. At one level of description, Augustine's guiding desires are continuously changing. At different stages his life is oriented around the pursuit of sex, aesthetic pleasure, philosophical insight, public honor, merely worldly friendship, and other ends that he eventually comes to regard as misguided. Yet Augustine thinks that we lose sight of the possibility of conversion (and, by extension, of the coherence of his and many other life stories) if we fail to see that the longing for God is present from the beginning of our lives, and that many human pursuits (including Augustine's pre-conversion pursuits) are unsatisfying displacements of a longing whose real nature is opaque to, or at least unacknowledged by, its possessor.[5]

Augustine, then, understands his own conversion not as the wholesale substitution of one set of desires for another, but as the attainment of a clearer and less adulterated vision of what he really longs for. This idea can seem hard to credit, since the pre-conversion "adulterations" of that vision were themselves desires, and it might seem that they must have been desires for something other than God. If the object of a desire were given by the state of affairs that actions springing from the desire are calculated to bring about, then clearly those earlier desires could not plausibly be regarded as desires for God. However, Augustine anticipates the "evaluative attention" account of desire in the sense that he thinks of desire as appreciative attention to some real or imagined object under the guise of the good. (The famous case of the purloined pears is no exception, for even if the fruit itself did not show up in the young Augustine's mind as good, the pose of rebellious independence and the approval of friends did.)[6] If we think

---

[4] Augustine, *Confessions* I, 2. Augustine is here echoing *Romans* I, 36.

[5] Augustine's picture of the desire for God is a religious correlate of Plato's recollection-based answer to the paradox of inquiry: just as Plato held that we must already have some inkling of truths in order to recognize them as true, so Augustine holds that we must already have an obscure longing for God's goodness in order to respond with appreciative desire to our first glimpses of God. Augustine is not speaking only of the saved, but of all humans, when he writes: "Man is one of your creatures, Lord, and his instinct is to praise you . . . since he is part of your creation, he wishes to praise you. The thought of you stirs him so deeply that he cannot be content unless he praises you, because you made us for yourself and our hearts find no peace until they rest in you" (*Confessions* I, 1).

[6] Augustine, *Confessions* II, 4–6.

of desires as apprehensions of actions, ends or persons as good, then we can make sense of the thought that the real object of Augustine's early desires was God by supposing that God answers best to the kind of goodness he imputed to the objects of those early desires. One might say, for instance, that his early desires involved a tendency to see various worldly pursuits as offering a deep or permanent satisfaction—a balm to an indistinct need—that worldly experience proves them unable to offer. His conversion might then be understood as consisting in the dawning conviction that his early, seemingly secular longings were misdirected towards activities that did not in fact answer to the evaluative picture implicit in them, and that something else, God, did answer to that evaluative picture and hence was the real object of those longings. A similar idea is implicit in the following saying (which is often, though apparently falsely, attributed to G. K. Chesterton): "A man knocking on the door of a brothel is knocking for God."[7]

The appeal of this approach to desire is that it helps us to see more clearly what distinguishes those curious sorts of desires that I have been calling dialectical. These desires have a vitally important yet somewhat elusive feature—a feature whose synchronic aspect might be called *depth* and whose diachronic aspect might be called *perfectibility*.[8] To say that a desire has depth is to say that its object exceeds the desirer's explicit articulation of it, and this affords the desirer with an occasion to perfect the desires by arriving at a fuller articulation of them.

As I've tried to show in the previous section, this point can be applied to a wide range of perfectionist pursuits and concerns, whether secular or sacred, and not just to longings directed at some perfect divinity or Platonic form. It obtains, for instance, in the pursuit of ideals of artistic or philosophical excellence. The objects of such desires are fugitive: as the light of self-understanding pierces more deeply into the desire, the desire itself extends so as to outdistance our achieved articulation of its object. This fugitive quality owes partly to the reflexive structure of the self. The self that pursues an understanding of its own guiding concerns will generally find that these concerns take on a more finely articulated shape as that pursuit advances.

To say that certain desires are dialectical is to say that repeated efforts to find words or actions suited to the goods they bring into view can provide us with an increasingly more adequate conception of these goods. By attempting to provide a faithful articulation of the goods one seems dimly to apprehend, one extends

---

[7] According to the American Chesterton Society, the line is not to be found in Chesterton's work. The most likely source is Bruce Smith's *The World, the Flesh, and Father Smith* (Boston: Houghton Mifflin Co., 1945), and Smith's actual words are: ". . . the young man who rings the bell at the brothel is unconsciously looking for God" (p. 108). http://www.chesterton.org/qmeister2/questions.htm

[8] This terminology and some of the ideas developed in this section were suggested to me by Chuck Mathewes in the course of several invaluable conversations about the themes of this chapter and their relation to Augustine.

the range of the appearances of value that structure one's experience. Dialectical desires are, in this particular, on all fours with apprehensions of aesthetic value. By articulating one's sense of the aesthetic value of the paintings one sees, or the novels one reads, one cultivates that self-same aesthetic sensibility by extending its reach and increasing its nuance and complexity (its *articulation*).[9] Likewise, by articulating the intimations of goodness or value that are partly constitutive of one's desires, one cultivates one's capacity for apprehending the good by extending its reach and increasing its nuance and complexity. This sort of progressive attempt to understand one's own fundamental concerns is a central element in the most coherent telling of the story of (almost) any distinctively human life.

We lose sight of this central human activity if we embrace the first two dogmas of desire as an exhaustive account of the ideational content of desire. On that approach, the ideational content of a desire would consist solely in the propositional representation of whatever states of affairs the desire disposes its possessor to make actual. If Augustine's behavior is at one point calculated to bring it about that he sleeps with prostitutes in Carthage, and at another point that he becomes famous for his philosophical teachings, and at a third point that he attains oneness with God, then the propositional approach will picture these successive guiding concerns as entirely distinct, related only because they happen to occur in the course of the same life. They do not form a series that can explain the unity of this life; rather, the unity of the life, given entirely on other grounds, is what constitutes them as a series. A life story told solely in terms of such a succession of guiding desires would be a series of unintelligible shifts in the protagonist's manner of throwing about his causal weight in the world. What seems from the first-personal standpoint to be a gradual deepening of one's understanding of what one wants is interpreted as a series of shifts in what one wants. What seems to be growth is reduced to mere change.

One way to bring out the problem at hand is to note that without further supplementation, the belief–desire model of action–explanation can serve up a rationalizing explanation of any series of performances, no matter how fractured or discontinuous the series might seem. Suppose an agent performs a seemingly bizarre and disconnected series of actions a_1 thru a_n at times t_1 thru t_n. Once we assign to the agent some interpretation, no matter how bizarre, of what he is doing at each of these moments, we can provide a rationalizing explanation of his actions in accordance with the belief–desire model simply by assigning to him a changing series of desires d_1 thru d_n, where d_1 is a desire by which the agent happens to be gripped at time t_1 to bring it about that he performs an action answering to his interpretation of a_1, d_2 is a desire by which the agent happens

---

[9] For an interesting discussion of the thought that the articulation of basic concerns both puts them into words and gives them more precise form, see Charles Taylor's essay "Responsibility for Self," in Gary Watson, ed., *Free Will* (Oxford: Oxford University Press, 1982), 111–26.

to be gripped at time t_2 to bring it about that he performs an action answering to his interpretation of a_2, and so on.

Unless we think that desires ought rationally to endure over time, or to change in accordance with some coherent thought process about what there is reason to do, there will be no problem whatever exhibiting the rationality of any possible series of actions. Many of these series will strike us as highly unusual, since we are used to interacting with people whose desires exhibit a reassuring stability. This is lucky, since otherwise we would have very little idea what to expect from others. So we will be *surprised* if we find people whose desires are constantly changing. But without further supplementation, the propositionalist model for the rationalizing explanation of action lacks the resources to condemn this as a kind of irrationality. Yet surely it *is* irrationality. Indeed, if it takes an extreme enough form it ceases to be irrationality and begins to spell the dissolution of any sort of agency at all. Hence surely the propositionalist picture of rationalizing explanation needs either to be supplemented or replaced entirely. The canons of practical rationality are not merely synchronic. Rationality demands that one's performances over time cohere with each other in the form of intelligible pursuits, and they cannot do so if the aims and priorities that seem to be expressed in them change over time in wholly arbitrary or thoughtless ways. Nor can the difference between sensible and senseless changes be spelled out in a wholly non-evaluative vocabulary.

What this suggests is that when we attribute desires to people and track changes in those desires, we are guided by diachronic standards of charitable interpretation. Thus desires cannot be a bedrock of given material, not itself subject to canons of rationality, upon which we can attempt to ground conclusions about what it is or is not rational for people to do. We are already in the thick of the activity of interpreting others as rational when we impute desires to them. Such interpretations are guided not only by our sense of what humans can reasonably find to be valuable (a point stressed in Chapter 1) but also by our sense of how their outlook on value can reasonably change under pressure of experience and reflection.

It might be thought that the propositionalist could provide a diachronically unified interpretation of Augustine's successive pursuits by attributing to him an enduring desire that his life be organized around and informed by the highest goods applicable to human life, then suggesting that his conversion consisted in a fundamental change in his beliefs about this highest good. No doubt Augustine had such a desire. But if the idea behind this suggestion is to illuminate the point and the coherence of Augustine's strivings by bringing them within the canonical belief–desire model, then the suggestion must be rejected. From the standpoint of the deliberator, the point of acting in ways calculated to make true that one live a good life, or a life organized around properly focal or authoritative goods, cannot lie in the fact that one happens to have a desire with this propositional content. One can offer a full rationalizing explanation of an action by showing

how the action came to look good to the agent who went for it, without needing
to mention that the agent desires to go for things that look good to him.

Here we see once again that goodness cannot be shoehorned into the propositional account as a contingent element in the propositional depiction of
the states of affairs one desires to bring about. Any property could enter into a
propositional desire in *that* way, yet apprehensions of the property of goodness
have a *special* role in explaining one's actions. We could have the propositional
desire that (it be the case that) we live in accordance with the good, yet find
ourselves in a depressed or dispirited condition that inures us to the more immediate attraction, or vivid appeal, of the goods that figure in this propositional
desire. To fulfill this propositional desire would require coming to feel a vivid
and unmediated attraction to the goods one is able to discern. Indeed, this is a
rather exact description of the predicament Augustine took himself to be in, just
prior to his conversion. He presents himself as badly wanting it to be the case
that he enter into intimate relation with God, yet as lacking the wholehearted,
attention-flooding longing for God that he regards as the primary constituent of
this desired condition.[10]

On reflection, it should not come as a surprise that this move fails. Consider
how we arrived at this point in the dialectic. We were considering the credentials
of a conception of rational action according to which we come to have reasons
to produce possible states of affairs when we desire them. Desires serve, on this
conception, to confer reason-giving force upon possible states of affairs that
would otherwise have no practical significance. If we already see some possible
action or outcome as good, this alone ensures that it has practical significance
in our eyes. This way of seeing the action or outcome is already sufficient to
rationalize our decision to perform the action or promote the state of affairs.
Desire serves, by the propositionalist's lights, to convert what would otherwise
be indifferent from the practical point of view into something it is rational to
pursue. The good does not stand in need of such a conversion. If one sees a
certain kind of activity as good, then one thereby sees it as something there is
some reason to do, and no mention of a desire is needed in order to provide a
rationalizing explanation of one's decision to go for it. And if one has decided
to engage in an activity, then one does not need an extra desire—the desire to
perform the activity well—in order to rationalize one's efforts to perform it in a
way that one regards as good rather than indifferent or bad. Nor is the addition
needed to explain such efforts. As noted above, a capacity to do what one sees as
good or worthwhile is a necessary condition of agency, not a contingent capacity
traceable to a desire that an agent might conceivably be without.

The alternative for which I've argued is to understand the ideational content
of a desire as an inchoate picture of some species or aspect of goodness. This
approach permits us to see how an initially obscure desire can be cultivated

---

[10] Augustine, *Confessions*, Book VIII.

over time so as to afford what its possessor regards as an increasingly clear understanding of a kind of goodness or value once seen through a glass, darkly. It can then make sense to speak of a person's life as centered around the progressive clarification of a single, self-defining longing that has strikingly different behavioral manifestations at different times.

To adopt this conception of desire is to reject a picture of the nature and point of human action that has a rather powerful hold not only on contemporary philosophy but on the contemporary culture in which that philosophy is embedded. On this ascendant conception, human action always gets its point from some pre-envisioned state of affairs that the agent seeks to bring about. It is this deeply embedded cultural prejudice in favor of production-oriented conceptions of action that stands in the way of making full sense of dialectical activities.

There is a place for propositional desires on this alternative, "evaluative outlook" account of desires, but a subsidiary rather than a primary one. Just as a visual perception (e.g. of a landscape) can give rise to a plethora of beliefs *that* things are thus and such, so too the quasi-perceptual evaluative outlooks (i.e. non-propositional desires) that provide us with our pre-deliberative sense of the good can give rise to a plethora of desires *that* things be thus and such. Yet we cannot hope to make the occurrence of these propositional desires intelligible, nor to exhaust their ideational content, merely by capturing them in propositional form. Propositional desires derive any justificatory import they might have from the evaluative outlooks that spawn them. These outlooks provide the desirer with a picture of the *point* of trying to bring it about that the world answer to one or another proposition. As noted above, a propositional desire considered in itself might give the desirer a *de facto* psychological propensity to bring it about that things are thus and such, but it does not provide him with a reason to do so.[11]

The contemporary antipathy to this picture of desire owes in part to the conviction that there are no truths concerning what it would be good to do or how it would be good to live, conjoined with a reluctance to suppose that we cannot sensibly take guidance from our own desires—i.e. do what we want to do—without implicitly undertaking the false supposition that there are. Here as elsewhere, one thinker's *modus tollens* is another thinker's *modus ponens*. In my view, we should hold on to the premise that desires have a mind-to-world direction of fit, and that the world is such that it is possible for desires to succeed in "fitting" it, on pain of losing our grip on the thought that our practical reasoning might go well or badly. Indeed, since counting a series of mental events as an episode of reasoning implies that it has answered at least passably well to the constitutive norms or ideals of reasoning, what is at stake here is our grip on

---

[11] Warren Quinn makes this point very effectively in the essay "Putting Rationality in Its Place," in *Morality and Action* (Cambridge: Cambridge University Press, 1993), 228–55; especially 236–7.

the idea that there is such a thing as practical reasoning. Or so I will argue in upcoming chapters.

A BRIEF HISTORY OF THE DIALECTICAL CONCEPTION OF DESIRE

The dialectical conception of desire that I have outlined here is currently out of favor, but it has not always been so. Augustine's discussion of the desire for God finds its place within a long tradition of Platonist, neo-Platonist, and Christian mystical discussions of the longing that attracts humans to the highest good, understood either as abstract form or as divine person. The propositional view cannot make good sense of this tradition, nor even of our readiness to recognize that it is a tradition of thought about what we call desire. We are prone to arrive at fundamental misunderstandings of this tradition of thought if we read it through the lens of currently ascendant ideas about desire. This tradition coheres far better with the dialectical account of desire that I have begun to set out in this chapter.

To get hold of this strand, it will help to begin with two quotes from the fourth century Platonist and mystical theologian Gregory of Nyssa, who died three years before Augustine wrote his *Confessions*. Here is what Gregory says about desiring God:

It is not in the nature of what is unenclosed to be grasped. But every desire (*epithumia*) for the Good which is attracted to that ascent constantly expands as one progresses in pressing on to the Good . . . This truly is the vision of God: never to be satisfied in the desire (*epithumia*) to see him. But one must always, by looking at what he can see, rekindle his desire (*epithumia*) to see more. Thus, no limit would interrupt growth in the ascent to God, since no limit to the Good can be found nor is the increasing of desire (*epithumia*) for the Good brought to an end because it is satisfied.[12]

Elsewhere Gregory writes:

Hope always draws the soul from the beauty which is seen to what is beyond, always kindles the desire for the hidden through what is constantly perceived. Therefore, the ardent lover of beauty although receiving what is always visible as an image of what he desires (*epithumia*), yet longs to be filled with the very stamp of the archetype.[13]

In these passages, Gregory portrays *epithumia* as a mesmerizing vision that, because of the seeming beauty or goodness of its apparent object, never satisfies but always heightens the selfsame *epithumia*, and thus continuously induces those possessed by it to bring its object more clearly into view. The word 'desire' seems

---

[12] Gregory of Nyssa, *The Life of Moses*, translated by Abraham J. Malherbe and Everett Ferguson (New York: Paulist Press, 1978), sections 238–9.

[13] Gregory of Nyssa, *The Life of Moses*, section 231.

an apt translation for the longing that Gregory has in mind, not only because his thought is immediately recognizable in English, but also because he uses the term 'epithumia' elsewhere in the same work to refer to attractions that fall comfortably within the ambit of what we call desire.[14] Yet the desire described by Gregory does not seem to aim at the refashioning of the world so as to bring it into correspondence with any proposition. The desire seems to consist in a mesmerizing attraction to a good wholly present rather than in a disposition to bring about some as-yet-unrealized state of affairs.

Any attempt to capture the desire's end in propositional form is likely to exhibit one of two failures. If love of the Good, or of God, is mistaken for the desire that one be good, or possess the good, or be worthy of the love of God, this would be tantamount to reversing the "direction of gaze" of the desire. What presents itself as an attraction to something *other*, longing for which might have the *indirect effect* on the desirer of making the desirer good, is misconstrued as a desire for its own indirect effect. This cannot be the desire in question, since one could have any one of these self-oriented propositional desires (i.e. that one be good, or possess the good, or be worthy of the love of God) without feeling the overwhelming and unmediated attraction to the good, or God, that Gregory is trying to characterize, and that might plausibly have the indirect effect of making one good.

Other likely sounding propositional translations of the desire for God fail because they only manage to capture the desire itself, in its most extreme pitch, rather than its object. The desire that I be one with God, or that I be one with the good, is best understood as a metaphorical expression of the desire that I be continuously filled with a proximate and unmediated awareness of God, or the good, as what they essentially are (e.g. as good). But such awareness just is the desire in question, in its most extreme pitch. Yet we cannot locate the object of the desire in the desirer's own conscious states without misunderstanding contemplative devotion as self-preoccupation. To save the embarrassment of concluding that the desire's object is neither good nor God but merely itself intensified, I think it best to say that if the desire is not illusory, it is directed at a person and not at a project. That is, its object is not a state of affairs to be brought about, but a luminous being already wholly present if not wholly

---

[14] For instance, in section 271 of *The Life of Moses*, Gregory writes: "But the people had not learned to keep in step with Moses' greatness. They were still drawn down to the slavish passions (*epithumia*) and were inclined to the Egyptian pleasures." In section 272, he writes: "Their unruly desires (*epithumia*) produced serpents which injected deadly poison into those they bit. The great lawgiver, however, rendered the real serpents powerless by the image of a serpent." Again, in section 280: "When those who were lusting (*epithumounton*) believed in the one lifted up on the wood, the earth stopped bringing forth serpents to bite them . . . It is then, when lustful desire (*epithumia*) leaves them, that the disease of arrogance enters in its place." Finally, in section 316: "And when you, as a sculptor, carve in your own heart the divine oracles which you receive from God; and when you destroy the golden idol (that is, if you wipe from your life the desire (*epithumia*) of covetousness) . . . then you will draw near to the goal."

appreciated. While it is true that this luminous being appears as something to be savored and neared, the desire that displays it as such is not best interpreted as the desire that one savor or near it. Such an interpretation would either commit the above-mentioned error of mistaking the desire for a solipsistic longing for its own intensification, or assign to the desire an object that one could desire without desiring God.

The reason we cannot compass the desire for God within the framework of propositionalism is not, as one might be tempted to suppose, that God's goodness is infinite. Infinitude in itself is no bar to propositional (as opposed, say, to pictorial) representation. The real reason is that the desire's object is not the sort of thing that can be picked out by a proposition, nor for that matter the sort of thing one could sensibly endeavor to bring about. It is a person and not a state of affairs. If Gregory's discussion of the desire for God is so much as coherent, what it shows is that the wellspring of human motivation can consist in a mesmerizing and self-augmenting vision of goodness—a vision that precedes and inspires determinate plans and projects. Further, there is an historically prominent sense of 'desire' that is broad enough to encompass such visions of goodness, even when these visions are taken in isolation from ensuing plans and projects.[15]

I have been using the phrase 'dialectical desire' to refer to desires that consist in self-augmenting attraction to persons or objects represented under the aspect of the intrinsically good. The notion that there are such desires, and that they mediate our relation to the highest good, has obvious resonances with the Platonic picture of the reasoning part of the soul's self-augmenting attraction to truth and to the form of the Good. The self-augmenting feature of this desire is brought out in a particularly vivid way by Plato's talk, in the *Phaedrus*, of the vision of true being as the proper nourishment for the soul, capable of strengthening the plumage of the soul's wings so that it becomes increasingly able to bear itself upwards and to partake of the self-same nourishing vision.[16] However, this conception of desire for the good might just as plausibly be said to have Aristotelian roots, as it has a distinct affinity with Aristotle's claims (in

---

[15] At the risk of illuminating the obscure with the indecipherable, the sort of desire at issue here has clear affinities with what Emmanuel Levinas calls "metaphysical desire." In Levinas' words: "The other metaphysically desired is not "other" like the bread I eat, the land in which I dwell, the landscape I contemplate . . . I can "feed" on these realities and to a very great extent satisfy myself, as though I had simply been lacking them. The metaphysical analysis of desire tends toward *something else entirely*, toward the *absolutely other*. The customary analysis of desires cannot explain away its singular pretension . . . The metaphysical desire has another intention; it desires beyond everything that can simply complete it. It is like goodness—the Desired does not fulfill it, but deepens it . . . This remoteness is radical only if desire is not the possibility of anticipating the desirable, only if it does not think it beforehand, if it goes toward it aimlessly, that is, as toward an absolute, unanticipatable alterity, as one goes forth unto death." See Emmanuel Levinas, *Totality and Infinity: An Essay on Exteriority*, tr. Alphonso Lingis (Pittsburgh, Duquesne University Press: 1969), 33–4.

[16] See *Phaedrus* 246d–249c.

Metaphysics Λ, part 7) that the unmoved mover is the highest good and the primary object both of thought and of desire, and that this object serves as the final cause of action not in the sense that things are done for its good (it can't be altered) but in the sense that things are done out of love for it.

The dialectical conception of desire for the divine enters into the early Christian mystical tradition at least a century before Gregory, in the neo-Platonist writings of Plotinus. For Plotinus, the human encounter with the Good is not a passionless intellectual exercise but rather the responsiveness of reason to something that mightily attracts it and that inspires a loving desire proper to us. The Good is "the desired of every soul."[17] To see the Good is to be filled with a "veritable love" and a "sharp desire" for it.[18] If you are gripped by such a loving desire, Plotinus claims, you will find within yourself "a Dionysiac exultation that thrills through your being" together with "a straining upwards of all your soul."[19] This is the sole route to becoming good, since one becomes good not by directly striving to be good but only as the byproduct of loving desire oriented immediately towards the divine mind—an object that all humans grasp, at least dimly, as the proper object of their longing and contemplative attention.[20] Indeed, Plotinus holds that all of nature strives towards contemplation of the divine mind, though the participation of inanimate nature in the divine mind differs from the best sort of human contemplation as sleep differs from waking.[21] Still, humans vary widely in their degree of wakefulness, and many strive to bring about material results in the world without realizing that the real object of their longing is not some state of affairs they might produce, but a perfection they are suited to contemplate and to participate in by means of contemplation.[22]

It is well beyond the scope of this chapter to provide even a minimally comprehensive history of the still-evolving theological conception of dialectical desire for God, whose early elaborations we've found in Plotinus and Gregory. Still, to get some sense of the longevity and centrality of this notion, it will help to look briefly at a few of its more influential manifestations. The dialectical notion of the desire for God crops up in Aquinas' discussion in *Summa Theologica* (II, I, 1–5) of the "last end" and our desire for it.[23] Aquinas speaks of man's last end as the proper object of desire, and he characterizes this last end formally as happiness and substantively as God. All men desire happiness[24] but not all see that "God alone constitutes man's happiness" and hence that the last end of man, hence the proper object of desire, "is not the good of the universe, but God himself."[25] The

[17] Plotinus, *First Ennead*, VI, 7. Quotes are drawn from Plotinus, *The Enneads*, translated by Stephen MacKenna (New York: Penguin Books, 1991).
[18] *Ibid.*, VI, 7.   [19] *Ibid.*, VI, 5.   [20] *Ibid.*, II, 4.
[21] Plotinus, *Third Ennead*, VIII, 1–5.   [22] *Ibid.*, VIII, 4.
[23] I thank Tobias Hoffman for directing my attention to these passages.
[24] Thomas Aquinas, *Summa Theologica*, translated by English Dominican Fathers, First Part of Second Part, 5, 8.
[25] *Ibid.*, 2,8, and 3,1.

last end, in other words, is not some way that the created universe might come to be, but a perfect being who is always already wholly present though never wholly grasped by the human mind. Aquinas notes that this last end of man can be characterized either as God or as the attainment or possession of God.[26] Yet, he makes clear, the first characterization is primary. Attainment or possession of God is good only because it constitutes a form of participation in a conceptually prior and independent good.[27] Hence, the goodness of God is more final than the goodness of any possible relation to God, and since the proper object of desire is the most final end, the proper object is God.

We can reach this same interpretive conclusion by focusing on Aquinas' denial that the final end could be a property or possession of the human soul. For Aquinas, happiness consists in attaining or participating in the final end, God. Yet, as Aquinas makes clear, " . . . the thing itself which is desired as end, is that which constitutes happiness, and makes men happy; but the attainment of this thing is called happiness. Consequently we must say that happiness is something belonging to the soul; but that which constitutes happiness is something outside the soul."[28] Aquinas holds that "it is impossible for man's last end to be the soul itself or something belonging to it."[29] Again, since the last end is the proper object of desire, the proper object of desire is God and not one's own attainment or possession of God.

Relatedly, Aquinas claims that we misunderstand the proper desire "to" God if we think of it as a desire to enjoy or delight in the contemplative vision of God. This would effectively reverse the "direction of gaze" of the proper desire for God. Desire for the highest good involves a movement of the intellect towards that good. Delight is necessarily attendant upon the intellect's approach to the highest good, and that approach is in turn propelled by a longing for the highest good.[30] Those whose sole desire is for this delight itself will be unable to attain it.[31]

It might seem that Aquinas' occasional references to resting in God, or sating one's appetite for God, mark an important departure from the views of Gregory of Nyssa, who denies that it is possible to bring contemplative appreciation of God to a fully perfect form, or to satiate the desire for God. Yet this difference turns out on inspection to be superficial, since Aquinas denies that the contemplation of God's infinite perfection can itself be perfected by a finite human mind.[32] Hence the human desire for God can augment itself without end. As Aquinas puts it, " . . . the more perfectly the sovereign good is possessed, the more it is loved, and other things despised: because the more we possess it, the more we know it. Hence it is written (Ecclus. 24: 29): 'They that eat me shall yet hunger.' "[33]

---

[26] Aquinas, *Summa Theologica*, First Part of Second Part, 1,8; 2,7, and 3,1.
[27] *Ibid.*, 2,7; see also 3,1.　　[28] *Ibid.*, 2,7; see also 3,5.　　[29] *Ibid.*, 2,7.
[30] *Ibid.*, 2,6, and 3,4.　　[31] *Ibid.*, 3,4.　　[32] *Ibid.*, 3,2; 4,3, and 5,3.　　[33] *Ibid.*, 2,1.

A recognizably Gregorian conception of desire for God can also be glimpsed in the writings of various fourteenth and fifteenth-century Christian mystics, as for instance in the below-quoted selection from Walter Hilton's *The Ladder of Perfection*. This selection is particularly interesting because it uses the Old English word 'desire' in a way that cannot be accommodated within the propositionalist framework. This usage was unsettling enough to the translator that he seized upon the Modern English term 'longing' to capture the idea being expressed. It is also worth noting that what is at issue, for Hilton, is a desire *to* something rather than *for* something. The archaic preposition suggests that desires are impulsions towards their objects rather than inclinations to possess their objects—an idea that is easily lost in translation (as it is in the translation I've used). Here is the selection in question:

If, then, you feel a great longing (*desire*) in your heart for Jesus . . . and if this longing (*desire*) is so strong that its force drives out of your heart all other thoughts and desires of the world and the flesh, then you are indeed seeking your Lord Jesus. And if, when you feel this desire for (*to*) God, for (*to*) Jesus . . . you are helped and strengthened by a supernatural might so strong that it is changed into love and affection, spiritual savour and sweetness and knowledge of truth . . . then you have found something of Jesus . . . and the more fully you find Him, the more you will desire Him.[34]

(Parenthetical interpolations are from the original Old English)

Hilton writes his book for aspiring contemplatives who aim to cultivate an abiding desire "to" God, a love on fire with contemplation. Such contemplation cannot be perfected in this life, but only in the bliss of heaven, when "all of the aspirations (*affeccion*) of the soul will be entirely Godward and spiritual."[35] In Hilton's view, this state does not leave behind the loving desire for God, but is continually buoyed and strengthened by such loving desire—it is "love on fire with contemplation."[36] The sole pathway to this contemplation is to cultivate a self-augmenting desire for God—to "seek desire by desire."[37]

Given the Platonic and Aristotelian roots of the dialectical conception of human desire for the highest good, and given its continued grip on Thomistic and Christian mystical theology,[38] it is no exaggeration to say that its elaboration and development has been the work of two and a half millennia. This historically influential tradition of thought is fundamentally at odds with the three dogmas

---

[34] Walter Hilton, *The Ladder of Perfection*, translated by Leo Sherley-Price (New York: Penguin, 1957), Book I, chapter 46.

[35] Hilton, *The Ladder of Perfection*, Book II, chapter 35.

[36] This is Hilton's name for the highest level of spiritual enlightenment, involving "ecstatic union with God." See Clifton Wolters' introduction to the above-cited edition of *The Ladder of Perfection*, xxiii.

[37] Hilton, *The Ladder of Perfection*, Book I, chapter 47.

[38] This notion of desire surfaces in the work of certain twentieth-century Christian theologians. See for instance Hans Urs von Balthasar, *Prayer* (San Francisco: Ignatius Press, 1986), 24–5; see also *Seeing the Form*, Volume I of *The Glory of the Lord: A Theological Aesthetics* (Edinburgh: T&T Clark, 1982), 120–2.

of desire set out in the last chapter, and one cost of our attachment to these dogmas is that they impede our efforts to understand the moral psychology of this tradition.

This same tradition has somewhat greater affinity with the "evaluative outlook" conception of desire favored by Scanlon and Stampe than with the straightforward propositionalist conception. Still, we must make minor emendations to the best-known expositions of the evaluative outlook account in order to accommodate dialectical desires. Stampe, for instance, holds that having a desire amounts to being struck by the seeming goodness of something, and to this extent his view seems like a natural home for dialectical desires. However, he goes on to say that the goodness in question is always attached to the prospect of some proposition's coming to be true. Hence he does not break with the thought that we can desire something other than the coming into actuality of a possible state of affairs.

Scanlon, for his part, thinks of desires in the "directed attention sense" as tendencies to see certain features of one's circumstances as reasons for doing or bringing about something or another, and this rules out the possibility of a desire directed at a good or value that cannot simply be reduced to reasons for action. Indeed, Scanlon's theory of value reduces all apprehensions of goodness or value to apprehensions of reasons.[39] I will argue against this view in Chapter 5. For now, it will suffice to note that the position seems strained when applied to aesthetic or religious experience, since such experiences seem to involve the apprehension of goods that bear on, but are not exhausted by, claims about what one ought to feel or do. Hence it is unsurprising that Scanlon's view is subtly at odds with Platonic and Christian mystical conceptions of desire for beauty, the good and God.

LOVING DESIRE FOR OTHER HUMAN BEINGS

I turn now to another kind of desire that cannot plausibly be shoehorned into the propositionalist mold: loving desires for other human beings. No doubt a wide variety of human urges and longings could be brought under the fungible description of "loving desire." I have no wish to stake out exclusive rights to the phrase. Still, I think that the conception of desire that I've set out above permits us to bring into focus a familiar and valuable mode of interpersonal attraction. The approach provides a way of crediting the thought that personal love essentially involves desire without committing us to the claim that it essentially involves a project of remaking the world in the image of one's thoughts. It leaves open the possibility of a desire consisting simply in mesmeric attraction to, and delight in, an element of the world already wholly given. When we desire a person in this

---

[39] Scanlon, *What We Owe to Each Other*, chapter 2, especially 95–100.

sense, the apparent goodness brought to light by the desire is the actual goodness of someone already wholly present, if not yet wholly appreciated or understood, and not the hypothetical goodness of some merely possible state of affairs. Such an attraction is not in the first instance a call to world-making. It might induce one to celebrate the other's presence in a variety of ways, but to be moved to genuine celebration is not to be moved by the thought of the *celebration*'s goodness but rather by the thought of the goodness that incites the celebration. More generally, such an attraction might issue forth in a wide variety of plans for alteration of the world, but the point of these subsidiary aims cannot be understood except in the light of the more fundamental attraction to a kind of goodness perceived as already wholly present. Indeed, the continued existence and perhaps even the intensification of this more immediate attraction might well figure as a condition for the desirability of whatever states of affairs this same attraction inspires one to attempt to bring about (e.g. that one lives with another, marries another, spends time with another, sleeps with another, and so on).

A proper and undistorted intimate relationship is a mutual and continuous gifting of the self to the other. The gift of self to another is misconstrued when thought of as an offer to produce or enact some future state of affairs with the other. The gift is present now; it is on offer now. It is not a promise of a future deliverable. It is not a proposition to be or do anything but a willing self-exposure, a free opening to another's gaze through which one permits oneself to be known in hopes of being appreciated and at risk of being scorned.

If we reflect on what it can mean in the best of cases to desire another person—i.e. to be drawn to them lovingly—the propositional translations of this desire all seem to omit something critical. Some fail because they distort the desire, often by portraying its object with a metaphor that cannot be taken literally without rendering the desire more possessive than ideally it ought to be (e.g. "that she be mine" or "that I possess her"). Others fail because they describe the desiring itself rather than its object. An instance of this second class of failures is the proposition "that I be one with her." If this last proposition is to pick out a possibility consistent with the welcome fact of the separateness of persons, it seems to mean something like: that I attain a vivid, immediate, and fully appreciative awareness of her value (and perhaps vice versa). Yet such vivid awareness just is desire, in its most intensive pitch. We cannot understand loving desires as desires for their own intensification without losing hold of the most basic facts about them—i.e. that the loving desire for one person has a different object than the loving desire for another person, and that the objects of such desires are not one's own future psychological states but something wholly other than oneself.

If we understand loving desire in this way, we are able to attain a deeper understanding of the "unselfing" influence exercised by the best and purest forms of loving desire. Such desires are attention-arresting modes of appreciation of something wholly other. They serve to remove us from the condition of distraction, and in particular from that most banal and obsessive of human distractions, the self. They also extend our concerns beyond our standing articulation of those concerns.

It is part of our relation to other persons that if we are able to love them at all, we must love them before we grasp fully who or what they are such that they are worthy of the attention we devote to them. To love another is to be drawn to another by a generous straining to bring into focus the goodness, hence desirability, of an as-yet-obscure object of desire. The lover stands ready to interpret the beloved's words and actions as signposts towards further discoveries about what it is good to be or to do, and this interpretive posture sustains and is sustained by attention-riveting appreciation of the other. At its best, this is a mutual and continuously reiterated process. It involves a readiness on the part of each to be guided by the example of the other in articulating an evolving understanding of the human good. This is an *ekstasis* of the most literal sort—a displacement of the self from the confines of the standing concerns that constitute the central element in what is sometimes called its "practical identity,"[40] and a readiness to discern new outlines for its own guiding concerns in the person of another. (I return to these matters in Chapter 7.)

It might be objected that I have suggested an improbably ample picture of what it can mean to desire another person, since we ordinarily reserve talk of desiring persons for cases of sexual attraction. Common usage might be preferred here for its refreshingly crass picture of human longings, and my view might be dismissed as quaintly romantic. Yet one must ask whether common usage might be shaped not by clarity about the real nature of human longings but by anxious insistence to mark off a safe boundary between sexuality and other, merely Platonic forms of interpersonal longing or attraction. Common language might be regarded here as the bearer not of our accumulated psychological wisdom but of our taboos. If we set these taboos aside, we can admit the pervasive sexual undertones to "Platonic" human relations, and we can acknowledge that sexual desires are often shot through with longing for a kind of access to another's being that cannot be secured but only symbolized by sex.[41] This insight dates at least to Lucretius, who writes:

> Venus plays tricks on lovers with her game
> Of images which never satisfy.

---

[40] I believe that this phrase was introduced into contemporary philosophical discussion by Christine Korsgaard in *The Sources of Normativity* (Cambridge: Cambridge University Press, 1996).

[41] Another problem with the objection at hand is that it makes it entirely mysterious why believers and unbelievers alike tend to accept the aptness of talk about desiring God. If desires for God are recognized as conceptually coherent and not necessarily sexual, and if Gregory's account of longings for God is recognizable as an account of something it makes sense to call *desire*, then there would seem to be conceptual space for desires for other persons that are not necessarily sexual but that are partly constituted, and continuously deepened, by appreciative awareness of another's goodness.

Looking at bodies fills no vital need
However nakedly the lovers gaze,
However much their hands go wandering
And still are empty—can they gather bloom
From tender limbs? And then the time arrives
When their embraces join, and they delight
In the full flower of love, or almost do,
Anticipating rapture soon to come,
The moment of the sowing. Eagerly
They press their bodies close, join lips and tongues,
Their breath comes faster, faster. All in vain,
For they can gather nothing, they cannot
Effect real penetration, be absorbed
Body in body, utterly. They seem
To want to do just this. God knows they try . . .[42]

Lucretius' ambition here is to show that sexual desire aims at something impossible, and thereby makes us ridiculous and needlessly vulnerable, hence that we ought to reshape our sexual longings so that they direct us towards ends that can actually be realized. It is worth pointing out, though, that this wonderful description of sexual longing seems most apt for cases of loving sex and not detached or impersonal sex. Given this, there are perhaps grounds for venturing that the sort of sexual longing described by Lucretius aims at symbolic enactment of the infinite nearing of loving desire. Understood in this way, the longing might be regarded as more nearly sublime than ridiculous. To reject such sexual longings because they aim at a physical impossibility would be like rejecting a statue of Pegasus on the ground that chunks of marble can't possibly take wing.

CONCLUDING REMARKS ON THE DOGMAS OF DESIRE

As I noted in the last chapter, talk of desire has become quite rare outside of philosophical circles, to the point where one of the more ordinary uses of the term 'desire' might well be, or at least be heavily influenced by, the contemporary philosophical use as guided by the dogmas of desire. Given this, there is some danger that philosophical accommodation of "ordinary" usage will lend undeserved impregnability to reigning philosophical orthodoxies. Still, we should take care not to exaggerate the degree to which the proponents of the three dogmas of desire can preen themselves on their fidelity to ordinary usage. The numerous philosophers who sign on to one or more of the above-mentioned dogmas of desire tend to use the term 'desire' in a very broad sense, encompassing

---

[42] Lucretius, *The Way of Nature*, Book IV, 1100–12.

all mental states whose world-to-mind direction of fit suits them to explain actions (when paired with suitable beliefs).[43] These philosophers are typically quite aware that this usage departs strikingly from ordinary usage, and they are right to insist that this alone is not an objection to their view. Philosophers ought to adopt whatever conception of desire permits them to generate the most illuminating account possible of human agency, even if this conception comes loose in certain particulars from ordinary talk of desire. The tenability of the conception of desire elaborated in this essay depends upon whether they help us or hinder us in our efforts to formulate a coherent account of human actions and the lives they compose.

The three dogmas of desire come naturally to us because they cohere with the thought that the point of human action, if there is one, would have to lie in the states of affairs that the action is calculated to bring about (if only by constituting that state of affairs). It would be interesting to speculate on how exactly this conception of the point of action has colonized the most fundamental concepts through which we bring agency into view, crowding out the tradition of thought sketched in this chapter. The story is no doubt multi-faceted, but one thing that must surely enter into it is the historic rise of vast social organizations that assign specialized roles and tasks to each participant. These institutional forms of coordinated activity have multiplied in large part because they are immensely productive, yet they cannot function smoothly unless each participant can be counted on to deliver up whatever state of affairs is required to set the stage and grease the wheels for the work of others. Within such institutional contexts, coordinated tasks are specified in terms of the deliverables towards which they are directed, and participants are assessed in terms of their reliability in producing these deliverables. As Alasdair MacIntyre has argued, a society with institutions of this sort will see little point in cultivating or praising the specifically Greek virtues, since these virtues have their value as preconditions for complete and unimpeded engagement in intrinsically valuable (shared) activities, and not as grease for the wheels of large enterprises.[44] A very different and recognizably instrumental order of virtues tends to rise to prominence within a society characterized by this form of organized cooperation: efficiency, punctuality, reliability, industry, a strong and unquestioning "work ethic," and the like.

Whatever its causes, the production-based conception of human action has taken hold, and has manifest itself within professional philosophy in the form of the three dogmas of desire. I've tried to show that this tempting understanding of the point of action does not permit us to make good sense of our lives

---

[43] See for instance Bernard Williams, "Internal and External Reasons," in *Moral Luck* (Cambridge: Cambridge University Press, 1981), 101–13. See also Michael Smith, *The Moral Problem*, 113–14.

[44] Alasdair MacIntyre, "Moral Philosophy and Contemporary Social Practice: What Holds Them Apart?" in *The Tasks of Philosophy: Selected Essays* (Cambridge: Cambridge University Press, 2006), 104–24.

and their unity, of our desires for other human beings, or of our wholehearted activities and the pleasure we take in them. I also hope to have shown that the rival "soul-picture" I've begun to articulate can make better sense of these phenomena, while opening up "new places for philosophical reflection" of the sort mentioned by Murdoch in the epigraph to the Introduction. In particular, I hope to have begun to open up fruitful places for philosophical reflection about the nature of practical thought, the way it surges forth in action, and the role of the virtues of character in enhancing the acuity and reliability of practical thought. These are the themes to which we turn in the next chapter.

3

Fluency in Practical Thinking

For an instant it may seem as if the things between which a choice is to be made lie outside of the chooser, that he stands in no relationship to it, that he can preserve a state of indifference over against it. This is the instant of deliberation, but this, like the Platonic instant, has no existence, least of all in the abstract sense in which you would hold it fast, and the longer one stares at it the less it exists... One sees then, that the inner drift of the personality leaves no time for thought experiments: ...

(Søren Kierkegaard)[1]

Judgment is not the valve, or the hand on the valve, that lets the flow of good into life. To the extent that judgmental activity may serve the good, it presupposes that very spirit essential to the grounding of any phase of action. We may only hope that the good may inform our judging as well as anything else we may do; we may not expect to control the good by rendering it subject to judgmental control, as if the possibility of justified action were contingent upon making grounds for action explicit for judgment as we would adduce explicitly the grounds supporting a truth.

(Henry Bugbee)[2]

PRACTICAL REASON AND THE SUBJECT MATTER OF ETHICS

The task of philosophical ethics is to shed light on the nature, source, and content of a certain class of norms or ideals of practical thought. Our understanding of the subject matter, then, will depend to a great degree on our picture of how thought makes itself practical. If we wish to know how ethical theorists conceive of the practical thought with which their discipline is concerned, we should look at the cases they use to explain and assess their own normative views and those

---

[1] Søren Kierkegaard, *Either/Or, Volume II*, translated by W. Lowrie (Princeton: Princeton University Press, 1959), 167–8. I draw this quote from Richard Moran, "Vision, Choice and Existentialism," *Notizie di Politeia* 12 (2002), 88–101, quoted passage on 100–1.

[2] Henry Bugbee, "The Moment of Obligation in Experience," *Journal of Religion* 33 (1953), 1–15; 7.

of their rivals. These, after all, are the cases that theorists imagine us navigating with the help of their favored norms or ideals.

Those familiar with the more influential works in contemporary ethical theory will have no trouble listing half a dozen cases of this sort. A wandering anthropologist must decide whether to kill an innocent prisoner or stand by while twenty prisoners are gunned down by a local strongman in a remote South American village.[3] A lawyer must decide whether to dispose of a secret yet legally binding will that would redirect her recently deceased client's vast wealth from worthwhile medical research to a worthless nephew.[4] A grown daughter must decide whether to ask doctors to keep her unconscious mother on life support for yet another year or to withdraw treatment and let her mother die.[5] A man comes across two people trapped in collapsing wreckage caused by an earthquake and must decide whether to save one person's life by moving another person's body without her consent in a way that would destroy her leg.[6] The driver of a run-away trolley car is bearing down on five people tied to the track and must decide whether to save the lives of these five people by diverting the trolley onto a second track to which one person is tied.[7] Yet another run-away trolley car is bearing down on five people tied to the track and a bystander must decide whether to push a fat man into the path of the train, killing him to stop the train and save the lives of the five.[8]

A quick perusal of this list of cases will certainly leave one hoping fervently not to end up in the starkly catastrophic terrain of a moral theorist's thought experiment, and for the most part we do somehow manage to avoid such quandaries. More tellingly, even when we do have the misfortune of facing such emergency decisions, we are unlikely to have the remarkable clairvoyance about the future that is so blithely attributed to the protagonists of these brief fictions. A *real* wandering anthropologist could only guess whether his decision to kill one captive really would save nineteen, or whether he might possibly save more by doing something unexpectedly noble such as joining the line-up of captives. A *real* lawyer would be foolish to take it as certain that a breach of professional ethics would remain secret or produce its intended benefits. And what sane passer-by would ever find it simply obvious that a fat man's

---

[3] Bernard Williams, "A Critique of Utilitarianism," in Williams and J. J. C. Smart, *Utilitarianism: For and Against* (Cambridge: Cambridge University Press, 1973), 98–9.

[4] Christine Korsgaard, *The Sources of Normativity* (Cambridge: Cambridge University Press, 1996), 86.

[5] Rosalind Hursthouse, *On Virtue Ethics*, 69. A similar case appears in Michael Slote, "Agent-Based Virtue Ethics," in Roger Crisp and Michael Slote, *Virtue Ethics* (Oxford: Oxford University Press, 1997), 259.

[6] Derek Parfit, *Manuscript.*

[7] Philippa Foot, "The Problem of Abortion and the Doctrine of Double Effect," in *Virtues and Vices and Other Essays in Moral Philosophy* (Oxford: Oxford University Press, 2002; first published by Blackwell, 1978), 23.

[8] Judith Jarvis Thomson, "Killing, Letting Die and the Trolley Problem," in *The Monist* 59 (1976), 204–17 and "The Trolley Problem," in *Yale Law Journal* 94 (1985), 1395–415.

body would stop a trolley in its tracks? The protagonists in these cases are portrayed as capable of attaining confidence about these matters in a flash, at the speed of a runaway train. Whereas when we face similar problems outside of philosophical thought experiments, we are likely to be deeply uncertain about the workability of our schemes for remaking the world so as to bring about some favorable result, and this uncertainty seems crucially relevant to a proper and laudable reluctance to trample the standards of our profession or to kill or maim others in hopes of producing good results. Unless these thought experiments are used to draw attention to the uncertainty with which we make actual decisions, their use is likely to corrupt rather than to sharpen our habits of moral deliberation, partly by encouraging us to reconsider the unthinkability of certain classes of actions that we humans would do best to regard as beyond the pale, and partly by encouraging us to conclude—on the strength of a handful of highly unusual cases in which averting some calamitous consequence might justify us in transgressing the ordinary bounds of human relationships—that the authority of morality is grounded ultimately in its tendency to produce good consequences.

These are serious problems, and philosophical susceptibility to them is clearly connected to acceptance of the world-making conception of agency critiqued in Chapters 1 and 2. But in this chapter I want to explore a more basic and, I think, more telling problem with these cases. The problem is that in their narrative structure, they implicitly manifest a commitment to a partial and potentially misleading conception of practical thinking—one that we have good reason to reconsider before we put it to use, implicitly or explicitly, in framing our inquiry into normative ethics. On the conception in question, practical thinking (or practical reason, to use the phrase preferred by many contemporary ethical theorists) can be represented without distortion or loss as occurring in a moment of stasis prior to action, taking as its input some representation of the circumstances at hand, and yielding some action or intention that the circumstances make apt (or some judgment concerning which action or intention would be apt in the circumstances). This conception of practical thought provides the basic narrative structure for the hypothetical cases listed above. These cases begin with an agent who is aware that s/he is in circumstances with certain generically describable features and they raise the question which generically describable action the agent ought to choose. The background supposition is that even the most automatic or inarticulate episodes of practical thinking can be represented, in a way that makes clear their fundamental logical structure, as a movement from a description of one's circumstances to a conclusion about what is to be done in these circumstances. Call this the received picture of practical reason.

This seemingly innocuous picture of the logical form of practical reason goes hand-in-hand with an allied picture of what a successful normative ethical theory would consist in, if there could be such a thing. Such a theory would set out the ethical norms that govern practical reasoning and it would shed light on the authority of these norms. Since the task of practical reason is to move from generic descriptions of circumstances to the decisions that are justified by the circumstances so conceived, the task of normative ethical theory must be to inquire into the justificatory connections between types of circumstances and types of actions. And if thought experiments of the sort set out above really can serve to elicit our sense of these justificatory connections, then the connections in question must link generically describable circumstances to generically describable actions that the protagonists might be imagined as choosing. On this picture, whether a proposed action is morally permissible or morally required will depend solely upon whether the generic features of the circumstances provide a decisive moral reason to perform or to avoid actions of the proposed type.[9] The substantive content of morality can be captured, on this view, in the form of general principles specifying what kinds of actions can and cannot be done, morally speaking, in what kinds of circumstances.[10] In the words of one prominent theorist, a complete moral theory would be "a system of general principles of moral evaluation that, when combined with the relevant bits of specific information, generated accurate overall moral verdicts about particular actions."[11]

This is a widely accepted view of what a successful moral theory would be like.[12] It is the predominant view not only among partisans of normative ethical theory but also among its opponents. There are, for instance, growing numbers of "particularists" who reject the possibility of normative moral theory on the ground that the moral proprieties of practical reasoning cannot be captured in tractable and invariant principles. Particularists often make their case by showing that certain properties that might seem to have invariant reason-giving force in fact shift their justificatory valence in some imaginable circumstance. It is said, for instance, that prospective pleasures ordinarily count in favor of the actions that produce them, but that the fact that one would take pleasure in causing an innocent person to suffer is an additional reason not to do it. Such examples are often very convincing, but these examples can only play their role in philosophy texts if they are stated in generic language, hence they can do no more than provide exemplars of the sort of context-induced

---

[9] For a representative affirmation of this ubiquitous view, see Marcus George Singer, *Generalization in Ethics* (New York: Atheneum, 1961 and 1971), 13–15; see also W. D. Ross, *Foundations of Ethics* (Oxford: Oxford University Press, 1939), 146.

[10] For clear affirmations of this conception of reasons and their relation to principles, see: Singer, *Generalization in Ethics*, 14–15; Hare, *Freedom and Reason*, chapters 2 and 3; and Scanlon, *What We Owe to Each Other* (Cambridge: Harvard University Press, 1998), 73–4, 197–202.

[11] Samuel Scheffler, *Human Morality* (Oxford: Oxford University Press, 1992), 39.

[12] One could find many theorists who explicitly affirm this conception of ethical theory. Here are two: Frances Kamm, *Morality, Mortality: Volume I: Death and Whom to Save from It* (Oxford: Oxford University Press, 1998), 7; R. M. Hare, *Freedom and Reason* (Oxford: Oxford University Press, 1963), 1–4 and 89.

valence shift that the particularist takes to be an omnipresent possibility. As my colleague Jim Cargile recently put it to me, particularists betray a curious readiness to generalize when they leap from these examples to the general conclusion that nothing has invariant justificatory force. For present purposes, though, a more pressing concern is that this argument for particularism accepts what is most dubious about generalism, since it is premised on the idea that the paradigmatic task of practical reason is to move from a representation of one's circumstances to a conclusion concerning what is to be done in those circumstances.[13]

I do not mean to suggest that this conception of practical reason has gone entirely unchallenged. A growing number of thinkers, including some with particularist sympathies, have joined Iris Murdoch in emphasizing the work of attention by which we continuously refine our sense of how best to live.[14] Yet even this theme has sometimes been taken up as a suggested refinement of the currently predominant picture of deliberation rather than as an alternative to it. On this interpretation, Murdoch's point is that it is a ceaseless and difficult task to arrive at the most perspicuous or practically illuminating description of one's circumstances—that is, the description that makes maximally clear what sort of action the circumstances call for.[15] Excellence in this task will require a nimble and discerning evaluative sensibility. This way of reading Murdoch leaves in place the notion that the task of practical thought is to discern justificatory links between circumstances and actions. It simply insists that these links will be discernible in real time only to those whose perception gives salience to precisely those features of our changing circumstances that have the most telling justificatory links to action. This point is readily incorporable into a broadly Kantian conception of ethics and it has been embraced by some of the most influential contemporary Kantians.[16] Yet there are more radical insights in Murdoch's work that cannot be tamed so easily, including the insight that ethically significant activities cannot

---

[13] One of the most influential contemporary particularists, Jonathan Dancy, writes, "If I have some duty to do this [i.e. some] action, here must be some feature of the situation that makes it so. If in some more general way I ought to do it, still there must be some feature of the situation that makes it so." See Dancy, *Ethics without Principles* (Oxford: Oxford University Press, 2004), 33. Elsewhere Dancy writes, "To justify one's choice is to give the reasons one sees for making it, and to give those reasons is just to lay out how one sees the situation . . ." This quote is from Jonathan Dancy, *Moral Reasons* (Oxford: Blackwell Publishers, 1993), 113.

[14] This is a central theme of Iris Murdoch's visionary essay "The Idea of Perfection," which can be found in *The Sovereignty of Good* (London: Routledge and Kegan Paul, 1970). Murdoch, in turn, traces her notion of attention to the work of Simone Weil.

[15] This is the strategy adopted, for instance, by Elijah Millgram in his attempt to show how particularism might be grounded in Murdoch's conception of practical reasoning. See Millgram, "Murdoch, Practical Reasoning, and Particularism," in *Ethics Done Right: Practical Reasoning as a Foundation for Moral Theory* (Cambridge: Cambridge University Press, 2005), 168–97, especially 187.

[16] See for example Barbara Herman, "The Practice of Moral Judgment," in *The Practice of Moral Judgment* (Cambridge: Harvard University Press, 1993), 73–93 and Onora O'Neill, "The Power of Example," *Philosophy* 61 (1986), 5–29.

be broken down without remainder into discrete acts, each of which springs from a practical judgment or choice, and that thinking is itself an ethically significant activity that resists such decomposition.[17] I believe that we must develop and extend these claims if we are to appreciate the most valuable insights of Ancient virtue ethics.

We can bring out the difficulties with the ascendant conception of practical reason by dwelling on the role of practical thinking in initiating and sustaining the sort of dialectical activities considered in Chapter 2. These activities present as fundamental a challenge to contemporary notions of practical thought as to contemporary notions of desire. They require continuous practical thought about the evaluative properties of one's unfolding activities—properties that cannot be reduced to justificatory relations between circumstances and actions. Once we bring this sort of practical thinking into view, we are presented with a choice. We must either deny that such thinking can be ethically better or worse, or revise our understanding of ethical theory so as to encompass and illuminate ethically significant variations in this sort of thought. In this chapter, I make a case for the latter alternative. In subsequent chapters, I will try to show that this sets the stage for a compelling account of the virtues and their relation both to the good life and to the norms that we moderns compass under the term 'morality.'

THE RECEIVED PICTURE OF PRACTICAL REASON

As suggested above, it is standard practice in contemporary ethical theory to represent practical reasoning as a discrete and occasional process that occurs in the interval between two relatively well-defined temporal boundaries. What precedes and sets the stage for an episode of practical reasoning is the ongoing monitoring of one's surroundings through which one arrives at a concrete conception of one's circumstances. What follows an episode of practical reasoning and stands as its proper consummation is the initiation of an intentional action (or, at least, the formation of an intention to act). The task of practical reasoning, on this view, is to move from an achieved understanding of the circumstances to the adoption of an intention.

This picture of what qualifies certain episodes of thinking as practical can seem—and has seemed to many—to be the merest deliverance of common sense. This is not to say that it is philosophically unproblematic. Its proponents generally recognize that there are puzzles lurking on the boundaries of this bit of common sense, and that there is philosophical work to do in tidying it up. For instance, when we think about what others ought to do in the circumstances they

---

[17] These are two central themes of Murdoch's "The Idea of Perfection," in *The Sovereignty of Good*, 1–44.

face, or about what we ourselves or others ought to do in various hypothetical circumstances, it seems that we are engaged in practical rather than theoretical reasoning even though our cogitations will typically culminate neither in action nor the adoption of a new intention. Still, such puzzles are not generally regarded as insuperable objections to the basic idea that there is such a thing as practical reason only because reasoning sometimes culminates in the adoption of a motivationally efficacious intention, and that no episode of reasoning counts as practical except in virtue of its relation to actual or possible episodes that do culminate in such intentions. It is also widely admitted that actions sometimes take place with little or no explicit deliberation, but this too is regarded as perfectly compatible with the reigning conception of practical deliberation. The thought is that if the implicit practical reasoning behind these relatively spontaneous actions were made explicit, it would be seen to share the basic logical structure of explicit episodes of deliberation. That is, it would begin with a conception of circumstances and generate actions that are intended under some description, and it would count the circumstances so conceived as sufficient justification for the action so described.

The first of the temporal boundaries of practical deliberation constitutes a working interpretation of the philosophical thesis that reason has two modes of deployment, theoretical and practical, and that these two kinds of reasoning bear on action in very different ways. If mistakes are made in bringing one's circumstances into view, these will ordinarily be errors of theoretical reasoning and not errors of practical reasoning. I say "ordinarily" here because the boundary might well have to be complicated if we are to provide a plausible treatment of negligence and culpable ignorance. However, even if there are practical norms that govern which features of one's circumstances one ought to make it one's business to know about, one's grasp of these features is itself regarded as an achievement of theoretical rather than practical reason. It is of course true that those who are not initiated in the jargon of post-Kantian philosophy are likely to regard 'theoretical' as an overblown adjective for the sort of continuous and usually quite effortless attentiveness by which we keep track of our changing circumstances. But the point of this jargon is to mark a division between the sort of reasoning that yields true beliefs about the way things are and the sort that yields practically efficacious verdicts about what to do given how things are. The basic thought is that we cannot hope to arrive at sensible conclusions concerning what to do unless we know what circumstances we face, hence that practical reason can get traction with its assigned task only after theoretical reason has supplied it with a working conception of the prevailing circumstances.

There is great controversy about how best to picture the second temporal boundary of practical deliberation—the moment when deliberation comes to an end. Aristotle seems to have pictured explicit practical syllogisms as ending in action, and some theorists continue to assert that we must hold this view on pain of losing hold of the thought that the reasoning in question really does issue in a practical conclusion rather than, say, a motivationally inert belief concerning what ought to be done. It seems clear, though, that what we typically find choice-worthy in deliberation is not the mere initiation of a course of action but the course of action as a whole, and that the whole course of action is typically guided in some sense by the deliberation. Deliberation exercises an intelligent control over the motions that it initiates. Hence the conclusion of deliberation would seem to be something with greater staying power than the mere initiation of action.

Terms such as 'intention' or 'plan' are often ushered in, at this stage, to denote the action-controlling pro-attitudes that deliberation leaves in place as its proxies for controlling whatever temporally extended course of action is deliberately undertaken. Intentions and plans are typically analyzed, in turn, in ways that cleave closely to the propositionalist picture of motivation discussed in Chapters 1 and 2. Plans are regarded as complex intentions or hierarchically ordered arrays of intentions, often covering a considerable time span. Intentions, in turn, are generally taken to be world-to-mind propositional attitudes whose propositional objects pick out the states of affairs that one aims to bring about.[18] Some theorists hold either that talk of intentions can be reduced to talk of beliefs and desires, or that intentions just are desires (e.g. those desires on which one believes one will act).[19] This reductive approach seems destined to founder on the fact that intentions involve an element of willed commitment that need not be present in any array of beliefs and desires. As Carlos Moya puts it, intentions differ from desires in that one is committed to fulfilling one's intentions (or at least trying to

---

[18] There is some disagreement about whether intentions are propositional attitudes, but those who reject this view tend not to stray from the guiding thought that intentions are determinations to bring about some state of affairs, and that the state of affairs that would fulfill the intention can be captured with a descriptive proposition. Thus, for instance, Hector-Neri Castaneda argues that intentions are attitudes not towards propositions but towards practitions, and hence belong in the same family as prescriptions. However, one of his main reasons for affirming this view is that intentions cannot be true or false, and this indicates that he denies that intentions are propositional because he thinks that entertaining a proposition always involves thinking that proposition to be true. Here he departs sharply from the propositionalists whose views I canvassed in Chapter 1, since they think that desires are propositional attitudes that involve no supposition of truth. Yet the departure seems to be primarily terminological. After all, Castaneda's practitions themselves have a grammatical structure, with a subject term picking out an agent and a predicate specifying an action that the agent might conceivably do. If we know what practition forms the object of an intention, we can easily specify the proposition picking out the world-state that would fulfill the intention. Indeed, Castaneda shows considerable sympathy for the view that all action owes its intelligibility as action to its status as an effort to bring about some specifiable state of affairs. See Hector-Neri Castaneda, *Thinking and Doing: The Philosophical Foundations of Institutions* (Dordrecht and Boston: D. Reidel Publishing Company, 1975), 41, 98, 149–77.

[19] See for instance Donald Davidson's early view in "Actions, Reasons, Causes," in *Essays on Actions and Events* (Oxford: Oxford University Press, 1980), 3–19. Davidson later adopted a more complicated view. See also Alvin Goldman, *A Theory of Human Action* (Princeton: Princeton University Press, 1970), 51; and Robert Audi, "Intending, Intentional Action and Desire," in Joel Marks, ed., *The Ways of Desire* (Chicago: Precedent Publishing, 1986), 17–38.

do so), and this commitment imposes a normative pressure on practical thought and action that mere desires do not.[20] Michael Bratman has attempted to capture this phenomenon of commitment in more clearly naturalistic terms. On his view, intentions differ functionally from desires in that they exercise a persistent controlling influence over one's actions and over the formation of further intentions.[21] It is because of this persistent controlling influence that intentions can serve as the proxies of the episodes of deliberation from which they emerge, generating subsequent decisions that conduce to the completion of the temporally extended course of action that has been decided upon. This role of intentions can be accommodated within the received picture of deliberation provided that adopted intentions are counted among the circumstances whose justificatory force it is the task of practical deliberation to discern and act on.

Once it is seen that practical reason sometimes ends with the adoption of an intention, it is tempting to generalize this picture to all cases, including those in which practical reason yields an immediate and evanescent action. After all, it seems that no behavior can properly be counted as action unless it is performed on an intention, and that it is precisely the intention rather than the action considered in the abstract that practical reason affirms as worthwhile. Suppose, for example, that someone intentionally pulls a trigger, thinking the gun to be unloaded, and' thereby unintentionally fires a gun and shoots a friend. If we wish to reconstruct the practical reasoning that produced this action, we must determine what the agent took to be sufficient reason to pull the trigger, since this was intended. It would make no sense to try to determine what the agent took to be sufficient reason to shoot the friend. This was done but not intended.

On the received view, then, practical reasoning begins with a representation of one's circumstances and culminates in an intention that takes as its object a description of an action or temporally extended plan of action. If this is to be an exhaustive characterization of practical reasoning, the intention's object must be entirely non-evaluative. After all, an intention to perform a brave action or to write a good book will yield a determinate action only when conjoined with an understanding of what counts as bravery or literary excellence, and arriving at such an understanding requires a further stretch of thinking. Since the role of this further thinking is to arrive at a determinate and motivationally efficacious picture of what it makes sense to do, it must surely be counted as practical rather than theoretical. If one held otherwise, it would be hard to avoid the disastrous conclusion that one could instantaneously complete one's lifelong task of practical reasoning simply by adopting the intention to live a good life, leaving only the theoretical task of determining what a good life consists in.

[20] Carlos J. Moya, *The Philosophy of Action: An Introduction* (Oxford: Polity Press, 1990), 56–60, 136–41.

[21] Michael Bratman, *Intention, Plans and Practical Reason* (Cambridge: Harvard University Press, 1987), 18–19.

Hence proponents of the received view are under strong pressure to suppose that practical reason must culminate not merely in intentions but in intentions whose objects are purely non-evaluative propositions.

Attachment to this background notion of practical reason can manifest itself in strikingly imperceptive reconstructions even of those episodes of practical thinking that do result in clear intentions to act in some way or another. For instance, the historic Socrates is portrayed by Plato as arriving at the conclusion that he ought not to flee Athens in order to avoid his punishment because it would be tantamount to breaking a promise or disobeying a parent. In his widely used introductory text on ethics, William Frankena puts forward this example as a paradigmatic instance of moral thinking, but he locates Socrates' moral thought entirely in his acceptance, and application to the facts of the case, of principles prohibiting the breaking of promises and the disobeying of parents. What drops through the cracks, as wholly irrelevant to ethics, is the effort of thought through which Socrates comes to see a kind of badness in fleeing Athens that is relevantly similar to the sort of badness involved in breaking promises or disobeying parents.[22] Cora Diamond finds in this passage from Frankena "a particularly wild misunderstanding of a kind of moral activity." She persuasively insists that Socrates' effort to bring his circumstances and alternatives into view is ". . . as much a significant moral doing as is his choosing to stay rather than to escape, or, rather, it in fact goes to any full characterization of *what* Socrates is doing in staying. . . ."[23] What drops from view on the received picture of practical reasoning is the struggle to deepen one's understanding of the meaning of one's activities—that is, of the good to be found in them, hence of what one is doing by engaging in them.

If we consider the nature of value through the lens of the received view of practical reasoning, it will appear eminently sensible to reduce talk of the goodness or value of courses of action to talk of natural properties and their justificatory links to various courses of action. It is against this stage-setting that we might be tempted to analyze moral standards as "constructions" of practical reason that tie circumstances to action types, and that can serve the role of coordinating social expectations even in pluralistic societies because they locate the triggering conditions of various moral requirements and prohibitions in features of the world that are there to be apprehended by a wholly non-evaluative and purely theoretical use of reason. Contemporary Kantian constructivism, then, owes its appeal in large part to the conception of practical reason that I've outlined.

It is also against this background picture of practical reason that it can look eminently sensible to join contemporary noncognitivists in denying that there

---

[22] William Frankena, *Ethics*, 2nd edn (New York: Prentice Hall, 1973 and 1963), 2–4.

[23] Cora Diamond, "Missing the Adventure: Reply to Martha Nussbaum," in *The Realistic Spirit* (Cambridge: MIT Press, 1991), 311.

are any real justificatory reasons or values at all, whether found or constructed. If what we call reasons are discernible by a not-yet-evaluative exercise of reason and the ends of action can be formulated in non-evaluative language, then Ockham's razor can seem to count in favor of insisting that talk of justificatory reasons for certain actions simply expresses a motivationally efficacious attitude generated by those natural properties that induce us to perform those actions, and that talk of goodness or value expresses the attitude we take towards those states of affairs that we desire or intend to produce. This will involve a disastrous cost in the metric of evaluative articulacy only if the requirements of morality cannot be captured in principles specifying which naturalistically describable action types are permitted or prohibited in which naturalistically describable circumstances. If we accept the received view of practical reason, the cost is unlikely to be acknowledged, and the full appeal of realism will remain hidden. To the extent that contemporary particularism has attempted to argue for realism on this alien playing field, its critique of contemporary ethical theory has been insufficiently radical.[24] We must begin with a revisionist conception of how thinking becomes practical if we are to put forward either an appealing form of ethical realism or a convincing case for the particularist insight that the content of a fully adequate ethical understanding cannot be captured in a tractable set of principles.

At any rate, if one adopts the received picture of practical reason, it is but a short step to the affirmation of generalism. After all, on the received picture, the task of practical reason is to move from a conception of the circumstances delivered by theoretical reason to a performance that counts as intentional under some determinate description, hence one that is regarded by the agent as choice-worthy under that description. It is hard to see how one could reason in this way without implicitly accepting the principle that the circumstances one thinks to obtain are sufficient reason to perform the action type one intends. One cannot begin deliberation from an ostensive specification of the circumstances, since this would sweep in features of the circumstances of which one is wholly unaware, and one clearly is not premising one's practical judgment on these features. Nor can one's deliberation yield an intention with a demonstrative rather than a descriptive content—e.g. an intention to do *this* action—since an intention cannot guide an action if its content is fixed by the contours of whatever action it ends up yielding. Hence the reasoning must run from a general description of circumstances to a general description of actions. Particularist protestations aside, it is hard to see how one could regard such reasoning as justified without committing oneself at least to a *ceteris paribus* principle according to which actions of the kind intended are justified in circumstances of the kind apprehended.

These, at any rate, are the sorts of considerations that induce Kantians to maintain that all actions are performed on subjective principles of action, or

---

[24] As I tried to show above, such a tendency is clearly visible in the work of the prominent particularist Jonathan Dancy.

maxims.[25] In his influential lectures on Kant, John Rawls maintains that maxims contain a generic description of the action under which it seems worthwhile, and a generic description of the circumstances and purposes that seem to justify the action.[26] To act on a maxim is to make the practical judgment that the circumstances and purposes (which might include previously adopted plans and intentions) mentioned in the maxim are sufficient justification for actions of the type mentioned in the maxim. For the Kantian, maxims form the focal element of explicit episodes of moral reasoning and the proper target of moral assessments of actions. An action is morally justified if and only if its maxim can consistently be willed as universal law. Maxims also play a vital role in Kantian action theory, explaining the sense in which we are active in those bodily motions that count as actions. Agents and actions come into view together—crystallizing, as it were, from the world of things and events—when we interpret a conscious being as taking some set of circumstances to be sufficient reason for some type of performance. Actions, then, are born of exercises of practical reason, and these always take the form of the adoption of a maxim and the simultaneous acceptance of the picture implicit in that maxim of the justificatory relation between generic features of circumstances and types of actions.[27]

The received picture of practical reason, then, might fairly be called the Kantian picture, though it has by now left its mark on nearly every prominent position in contemporary ethics. I've already pointed to the way in which it structures (or, better, distorts) the thought of certain self-styled Aristotelian particularists, and to the way it has shaped certain misinterpretations of Murdoch's broadly Platonist view. It is a comparatively straightforward matter to show that it also structures most utilitarian ethical theory. Utilitarians can be divided into those who affirm a single principle of choice (act utilitarians) and those who affirm a single highest-order principle from which subsidiary principles can be derived. The act-utilitarian holds that one is always to reason from one's circumstances, and in particular from theoretical knowledge of the opportunities for utility-production made available by one's circumstances, to the action that promises to produce the most utility in the circumstances. The rule-utilitarian holds that one is to act on principles whose general acceptance would maximize utility. These principles, in turn, are generally thought to specify what kinds of actions are to be performed in what kinds of circumstances (e.g. when you have made a

---

[25] Kant introduces the notion of maxims of action in Immanuel Kant, *Groundwork of the Metaphysics of Morals*, Ak. 401 and 420.

[26] John Rawls, "Themes in Kant's Moral Philosophy," in *John Rawls: Collected Papers* (Cambridge: Harvard University Press, 1999), see especially 497–9.

[27] While this view is, I think, accepted by most contemporary Kantians and Kant scholars, Allen Wood seems to suggest—though with little elaboration or textual evidence—that it is a mistaken reading of Kant. On Wood's view, it is possible for desires to induce us to act contrary to our own maxims, and this need not imply that we have adopted some other, contrary maxim. See Allen W. Wood, *Kant's Ethical Thought* (Cambridge: Cambridge University Press, 1999), 52.

promise, keep it), though in the limiting case they might specify actions that are never to be performed in any circumstances (e.g. never lie).

There is an additional source of support for the thesis that *moral* principles in particular must be codifiable in non-evaluative language, even if other principles of practical reasoning are not. This thesis coheres with a culturally ascendant and recognizably liberal conception of the nature and point of a moral code. On this conception, moral codes are analogous to legal codes in that they are not meant to provide comprehensive guidance for living a good life but are only to specify basic terms and conditions of social cooperation that all people can reasonably be required to meet. Since people differ irreconcilably about what sorts of lives are good, and even about what concepts to use in expressing a conception of the good life, moral principles ought not to be framed with any parochial set of evaluative concepts. We could draw upon such concepts if pluralism about the good were something to be lamented or if we could confidently assert that one vision of the good were true. But variations in conceptions of the good life are plausibly regarded as the inevitable historical result of sincere efforts to make sense of human life, and it can seem objectionably intolerant to frame the basic terms of social cooperation in ways that presuppose the truth or superiority of one such conception. Moral principles, then, must say what is prohibited and what is required in terms whose meaning is plain to all. This assures that all participants in social cooperation will be able to understand these principles and to hold themselves and others to the requirements they express.

It is not normally appreciated that the narrative form of the thought experiments that are used to frame theoretical inquiry into morality already bear the marks of this complicated and culturally specific nexus of liberal commitments. I believe, however, that this is precisely the underlying set of presumptions that structure our sense of the nature and limits of the subject matter of morality. These presumptions incline us to look for a moral theory that can tell us, in clear non-evaluative terms, what kinds of actions can and cannot be performed in what kinds of circumstances. It is against the backdrop of this intricately ramified worldview that it can seem central to the theoretical ambitions of moral philosophy to get straight on such questions as whether to push a fat man before a speeding train in circumstances where this will reduce the number of imminent human deaths.

DIALECTICAL ACTIVITY AND PRACTICAL THINKING

Practical thinking does not typically grind to a halt when we intentionally throw ourselves into dialectical activities. It often continues in the form of an effort to deepen and refine our picture of how best to engage in that activity. How might we conceive of the continuous role played by practical thought in sustaining such activities?

On one conception, temporally extended courses of action are launched by intentions or plans that specify an end to be produced. As circumstances change and new information comes to light, continuous course corrections are made with an eye to ensuring efficient production of the end while avoiding new courses of action that will undermine this intention. This approach amounts to a natural extension of the belief–desire conception of action, according to which actions borrow their point from the propositionally specifiable states of affairs that they are calculated to bring about. The extension consists in the recognition of intentions (and the complex congeries of intentions we call plans) as a second kind of world-to-mind propositional attitude from which actions can arise.[28]

[28] I've tried to capture something of a reigning consensus, but in fact there are subtle disagreements about these matters among those who assign intentions a central role in the etiology of actions. Moya, for instance, is somewhat equivocal about whether intentions are propositional attitudes. On page 62 of *The Philosophy of Action*, he says that a starting point for understanding the "aboutness" of all mental states, including intentions, is to think of them as propositional attitudes. However, he cautions that this is only a rough characterization, and might not be very illuminating. On page 137 he holds that the content of any *future-directed* intention is "a proposition in the first person that contains at least one verb of action in the future tense." He suggests elsewhere (58) that some intentions are propositional attitudes that commit one to the production of some aim or to following some plan or standard, and that these sorts of intentions must be operative if one is to act intentionally at all. Once these propositional intentions are in place, it is possible to develop subsidiary "indexical" intentions that specify their content in ways that are responsive to one's running apprehension of one's changing circumstances (59). His idea seems to be that if I intend to eat an apple (or, to use the rather awkward propositional form, if I intend that I eat an apple), I might find myself in the vicinity of some apples and develop the intention to eat *this* apple even though I lack any non-indexical representation of that which I intend. If this is the sole source of his hesitation about the idea that intentions are propositional attitudes, it does not call into question the production-oriented framework that stands in the way of generating an illuminating conception of dialectical activities, since intentions will still be satisfied by rearranging the world in ways that make certain propositions or indexical claims true. Michael Bratman's position is similarly complicated. He holds that intentions are like desires in being pro-attitudes, but that they differ from desires in several ways, the most important of which is that in the absence of *akrasia* they are conduct-controlling. To the best of my knowledge, he does not say whether intentions are attitudes towards propositions, but this is the default view of the intentionality (i.e. the "aboutness" or representational content) of desires and other mental states, so the fact that he does not contest this view would seem to suggest that he either accepts it or at least does not view it as obviously mistaken. See Bratman, *Intention, Plans and Practical Reason*, 14–20. (Bratman retains the same theoretical view of intentions in his most recent work. See Bratman, *Structures of Agency* (Oxford: Oxford University Press, 2007), 26n.) As for Davidson, he argues in the 1978 essay entitled "Intending" (reprinted in *Essays and Actions and Events*, 83–102) that intentions and desires are both species of the genus of pro-attitudes, but that intentions involve an all-things-considered, unconditional judgment that the intended aim is desirable (99–102). In replying to critical commentary on this view, he makes clear that these pro-attitudes are indeed propositional attitudes and that they are like desires in involving a disposition to act in ways calculated to make true their propositional objects. John Searle, for his part, holds that intentions have the same deep structure as beliefs and desires. All of them take propositions as their objects, and intentions and desires are satisfied when their propositional objects are true (though in the case of intentions, the world must come to make one's proposition true through the causal efficacy of the intention itself). See John Searle, *Intentionality: An Essay in the Philosophy of Mind* (Cambridge: Cambridge University Press, 1983), 79–83 and 105–6.

This approach preserves an episodic picture of the practical deliberation that yields fresh intentions while allowing for a second, more continuous sort of practical thinking that makes whatever course corrections are necessary to realize these intentions. Still, this view has no place for the distinctive sort of practical thinking that accompanies and carries forward dialectical activities. This latter sort of thinking gives rise to corrections in one's unfolding activities, but it would not be natural to call these "course corrections" since this phrase would imply that one already has a clear idea of the end to which one seeks a sensible course. The mid-stream adjustments characteristic of dialectical activity are changes in one's idea of one's end. Since the end is not a state of affairs to be brought about but the activity itself in its ideal form, what changes is one's sense of what exactly one is doing and what it would mean to do it well.

It will be pointed out that our intentions sometimes control subsequent deliberation by inducing us to arrive at more specific formulations of their objects. For instance, if one intends to get some exercise and an opportunity arises to plan a weekly jog with a friend, one might specify the content of one's previously rather vague plan by adopting the intention to jog weekly with this friend. This sort of deliberation can be accommodated within the received picture of practical deliberation in a relatively straightforward way, by counting one's existing plans and intentions among the circumstances that can justify the adoption of new intentions (or, as in this case, more specific versions of existing intentions).[29] Further, it seems in general that there is practical reason to find ways of fulfilling those intentions one has already adopted, since a wholesale failure to do so would spell one's dissolution as an agent. Still, this sort of deliberation is wholly unlike the sort of deliberation that carries forward dialectical activities, since one's deliberative gaze is directed towards opportunities presented by one's changing circumstances for specific means of realizing vague intentions. One could specify an intended end in this way even before one has begun to act on the intention, as in the above example. The refinement of the intention need not be guided by a deepening sense of the intrinsic value of the intended activity. Indeed, the intended activity could be seen as having a merely instrumental value. By contrast, the sort of practical thinking that deepens and extends dialectical activities is directed at the activity itself and focuses on arriving at a more illuminating picture of the intrinsic goodness latent in the activity, hence of what would count as full and proper engagement in it.

[29] In fact, this possibility is explicitly accommodated in the Kantian notion of a maxim, at least on Rawls' reconstruction of it. As noted above, Rawls holds that there is a placeholder in Kantian maxims for the purpose for which an action is performed, and this purpose might naturally be regarded as an existing plan or intention which, in combination with (other) prevailing circumstance, provides sufficient reason to adopt and act on some other, more specific intention. It is not at all obvious that all action, or even all morally relevant action, will be chosen in order to serve a purpose. Yet certainly some actions will do so.

The idea of specification, then, is simply inadequate to the task of displaying the unity of temporally extended dialectical activities. As just shown, it encompasses forms of ongoing thought that are not dialectical. Yet it is not merely too broad a concept to capture what is distinctive about dialectical thought. It leaves out certain key instances of dialectical thought. An example is the sort of lifelong quest described by Augustine in his *Confessions* and discussed in Chapter 2 of this book. It will hardly do to hold that the life of religious devotion is merely a more specific version of the guiding project that steered a younger Augustine to brothels and philosophy seminars (a pair that are rarely acknowledged as kin). And even in those cases where the moments of a dialectical activity can be counted as successive specifications of an initially vague intention, this conceptual framework leaves out the more fine-grained practical thinking that determines why the activity ended up taking one of the many specific forms that it might have taken. There is a richer sort of continuity in certain chains of practical thinking that move from general to specific plans—a kind that involves the increasing clarification of an initially opaque sense of goodness or value. We cannot make optimal sense of why such thought unfolds as it does, or of what unifies the changing activities that it produces, if we speak only of specification and not of increasing clarity or depth.

A second way to fit dialectical activities within the received view would be to hold that such activities are modified on the fly by repeated episodes of practical deliberation, each yielding a fresh intention to act in a new and slightly different way. As noted above, if practical reasoning is to consist solely in the adoption of such a series of intentions, these intentions must provide a non-evaluative specification of the actions at which they aim. Otherwise there would be further practical thinking involved in interpreting the evaluative predicates featured in one's intentions. This picture runs into the same difficulty that arises when we try to fit dialectical activities into the propositionalist conception of desire. It effectively fractures dialectical activities into a series of disparate acts related only by spatio-temporal contiguity. If we are to keep these evolving intentions in view as the successive moments of a single temporally extended activity, we must understand them as attempts to approximate a single ideal or standard of excellence. Otherwise what will appear from the eyes of the agent or the sympathetic biographer as the attainment of greater clarity, depth, or excellence in a single evolving activity will show up as a series of unrelated shifts in one's behavior.[30]

---

[30] After I first elaborated my conception of activity and worked up my argument to the effect that contemporary theories of motivation and practical reason provide us with a fractured view of these activities, I discovered that my main criticisms were anticipated by John Dewey in his seminal 1896 paper "The Reflex Arc Concept in Psychology." In that paper, Dewey conceives of human actions as the product of a "sensori-motor circuit" (359) composed of two running activities: a continuous, practically structured, and active apprehension of one's circumstances and a continuous production of apt bodily motions. Dewey claims that the relation between apprehension and action is not a

It would be a mistaken, then, to adopt the influential suggestion of John Searle that activities are carried forward by a series of "intentions in action," understood as propositional attitudes with a world-to-mind direction of fit that take bodily motions as their subject matter.[31] We can bring out the nature of this mistake by returning to the case discussed in Chapter 2 of the blues singer who is searching for the right phrasing and intonation for the next line of a song. The singer needn't be imagined as representing certain motions of the tongue and throat in such a way as to cause these motions to occur. In most cases it is only inexperienced singers in early stages of training who have to think explicitly about the bodily mechanics of sound production, though these awkward techniques are sometimes revisited to remedy bad habits. For a master singer, the relevant bodily motions are generally conjured into being as the unconscious byproduct of a striving towards something else—for instance, towards the evocation of a fully felt and wholly apt mood, or the voicing of an interpretation that avoids sentimentality, woodenness, awkward rather than pregnant pauses, and so forth.[32] As one proceeds, one might become more articulate about what one is after, and one might become more successful at attaining it in practice. In many cases, these two achievements will be related dialectically, with advances in each facilitating advances in the other. But throughout these changes in one's mode of engagement in the activity, it will often make sense to say that one's intention remains the same. One intends to enact a valuable performance whose contours one has intimated from the start. The activity changes, under the best of circumstances, due to refinement in one's grasp of what one is after. These changes count as the successive moments of a single activity because they are successive interpretations of a single irreducibly evaluative intention.

---

one-way street but a circuit, with activities continuously conditioning the apprehensions that inspire and guide them. One's apprehension of one's circumstances is already practically structured, in the sense that it highlights the lines of sensible action that are afforded or closed off by one's circumstances. For instance, if one is burned by a flame, one's apprehension is altered so that one no longer sees a mere flame but rather "a-light-that-means-pain-when-contact-occurs" (360). Ongoing activities also shape the salience and meaning of contemporaneous perceptions. In this vein, Dewey considers what it is like to hear a loud, unexpected sound while engaged in different activities. "If one is reading a book, if one is hunting, if one is watching in a dark place on a lonely night, if one is performing a chemical experiment, in each case, the noise has a very different psychical value; it is a different experience" (361). Because the psychologists of his time conceive of environmental stimuli in isolation from the actions they cause, Dewey claims that they fail to see the unity of our activities, leaving us "nothing but a series of jerks, the origin of each jerk to be found outside the process of experience itself. . ." (360). See John Dewey, "The Reflex Arc Concept in Psychology," *Psychological Review* 3 (1896), 357–70. (Note: Thanks to Chris Collins for having directed my attention to Dewey's essay.)

[31] John Searle, *Intentionality*, chapter 3.

[32] Harry Frankfurt makes what looks to be a similar misstep when he claims that "When a person intends to perform an action, what he intends is that certain intentional movements of his body should occur." See Frankfurt, "The Problem of Action," in *The Importance of What We Care About* (Cambridge: Cambridge University Press, 1988), 73.

In summary, if we are to keep in view the cross-temporal unity of dialectical activities and make room for the sort of practical thinking that seems to be at work in them, the intentions that guide these activities must be assigned an irreducibly evaluative content. This, however, opens the way for a new kind of practical thinking—a kind that strains for clearer and deeper *understanding* of the forms of human excellence that animate one's activities and that one seeks to actualize in those activities. As emerged in Chapter 2, one cannot bring it about that one is engaged in certain dialectical activities simply by sincerely adopting the intention to perform them well, then making every effort to enact this intention. To succeed in engaging in many dialectical activities, one must have at least an intimation of the goods internal to the activity, and one's activity must be inspired by that intimation. One is not befriending another if one does not have at least an intimation of the other's value that might be deepened by further interaction, nor is one philosophizing if one lacks even an intimation of the value of philosophical inquiry. When one does manage to engage in such activities, one's doings are guided by practical thought in the sense that they are apt responses to a motivating apprehension of goodness or value, and not merely in the sense that they emerge from an intention that can be adopted at will. Practical reason and the will cannot be identified with each other, after the Kantian fashion.

Taking this last point into account, we might re-conceive of the practical thinking that guides dialectical activities as itself a continuous activity that accompanies and continuously refines the ongoing activities whose constitutive goodness it takes as its subject matter. This sort of practical thinking can be regarded as active understanding—provided at least that we keep the emphasis on the gerundival form of the term 'understand*ing*,' thereby conceiving of it as something we are continuously engaged in, continuously doing, rather than as a fixed achievement of the sort that can be attributed to us even while we are dormant. When we throw ourselves into these activities, we might have only a vague intimation of their intrinsic goodness or value. The task of practical thinking is to actualize and to continuously deepen one's running understanding of one's own unfolding activities, so as to keep these activities in view as something it is good to be doing while simultaneously attaining a clearer sense of which ways of carrying them forward would more fully answer to the ideals or excellences by which we understand these activities. Such thought proceeds by way of a dialectical interaction between a series of increasingly vivid intimations of these ideals or excellences, and a series of reifications of these intimations in the form of stretches of activity inspired by them, each stretch providing further opportunity for sharpening one's grasp of how best to engage in the activity. It proceeds, then, through attention to the nature and point of what one is doing, and not primarily through attention to one's circumstances. What supplies such thought with normative guidance is not a set of principles that detail justificatory links between circumstances and action-types, but rather faithfulness to an intimated value that is itself internal to—even if only imperfectly realized by—one's unfolding activity.

The idea here is a cousin, or maybe a second cousin, of Marx's thought that we elaborate ourselves dialectically by laboring on the world, finding ourselves confronted by our own thoughts (especially thoughts concerning what sort of world would be ideally fit for human habitation) reified in the form of the work we have done on the world, then critiquing and refining those reified thoughts in preparation for another round of self-*elabor*ation.[33] One key difference is that I am extending this general picture to cases in which the point of action is precisely not to remake the world so that it answers to some pre-envisioned picture, but rather to actualize the defining *telos* of some intrinsically valuable activity. Hence I am thinking of the external element of the dialectical as one's own unfolding activity and not as something brought about by one's activity. Because of the difficulty of bringing this external element of the dialectic into clear view, properly structured interactions with other persons will play a pivotal role in the sort of dialectic under discussion. This intersubjective element is discussed in Chapter 7.

Knowing how best to continue an activity requires not only a grasp of what in general it would mean to do the activity well, but also and more particularly a grasp of the best and highest possibilities made available by the portion of the activity that has already run its course. The continuous task of practical thinking, then, is analogous to the one faced by an author who has written half of a book and who must discern the most compelling complete book for which the finished half could serve as a beginning. What has already been written constrains what it could possibly make sense to write next, but the meaning of what has been written is itself up for grabs, since its proper interpretation will depend partly on as-yet-undetermined features of the complete story. It can make sense for a writer in this position to turn his gaze at the already written portion of the novel to try to discern the best and most interesting of the many complete stories latent in it, as its unfinished possibilities.

To take an example closer to home, this task of practical thinking is comparable to the task faced by the philosopher who is in the midst of explaining an inchoate line of thought and who is continuously searching for the right words to stretch his unfolding sentences towards an intimation of insight lying at the horizon of his understanding. In such cases, one does not yet have in mind a fully determinate thought for which one is attempting to find the right words. There must be such cases if it is possible for philosophical dialectic to be a form of active inquiry—that is, a path to increased insight rather than merely a means of communicating already achieved insights. In such cases, one has the sense of trying to wrest the thought that has inspired one's interest from a partially veiling

---

[33] See Karl Marx, "Alienated Labor," the last section of the first manuscript in *The Philosophical and Economic Manuscripts of 1844*.

obscurity and to bring it into words that vindicate one's incipient excitement about it. If this is one's task, the already completed temporal part of one's ongoing activity cannot be regarded as a mere circumstance to be grasped by purely theoretical reflection so as to set the stage for deliberating about what to say next. One's task, instead, is to uncover the best and most interesting thought that one's words are already reaching for. My suggestion is that practical thinking sometimes takes this same form. If it does, then excellence in practical thinking cannot consist solely in discerning and acting on justificatory links between the non-evaluative facts and non-evaluative specifications of intentional actions. It sometimes requires a continuous effort to bring into view the best and highest possibilities latent in one's unfolding activities. This focal object straddles the supposed divide between the circumstances of choice and the action being chosen. The task is to grasp what one is already doing in such a way as to lift it, moment by moment, closer to the ideal form in whose light it is understood.

It might be objected that the goal of philosophical thought and other forms of theoretical inquiry is in fact graspable from the outset, though only in abstract form. Inquiry, it will be said, aims at true belief (or justified true belief). I will argue in the last chapter of this book that this is an impoverished view, and that the proper aspiration both of theoretical reflection and of practical thinking is active understanding of matters of importance. This is the sort of excellence whose precise nature and value one cannot hope to appreciate all at once but only bit by bit, as one grasps its contours and learns to answer to it. Inquiry, then, will turn out to be a dialectical activity in the sense at issue in this chapter.

Other readers might object that even if philosophical inquiry is dialectical in the sense under discussion, it is an unusual case and not a fitting model for other intrinsically valuable human activities. Yet, as I argued in Chapter 2, there is nothing rare nor *recherché* about engagement in dialectical activity. It is the stuff of everyday life. When we take a walk in the woods, spend time with relatives or friends, read books or explore foreign lands, we generally regard what we are doing as intrinsically valuable, and our sense of this intrinsic value has arisen and has been deepened and extended precisely by engaging in that sort of activity. This is particularly obvious in the case of activities that we improvise jointly with other people, such as conversations or friendships or love affairs, since carrying them forward requires that we interpret and respond to another's sense of their point or value, as manifest in the other's words and deeds. But even when we are acting alone, there is enough distance between our externalization in action of our sense of how best to engage in the activity, and our evaluation of that externalization, to speak of dialectical progression.

I argued in Chapter 2 that desires figure in dialectical activities as pre-deliberative appearances (or, in the best cases, apprehensions) of goods present — even if only as potentialities — in one's ongoing activities. This suggests a way of specifying the proper task of the practical thinking through which we carry forward dialectical activities: its task is to refine the outlook embedded in our operative desires so as to increase its articulacy and to make it more discriminating. To put the point in Aristotelian terms, the task is to refine the *phantasmata* that inform our desires by supplying a conceptually structured apprehension of the good that might lie in our doings.[34] Some commentators have emphasized that Aristotle assigned a cognitive role to such *phantasmata*. He thought of them as shaped by an achieved practical understanding of the good, and as susceptible to being reshaped by changes in that understanding.[35] If this is a tenable picture of the practical thinking that guides dialectical activities, then the proper movement of this thought is towards a deeper and more revealing understanding of the intrinsic value of the activities in whose midst we find ourselves. Such thought does not ordinarily protrude as a separate introspectible concomitant of the activity. Rather, it ordinarily takes the form of concentrated attention to or absorption in what one is doing. Such attention can change the content of the operative desire—that is, the seeming of goodness in which it partly consists—without the outbreak of any explicit deliberation and without an introspectively discernible choice to carry forward with the activity in this or that way. In such cases, the content of our practical thinking is embedded in the evolving desires that sustain the activity and shape those elements of it that are up to the agent. It is through these desires that the agent's evaluative outlook is expressed in the activity.

I have emphasized that the main object of the practical thinking by which dialectical activities are carried forward is not the circumstances in which one finds oneself but rather the activity itself, conceived in light of its constitutive goods or ideals. This does not mean that circumstances are irrelevant to such deliberation. It would ordinarily be a misstep to go on with an engrossing conversation in the midst of an unnoticed emergency, though there can be something impressive about those who are prone to such missteps. (It is certainly not flattery, but neither I hope is it *mere* disparagement, to be called an absent-minded professor.) One ought to have a background awareness of when circumstances call for the activity to be discontinued, though clearly this desirable sort of attentiveness to circumstances is radically insufficient to determine how best to perform the activity itself. Further, whenever one does carry forward an activity, one implicitly commits oneself to the judgment that the circumstances do not count as a decisive reason to abandon the activity. In this sense, a judgment about the reason-giving force of circumstances is always in place when one acts. This, however, does not mean that an agent's reasons for action are always found in the

---

[34] See Martha Nussbaum, *Aristotle's de Motu Animalium* (Princeton, NJ: Princeton University Press, 1978), 232–3.

[35] See Dorothea Frede, "The Cognitive Role of *Phantasia* in Aristotle," in *Essays on Aristotle's De Anima*, Martha Nussbaum and Amelie Rorty, eds. (Oxford: Clarendon Press, 1992), 279–96, especially 291.

circumstances; it means only that the agent cannot have found the circumstances to provide a decisive reason for refraining from her actions. It is true, too, that many activities will require a more expansive sort of attention to circumstances. For instance, someone engaged in conversation with a friend ought to listen attentively to what the friend says and ought to notice when his words induce a look of confusion or boredom. However, this does not count as bare information of the sort that might be delivered by a purely theoretical use of reason, since it must be structured by a constantly evolving sense of the practical concerns made live by the unfolding activity itself.

If we inspect our running experience in such cases, we will typically find no sign of a *purely* theoretical datum. What we will find, instead, are a series of apprehensions that already bear the marks of our practical concerns. A carpenter re-sawing a board hears variations in the pitch of the band saw as guides for varying the lateral pressure she puts on the board and the speed at which she feeds it to the blade. If she is experienced, she makes these adjustments spontaneously, with a skill whose contours might be hinted at with some rules of thumb yet could not be exhaustively captured in an actionable principle. A mechanic's apprehension of the sound produced by the same saw might highlight a subtle grinding noise that the carpenter entirely misses and that is a telltale sign of worn bearings. A "sound artist" listening to this same motor might gain a clearer apprehension of the proper completion of an ongoing composition as she hears how the saw's keen-edged, wavering whine would offset or complete other elements of a half-finished composition of "found sounds." There is a sense in which all three are hearing the same sound, but this must not be taken to imply that they all have the same perceptual *experience* and only then notice and highlight elements of it with their idiosyncratic ideas of practical significance. The sound shows up in experience already wearing the marks of the practical concerns associated with their activities.[36]

If we are fully to reckon with the sort of deliberation by which dialectical activities are carried forward, we will be forced to abandon the idea that deliberation can be separated into two sharply distinguished activities: an exercise of theoretical rationality whose aim is to arrive at a true characterization of one's circumstances, one's alternatives, and the likely effects of pursuing those alternatives; and a moment of practical deliberation culminating in a decision to opt for one or another of the alternatives left open by one's circumstances so construed. When we are engaged in activity, our awareness of our surroundings already bears the marks of our practical concerns. Furthermore, as I have stressed, practical thinking often requires making sense of an activity in which one is already engaged, and the requisite sort of "sense-making" will itself require an effort to interpret those ongoing doings in such a way as to bring to light their best and highest possibilities. Such thinking cannot plausibly be regarded as

---

[36] See John Dewey, "The Reflex Arc Concept in Psychology," 361.

mere theoretical stage-setting for practical deliberation. It does not yield a set of theoretical facts about one's circumstances; instead it yields a conception of the highest goods latent in what one is already doing, a conception that settles the practical question how best to carry forward with the activity.

When we perform actions solely because we see value in their expected effects, we are in an important sense absent from our own activities. It is the future that calls for appreciation, not the present, and if we could somehow magically dispense with such a stretch of life and propel ourselves forward immediately to the future pay-off, we would have no reason not to shorten our lives in this way. Whereas we are wholly present in our lives, concentrated within their unfolding moments, when we are engrossed in dialectical activity. Our attention is turned towards those evolving doings themselves, and the "pay-off" is seen to lie in a temporally extended stretch of activity that one is already in the midst of. Hence one does not absent or reserve oneself from one's activities when one focuses on the good or value in whose name one carries them forward; rather, one consummates these activities with a vivid and continuously deepening apprehension of the intrinsic value latent in them. As I will argue in the next chapter, this is the possibility Aristotle had in mind when he spoke of unimpeded *energeiai* both as the most pleasurable sort of activity and as the full actualization of the defining human capacity for self-direction in light of an apprehension of value. To dispense with a stretch of life during which one is wholeheartedly engaged in such activity would hardly be a boon, even if one is still striving to answer more completely to the activity's constitutive ideals. This suggests a certain diagnosis of the modern mania that perceives the point of a life's work in some set of listable achievements, the point of parenting in the production of children with some desired set of characteristics and capacities, and the point of intimate relationships in some status to whose production and stabilization the participants ought to commit themselves. This outlook is a formula for indefinitely postponing the good life by dint of a ceaseless, determined pursuit of its static simulacrum. It might be regarded as a secular analogue of the vice of idolatry.

There is a close kinship between the sort of engaged practical thinking that carries forward dialectical activities and what we would ordinarily call contemplation about the good life and its constituent activities. What distinguishes the sort of thought under discussion is that it forms a seamless part of the activity on whose good it is focused. As this sort of thought deepens, the quality of the accompanying activity is altered, since it is lit up from inside (so to speak) by a more penetrating understanding of its value. We might move, for instance, from interacting with fellow human beings with a vague and still immature sense of the intrinsic goods realizable in various forms of human community, to interaction guided by a keen and penetrating appreciation of the intrinsic goodness of other human beings and of relating to them in a spirit of mutual respect, acknowledgment, or love. This sort of understanding simultaneously opens the possibility of a more thorough sort of at-homeness in the human world and of a more keenly articulated alienation from it. The value of such appreciation, then, cannot be grounded merely in the sense of ease that it might produce. Nor can its value be thought to lie in its status as an efficient means for producing utility. It is not a mere means to the best sort of activity but an essential part of it.

DIALECTICAL ACTIVITY AND THE SUBJECT MATTER OF ETHICS

Some might recognize that dialectical activities involve a distinctive kind of practical thinking yet insist that ethical theory need not concern itself with such thought. This stance would cohere with the above-described liberal conception of the point of morality, and might be buoyed further by the thought that we cannot be morally faulted for failing to do that which we cannot do at will. This common conception of the preconditions of moral assessment suggests that we cannot be morally faulted for shortcomings in our running appreciation of the value of various human activities, since appreciation cannot be achieved at will.

At this point we must remind ourselves that the proper boundaries of philosophical ethics cannot definitively be settled in advance of our engagement in ethical reflection. The way to determine these boundaries is to see what range of norms, ideals, and modes of human excellence admit of being grasped as a unity through the lens of a genuinely illuminating account. Enthusiasts of the Aristotelian revival in ethics have sometimes lost sight of this basic feature of the subject. They have been too ready to wrest from the ethical thought of Aristotle a theoretical treatment of morality as that subject matter is conceived by Kantians and utilitarians.[37] Yet surely a body or writing that presents justice and wit as virtues of a single underlying kind, and that regards virtues falling into this rather unfamiliar category as necessary not only for excellence in the communal life of a polity but also for a form of human flourishing that can be translated without obvious error as happiness, can open our eyes to the possible benefits of theorizing about a different range of normative phenomena than is compassed by Kantianism or utilitarianism. If we turn to Aristotle in search of an alternative conception of right action—or, even worse, in search of moral principles fitted to resolve discrete deliberative problems (a "quandary ethics,"

---

[37] See for instance Rosalind Hursthouse, *On Virtue Ethics*, 3–4; Michael Slote, "Agent-Based Virtue Ethics," especially 258–62. This conception of virtue ethics has been even more prominent among those who have sought to offer general characterizations of the movement than among its proponent. See especially: Gary Watson, "On the Primacy of Character," 450–2; Gregory Trianosky, "What Is Virtue Ethics All About?" 336–8; Robert Louden, "On Some Vices of Virtue Ethics," 227–36.

as Edmund Pincoffs calls it)[38]—we pass up the opportunity to illuminate some of the more deeply entrenched prejudices and blind spots of our culture and the philosophy that grows out of it.

I have tried to set the stage for a more illuminating retrieval of Aristotelian virtue ethics by resurrecting a broadly Aristotelian conception of agency, and in particular of the way that practical thinking surges forth in those activities that we regard as intrinsically valuable. It is Aristotle's view, after all, that the highest human good lies in sustained activity—and in particular, the life of activity that constitutes *eudaimonia*—and not in passive experiences nor in achieved states of character. While Aristotle is routinely called a virtue ethicist, he did not ground value in the virtues of character themselves, but rather in the intrinsically valuable activity that flows from the virtues under minimally propitious conditions. Given this, we must resurrect a broadly Aristotelian notion of intrinsically valuable activity if we are to grasp the nature and value of Aristotelian virtues, and by extension the sort of alternative that Aristotelianism can offer to Kantian and utilitarian moral theories.

If an investigation of Aristotelian activity helps us to understand human happiness or flourishing (i.e. *eudaimonia*, under one or another of its standard translations), then it will have a direct and obvious relevance for ethical theory. It is widely accepted, after all, that it is ethically laudable to concern oneself with the advancement of human flourishing, hence we have a clear ethical ground for trying to understand what flourishing consists in. I believe, however, that a broadly Aristotelian conception of activity has a more direct and more interesting relevance for ethical theory. It can shed light on the proper mode of attention to, and investment in, many activities that are widely regarded as ethically good.

Consider the case of a parent embarking upon a conversation with a teenage child who has become withdrawn, very nearly estranged from the family, and who seems both pained by this detachment and stubbornly insistent upon it. The parent wishes to mend the relationship but realizes that this mending does not call for the production of some inactive state of affairs; rather, it must be realized in precisely the sort of shared activity now getting underway. The best outcome, then, is for the conversation to count as a fit constituent of a temporally extended and ethically laudable parent–child relation. Yet the parent might be quite uncertain what the conversation would have to be like if it is to be a fit constituent of such a relationship. It might be clear that this will require listening to the teenager and forging some sort of common ground or mutual understanding. Still, it might be quite unclear in what ways this process should be similar to and in what ways different from the reciprocal forging of common ground and mutual understanding that marks a good friendship

---

[38] See Edmund L. Pincoffs, *Quandaries and Virtues: Against Reductivism in Ethics* (Lawrence, Kansas: University Press of Kansas, 1986), chapter 2, especially 13–15.

between adults. What counts as a proper accommodation of the fact that one's conversational partner is a teenager? What counts as proper parental concern, and how is this to be distinguished from condescension or stultification of the child's yearnings for independence? In what ways might one's words and tone manifest an objectionable tendency to mistake the battles, achievements, and failures of one's child for one's own, and how might such vicarious feelings distort the relationship or harm the child? All of these ethically pregnant questions are in play, and many others besides.

Even if one cannot answer such questions definitively, still one might have a vague sense of what a genuinely good parent–child relationship would be like. This sense might be sufficient to provide guidance for one's first and still halting efforts to talk and to listen. As the conversation unfolds, it might become clearer what is called for, in something like the way that the blues singer described in Chapter 2 is able to become clearer about how she wants to sing by hearing her progressive attempts to give voice to the as-yet-obscure object of her desire. It seems possible, then, for the conversation to have all the attributes of a dialectical activity, and to involve the distinctive sort of practical thinking that carries forward such activities.

On reflection, it seems not only possible but morally laudable for the parent's engagement in this sort of conversation to be accompanied and guided by a continuous straining to see and to actualize the highest possibilities latent in the unfolding conversation—and, more generally, in parent–child relations. Indeed, while it might be a mistake to blame a parent for not managing to resuscitate such a damaged relationship, there would be something morally amiss with a parent who did not try mightily to do so. In the absence of a special story, there would also be something morally amiss with a parent who wholly lacked the sort of running appreciation of the value of the child and of the relationship that is necessary (though hardly sufficient) to turn the most devoted "trying" into something approaching a success. This last point is crucial, since this dawning appreciation is precisely the kind of practical thinking that cannot adequately be represented in the maxim-based Kantian model.

To illuminate this point, it will help to note that to attend to a conversation in this way is to be fully present in the conversation—as opposed, say, to being distracted or detached from the conversation itself by the orientation of one's evaluative attention towards some desired effect that one's words are calculated to bring about. Part of what makes certain conversations fit constituents of ethically laudable relationships is that the parties to them are present to each other in this rather elusive sense. If the evaluative attention of the parent is focused entirely on the not-yet-present value of the child's possible future traits or achievements, and not at all on the already-wholly-present value of the child, the parent–child relationship will thereby be impoverished. To refuse a world-making conception of the point of human action is not, then, to encourage an other-worldly outlook on life. On the contrary, it is a fitting preparation for full presence in worldly activities and worldly relationships.

Here we catch sight again of a point that we encountered in our earlier discussion of philosophical thought and the desires that drive it: there are some activities that we cannot engage in except in caricature or parody if we are not continuously responsive to the goods internal to them. One such activity is that particularly valuable sort of shared conversation between parent and child that is sometimes called a "heart-to-heart" or a moment of genuine "connection." Dwelling on the ethical stakes of proper and complete absorption in such an activity provides a point of entry for contesting the sense that Aristotle (or at least the Aristotle of our translations) makes a category mistake when he counts the *ethical* virtues as necessary for, and ideally conducive to, a genuinely *happy* life.

Authentic presence in conversation or speech is a special case, and an especially illuminating case, of authentic presence in action. Whether in speech or in action, we know this sort of presence by its signs, among which must be counted a kind of suppleness in our unfolding engagement in our activities. We feel the quality of a human being in his unscripted and spontaneous activities far more viscerally than in those premeditated performances that would take on a less tidy form if not for prior rehearsal, or coaching, or pre-commitment to a few simple rules of action. Here we run across what seems to be a common feature of all those human activities in which excellence (and not e.g. mere proficiency) is a distinct and worthy possibility. It might be possible to attain a certain level of competence in such activities by pre-commitment to a plan of engagement, but to approach excellence seems to require a running awareness of goods that come to light through the activity, and that could not be captured by any plan to which one might usefully pre-commit.

It is not always recognized that fully consummated Aristotelian activity requires something other, or something more, than the deliberate enactment of a plan of action. Rawls, for instance, puts forward "the Aristotelian Principle" that "other things equal, human beings enjoy the exercise of their realized capacities (their innate or trained abilities), and that this enjoyment increases the more the capacity is realized, or the greater its complexity."[39] If the enjoyment of an unimpeded activity really were merely a matter of exercising complex capacities, there would be no problem in securing this enjoyment by including an array of complex activities in one's life plan and then devoting one's practical attention to the efficient fulfillment of that plan. But success in the enactment of any actionable intention is compatible with a kind of absence from the activities that enact those intentions—that is, with a deadness in or detachment from one's own doings. Nor can lively engagement be brought into the picture as the object of a more complicated plan. The problem is that the lively engagement that matters is the sort that emerges from appreciation of the value of the activities themselves,

---

[39] John Rawls, *A Theory of Justice* (Cambridge: Harvard University Press, 1971), 426.

and this is something different from appreciating that they are included in one's plan of life, or appreciating that they have abstract properties such as complexity that make them fitting elements of a life plan.

As will be argued in Chapter 4, what completes activity is the active and continuous apprehension of the activity's intrinsic value. This cannot be attained merely by throwing oneself into an activity that has the non-evaluative property of complexity, or that requires us to make nuanced distinctions, since nuance and complexity can be displayed in activities that are patently valueless. Collecting saucers of mud does not become valuable simply because one makes nuanced distinctions among the textures and shapes of the clumps of mud one is collecting. Such activities as artistic creation, philosophical reflection, and interpersonal conversation are valued and experienced as pleasurable not merely because they actualize a *complex* array of native or trained capacities but rather because they actualize capacities that seem to us to be worth actualizing. The value of these activities is not always increased when we increase their complexity. We might find certain works of art valuable partly because of their simplicity. The activities that fully actualize the capacities that we have most reason to actualize, and that thereby contribute to the goodness of our lives, are those that inspire and are carried forward by a vivid and non-delusive sense of their intrinsic value. Yet this sense is itself cultivated by thoughtful practical attention to these activities, as experienced from the inside. This means that the sort of practical thinking needed to secure this centrally important kind of good must extend beyond the efficient pursuit of a plan so as to include the continuous running appreciation of intrinsic values realized by elements of that plan. This is the sort of practical thinking that cannot be fitted without distortion into the received picture of practical reason, and that so often falls through the cracks of contemporary philosophical discussions of ethics and practical reason.

One lesson of the above-discussed parent–child conversation is that excellence in deliberation cannot exhaustively be characterized as expertise in seeing which actions are to be performed and choosing to perform them. There is a specifically ethical excellence that cannot be produced at will, and that involves an immediate appreciation of the value of the human beings with whom one is confronted—a value that gives one reason to do many things but that is not exhausted by these reasons. This sort of moral excellence cannot be captured by any theory that locates the point of human actions solely in their consequences. This is unsurprising. What is more surprising is that there is no straightforward way of capturing this sort of excellence in the Kantian tradition of ethical thought that has served for the better part of the past two centuries as the most prominent alternative to ethical consequentialism.

For Kant, the moral quality of our practical reasoning is entirely a matter of the content and provenance of the maxims on which we act. If we act only on universalizable maxims, and if we do so not by accident but from a higher-order commitment to act only on universalizable maxims (that is, a commitment to the Categorical Imperative), then our practical reasoning is morally beyond reproach. This conception of practical reasoning cannot properly accommodate the sort of thinking through which we monitor our own unfolding activities and discern the highest possibilities latent in them. Our apprehension of these activities could enter into our maxims only as part of a morally innocent account of our circumstances or as part of a proposed course of action that the maxim represents as justified by our circumstances. The former alternative is unworkable, since an apt interpretation of these unfolding activities can itself be an ethical achievement. The latter alternative is also unworkable, because the next stretch of activity towards which our intentions are directed is represented in an irreducibly evaluative light that does not bring practical thought to an end but rather provides it with the intimation of value that it must continue to clarify. Nor is it apt to think of the relation between the stretch of activity that has already unfolded and the next stretch as a reason-giving relation. This element of the past figures not primarily as a reason to carry on in some particular way but as an imperfect instantiation of our working sense of how best to engage in the activity. As such, it is suited to play a role akin to that played by an artist's sketch when it inspires another, more nearly adequate sketch of what the artist is after. Put another way, it confronts the agent as the reification of her evolving conception of an excellence specific to her ongoing activity, and presents her with the task of interpreting it in such a way as to extend and deepen that evolving conception and the activity that flows from it.

By contesting the notion that practical thinking *ends* when we embark upon an intentional action, we have uncovered a fresh objection to the notion that it *begins* with an already formulated and purely theoretical picture of the circumstances in which we must choose an action. Practical thinking cannot be contained within *either* of its supposed temporal boundaries; it is not properly regarded as a discrete and episodic human activity but as a continuous straining to see the point or value of activities that are already underway, including one activity that is always implicitly underway as long as any practical question is alive for us—that is, the activity of attempting to live a fitting human life.

It is hardly surprising that there is a conflict between Kantianism, with its constructivist leanings, and the broadly Aristotelian realism implicit in my discussion of dialectical activities. The surprise lies in the fact that the Kantian conception of practical reasoning, which is often taken to be mere stage-setting for substantive claims about the requirements of morality, already closes off the very possibility of the sort of practical thinking that Aristotelian ethics regards as most distinctively ethical. What is at issue in the confrontation between Kantianism and Aristotelianism, at the most fundamental level, is how exactly thought becomes practical. When Aristotelianism is forwarded as one of a number of possible theories of the proprieties that govern episodic deliberation about what to do next, or what to do in this or that imaginable circumstance, this fundamental confrontation is sidestepped.

THE MISINHERITANCE OF ARISTOTELIAN PRACTICAL THINKING: A CASE STUDY

The methodological strategy of this book has been to cast light on the formal structure of practical thinking by inquiring into the structures of intelligibility that permit us to bring temporally extended successions of bodily motions into view as coherent human activities and, in the long run, coherent human lives. Another contemporary philosopher who has adopted a similar method is Candace Vogler.[40] Despite this similarity, Vogler ends up affirming a narrowly calculative conception of practical reasoning that excludes practical thinking about the proper ends of action. Vogler's work is particularly relevant because she purports to find her conception of practical reason in Aquinas, and she claims that Aquinas arrived at this view via a plausible reading of Aristotle.[41] Hence Vogler's work offers a rival conception of what it might mean to retrieve an Aristotelian conception of practical thought.

According to Vogler, the fine-grained running features of temporally extended action are intelligible as action only insofar as they can be seen as intentional efforts to serve or further the agent's ends or purposes. This implies that reason can give rise to action, hence count as practical, only by giving rise to bodily motions calculated to serve or further some end. Reason must be calculative to be practical.[42] In claiming that practical reason is calculative, Vogler does not mean to limit it to the narrowly instrumental sort of calculation that aims to determine how best to bring about some desired consequence. Her notion of calculation is broad enough to encompass the intentional choice of actions as constitutive parts of temporally extended ends.[43] What is crucial, though, is that practical reason cannot get started without an already determinate idea of an end, since otherwise it would not be possible for the agent to make calculations concerning what would conduce to or constitute the end. As Vogler puts it, "without some determinate end in view, there is *no* reason to do anything."[44] On the calculative view, then, practical reason cannot be used to critique, refine,

---

[40] This is the basic methodological commitment of Candace Vogler's *Reasonably Vicious* (Cambridge, MA: Harvard University Press, 2002). Vogler announces this commitment on page 7 of her introduction, where she writes: ". . . I think that a whole view of practical reason can be spun from a simple insight into the structure of intentional action . . ."

[41] Vogler is forthright in attributing her calculative view to Aquinas but somewhat more equivocal about whether Aquinas was right to trace his view to Aristotle. At one point, she says that this latter question is best left to the scholars, but later in the text she says that she is inclined to think that Aristotle did hold key elements of the view. See Vogler, *Reasonably Vicious*, 4 and 128.

[42] *Ibid.*, chapters 1 and 2.   [43] *Ibid.*, 2, 23, and 127–8.   [44] *Ibid.*, 49.

or deepen an as-yet-inchoate sense of the ends that one ought properly to have. This is the position that Vogler claims to find in Aquinas and possibly also in Aristotle, and this is the position that she herself affirms.

Vogler further elaborates this view by affirming the view, common to Aristotle and Aquinas, that all actions are chosen under the guise of the pleasurable, the useful, or the fitting. A plausible case can be made for a calculative view of the reasoning behind the first two species of actions, provided that we remember that many valuable human pleasures are byproducts of activities chosen in the name of their intrinsic value.[45] However, when we engage in an activity out of a sense of its fittingness, our reasoning does not always remain within the bounds of the calculative. Such thinking would be calculative only if it began with a determinate idea of how it is fitting for human beings to act and proceeded to make calculations about how best to perform or promote such action. I have tried to show that we can bring temporally extended activities, and indeed whole lives, into view as coherent unities only if we understand them as driven forward by non-calculative practical thinking about their value. The thinking in question moves from vague intimations of the activity's proper form or end, towards more determinate and satisfying apprehensions of the end. This is how we learn what befits us as parents or children, friends or neighbors, philosophers or poets, political leaders or school teachers, athletes or musicians. Indeed, this is how we make sense of the comprehensive and inescapable activity of living a fitting human life: we are thrown into this task without benefit of a clear and determinate idea of our end, and have no choice but to clarify our sense of how it befits us to live in mid-stride, as our lives unfold. If we try to understand these activities through a wholly calculative conception of practical reason, those evolving patterns that we might naturally regard as maturation and growth will be fractured into a series of unrelated changes in our mode of behavior.

These dialectical activities provide a *prima-facie* counterexample to Vogler's general picture of the nature of human action and the general form of practical reason. If Vogler were right to suggest that her calculative conception of practical reason was held by Aquinas and possibly also by Aristotle, these activities would also indicate a shortcoming in their doctrines. It seems to me, however, that neither of these thinkers held a purely calculative conception of practical reason. We can diagnose Vogler's interpretive error by looking at how she understands Aquinas's conception of befitting-style reasons for action. On Vogler's reading, considerations of befittingness are all grounded ultimately in our last end, which provides the destination towards which all of our worldly efforts should be oriented. The destination in question is "everlasting contemplation of God."[46] This condition of eternal beatitude is

---

[45] This point is discussed at length in Chapter 4 of this book.
[46] Vogler, *Reasonably Vicious*, 34.

"virtue's ultimate reward," Vogler writes, and therefore "virtue remains useful and fitting, even when it looks as though acting from it will bring disaster to one's mortal life."[47]

It is true that if we premise Aquinas's cosmology, the *usefulness* of virtue can be seen via a purely calculative exercise of reason. A passing acquaintance with the everlasting rewards of virtue would be sufficient to ground the calculative conclusion that it would be useful to be virtuous. The discernment of the *fittingness* of virtuous action is quite a different matter. To discern an action's fittingness is to understand its proper place in the divine plan and in one's proper calling as determined by that plan, and this is not a matter of mere calculation.

This point can be obscured if we limit our attention to the abstract question whether it is fitting for us to act virtuously. For the Thomist, it is obvious that it is fitting for us to be virtuous, since the term 'virtuous' functions as an abstract designation of the fitting, as specified by a divinely ordained human ideal. We can know in the abstract that we ought to act virtuously without knowing concretely what does and does not count as virtuous, hence without answering the concrete question what it is and is not fitting for us to do. We must settle this concrete question in order for our practical reasoning to guide our actions, yet answering this question requires insight into the nature of God, and in particular into the nature of divine goodness. Aquinas pictures this as something that dawns slowly—if it dawns at all—as we attempt to deepen and extend our understanding of God, perhaps by praying or by dwelling on and attempting to interpret and understand the parables and aphorisms of the gospel, or perhaps by reading Aquinas's writings on the virtues and vices. On Aquinas's view, then, befitting-style practical reasoning could be regarded as calculative only if one had already attained a clear grasp of God's goodness, hence of what it would be for us to be good or to live in accordance with God's plan. It could be regarded as calculative, in other words, only if the work of contemplation were already complete. Yet for Aquinas this work cannot be brought to completion in this worldly existence. It is central to the human condition that we are never more than on the way to God—never, that is, in possession of an achieved understanding of God.[48]

Aquinas is at pains to make clear that understanding is not merely a speculative but also a practical faculty, since the same power that permits contemplation of

[47] *Ibid.*, 35.

[48] In the words of the Thomist theologian and philosopher Josef Pieper, "It seems to me that St. Thomas's doctrine means that hope is the condition of man's existence as a knowing subject, a condition that by its very nature cannot be fixed: it is neither comprehension and possession nor simply non-possession, but 'not-yet-possession.' The knowing subject is visualized as a traveler, a *viator*, as someone 'on the way.'" See Josef Pieper, *The Silence of St. Thomas: Three Essays*, translated by John Murray and Daniel O'Connor (Chicago: Henry Regnery, 1965; original copyright 1957 by Pantheon Books), 69.

our place in the divine order, and of the higher law, also permits us to consult that order and to act in accordance with that law.[49] Understanding is a part of the practical virtue of prudence, and we must make use of understanding if we are to direct our will consistently towards the good.[50] The vicious cannot be prudent, because they lack understanding of the final end in whose light it is possible to make adept use of the faculty of practical reason. At best they can engage in the clever and efficient pursuit of bad ends.[51] The understanding required for prudence in practical reasoning is not only understanding of the final end but also of more specific principles of action and of the particulars that fall under these principles.[52] To use one of Aquinas's examples, prudence requires that one understand the content and the normative force of the abstract principle that one should do evil to no man, and one does not have a full grasp of this principle unless one can discern its concrete implications. Such understanding requires a concrete grasp of human beings and their value, hence of what does and does not count as doing evil to a human being. To strive for this sort of understanding is to strive to deepen and extend one's apprehension of the divine goodness in whose light we are called to live. This sort of practical thought cannot be called calculative because it moves towards clarity about what befits us rather than calculating the implications of an achieved idea of the befitting.

Aquinas does say that we choose virtuous actions "for the sake of" something, and this might suggest that the choice is guided by a recognizably calculative species of "means–end" reasoning. Yet he explains that in this case, the phrase "for the sake of" makes reference to a formal end rather than a final end or destinations towards which we are called upon to proceed. We are meant to choose and delight in virtuous actions out of awareness of their good form, or "for the sake of their inherent goodness."[53] The end of these actions is immanent in them. As stressed in the brief discussion of Aquinas in Chapter 2, the most final end is not the sort of thing that it would make sense to try to produce or possess. Contrary to Vogler's interpretation, the most final end is God and not contemplation of God.[54] The last end, in other words, is not some way that things might come to be, but a perfect being who is always already wholly present though never wholly grasped by the human mind. This is a point that we must take on board if we are to understand the straining of evaluative attention that constitutes the contemplation for which human beings are destined. Orientation towards the final end is the beginning of contemplation, and it involves a straining to appreciate the goodness of God, hence it consists in and continuously augments one's love of God. For Aquinas, virtuous action

---

[49] Aquinas, *Summa Theologica*, II–II, 8,3.   [50] *Ibid.*, II–II, 8,4, and 49,2.
[51] *Ibid.*, I–II, 58,5 and II–II, 47,13.   [52] *Ibid.*, II–II, 49,2.   [53] *Ibid.*, I–II, 70,1.
[54] *Ibid.*, II–I, 1,8; 2,7, and 8; 3,1; 3.5. See also the discussion of these passages in Chapter 2 of this book.

is a manifestation of this love-driven straining to see the good. Indeed, Aquinas holds that the master virtue is charity, understood as participation in the infinite love of the Holy Spirit.[55] There can be no true virtue without charity, and charity gives form to all virtuous acts—all such acts are informed by divine love. For Aquinas, this represents a proper orientation towards the final end of human beings—which is to say, towards God—both because it is a mode of participation in the love of the Holy Spirit and because one is to love one's neighbor under the aspect of God, in the same movement of affection that is one's love of God.[56] This is not to say that for Aquinas, virtue requires something other than understanding—that is, love. Rather, it is to explicate the sort of understanding that brings virtue into being. There is no possibility of understanding God without apprehending God's goodness, nor of apprehending God's goodness without love. A full and adequate appreciation of the nature of that goodness just is love. Straining to act virtuously, then, requires the same quest for clearer understanding of God that contemplation requires. This is why Aquinas insists that understanding is neither merely speculative nor merely practical but both at once.

Nor is it plausible to suppose that the quest for a clearer and deeper understanding of the intrinsic goodness of virtuous activity comes to a screeching halt when we engage in the sort of practical reasoning that either initiates or carries forward some activity. If we are truly concerned about the fittingness of our activity, we have good reason to monitor our ongoing activities with an eye to determining whether pride or anger or jealousy are distorting our sense of how to act. Our quest to attain a deeper understanding of the fitting, then, ought to be and can be a continuous mental activity—call it *the activity of ethics*. It is through the activity of ethics that we might hope to deepen and extend our sense of how best to answer to the ideals to which we are answerable as human beings and more particularly as friends, neighbors, citizens, parents, children, and devotees of various practices and vocations. Perhaps we can arrive at a fully mature conception of how to live in no other way than by throwing ourselves into the general kinds of activity (or interactivity) recommended by those with more experience, in hopes of coming to see the value of these activities "from the inside," thereby refining our sense of how best to carry forward with them.

Myles Burnyeat has persuasively argued that this was how Aristotle understood the process of coming to understand the nature and value of virtuous activity.[57] On Burnyeat's reading, Aristotle stresses the importance of a good upbringing, where this consists primarily in the cultivation of good habits, since one cannot learn to value virtuous activity except by acting in outward conformity with virtue and coming to appreciate, from the participant perspective, the intrinsic

---

[55] Aquinas, *Summa Theologica*, II–II, 24,7.   [56] *Ibid.*, II–II, 25,1.
[57] See Myles Burnyeat, "Aristotle on Learning to be Good."

goodness that can be enjoyed by acting in this way. Until one throws oneself into a good activity, one can have only a second-hand and approximate grasp of its value. One might take it on the word of others that there is intrinsic value in virtuous activity, but this could confer neither an appreciation of the value of virtue nor a reliable capacity to distinguish virtue from vice. One learns for oneself that virtuous action is intrinsically valuable, and learns which activities are virtuous, by habituation in outwardly virtuous patterns of action. For instance, a child might initially see fairness as having little point except as an instrument for currying favor with parents or securing other extrinsic rewards. Yet given a minimally decent upbringing, many children eventually see from the inside how human interactions are transfigured and take on an unexpected and pleasing value when conducted in a spirit of mutual recognition and respect. As Burnyeat summarizes the point, "It turns out that Aristotle is not simply giving us a bland reminder that virtue takes practice. Rather, practice has cognitive powers, in that it is the way we learn what is noble or just."[58]

If Burnyeat's reading is correct, as I believe, then Aristotle does not have a purely calculative idea of the practical thought that lies behind those actions chosen in the name of the fine or noble (i.e. the *to kalon*, Aristotle's correlate of Vogler's category of the fitting). It is true that such actions would be regarded as choiceworthy because they are fitting constituents of a fully *eudaimon* life, but we do not have a fixed and determinate idea of a fully *eudaimon* life from which we can make calculations about what concrete actions are fit constituents of such a life. Our idea of a fully *eudaimon* life is expressed in our choices concerning what it would be best to do next, and it is precisely by making such choices and assessing them "from the inside" that we refine our sense of what is and what is not a fitting constituent of the *eudaimon* life. What is called for here is not calculation but *phronesis*, or wisdom. Hence, we cannot inherit Aristotle's notion of the relation between thought and action—and in particular, of what Burnyeat calls the "cognitive powers" of practical activity—if we adopt a narrowly calculative conception of practical reason. One might miss this aspect of Aristotle's thought if one places too much weight on his discussion of the practical syllogism, but it is central to Aristotle's purposes to insist that *phronesis* is not merely a matter of the content of one's explicit syllogisms but also of the patterns of evaluative attention or sensitivity that set the stage for explicit episodes of practical deliberation.[59]

---

[58] Burnyeat, "Aristotle on Learning to be Good," 73. Perhaps Aquinas is making a similar point when he claims that docility is part of prudence because it conduces to patient learning from elders, something which is necessary if one is to internalize the insight into the proper ends of action that elders have accumulated as a result of their long experience. See Aquinas, *Summa Theologica*, ii–ii, 49,3.

[59] Michael Frede puts his finger on this crucial point when he says that for Aristotle, as for Socrates, Plato, and the Stoics, practical reason provides us with "the ability to recognize what is good and to move us towards it." See Michael Frede, Introduction to *Rationality In Greek Thought*, eds. Michael Frede and Gisela Striker (Oxford: Oxford University Press, 1996), 17.

Vogler suggests that the secular ethical theorist can make use of the category of the fitting only in support of actions that fit into patterns that the deliberator has actually established in the past and now seeks to maintain.[60] If this were true, then the category of the fitting could not be used to vindicate the rational credentials of a recognizably ethical way of life. As Vogler points out in passing, it would be fitting on this approach for "the envious person to be a spoilsport."[61] If this really were the only way that the secular theorist could draw upon this category of reasons, then on full reflection the secular theorist would have to discard the category as empty. Suppose that some deliberator simply finds herself with a functional desire to produce more instantiations of some habitual type of action, yet sees these instantiations as wholly pointless. This would be sufficient for the possession of an obsession but not for the possession of a pattern worth continuing. We must see something in continuing the pattern in order to have intelligible grounds for thinking that we have reason to continue it. Perhaps this is why Vogler says that it is fitting to perpetuate only those patterns we seek to continue. But once this is admitted, it is not clear why past patterns should matter at all. The justificatory weight seems to lie entirely in what we think we see in the pattern such that we seek to sustain it, and not in the fact that we have exemplified it. To return to Vogler's example, it is no reason to be a spoilsport that one has consistently exemplified envy in the past. Practical judgments cannot be established as reasonable by dint of mere obstinate repetition. To tie the category of the fitting to actual patterns of action is to debunk it, not to make it safe for secular use. This is not to say that the category is usable only by religious believers; it is only to say that its intelligible use presupposes a minimally substantive account of how it is good to live.

Vogler's conception of practical rationality manifests the same fundamental problem that we see in contemporary decision-theoretic conceptions of rationality. These conceptions encourage the thought that one's outlook on value ought rationally to be complete and determinate before one begins the work of deliberation about particular cases. They provide no insight into the most fundamental work of deliberation, which is the formation and revision of a tenable conception of the good. Instead, they reduce deliberative rationality to skill in estimating probabilities and performing calculations. But the work of proper deliberation is not the work of an accountant. It is the work of a seeker after the good, and it often requires a fresh straining to form a more just and palpable sense of the goods bearing on one's ongoing activities. One of the most appealing aspects of Aristotelian virtue ethics is that it provides us with an illuminating way to evaluate and to improve our efforts to bring the good into view—or so I will argue in the chapters ahead.

---

[60] Vogler, *Reasonably Vicious*, 42.   [61] *Ibid.*, 50.

THE UNDELEGABILITY OF MORAL THINKING

One of the more puzzling features of moral thinking—a feature to which Raimond Gaita has usefully drawn attention—is its undelegability.[62] The task of moral reflection cannot be delegated to others who are experts in it in the way that merely technical or calculative practical problems can be. To use Gaita's example, if I have become disoriented and run out of food and water during a mountain-climbing excursion, I would do well to consult with an expert about how best to get off the mountain and back to safety. But if I am uncertain about what to do, morally speaking, I would not do well to pass off the problem to someone I regard as a "moral expert" and take over their answer without coming to see its cogency for myself.[63]

If moral reflection were technical, means–end reflection about how to bring about some already understood end, its undelegability would be all but inexplicable. Hence the undelegability of moral reflection presents yet another decisive objection to utilitarianism. After all, if the point of moral reflection were to determine which action promises to maximize aggregate pleasure or desire-satisfaction, it would seem silly not to delegate this reflection to those armed with full knowledge of the latest polls and relevant expertise in economics, politics, and social psychology. Utilitarianism cannot make good sense of the deep-seated conviction that moral deliberation is an unshirkable task for each individual. The same objection applies to any purely calculative conception of ethical reasoning. If ethical reasoning were solely a matter of accurate calculation, then presumably we could faultlessly outsource the calculations to an expert just as we outsource the calculative steps of checkbook-balancing to an adding machine.

It might be thought that ethical deliberation cannot be delegated because it is about ends and not merely about means, and we cannot rely upon experts to specify our ends. However, there are cases in which it seems perfectly acceptable to delegate the task of clarifying one's ends, if not of setting them from scratch, and ethical deliberation often bears upon ends only in the sense that it yields a clearer and more determinate picture of an end that one already holds (e.g. the end of being fair in one's dealings with others). For instance, if I want to listen to good jazz but have no idea what jazz is good, I might sensibly delegate the task of buying jazz recordings to someone who is reputed to be a particularly keen critic of jazz. Still, it will remain true that if I do not come to appreciate the value that the putative jazz expert hears in the recordings she selects, my experience with them will not be nearly as valuable as it might be.

---

62 Raimond Gaita, *Good and Evil: An Absolute Conception*, 2nd edn (London: Routledge, 2004 (first edition MacMillan 1991)), 100–9.
63 *Ibid.*, 102–3.

Here we catch sight of something that really can't be delegated: the sort of evaluative attention that accompanies certain activities and constitutes them as the valuable activities that they are. This suggests one potentially fruitful diagnosis of the undelegability of some kinds of practical thinking, including what we ordinarily call moral thinking. There is no problem in asking someone with a great deal of life experience and wisdom for guidance when we face a morally perplexing decision. Whatever is meant by the undelegability of moral thought, it does not rule out the seeking and accepting of advice. However, if the advice were merely followed but not *understood*, the resulting performance would be altered for the worse by the very fact that it is not accompanied and guided by a living sense of its point or value. This is what makes it absurd to consider delegating the practical thinking behind the running activity that constitutes a good day of parenting, or a kind and decent interaction with a fellow human being, or even a good game of chess. The understanding that accompanies and guides such activities is an essential constituent of the best form of the activity. Without the understanding, only a paltry simulacrum of these activities would be possible.

Some might object that the problem with delegating practical thinking is not that it severs the connection between practical understanding and action but that it undermines one's autonomy. This would be a distinction without a difference if acting autonomously came to the same thing as acting from a first-personal understanding of the point or value of what one is doing. We will need a different conception of autonomy to elaborate the objection at hand. Many philosophers have held that to act autonomously is to act from a plan or principle that one has chosen or endorsed. If we premise this conception of autonomy, it becomes entirely unclear why there should be any conflict between autonomy and the delegation of deliberative tasks. After all, it seems possible to endorse and choose to act on the principle of doing whatever someone else directs us to do, within certain bounds. If this can't be done autonomously, then it seems that it would be an abandonment of autonomy to commit oneself to following the directives, within reasonable bounds, of a teacher or workplace manager. Yet whatever might be wrong with following the directives of teachers or managers, clearly it does not involve the same sort of self-abandonment that would be involved in outsourcing one's moral thinking.

This brief discussion hardly shows that there is no conception of autonomy that could ground an alternative explanation of the undelegability of moral thinking. There is, however, a further obstacle faced by an autonomy-based explanation of this phenomenon. Intuitively there seem to be cases of undelegable practical thinking that have nothing to do with autonomy yet that can be explained on that approach I have sketched. For instance, there seems to be something badly deficient about "playing chess" while delegating to another the entire task of thinking about which moves to make. Intuitively it seems that one could perform this charade autonomously. The deficiency seems not to consist in a loss of autonomy but in a failure actually to play chess. To engage in certain valuable activities, and to be optimally present in those activities as they unfold, requires a first-personal understanding of one's doings and their point. I have suggested that ethically laudable relations with other human beings are like that. Their existence is conceptually dependent upon a running awareness, on the part of participants, of their point or value. Such thought cannot be delegated because such relations are not optional and cannot exist unless we do this thinking for ourselves. In upcoming chapters, I will argue that Aristotle recognized the importance of such thinking, and its constitutive relation to the most valuable human activities, in his discussions of pleasure and of friendship.

CONCLUDING REMARKS ON PRACTICAL THINKING

The phrase "practical reasoning" seems almost expressly designed to direct attention away from the sort of continuous thought through which we become entwined in and carry forward with the temporally extended activities that we find intrinsically valuable. Each term of the phrase has the potential to mislead us, and when the two terms are conjoined in an attempt to delimit the proper subject matter of ethical theory, they are almost certain to set us down an artificially narrow pathway. It would be better to speak of excellence in practical thinking rather than of norms of practical reason, but even then we must be careful to avoid too stark a picture of the theory–practice distinction when we flesh out the idea of the practical.

The term 'reasoning' is generally understood to refer to a structured transition of thought that begins with a well-formulated problem and moves through a series of steps, with an eye to arriving at a justified resolution. What brings an episode of reasoning to a successful conclusion is the identification of a good *reason* for resolving it in one way or another. The effort of thought through which we apprehend the goodness internal to an intrinsically valuable activity can easily be distorted if it is viewed as a quest for reasons to resolve an already well-formulated problem in one way or another (e.g. to say 'yes' or 'no' to a determinate action we desire to perform). It is true that when one apprehends the value internal to an activity, one thereby grasps a reason for doing it. But what thought does in such cases is to bring a kind of intrinsic value into view, and (as will be argued in Chapter 5) this process cannot be reduced to the identification of practical reasons. Hence there is a kind of practical thinking that continuously seeks an understanding of intrinsic goods or values, and that seeks this understanding through experience rather than through discursive reasoning. Aristotle uses the term *nous* to name this grasp of the proper starting points of practical reflection. If we conceive of ethical theory as an inquiry into certain norms of practical reasoning, we will be inclined to overlook this ethically vital sort of thought.

The term 'practical' is also potentially misleading. This term gets its sense as one half of a binary opposition between practical and theoretical reason. The basic idea behind the distinction, in its modern or Kantian incarnation, is to mark off two mutually exclusive modes of deployment of human reason, one ordered towards forming true beliefs about the world and the other towards determining what ought to be done. This framework threatens to distort rather than to illuminate the sort of thinking that sustains dialectical activities. Such thought strains towards insight into the value of unfolding activities. If there are facts to be discerned in this domain, then it counts as an effort to arrive at a faithful conception of these facts. Yet it also shapes those running activities, and it does so not merely by causing them to be different than they would otherwise be, but by inducing revisions that the thought itself makes apt. If we counterpose practical thought with thought aimed at the attainment of true beliefs, and if we take ethical theory to concern itself solely with proprieties of practical thought so conceived, we run the risk of overlooking the sort of thought I have been discussing. On the other hand, if we keep an open mind about how best to draw the theory–practice divide when we turn to the task of specifying the norms bearing on what is ordinarily called theoretical inquiry, we will begin to see some striking commonalities between the virtues of ethical and of epistemic activity—commonalities that cast doubt on the notion that ethics and epistemology can be pursued in isolation. (I will return to this theme further down the road, in the book's final chapter.)

4

Savoring Time: Pleasure and Unreserved Activity

> . . . he solves the great riddle, to live in eternity and yet to hear the cabinet clock strike in such a way that its striking does not shorten but lengthen his eternity, a contradiction that is just as profound as, though far more glorious than, the one in the familiar situation described in a story from the Middle Ages, about a poor wretch who woke up in hell and shouted, "What time is it?"—whereupon the devil answered, "Eternity!"
>
> (Søren Kierkegaard)[1]

> Most of us labor for the sake of things in space. As a result we suffer from a deeply rooted dread of time and stand aghast when compelled to look into its face. Time to us is sarcasm, a slick treacherous monster with a jaw like a furnace incinerating every moment of our lives. Shrinking, therefore, from facing time, we escape for shelter to things of space. The intentions we are unable to carry out we deposit in space; possessions become the symbols of our repressions, jubilees of frustrations.
>
> (Abraham Heschel)[2]

PLEASURE AND CONTINUOUS PRACTICAL THINKING

If we turn to Aristotle in search of an illuminating discussion of the sort of appreciative discernment of value that accompanies and carries forward intrinsically valuable activities, we might profitably begin with his elusive yet intriguing passages on pleasure. In the most revealing of these passages, Aristotle characterizes pleasure not as a separate sensory effect of our doings, but as an active attention to our own unfolding activities that renders these activities complete or unimpeded. On Aristotle's view, it is not just any human doing

---

[1] Søren Kierkegaard, *Either/Or, Part II*, translated by Howard V. Hong and Edna H. Hong (Princeton: Princeton University Press, 1988), 138–9.

[2] Abraman Heschel, *The Sabbath, Its Meaning for Modern Man* (New York: Farrar, Straus and Giroux, 1977, original copyright 1951), 5.

that can be completed by appreciative attention. This is possible only when the agent views the activity as non-instrumentally valuable, and not when the agent sees the activity's point as lying solely in an effect that it is calculated to produce. Nor does this sort of attention leave our activity unchanged. What is in question is not mere self-spectatorship, but rather an attentiveness that metamorphoses the activity that it accompanies, lending the activity a character and value that it could not have if performed mechanically or mindlessly.

As emerged in the previous chapter, there are some activities that cannot be engaged in except in parody if we are not continuously attentive and responsive to the goods internal to them. Many of these activities are morally significant. For instance, such attention is essential to that form of shared conversation between parent and child that we might refer to as a "heart to heart" or a moment of genuine connection, and one cannot be fully responsive to the demands of the parent–child relation if one is incapable of such attention in those moments of crisis that call for it. If we dwell on the ethical stakes of proper and complete presence in unfolding life activities, this provides us with a point of entry for contesting the sense that Aristotle makes a category mistake when he counts the ethical virtues, including such virtues as justice and generosity, as necessary for and ideally conducive to something that might be translated without blatant infelicity by the English term 'happiness.' Aristotle's *eudaimonistic* treatment of these virtues might look more plausible if we could make sense of his claim that the ideally virtuous person not only finds virtuous actions to be "the thing to do" but also finds them pleasurable. Yet until we appreciate the very unusual idea of pleasure with which Aristotle is working, it will remain hard to see what could possibly have tempted Aristotle to believe such a thing.

If pleasures were mere sensations, related to virtuous activities only as their conceptually separate effects, Aristotle's claim would be entirely implausible.[3] It seems offhand that one could have the full measure of the virtues of practical thought, yet be "wired" in such a way that one's reliably virtuous actions did not cause such sensations to occur. Yet Aristotle held that anyone with the virtue of practical wisdom (*phronesis*) would have the full array of ethical virtues and therefore would find virtuous actions pleasurable. What conception of pleasure, and what allied conception of practical thinking, might make this view plausible?

The basic idea behind the Aristotelian conception of pleasure is this: to take pleasure in an activity is to attend to it in such a way that one's engagement in

---

[3] This sensory conception of pleasure was embraced by John Locke in *An Essay Concerning Human Understanding*, II, xx, 1; it was also put forward by G. E. Moore in *Principia Ethica* (Cambridge: Cambridge University Press, 1962), 12. A more recent defense can be found in Irwin Goldstein, "Why People Prefer Pleasure to Pain," *Philosophy* 55 (1980), 349–62.

it becomes wholehearted or unimpeded.[4] This conception of pleasure has had some very able contemporary proponents. However, I do not think that they have made adequately clear what *kind* of attention it is that can perform the surprising feat of transforming otherwise indifferent activities into pleasurable ones, nor why we should expect that those who are fully virtuous will generally extend the requisite sort of attention to their virtuous activities. The central task of this chapter is to correct for these shortcomings by building upon Gilbert Ryle's suggestion that taking pleasure in an activity is tantamount to engaging in the activity while fervently desiring to do it and it alone.[5] If Ryle's claim is correct—and I think that, with minor qualifications, it is—we can use the notion of desire set out in earlier chapters to generate corollary insights into the sort of attention that makes activities *pleasurable*. This is the strategy followed in this chapter. The aim is not merely to articulate a compelling account of certain pleasures, but also to shed light on a series of puzzling questions about the place of pleasure in virtuous character, practical reason, and the good life.

A subsidiary aim of this chapter is to dispel the widely accepted thesis that most human pleasures (including those that are generally taken to be higher, or more meaningful, or more central to a life well lived) are reasons for performing whatever actions tend to produce them. This thesis is an important pillar of the production-centric conception of action considered and rejected in Chapters 1 and 2, since it supports a production-oriented posture towards at least one centrally important human good. The view is mistaken. Prospective pleasures are rarely reasons for action, though they are often reliable *indicators* of other reasons. This does not mean that they make no contribution to the goodness of the lives in which they occur. They often do. In many cases, however, their goodness is conditioned on their consonance with an independent realm of non-hedonic values, and they can be enjoyed only by those who act in the name of these non-hedonic values. The value of these pleasures hinges, paradoxically, on the falsity of the twin hedonistic theses that all pleasures are valuable and that only pleasures are valuable.

---

[4] See Aristotle, *Nicomachean Ethics*, Books VII and X; Gilbert Ryle, *The Concept of Mind* (Chicago: University of Chicago Press, 1949), 107–10; and Gilbert Ryle, "Pleasure," in *Collected Papers, Volume 2: Collected Essays 1929–1968* (New York: Barnes and Noble Inc., 1971), 326–35.

[5] The Aristotelian conception of pleasure had able champions in mid-twentieth-century Anglo-American philosophy, but it has since fallen into relative decline. The most distinguished and influential proponent of the view was Ryle, but broadly Aristotelian conceptions of pleasure can also be found in W. B. Gallie, "Pleasure," *Proceedings of the Aristotelian Society*, Supplementary Volume (1954); and C. C. W. Taylor, "Pleasure," *Analysis*, Supplementary Volume (1962), 2–19. I say that it has been largely forgotten, not entirely forgotten. Contemporary examples of the view can be found in Robert M. Adams, *Finite and Infinite Goods: A Framework for Ethics* (Oxford: Oxford University Press, 1999), chapter 3; and Elijah Millgram, "Pleasure in Practical Reasoning," *The Monist* 76 (1993), 394–415.

DESIRES AND JUSTIFICATORY REASONS

One lingering question about the "evaluative outlook" account of desire set out in earlier chapters is what exactly it means for something to *present itself as good or valuable* (or to be *heard as* or *seen as* good or valuable). It is not hard to find examples of this phenomenon. For instance, what distinguishes the sympathetic person from the sadist is that the sympathetic person notices the suffering of other human beings and *sees* it *as* something bad, presumably because she sees other human beings as creatures whose flourishing has great value. The sadist also notices the suffering of others but *sees* it *as* something good. We seem, then, to have an intuitive grasp of the phenomenological difference between these desires, but it is exceedingly difficult to provide an illuminating account of it.

Everyday talk of "seeing as" can easily lead us astray here. For instance, the phrase "As I see things" is ordinarily used to make known what one judges to be true while also signaling a lack of certainty or a readiness to consider alternatives. But hedged judgments are not the sorts of "seeings as" that partly constitute our desires. These latter "seeings as" are seemings or appearances and not tentative judgments.

Scanlon thinks of desires (or at least what he calls "desires in the directed-attention sense") as tendencies to *see* certain circumstances or considerations *as* reasons for some action or outcome.[6] He goes on to suggest that to see a consideration as a reason is to have a tendency to judge that it is a reason.[7] This equation sets the stage for a quick and decisive refutation of the traditional view that desires are direct sources of justificatory reasons.[8] When one is engaged in deliberation, it would be question-begging to take one's tendency to judge that some action is worth doing as a reason for that action. The problem is not simply that this so-called "justification" won't satisfy other people. If I am genuinely concerned about the justifiability of a proposed action, the mere psychological fact that I have a tendency to judge that there is reason to perform it ought not to satisfy even me. The question I must answer is whether I *ought* to judge the action worthwhile, not whether I *tend* to judge it so. This leads Scanlon to conclude that while desires may explain our actions, they do not supply us with justificatory reasons for doing what they incline us to do.

This argument depends upon a dubious conflation of seeings-as and tendencies to judge. Optical illusions are often taken to be paradigm cases of "seeings-as." Intuitively, it seems that one could *see* a pair of Muller–Lyer lines *as* unequal

---

[6] Scanlon, *What We Owe to Each Other*, 37–41.   [7] *Ibid.*, 43–4.
[8] A structurally similar argument is found in Scanlon, *What We Owe to Each Other*, 43–4.

yet have no *tendency to judge* them unequal.[9] One might have become wholly convinced of their equality by painstakingly measuring them several times. This suggests that while seeings-as might ordinarily give rise to tendencies to judge, they cannot be equated with such tendencies.

There is a further reason to reject Scanlon's equation. One potential advantage of the evaluative-attention conception of desires is that it can vindicate the common-sense notion that we sometimes do what we have no desire to do. If desires were nothing more than tendencies to attend to certain considerations and to judge that they are reasons for acting in some way, this potential advantage is compromised. Suppose I am resolutely determined to perform my fair share of some task that I find tedious or even slightly revolting—for instance, cleaning a group bathroom—and I proceed to do so. My determination to do my share might reliably prompt me to notice considerations that count in favor of cleaning the bathroom (e.g. it's dirty and I haven't done the past few cleanings) and to clean the bathroom out of acknowledgment of these reasons. In that case, it would be sufficient to ground a tendency to judge that these considerations are reasons to clean the bathroom, yet the action seems to be a paradigmatic case of doing what I have no desire to do. Hence Scanlon's view cannot vindicate the boundaries of the common-sense notion of acting without desire. Indeed, the problem might be worse, since whenever I perform any action, I must be judging implicitly that something counts in favor of performing it, and if I make a judgment it can hardly be said that I have no tendency whatsoever to make that judgment. Hence Scanlon's notion of seeing-as seems to rule out the very possibility of doing what one has no desire whatsoever to do.

If the relationship between evaluative seemings and tendencies to judge is not one of strict equivalence, a natural alternative is that the seemings in question make it appear as if the corresponding judgments are true. Yet if we retreat to this position, we thereby short-circuit Scanlon's quick argument against the reason-giving force of desire. A tendency to make a judgment cannot justify that same judgment, but an appearance to the effect that things correspond with a judgment might well justify that judgment. We might have good reason to suppose that things are as they appear. This is precisely the possibility seized upon by Stampe, who forwards an evaluative attention account of desire quite similar to Scanlon's yet regards it as a basis not for refuting but for vindicating the justificatory authority of desires *per se*.

Stampe prepares the way for his argument by claiming that whenever a person desires that *p*, it seems to that person as if it would be good that *p*.[10] Thus far Stampe's position is very similar to Scanlon's, the primary difference being that

---

[9] The Muller–Lyer illusion involves two parallel lines of equal length, one of which is bounded by arrow lines pointing outwards and the other bounded by arrow lines pointing inwards. The latter line is generally seen as longer.

[10] Dennis Stampe, "The Authority of Desire," 356–7.

Stampe equates desires with appearances of *goodness* rather than appearances of *reasons for action*. Stampe's view seems preferable in this particular, since one can desire that the world *be* a particular way without tending to see anything whatever as a reason to act in any way. I might desire, for instance, that there be a God, or that the physical universe have an elegant order, yet these desires seem dissociated from any particular course of action.[11]

Stampe's case for the justificatory authority of desire goes by way of a controversial claim about seemings. In his view, we would not count a psychological state as one in which things *seem* a particular way unless we believed it to be a reliable indicator that things *are* that way.[12] This strikes me as false. When I am jealous, it seems to me that the affections of someone I love are being redirected at another, yet clearly I could continue to be jealous even after reaching the conclusion that such impressions are extremely unreliable. Similarly, it seems possible to have desires that I judge to be entirely unreliable as guides to the good. If Stampe were right, I could not judge this without immediately inducing a fundamental shift in what I desire. This is not only implausible on its face; it also raises the puzzling question what *kind* of psychological state it is that one must believe to be a reliable indicator of goodness in order to have a desire. It is tempting to say that the state is already a desire—i.e. a vivid appearance of goodness—but Stampe cannot say this on pain of circularity. I conclude, then, that Stampe fails to vindicate the claim (or, as I'm tempted to say, the *dogma*—call it the fourth dogma of desire) that desires *per se* are reasons to act.

If desires are evaluative outlooks on goods or reasons, then we have reason to act on a desire if and only if we have reason to trust the evaluative outlook in which it consists. Sometimes we have good reason to distrust our desires, which is to say (*contra* Stampe) that we have good reason to deny their justificatory authority. In other cases, we have good reason to trust our desires. It seems strained to insist (with Scanlon) that these desires are not reasons for action, since reasons transmit their justificatory force to reasons for believing that they exist. (A reading of $102°f$ on a trusty thermometer can be a good reason to administer fever-reducing medicine to a child, but only because it reliably indicates a fever.)

---

[11] Such examples leave me unconvinced by Scanlon's proposal that values can always be reduced to reasons. See Scanlon, *What We Owe to Each Other*, chapter 2.

[12] Stampe, "The Authority of Desire," 364. My conjecture is that Stampe falls into error here because he fails to note that when we speak of how things *seem* to us, we are sometimes reporting a vivid impression and sometimes expressing guarded judgments about how things actually are. If I say, "It seems to me that Reagan was a second-rate president," my comment would naturally be understood as falling into the latter category, and in this case it would indeed be odd for me to add, "But I believe that he was an excellent president." This example, however, does nothing to bolster Stampe's claim that seemings must coincide with judgments, because the imagined comment is not a description of my psychological state but a guarded evaluation of Reagan. If I were asked to justify the comment, it would cut no ice to show that I did indeed have the vivid impression that Reagan was an inferior president; my task would be to adduce grounds for thinking Reagan a bad president.

The justificatory authority of a desire stands or falls with the supposition that the desire accurately reflects real reasons.

This conclusion is perhaps not terribly controversial. However, the "evaluative attention" view of desires has another, quite surprising and controversial implication concerning practical justification. It implies that even when desires *are* reasons for action, they are not the *sort* of reasons that philosophers have generally thought them to be. Desires are subjective outlooks on what presents itself as an independent world of value. Desires do not present themselves as reasons for action, and the candidate reasons they do present are not guaranteed the status of reasons simply because of the vivid way they are recommended to our attention. When we say 'yes' to a desire, we are endorsing the reason-giving status of the values brought into view by the desire, while endorsing the desire itself only as a reliable indicator of value. Without desires, we might not know where to begin thinking about which of the innumerable actions open to us might be worth doing.[13] This might show that we need desires to rescue us from disorientation, and that we cannot distrust all desires without inducing practical paralysis, but it does not show that desires are always reasons, nor that they are independent or self-standing reasons.

AN ARISTOTELIAN ACCOUNT OF PLEASURE

One possible motive for denying that desires themselves are reasons for action is that when one does something that seems entirely senseless—say, spends an entire day dropping and picking up a boxful of toothpicks—one cannot communicate one's reason for doing what one has done by saying "I just wanted to do it" or "I just felt like it." Such phrases merely invite the further question what could possibly make such senseless behavior seem worthwhile. Until we can answer this latter question, the mere mention of a desire will not help us to see what the agent's reason could be.

Suppose our toothpick-dropper were to add, "I took pleasure in it." Would this help us to see what reason he has for spending the day dropping and picking up toothpicks? This depends upon how we interpret his comment. We might understand him as reporting that when he engages in this activity, it causes an agreeable sensation in him, and he does it in order to produce this agreeable sensation. He does it, in other words, as an exercise in world-making. While this would indicate an odd and unfortunate psychological make-up, still it would begin to explain his reason for engaging in so curious an activity, since we do have a sense of the value that human beings see in agreeable sensations. However, this is not what we usually have in mind when we speak of taking pleasure *in*

---

[13] For a very interesting discussion of this topic, see Barbara Herman's *The Practice of Moral Judgment* (Cambridge: Harvard University Press, 1993), especially chapters 4 and 7.

activities.[14] When I say that I took pleasure, say, in a conversation or a stroll in the park, I am usually unable to recall any particular sensation that could plausibly be identified as the pleasure I took. Even if I do recall some distinct and agreeable feeling—a flush of well-being during the walk, or a flash of intellectual excitement during the conversation—I might well deny that I took pleasure only when I felt that feeling. I am likely to insist that I took pleasure in the whole walk, or the whole conversation. Further, any sensation caused by an activity could outlast the activity, yet it makes no sense to speak of taking pleasure in a walk after it is over.

On the strength of these and other related observations, Gilbert Ryle concludes that to take pleasure in an activity is not necessarily to feel any particular sensation while doing it, but rather to perform it in a particular way—to be absorbed or unreservedly engaged in it; to perform it with wholehearted enthusiasm or rapt attention.[15] If the toothpick-dropper means something along these lines when he explains his activity by saying that he took pleasure in it, then his comment merely leads to the question "What in the world is the pleasure of *that*?" Until we answer this latter question—that is, until we understand what he *saw* in the activity that drew his attention and ignited his enthusiasm—the mere fact that he took pleasure in it will not help us to grasp his reason. But once we have satisfactorily answered this latter question, we do not need the further fact of the pleasure to grasp his reason. Like desires, so too these pleasures present themselves as outlooks on an independent realm of value and not as original sources of reasons.

This picture of pleasure has clear affinities not only to Ryle's view but also to Aristotle's. There is a long-standing controversy about whether Aristotle thought of pleasure as *identical* with unimpeded activity or as some *additional* thing invariably conjoined with unimpeded activity.[16] However, even in those passages that seem to imply the latter view, Aristotle makes clear that pleasure never arises without activity, and that no activity can be complete and unimpeded without pleasure, since it is precisely the pleasure that completes the activity.[17] Aristotle is notoriously obscure about *how* pleasure completes activities, but he seems to have recognized that pleasure involves lively attentiveness to what we are doing. He notes that we are not continuously pleased by anything, partly because we grow tired after a while. When we do, the faculty that we are using is no longer in its best condition, and this makes the activity less complete and

---

[14] My project is not to analyze the ordinary usage of the phrase "taking pleasure in φ-ing," but to shed light on a distinctive sort of pleasure to which, I think, this phrase generally refers.

[15] Ryle, *The Concept of Mind*, 107–8.

[16] Gerd van Riel, "Does a Perfect Activity Necessarily Yield Pleasure? An Evaluation of the Relation between Pleasure and Activity in Aristotle, *Nicomachean Ethics* VII and X," *International Journal of Philosophical Studies* 7 (1999), 212. See also Aristotle, *Nicomachean Ethics*, 1153a13ff; 1174b25ff.

[17] Aristotle, *Nicomachean Ethics*, 1175a20–1.

hence less pleasant.[18] He then says that for the same reason, we are not able to take full pleasure in activities that have grown familiar. Our thought towards new activities is at first "stimulated and intense," but over time it becomes "lax and careless," and so the pleasure fades.[19] Now, it could be that the "same reason" he has in mind is that we grow tired, but our thought could become lax and careless even if we were not tired. So presumably, what he has in mind is that tiredness and lack of novelty both have the same effect on us—the effect of making our attention lax and careless rather than stimulated and intense. This is what accounts for the diminution of pleasure.

Both Aristotle and Ryle draw attention to a basic connection between what pleases us and what we love or desire. As Aristotle puts it, "each kind of person finds pleasure in whatever he is called a lover of."[20] Ryle, for his part, asserts that taking pleasure in an activity, or enjoying an activity, is often nothing more nor less than doing it while wanting to do it and not wanting to do anything else.[21] If taking pleasure in an activity sometimes consists in performing the activity while fervently and unequivocally desiring to do it and nothing else, then there is reason to expect any genuine insight into the nature of desire to yield corollary insights into the nature of pleasure.[22] I believe that the dialectical conception of desires offered in Chapter 2 does yield a convincing account of certain pleasures. It suggests that to take pleasure in an activity is to engage in that activity while being absorbed in it, where this absorption consists in single-minded and lively attention to whatever it is that seems to make the activity good or worth pursuing. For instance, taking pleasure in a conversation might involve lively attention to the humorous things one's partner is saying, or the intimacy manifest in her facial expressions, along with a tendency to see these things as in some way good or valuable. Such pleasure can be more or less complete depending on how thoroughly we are absorbed in our activities and how vividly we are impressed with their value.

This suggests a way to spell out Aristotle's claim that the pleasures that complete activities involve "stimulated and intensely active" thought "towards" that activity.[23] Certainly Aristotle's suggestion does require further elaboration, since "stimulated and intensely active" thought alone is not enough to make

---

[18] Aristotle, *Nicomachean Ethics*, 1175a5.   [19] *Ibid.*, 1175a4–10.

[20] *Ibid.*, 1099a8–9.

[21] Ryle, *The Concept of Mind*, 107–8. The key passage reads, "In this sense, to enjoy doing something, to want to do it and not to want to do anything else are different ways of phrasing the same thing." Ryle makes clear that the sense of 'enjoy' he has in mind is also often captured by the phrase 'take pleasure in.' (And while the quoted passage could naturally be read as a statement of equivalence between three phrases, it seems uncharitable to attribute to Ryle the absurd idea that wanting to do something is the same as not wanting to do anything else.)

[22] Indeed, if Ryle is right to suggest that this connection is a "linguistic fact," then any account of desire that failed to yield such insights could apply only to a special, philosophical notion of desire.

[23] Aristotle, *Nicomachean Ethics*, 1175a4–10.

our activities pleasurable. For instance, if I were directed on pain of death to rivet my attention on some task that I find entirely pointless, I might perform the activity very attentively indeed, but this would hardly guarantee that the task would be pleasurable. What pleasure requires is not mere focused attention, but focused attention of a particular sort. As a first approximation, one might say that it requires the kind of attention that arises spontaneously, without deliberate choice or force of will. However, this is still not sufficient, since activities can capture my attention quite against my will without giving rise to anything remotely resembling pleasure. For instance, I might find myself unable to keep myself from listening to loud music that I find entirely appalling. At the level of metaphor, one wants to say that pleasant activities *attract* or *draw* our attention, while unpleasant activities *arrest* or *extort* our attention. If taking pleasure involves desires of the sort I've sketched, this metaphor can be unpacked a bit. When music arrests rather than attracts my attention, I focus on it, but its features do not present themselves *as* good; indeed, they often present themselves *as* bad.

Taking pleasure in an activity, then, requires a vivid awareness of its goodness or value. This, however, is still not sufficient to yield pleasure. If I am told to break rocks in a chain gang on pain of corporal punishment, I might vividly imagine the beating I would receive if I stopped breaking rocks, and I might see what I am doing as extremely valuable precisely because it will help me to avoid such a beating. Yet this pattern of vivid attention could hardly be expected to transform hard labor into pleasurable activity. There are at least two reasons for this. First, in order to take pleasure in my activities, I must not only want to do what I am doing; I must also have no desire to do anything else. That is, I must not only be vividly aware of what is good about what I am doing; I must also lack vivid awareness of what is bad about it. If I were performing hard forced labor, my own fatigue and muscle pains, and perhaps also the indignity of my situation and the injustice of the demand to which I am acquiescing, would likely force themselves to my attention as bad. Second and more fundamentally, even if my attention were riveted solely on the prospective beating that gives me reason to work and were oblivious to any conflicting practical considerations, this alone would not be likely to render my activity pleasurable. If doing what one desires to do is to yield pleasure, the desire must not only be unequivocal; it must also involve a tendency to see something *non-instrumentally* good or worthwhile about the desired activity itself. If one were struck only by the instrumental value of the activity (its value, that is, as a technique of world-making) one's evaluative attention would be directed not at the activity but at its expected results—that is, at something other than what one is doing. This sort of attention does not complete our activity nor render it unimpeded; it absents us from our activity and renders it burdensome.

Ryle goes subtly astray, then, when he equates taking pleasure in an activity and performing the activity while desiring to do it and nothing else. Aristotle does better when he traces pleasures to what we love rather than to what we unequivocally desire. It is consummately rational for desires to transfer across means–end relations, and they tend to do so whenever these relations are vividly imagined. The same cannot be said of love, nor of subjective tendencies to be delightedly absorbed in what we are doing. It is both common and rational to be vividly aware that one's current activity is an indispensable means for doing something else that one loves and would be fully absorbed in, while neither loving nor becoming absorbed in what one is doing. Indeed, if our sole reason for engaging in some activity is that we think it will produce some valuable effect, this might well *prevent* us from becoming absorbed in the activity itself.

This does not imply that it is impossible to take pleasure in any activity oriented towards the production of some future state of affairs. For instance, a surgeon might take a running pleasure in the active use of his surgical skill without forgetting that surgery has value only as a means to good health. There is an important difference between making use of skills that one has honed by dint of hard study and practice in order to bring about a valued end like health, and mustering one's capacity for brute manual labor in order to avoid a beating or receive a subsistence wage. It would be implausible in the extreme to suppose that the former category of goal-directed activities can never be completed and rendered pleasurable by a vivid running appreciation of their value. They are, after all, integral parts of a way of living that can plausibly be regarded as intrinsically valuable. It is much harder to see how the latter sort of activity could be completed and rendered pleasurable by a vivid appreciation of its point or value. The point lies entirely in the future, and attention to it cannot but absent one from one's doings. It is taxing in the extreme to engage in activities that seem to have no intrinsic point, and we are strongly inclined to impose or invent one wherever it is entirely lacking. Thus, prisoners in chain gangs have been known to marry their dreary labor to some other activity capable of holding their attention, like rhythmic singing that moves in unison to the hammer's swinging, in order to lend intrinsic appeal to their doings taken as a whole.

Taking pleasure, then, requires a single-minded desire to engage in the activity for its own sake. This, however, is not sufficient to produce pleasure. As noted above, desires involve mere *tendencies* to attend to seeming goods or reasons. Pleasure is different. One must have an *occurrent* desire to engage in one's activities in order to derive pleasure from them. Further, pleasure is not vitiated by desires to do something else provided that these desires are not occurrent. One can fully enjoy a weekday at the park even if one desires to spend all weekdays hard at work, provided that the latter desire takes the day off too. On the other hand, an occurrent desire can rule out wholehearted engagement in what one is doing even if there is no conflict between fulfilling the desire and engaging in one's current activity. An anxious desire to impress colleagues during an upcoming presentation might rule out giving full attention to, or taking unmitigated pleasure in, almost anything one does.

To take pleasure in an activity, then, is to engage in it while having only one occurrent desire: a desire to engage in that activity for its own sake. One need not fulfill this attentional condition *perfectly* in order to take pleasure in an activity. Pleasure comes in degrees: we find mild enjoyment in some activities and boundless pleasure in others. But when we do have a desire of this sort to do what we are in fact doing, what we have is a vivid and appreciative awareness of aspects of our activity that seem to make it intrinsically valuable. To appreciate our own activity in this way is to live a stretch of life unreservedly, without those distractions or inner doubts that leave us at odds with ourselves and alienated from our doings. It is not hard to see why relishing or savoring one's doings in this way deserves to be called pleasure.

If this is what we mean when we speak of taking pleasure in activities, it is obvious why we are not capable of taking pleasure in just any activity. Sometimes we are distracted by something exogenous to our activity, as when the noise of arguing neighbors, or lingering anger over some insult, leave us unable to attend to the book we are trying to read. Such distractions are widely recognized as obstacles to pleasure, and it counts in favor of the Aristotelian view that it offers so simple and direct an explanation of this. Human attention is quite limited. We are sometimes incapable of enjoying anything because our field of attention is too crowded with preoccupations to permit focused attention to our own doings.[24] Other impediments to pleasure are endogenous to our activities. For example, I could not engage without impediment in dropping and picking up toothpicks. Here again, the Aristotelian account offers a simple and convincing explanation, for when I try to say what keeps me from taking pleasure in this activity, the obstacle is that it seems entirely worthless. Furthermore, when I try to imagine myself taking pleasure in dropping and picking up toothpicks, I find myself conjuring up peculiar cases in which I have come to see a point in the activity—for instance, because some psychological catastrophe has led me to value imposing order on the world, and has blinded me to the Sisyphean futility of the cycle through which I create occasions for this favored activity.

One implication of this account of pleasure is that the vivid thought that what one is doing is bad cannot itself be an enticement to pleasure. This can seem like an underestimation of human perversity unless one carefully distinguishes the thought that one's activity is bad from the thought that one's activity is "bad"

---

[24] Contemporary psychological research dramatically drives home the limits of human attention. For instance, when participants in an experiment were asked to count the number of times a group of players in the videotape bounced a ball, almost half (46 percent) reported no recollection of dramatic unexpected events occurring in the videotape (e.g. a "gorilla" strolling across the playing area). See Daniel J. Simons and Christopher F. Chabris, "Gorillas in Our Midst: Sustained Inattentional Blindness for Dynamic Events," *Perception* 28 (1999), 1059–74.

(i.e. *others* regard it as bad). This latter thought often yields an exquisite pleasure, one of whose alloys is the joy of bucking oppressive social norms.

This, then, is the picture of absorption in and enjoyment of activity that goes hand-in-hand with the evaluative attention conception of desire, and especially with the dialectical version of that conception. This picture is fundamentally at odds with the propositionalist conception of desire. The propositionalist locates the point of human action entirely in some future state of affairs that the action is calculated to bring into existence. Propositionalist desires can spawn actions only if the proposition describes some state of affairs that does not (yet) obtain. This holds good even in the limiting case of desires that the world continue to answer to some description that is already true of it. This does not mean that the propositionalist cannot recognize the possibility of a desire that the world answer at present to some proposition to which one knows it already to answer.[25] Such a desire, however, could not figure in the rationalizing explanation of actual (as opposed to counterfactual) actions.[26] And while this sort of desire would imply an absence of restlessness, it would not imply any positive delight in how things are. Because it omits the phenomenological element involved in the "evaluation outlook" account of desire, propositionalism cannot make sense of human contentment. It can picture satisfaction only as the absence of restlessness. But this is the contentment of a sleeper or an oyster, not of a human being who is fully awake to the consummation of his longings.

The propositional account of desire, then, can make little sense of satisfaction. And if the account is to remain within the bounds set by the ambition to sculpt a notion of desire capable of propelling one into action, then even this thin and formal satisfaction—this unsatisfying satisfaction—must be regarded, like the future itself, as a fugitive quantity always retreating into the future, always just beyond one's temporal reach. If we can speak here of satisfaction, its moment is forever deferred. The problem at heart is that propositionalism offers a wholly production-oriented conception of the wellsprings of action. On this view, to dwell entirely within one's present doings—that is, to become wholly absorbed or lost in them—is to lose the motive force needed to sustain them. If we are to make sense of the possibility of full-fledged and enduring absorption in ongoing activities, this will require a different conception of our relation to our activities, and in particular of how we are motivated by a subjective sense of their value. A thoroughly production-oriented conception of the nature and point of human action is itself a serious obstacle to unimpeded and hence pleasurable activity.

---

[25] Some propositionalists have held that one could not have such a desire, but Chris Heathwood argues persuasively that they are mistaken. See Heathwood, "The Reduction of Sensory Pleasure to Desire," *Philosophical Studies* 133 (2007), 23–44, especially 32–4.

[26] To have such a desire would be to have the following counterfactual disposition: if one believed that the world did not answer to the relevant proposition, then other things equal one would act in ways calculated to remake the world so that it did correspond to the proposition.

DIALECTICAL ACTIVITY AND ARISTOTELIAN ENERGEIA

There is a close affinity between my claim that pleasure requires an appreciation of the *intrinsic* value of one's activities and Aristotle's claim that one can take pleasure only in an activity (*energeia*) and not in a process (*kinesis*). However, Aristotle's elaboration of this idea is not at all easy to interpret, and on the most common interpretation it seems to go subtly astray. By putting our finger on the difficulties of the account ordinarily attributed to Aristotle, we can advance our understanding of the role of pleasure in consummating human activities.

In Book IX of the *Metaphysics*, Aristotle proposes the following grammatical test to distinguish between processes and activities: if the present progressive description of the doing implies the past perfect, then it is an activity and not a process.[27] For instance, "I am seeing X" implies "I have seen X," hence seeing is an activity and not a process. By contrast, "I am building the house" does not imply "I have built the house"—indeed it implies that I have not yet built it—hence building a house is a process. This test is fundamentally flawed. The purpose of the test is to track a metaphysical distinction between two categories of human doings that differ in their degree of completeness in those moments at which they are taking place. But the grammatical test can easily come loose from this underlying metaphysical distinction, since its verdicts will be sensitive to arbitrary changes in our descriptions of our doings. For instance, listening to a lecture will be counted as a process, but listening to a lecturer's voice will count as an activity. Similarly, we could introduce a new verb, 'shmuilding,' and stipulate that it means "engaging in doings aimed at building." We could then redescribe any instance of building as shmuilding, and magically transform it into an activity.

If the problem is that the test tracks fallible grammatical indications of a metaphysical distinction, then the solution is to look through the grammar to the distinction towards which it gestures between two kinds of temporality that human doings can have. The question, however, is how exactly we are to make sense of this metaphysical distinction. This is where things go badly astray with Aristotle's view—or, at least, with the view commonly attributed to him.

On one common reading, what distinguishes Aristotelian activities from processes is that activities do not change their form through time while processes do. This is too simple. Seeing is an activity, but we could move our eyes from side to side, thus in a sense changing its form through time, without suddenly converting it into a process. If there is a sensible distinction in this immediate vicinity, it makes reference not to actual change but to whether change must

---

[27] Aristotle, *Metaphysics*, 1048b18–35.

occur in order for the doing to be what it is. If we are engaged in building, the form of our doing must necessarily change over time, since otherwise it could not possibly count as the building of something. This remains true even if we think of what we are doing as *shmuilding*, since *shmuilding* is activity aimed at building and nothing would count as activity aimed at building anything if it remained entirely static. By contrast, if we are gazing at the stars, the form of our activity need not change over time in order to count as that activity.

There is, however, a further problem with Aristotle's position. In the *Metaphysics*, Aristotle presents the grammatical test as a way of distinguishing activities from processes by determining which of our doings contain their own completion in each of their moments. A performance counts as an activity if it is complete in this sense. Yet in Book X of the *Nicomachean Ethics*, Aristotle holds that pleasure is a distinctive activity that accompanies other activities, and that no activity can be complete unless it is accompanied and completed by pleasure.[28] This raises the question how Aristotle could have held both that all activities contain their own completion in each moment and that no activity can be complete unless accompanied and completed by the separate activity of pleasure.[29] It won't help at this point to revert to the rather different conception of pleasure set out in Book VII of the *Nicomachean Ethics*, according to which pleasure is identical with complete activity. The problem is that not all activities that are complete in the sense at hand are the least bit pleasant. For example, seeing the corpse of a loved one would be complete in this sense.

Indeed, Aristotle clearly acknowledges that some performances have the sort of completeness that qualify them as activities yet lack the sort that makes them pleasurable. He holds that the perception of any perceptible object will always count as an activity, but no faculty of perception will be completely active unless it is "in good condition in relation to the finest of its perceptible objects." From this example, he extrapolates the general point that in any truly complete activity, the active faculty must be in the best condition in relation to the best possible object of that faculty.

It seems, then, that Aristotle quite self-consciously uses 'complete' (*teleion*) in two senses, one temporal and the other perfectionist.[30] An activity is complete in the temporal sense if it has no course to run but is instead present in its entirety in each of the moments in which it occurs. An activity is complete in the perfectionist sense if it is a perfect instance of its kind. When Aristotle categorizes performances as activities in light of their completeness, he has the former, temporal sense of completeness in mind. When he claims that pleasure

---

[28] See Aristotle, *Nicomachean Ethics*, 1174b20–4 and 1175a20.

[29] For a very helpful discussion of this interpretive puzzle and its possible resolution, see David Bostock, "Pleasure and Activity in Aristotle's Ethics," *Phronesis* 33 (1988), 251–72.

[30] Here I follow Bostock, "Pleasure and Activity in Aristotle's Ethics," 257–60.

is an activity that accompanies and completes other activities, he has the second, perfectionist sort of completeness in mind. Temporal completeness, then, is a necessary condition not only of pleasure but of perfectionist completeness. The idea, in a nutshell, is that no human activity can be perfect of its kind unless it springs from and is guided by a vivid running awareness of its value. The content of this sort of awareness will differ in accordance with the activities towards which it is directed. But this generic sort of awareness is essential to the complete perfection of any human activity

It matters, here, that the word for activity (*energeia*) can also credibly be translated with the English term 'actualization.'[31] In explaining the idea of an *energeia* in the *Metaphysics*, Aristotle takes pains to underline its etymological connection to the term '*ergon*,' which refers to the characteristic function or work of a functionally organized kind. He writes, "For the work [*ergon*] is a completion, and the actuality is the work, hence even the *name*, '*en-ergeia*,' is said with respect to the *ergon*, and aims at the completedness."[32] An activity, then, is the full actualization of the characteristic human function, which is to direct one's doings in a way that expresses a stable and complete conception of the human good. We actualize our defining potentialities, hence realizing our defining *telos*, in our complete activities. The human *telos* does not lie beyond such activities in the form of something to which they conduce. Rather, it is constituted by the right mix over a lifetime of activities completed in this way—which is to say, activities in which we are wholly and pleasurably engaged. This is what makes such activities quite literally *teleion* (i.e. *telos*-containing).[33]

This is an appealing interpretive approach, but if we adopt it without further revisions, we run headlong into what is perhaps the most notoriously difficult interpretive problem posed by the *Nicomachean Ethics*. Aristotle argues at the outset of the book that the highest good for human beings is the life of activity manifesting the virtues. He clearly regards such activities as valuable in themselves, and he holds that those who are properly constituted will consistently take pleasure in them.[34] Yet surely it can't have been lost on Aristotle that acts of exemplary kindness, justice, or courage unfold over time, running through different stages, and that these stages are often calculated to produce a result (e.g. that a need is alleviated, a promise kept, a city defended). These activities,

---

[31] This translation is potentially misleading, since 'actualization' usually refers to a movement towards a perfect state proper to a thing, and not to the obtaining of such a state. The rather awkward phrase 'being actualized' would perhaps be more exact.

[32] Aristotle, *Metaphysics*, 1050a21–2.

[33] In his discussion of Aristotle's notion of the *teleion*, Friedemann Buddensiek translates the term with the German neologism '*zielhaft*' (roughly, "end-containing" or "goal-containing") to mark this important linguistic connection between the notion of a telos and that of completeness—a connection that is ordinarily lost in translation. See the review of Buddensiek's *Die Theorie des Glücks in Aristoteles' Eudemischer Ethik* by Ludger Jansen in *Bryn Mawr Classical Review* 2002.03.19 (http://ccat.sas.upenn.edu/bmcr/2002/2002–03-19.html).

[34] For a representative passage, see Aristotle, *Nicomachean Ethics*, 1099a6–20.

then, do not seem to be complete in the temporal sense specified above—it seems to be essential to them that they change their form through time. Yet on the proposed interpretation of the Book X discussion of pleasure and activity, Aristotle holds that only activities that are complete in the temporal sense can be accompanied and completed (in the second, perfectionist sense) by pleasure. This might perhaps help to explain why he immediately offers what seems to be a second, fundamentally different conception of the highest good for human beings, consisting in prolonged engagement in a ceaseless form of contemplation—one that does not move towards the attainment of insight but dwells appreciatively upon that which is already known. But it leaves the reader wondering what is to be made of the discussions of the civic virtues, of practical wisdom and friendship that occupy the first nine books. Are we to reject the life of virtuous civic engagement as fundamentally unfitting or unfulfilling, and disregard Aristotle's repeated insistence that those who are properly brought up will find such activity pleasurable?

Perhaps the text does not force us to make so stark a choice. In his Book VII discussion of pleasure and activity, Aristotle distinguishes between activities of movement or change and activities of immobility or rest.[35] He clearly indicates that the immobile activities are more pleasant and more divine, but nonetheless he counts the others as activities and suggests that it is possible to take pleasure in them. Presumably the shared activities of a polity, insofar as they manifest the virtues of citizens, would count as activities of movement rather than rest, as would the centrally valuable activity that Aristotle calls friendship.

If we reject the idea that we can take pleasure only in those activities that can take an unchanging form, how then might we formulate a broadly Aristotelian distinction between those human doings that can be accompanied and completed with pleasure and those that cannot? In my view, the best way to do so is with reference to a slightly more complicated notion of temporal completeness—a notion that can be found, at least in embryonic form, in Book IX of the *Metaphysics*.[36] We can begin by distinguishing two importantly different ways that pictures of the future can confer value on present doings. If we see our present doings as valuable only as efficient means for producing some future result that we value, then it seems right that we will be unable to complete our present doings with pleasure. However, sometimes our conception of our future (and,

---

[35] Aristotle, *Nicomachean Ethics*, 1154b21–33.

[36] In preparing the way for his grammatical test, Aristotle distinguishes between the way in which activities and processes relate to the *telos* in light of which they are performed by saying that processes move towards a *telos* that does not yet belong to them, while the *telos* of an activity is contained in it. It is hard to square this passage with the case for the superiority of changeless contemplation set out in Book X of the *Nicomachean Ethics*, but it seems to me to provide the seeds of the most promising elaboration of the process/activity distinction while also serving as a potential corrective to the implausibly static conception of the human end offered in Book X.

for that matter, our past) can confer intelligibility and value on present doings by situating them in an unfolding narrative that we find intrinsically valuable as a whole. When we are falling in love, or kindling a friendship, or composing a symphony, or joining in the shared life of a well-constituted community or *polis*, the value of our doings does not lie solely in their instrumental contribution to the production of some expected end state—whether friendship, love, a completed symphony, or a healthy community.[37] It is true that we would lose track of the value of these doings—and perhaps even their intelligibility as doings—if we considered them in isolation from the time-extended narrative they collectively constitute. Yet this does not prevent us from wholehearted absorption in our activities themselves, any more than the fact that the individual sentences of a novel make no sense apart from their place in a larger story prevents us from becoming thoroughly absorbed in them.[38] When we engage in such activities, we have our past and future with us, as part of the framework through which we grasp the nature and value of what we are doing. This is quite different from the relation we have to our past or future when we turn our mind to them out of a sense that the goodness that gives point to our present doings lies exclusively there. If we have such a relation to the past (as in moments of depressive grief) or the future (as in moments of intrinsically meaningless labor), this absents us from our life as it unfolds and leaves us joyless in our doings.

By contrast, when our doings await completion in the non-instrumental way that the sentences of a novel await completion, this does not rule out seeing what we are doing as non-instrumentally valuable. It does rule out finding value in each time-slice of our activity considered in isolation from the rest. But that is because, when we abstract from the rest, we literally lose our grip on what we are doing. In such cases, it is not the *actual arrival* of some anticipated result that confers value on present activities; it is the *thought* of their relation to the past and future that makes present activities intelligible and brings their value to light. If taking pleasure in an activity is a matter of vividly apprehending its value as it unfolds, then there is no obstacle to taking pleasure in these sorts of activities. They can be brought to completion and made pleasurable by the sort of wholehearted engagement that Aristotle takes to be essential to human flourishing.

---

[37] Even if we could identify and assign value to some relevant and suitably fixed end state, still we might well think that the end state's value depended upon the way it was created. For example, a painting's value might depend upon its being the congealed form of my own artistic activity; likewise, the value of mutual love might depend upon its being the consummation of a history of shared activities.

[38] The pleasure of reading a good novel seems, by the way, to be a paradigm instance of the kind of pleasure I have been discussing, yet Aristotle's grammatical test would categorize reading a novel as a process and not an activity.

Indeed, these "narrative activities" are arguably better suited to be final human ends than such static activities as Aristotle-style contemplation (as distinguished from more familiar forms of contemplation that unfold over time, perhaps by attaining greater clarity or articulacy). When we distinguish between those lives that have come to an untimely end and those that have run a full course, we are not guided merely by the sort of temporal duration measured by clocks and calendars. We are guided, instead, by a sense of whether the life's central projects and commitments have run their course. It is tragic to devote a relatively lengthy life to having children and to succeed so late in life that one is unable to see them through their childhood. Our grip on the difference between fortunate and unfortunate lives, and on the related difference between timely and untimely deaths, is given partly by our sense of what does and what does not count as a proper completion of the many narrative threads that provide one's sense of what one is doing with one's life. To think of the proper ends of human lives as static activities is to lose sight of this narrative element in our understanding of well-lived lives. Perhaps it is also to lose sight of the role played by impermanence in lending to our passing moments the sort of evanescent sweetness we are able to savor, the sort that does not linger so long as to inure us to their value.[39] If we lose sight of these aspects of the human good, the result (as Aristotle all but recognizes) will be a conception of the final end that might perhaps be fit for divine beings but that is a misfit for human beings.

Nevertheless, there is an important insight in Aristotle's conception of the human good that has largely dropped from view in contemporary philosophy, but that has been a central theme of this work of Aristotelian retrieval. The insight is that the human good must lie in activities rather than, say, in experiences or states of character. It is true of many things that their goodness consists solely in having certain punctual properties rather than in being engaged continuously in certain kinds of activities. For instance, a good knife is a knife that has properties such as a comfortable handle and a sharp blade made of strong and durable material. Such a knife has an optimal capacity for cutting things. Things do not go worse for a knife if this potentiality is never "actualized" in cutting anything. Human beings are entirely different. It is essential to the sort of being we call human that it unfolds over time, and not merely in events that compose a series but in activities that compose a life.[40] This suggests that if we set out in search of final human

---

[39] This thought is not so much explored as incarnated in Wallace Stevens' incomparable poem "Sunday Morning." One question I am left with by this poem is just how it encourages us to view the impulse to capture beauty in poetry. Does this involve a suspect longing to make permanent that which can only be savored in evanescence? But one cannot pursue this question without making it even harder than usual to avoid the related question how we ought to view the philosophical longing to understand pleasurable activity. Is it a distraction from the unmet call to unimpeded activity, a pallid compensation for foregone pleasures, an exemplary form of unimpeded activity in its own right?

[40] Cf. Aristotle, *Nicomachean Ethics*, Book I, chapter 8, paragraph 2.

ends or goods—that is, goods whose value is not explained by their relation to other, more final or ultimate goods—it would be a recipe for confusion to direct our search at properties or states that a human being could have or be in during moments of inactivity (e.g. virtue, or knowledge, or pleasure conceived as a passive experiential state). Such states or properties are ontologically unsuited to be final ends for human beings, and can at best be propensities or potentialities for engaging in the activities that compose the good life for human beings.[41] Hence Aristotle is quite right to think of the value of the virtues as less final than the value of the activities that they make possible. This is not to suggest that the virtues have purely instrumental value, since it seems to be a conceptual requirement on the best sort of human activity that it arises from and manifests a stable, motivationally efficacious grasp of the sort of intrinsic goodness that it instantiates. For instance, the interactions that constitute a friendship seem to require, as a condition of being what they are and having the value they do, that the partners to them have a vivid and stable grasp of each other's value and the value of friendship. This grasp need not be highly articulate—people do not have to be philosophers to be friends—but its utter absence would just be the absence of friendship. But having a stable and motivationally efficacious grasp of the value of human beings and of friendship is part of what it is to be virtuous.

Here we have come across an apt methodological criterion for distinguishing activities from processes. If the distinction is to play its role in shedding light on the good life for human beings, then we ought to prefer a conception that picks out precisely those doings whose structure suits them to be constituents of the good human life, rather than merely being conducive to such a life. (As noted above, this conceptual connection is visible in Aristotle's chosen term for activity: an *en-ergeia* is that in which our *ergon*, or functional essence, is actualized.) We can do this by characterizing activities in contrast with the category of mere production or world-making (where 'world-making' is broad enough to include efforts to bring it about that the state of the world does not change), and not with the category of temporally extended doings that take different forms at different times. We will then have set aside, under the category of processes, those human doings that are regarded by those doing them as valuable only in virtue of what they bring about. This will put us in a position to accommodate Aristotle's insight that the human good consists in lifelong engagement in intrinsically valuable activities while avoiding the implausibly "presentist" conclusion that the most final and complete human good must be static over time, as is the contemplation of timeless truths that one already fully appreciates. This seems like a genuine step forward, since it does not seem to be accidental to the most important form of human doings—including for instance the most intimate relationships and the most compelling stretches of human contemplation—that they unfold in time.

---

[41] Aristotle argues explicitly for this conclusion in *Metaphysics*, 1051a4–19.

The mere fact that a doing is self-consciously oriented towards the production of a certain result does not settle the question whether it counts as a pure case of a process, hence as the sort of doing that cannot be accompanied and completed by Aristotelian pleasure. For example, there are certain rare and exemplary souls who bring to the "lowly" task of dishwashing such a vivid sense of its place in the human ritual of the shared meal and of intimacy with those who have dined by their side that by all appearances it is not for them a mere process but a genuine activity—one that might well be accompanied and completed with pleasure. There are others who race through the dishes with the sole thought of having done with them and whose exasperation suggests that they might gladly shorten their time on earth by fifteen minutes per day if it were possible to "fast forward" through the chore. There is a sense in which both sorts of people do the same thing when they wash the dishes, but there is also an obvious sense in which they do not. The evaluative outlook that they bring to the task is fused inseparably with their performance and conditions its quality and value. The washing of dishes becomes a fit constituent of caring and intimate relations among the members of a household when it is attended to as such. This evaluative attention need not have an explicit or articulate presence in the introspectible experience of the person doing the dishwashing. It can subsist as a largely inarticulate sense of the point of the activity under way and of its place in the life of the family. To the extent that it does, an ongoing performance that is clearly oriented toward the production of some state of affairs (in this case, the dishes being clean) might also be regarded without error or illusion as intrinsically valuable.

It might seem mistakenly subjectivist to draw the distinction in terms of how agents *regard* what they are doing rather than in terms of the intrinsic properties of their doings. On reflection, however, I believe that this element of subjectivity is crucial to the distinction at hand. It represents a proper theoretical accommodation of the fundamental fact that human doings are partly constituted by the conception of value from which they emerge. Such conceptions of value are in some ways like findings and in some ways like foundings. They are like foundings in the sense that they often play an essential role in lending to activities the value that they picture, as when a favor depends for its status as a gesture of incipient friendship on the agent's sense that friendship is a looming and valuable possibility towards which it makes sense to extend herself. They are like findings in the sense that they can wholly fail to answer to the doings towards which they are directed.

Indeed, the possibility of severe dissonance between one's doings and one's picture of their nature and point is a properly focal human preoccupation, grounded in fundamental facts about the human condition. Our freedom to shape our lives outstrips our capacity to understand the nature, context, and significance of our actions, hence we have no choice but to act without perfect clarity or certainty about what we are doing or why it might make sense to do it. This mismatch is the common structural feature of a great deal of comedy (e.g. Quixote and his windmills) and tragedy (e.g. Oedipus and his mother). It opens the possibility that we might see loving intimacy in relations that are shot through with condescension or deceit, noble service in contributions to an abjectly evil military cause, or sustaining purpose in a job whose terms are unjustly sculpted to serve the interests of another person or class. When our picture of the value of our doings comes loose in such ways from the context within which our actions unfold, these pictures cannot unilaterally found the valuable doings they envision. Nor can one confer nobility on objectively evil doings by entertaining a self-serving picture of their goodness. One's doings must be apt objects of the evaluative picture in whose light one is drawn to engage in them and perpetuate them if the pictured value is to be actualized in them. Put another way, the picture must be directed at a goodness that is in some sense already incipient in one's unfolding doings if it is to confer its shape upon one's unfolding life rather than merely upon one's fantasy life or one's illusions about one's life. Still, the picture is often capable of altering what it pictures.

In summary, activities are chosen in virtue of their constitutive rather than their instrumental relation to the *telos* in whose light they appear choice-worthy. The *telos* of an activity is the activity itself in its proper form and not some conceptually separate state of affairs that the activity promises to produce. If the contours of an activity's *telos* come into view only gradually, and only by engaging in the activity under reasonably propitious conditions, then the activity counts as dialectical in the sense set out in prior chapters. Aristotle's account of how we learn to be virtuous, and of the standing possibility of deepening our understanding of the nature and value of virtuous activity, suggest that he regarded many of the most valuable human activities as dialectical in this sense. This would help to explain his claim that we need experience to develop a perspicuous understanding of the activities that constitute the human good.[42] By providing an illuminating account of why experience is essential to this sort of insight, we can lend to Aristotelian naturalism a signal advantage over the scientistic naturalism affirmed by the non-cognitivist, according to which there is no principled barrier to the attainment, by a clever child, of the ethical insight displayed by a wise adult.[43]

[42] A broadly dialectical interpretation of Aristotle's conception of virtuous activity is offered by Myles Burnyeat in "Aristotle on Learning to be Good."

[43] Cora Diamond, "'We Are Perpetually Moralists': Iris Murdoch, Fact, and Value," in Maria Antonaccio and William Schweiker, eds., *Iris Murdoch and the Search for Human Goodness* (Chicago: University of Chicago Press, 1996), 79–109; especially 98–100. I develop this point in Chapter 5.

PLEASURES, EMOTIONS, AND VIRTUOUS CHARACTER

We can affirm that pleasure involves running appearances of goodness or value without implying that it requires one to *judge* or even to have a *tendency to judge* that what one is doing or experiencing is valuable.[44] Pleasure requires only a vivid appearance of value. Hence it is perfectly possible to take pleasure in an activity that one judges on reflection to be valueless. Nor is the requisite appearance of value guaranteed by the corresponding evaluative judgment. One might judge an activity to be intrinsically valuable yet fail to experience it as such due to such impediments as fatigue, grief, or depression. Pleasure turns on vivid evaluative seemings but not on full-fledged evaluative judgments.

This "proto-cognitive" analysis can be extended not only to desires and pleasures but also to emotions. All emotions turn on some evaluative thought, yet—contrary to certain ancient stoics and contemporary cognitivists—one need not judge the thought true in order to have the emotion.[45] For instance, one need not judge that there really *is* danger in the offing in order to feel genuine fear; it is sufficient that one be gripped by the vivid thought that one is in danger. One telling objection to straightforward cognitivism about emotions is that people often experience emotions that they judge to be ill-grounded, and the principle of charity of interpretation counts against attributing contradictory beliefs to people whenever they find themselves in this predicament—provided, at least that there is a viable alternative. A similar objection would undermine the flat-footedly cognitivist thesis that taking pleasure in an activity involves judging the activity to be worthwhile.

Philosophers are notorious for raising the simplest and most elementary questions, then proceeding to give the most complicated and improbable answers, so it is with some trepidation that I turn now to the question of why it is generally pleasant to do what one desires to do. This empirical correlation is sometimes thought to owe to the influences of past pleasures and pains on current desires. On this picture, we are psychologically "wired" in such a way that we tend to form desires to do that which has caused us pleasure in the past, and to avoid that which has caused us pain. Given this, we have inductive grounds for expecting that acting on our desires will yield pleasure.[46] No doubt this brute process can

---

[44] This, I think, is the most important point of disagreement between my view and that of the contemporary philosopher whose conception of pleasure is perhaps closest to mine: Elijah Millgram. For Millgram, taking pleasure in an activity is tantamount to taking the activity to be good or desirable, where this is the practical analog of *belief* or *conviction* about how things are. See Millgram, "Pleasure in Practical Reasoning," 399, 404, and 406.

[45] Perhaps the best-known of the contemporary cognitivist accounts is that of Robert C. Solomon. See Solomon, *The Passions* (New York: Doubleday, 1976).

[46] This picture does not rule out the idiosyncratic acculturation of desires, but it does point towards a particular view of this acculturation. It implies that acculturation requires some

explain the coincidence between some desires and some pleasures. However, the above-elaborated accounts of desire and pleasure afford a more direct explanation of such coincidences. If I desire unequivocally to engage in some activity, and my desire is partly constituted by a tendency to see something good about the activity itself, I will take pleasure in the activity so long as that tendency remains constant. The coincidence of desires and pleasures, then, sometimes owes to a general stability in our pre-reflective evaluative outlook.

This opens the possibility that both desires and pleasures might be modified by careful evaluative reflection, provided that this reflection eventually reshapes one's characteristic pre-reflective outlook. Such a process occurs routinely in the domain of theoretical reasoning. For instance, when we learn to deploy an ordinary concept like 'smile,' we also re-order our way of perceiving the world so that we *see* certain facial expressions *as* smiles, not as contortions of flesh that we must then *judge* to be smiles. This same process routinely occurs as we develop a mature sense of what there is reason to do. For instance, when a seasoned driver approaches an intersection with a red light, she sees the light immediately as something that calls for stopping, not as a visual signal that she must then *judge* to be a reason to stop. If this process were to run its course with respect to all facets of practical reflection, one's characteristic pleasures, emotions, and desires might be expected to come into harmony with one's considered judgments.

These ruminations begin to shed light on the Aristotelian idea that those who are morally good or virtuous can be counted on not only to do the right thing but to do it with pleasure. The virtuous will generally have a vivid sense of the intrinsic value of the human relations that their virtuous actions partly constitute, and this sense will generally be sufficient to complete their virtuous activities with pleasure. Since this sort of pleasure manifests a full understanding of, and wholehearted commitment to, the relevant ethical values, it is not hard to see why it redounds to the credit of the virtuous that they take pleasure in their virtuous activities. If we conceived of pleasures as the brutely non-cognitive sensory effects of our actions, this Aristotelian point would be highly implausible. It would be hard to see why it ought to redound to the credit of the virtuous that virtuous actions cause them to feel pleasure. This would seem like the mark of a successful program of psychological conditioning, not of an especially deep and abiding understanding of ethical goodness or commitment to it.

Still, it would be a mistake to make the unqualified claim that the virtuous invariably take pleasure in their actions. Some duties require that we disregard deeply important values, as when one is obligated to turn in a family member

psychological mechanism, such as Humean sympathy, that causes us to be pleased by behavior that pleases those around us and pained at behavior that pains them. Given such a mechanism, the tutelage offered us by our pleasures and pains will tend to reflect local norms ranging from questions of etiquette to questions of morality.

who has committed a series of violent crimes. If one performed such a duty with unreserved relish, this might well raise questions about the adequacy of one's grasp of the value of family relations.

THE SCOPE OF THE ARISTOTELIAN ACCOUNT OF PLEASURE

The Aristotelian view of pleasure is attractive partly because it provides a useful corrective to the idea that all pleasure consists in an agreeable sensation, conceptually distinct from whatever activity may have produced it. Still, *some* of the things we call pleasure do seem to consist partly or wholly in agreeable sensations.[47] Let us use the name 'sensory pleasure' to refer to these pleasures, and 'attentional pleasure' to refer to those pleasures that consist in vivid appearances of the value of our doings or circumstances. Surely it is not mere coincidence that the word 'pleasure' refers to both phenomena. But what then do these two kinds of pleasures have in common such that they have come to bear the same name?

We cannot hope to get very far with this question if we don't ask the prior question what exactly it is that all sensory pleasures have in common, such that *they* deserve the same name.[48] This is a puzzling question, since there does not seem to be a common experiential element present in such diverse experiences as sensual caresses, the sun's warmth on bare skin, the taste of *pâté de foie gras*, and the smell of freshly cut clover, yet absent in the feeling of skin brushing up against a wall, the taste of burnt coffee, and the smell of rotten eggs. If sensory pleasure were such a common element, it would be a mystery how we manage to distinguish the quantum of this common sensation associated with, say, the drinking of beer from the quantum associated with the sun's warmth when drinking beer in full sunlight. Yet we are often able to say with confidence which of two contemporaneous sensory pleasures we find more pleasant and which we find less pleasant, hence it seems implausible to suppose that sensory pleasures all contain a single discernible sensation in virtue of which they count as pleasures.[49]

---

[47] This is something that Aristotle clearly recognizes. He distinguishes between those pleasures that accompany and complete the activities associated with them, and those appetitive pleasures that are the separable effects or ornaments of the activities associated with them, and he argues that temperance is the virtue of moderation with respect to these latter, appetitive pleasures. See *Nicomachean Ethics*, 1099a6–20; 1104b5–6; 1117b28–35; 1153a27–b2.

[48] In distinguishing between these two questions, and suggesting that they need to be answered together, I follow Fred Feldman's "Two Questions about Pleasure," in *Utilitarianism, Hedonism and Desert: Essays in Moral Philosophy* (Cambridge: Cambridge University Press, 1997), 82–105.

[49] I owe this argument to Fred Feldman, who traces it in turn to Anthony Kenny. See Feldman, "Two Questions about Pleasure," 87–8.

If we are to explain the unity of the category of sensory pleasures, then, we must do so by reference to something other than the intrinsic qualities of the sensations associated with them. One common strategy is to analyze sensory pleasures (or, in some cases, all pleasures) as sensations that the subject desires to have or to continue having, simply on the basis of their sensory qualities.[50] The adequacy of this approach will depend upon how we conceive of desires. If desiring something is just a matter of being in a functional state that disposes one to act in ways calculated to bring that thing about, then clearly this analysis fails. It is conceptually possible to have this sort of desire to bring about unpleasant and even downright painful sensations with no further end in view. Indeed, this seems like a familiar experience, as when we find ourselves obsessively probing a sore tooth. More generally, if the object of a desire is simply the state of the world that answers to the desire's propositional object, then the analysis will fail. We could in principle desire that (it be the case that) we feel any feeling, even a sharply painful one. The propositional conception of desire abstracts from the phenomenology of desire, hence cannot guarantee that a feeling desired in itself will have the phenomenology of a pleasure.

If we conjoin this desire-based analysis of pleasure with the "evaluative outlook" account of desire, then it can yield a far more plausible account of sensory pleasures. Sensory pleasures will be sensations that inspire a vivid running sense of their non-instrumental goodness (that is, a desire), while sensory pains will be sensations that provoke a vivid running sense of their non-instrumental badness (that is, an aversion). As in the case of the evaluative attention that completes activities, so too here the evaluative attention does not leave its object unchanged. Because desires are patterns of amplified phenomenological salience, a desired sensation will have an amplified phenomenological presence. It will be lit up in our experience, not just as present but as good.

Sometimes this sense of goodness will lack the sort of internal complexity that will make it articulable to others. The sensation will just feel good, and there's the end of it. But in fact there are few sensory pleasures about which so little can be said. The human sensorium tends to complicate itself over time as we position the occurrence of our sensations within an evolving picture of the meaning of our circumstances and activities. Consider the case of sexual pleasure, which is usually listed among the purely sensory pleasures.[51] The pleasure of sex is often heightened by vivid appreciation of the mutual care expressed by each

---

[50] One influential proponent of this view has been Richard Brandt, who first set it out in *Ethical Theory: The Problems of Normative and Critical Ethics* (Englewood Cliffs: Prentice-Hall Inc., 1959). The view was also affirmed by William Alston in his entry entitled "Pleasure," in Paul Edwards, ed., *The Encyclopedia of Philosophy* (New York: Macmillan Publishing, 1967), Volume 6, 341–7. For a brief history of this view of pleasure, see Fred Feldman, "On the Intrinsic Value of Pleasures," in *Utilitarianism, Hedonism and Desert . . .*, 127–31. A recent defense of the view is found in Chris Heathwood's "The Reduction of Sensory Pleasure to Desire."

[51] See for example Thomas Nagel, *The View from Nowhere* (Oxford: Oxford University Press, 1986), 156.

caress. Indeed the latter word — 'caress' — refers to touches backed by cherishing, and we cannot generally capture what we value in a sexual touch if we ignore the motivational backdrop that this term brings to the fore. Considered from a purely physical point of view — e.g. as patterns of skin contact with particular textures and pressures — the same touch that is pleasurable in a voluntary sexual encounter might be entirely unpleasant in the context of a sexual assault.[52] The pleasure of something as basic as a sexual caress, then, requires that one see the activity that causes the pleasure as good — and not just generically good, but good in a specific way, good as the intentional expression of another's love. This is one of many instances of sensations that owe their status as pleasures at least in part to a temporally extended narrative context.

This is not to deny that one *could* appreciate sexual relations simply as a causal mechanism for producing intensely agreeable physical sensations. The point, rather, is that sexual pleasure is often more complex than this. If we think of sensory pleasures as feelings towards which we have desires of the evaluative-attention sort, then we have a useful starting point for grasping this complexity. In order to develop such an account, one would have to explain how the appreciative awareness of the *circumstances that occasion* a sensory pleasure could focus one's attention on *the pleasure itself* and heighten one's appreciation of *it* (hence completing and perfecting it as a sensory pleasure). I can only gesture towards a solution here, by drawing an analogy between the pleasure of a sexual caress and the pleasure of a gift. To see an object as a gift is to see it as a symbol of another's affection or love. This, however, does not mean that when one appreciates something as a gift, one's evaluative attention strays from the gift to the affection that confers value upon it; rather, the gift presents itself as a symbol of the valued affection, and this imbues the object itself with a value that otherwise similar objects lack. Likewise, to savor a touch as a caress is to feel it as a symbol of another's affection, but this does not redirect one's evaluative attention away from the feeling of the touch; rather, the felt touch presents itself as a symbol of the valued affection, and this imbues the experience of the touch itself with a quality and a value that the experience of otherwise similar touches would lack. These reflections help to explain why it is best to say that sensory pleasures are sensations that inspire a vivid sense of their non-instrumental goodness rather than of their intrinsic goodness. The latter stance would overlook the way in which sensations can owe their pleasantness to their place in a temporally extended narrative such as an unfolding relationship.

On reflection it seems that many sensory pleasures are commonly deepened and completed by vivid awareness of the value of the circumstances that produce them. The pleasure of eating a piece of cake might be heightened when one sees it as a sign of the affection with which one's elderly uncle baked it. The pleasure

---

[52] This was pointed out to me by Bennett Helm.

of the sun's warmth on bare skin might be deepened when *felt as* a sign of one's at-homeness in the world—a token, as it were, of the world's suitability for human habitation. On a thoroughly non-cognitivist account of these pleasures, it would remain puzzling how their coloration and intensity could possibly be altered by differing evaluative outlooks on their occasions. The puzzle can be resolved if one brings these pleasures within the scope of the Aristotelian analysis. All pleasures are vivid seemings of goodness. Sometimes the goodness is found in one's circumstances, sometimes in one's ongoing activities, and sometimes in one's passive experiences. There are cases of pure sensory pleasure that fall into the last category. However, many things that we might initially be tempted to call sensory pleasures in fact show up as valuable in virtue of their connection to circumstances and activities—a connection that might, for instance, induce us to see them as expressive of another's love, or of affinity with another's sensibility, or of the world's fittingness for our lives.

On reflection, then, there is a surprising similarity between the pattern of attention that completes and heightens sensory pleasures and the pattern associated with attentional pleasures. It should be clear, at the outset, that sensory pleasures do require a kind of attention. We cannot have a sensory pleasure yet be entirely unaware of it. Furthermore, just as we manage physical or emotional pain by trying to "get our mind off of it," so too we can heighten sensory pleasures by minimizing distractions, clearing our minds of background worries, and concentrating our attention on the pleasant feeling. It's hard to relish a good wine while being circled by a buzzing mosquito, or to savor a cool breeze while being pestered by a fussy child. Indeed, it would make no sense whatever to say that a sensory pleasure was perfect, considered as a pleasure, but unfortunately one could not attend to it because one was distracted by something else. Sensory pleasures remain deficient *as pleasures* unless one completes them by directing appreciative attention at them (i.e. by *savoring* them or *giving oneself over* to them). And sensory pains can be mitigated as pains by directing one's attention at other things (i.e. by putting them wholly out of mind or, barring that, refusing to give one's attention entirely over to them).

This suggests a close affinity between sensory pleasures and attentional pleasures, since both require vivid appreciation of something that presents itself as good in order to be completed and perfected as pleasures. The difference seems to be that in the case of sensory pleasures, the thing that must be vividly appreciated is itself a feeling. There is, however, a serious worry in the offing. If we consider the most primitive pleasures, there is no doubt a feeling that shows up as good, but when we try to say what sort of goodness or value we see in it, the answer seems to be that it seems pleasurable. This is not a matter of reporting that it contains a felt element that is common to all and only pleasures, since (as argued above) there seems to be no such thing. Nor is it a matter of saying that it is simply the sort of feeling that creates an urge for its own continuation, since this is consistent with its being painful. The most plausible interpretation seems to be that it is simply a matter of finding it brutely or primitively good. This is the sort of goodness that cannot be expounded upon and that cannot be reduced to natural reason-giving properties. A feeling with this sort of primitive goodness counts as a pleasure provided that it is accompanied and completed by some minimal level of appreciative attention.

Perhaps we can speculate a bit more about the value of these primitive pleasures. They are sensations that concentrate one wholly in one's current experience, calling one into full presence. Pain, by contrast, induces a recoil from experience, a wish to be absent from it or numb to it. This thought gains support from the observation that we are able to take in and be fully present to pleasures of only a limited intensity. When pleasure passes beyond a certain pitch of intensity it passes over into something quite like pain, as when we recoil from intense tickling. If this speculation is on target, then there is a further similarity between sensory and attentional pleasures. Both derive their status as pleasures, and as valuable, partly from the concentration of presence that they essentially involve.

Still, there is a very fundamental difference between sensory pleasures and those pleasures that we take in our own unfolding activities. Sensory pleasures involve appreciative attention to sensations with respect to which we are largely passive. Our activity consists solely in the kind of attention we give to them—e.g. in savoring them or indulging them, as the case may be. Attentional pleasures taken in our own unfolding activities serve by contrast to complete those activities, and to bring them to completion by the continuous and optimal exercise of precisely that capacity for appreciation of value in virtue of which we are capable of such activity at all. These pleasures are properly regarded as the consummation of our nature as agents with lives to lead. This lends credence to Aristotle's claim that moderation is virtuous only in the case of sensory pleasures, and not in the case of attentional pleasure taken in contemplation, friendship, or virtuous activity itself. On the contrary, it is a misfortune of human beings that they are not capable of sustaining these latter pleasures ceaselessly. The problem with mistaking sensory pleasure for one's proper and final end is, at heart, that it expresses a fundamentally passive conception of one's *telos*. It is conceptually possible, after all, that one could experience uninterrupted sensory pleasure from birth to death without ever doing anything at all. If sensory pleasure were the proper human end, the capacity for agency would be valuable merely as an instrument for producing this experience.

Given the role of desire in dialectical activity, we can say something further about the connection between attentional pleasures and the consummation of the human capacity for activity. The desires that draw us into a dialectical activity are running intimations of that activity's goodness, intimations that continuously outstrip our achieved approximation to that goodness, and that therefore guide our continuous effort to carry on in ways that more closely approximate the activity's constitutive ideal. This is what it is to vividly apprehend the intrinsic value of one's unfolding dialectical activities, hence this is precisely the sort of attentional relation to one's activities that renders them unimpeded and pleasurable. Yet this attention is itself a kind of activity—it is evaluative thinking in its active and awake form, continuously apprehending more fully the proper form of the activities that it has spawned. Because it continuously appreciates the constitutive *telos* of one's actual activities, it draws one into those activities and renders them unimpeded. But because it apprehends a form of goodness that exceeds what one has actually managed to answer to in one's activity, it is not a mere mode of self-congratulations but a form of practical thinking. This provides a point of entry for retrieving Aristotle's curious idea that pleasure is an activity. The sort of pleasure in question involves a continuous straining to apprehend an intimation of goodness in whose light one's activities are unfolding. It makes possible, by partly constituting, a particularly valuable sort of activity—activity inspired rather than merely disciplined by an intimation of value.

By way of illustration, we might return once again to the example that remains close to hand throughout—that is, the example of philosophy. When our philosophizing goes well, we are carried forward into fresh thoughts by an intimation of something good or valuable lying in a particular direction, something we are not yet quite able to formulate precisely because it lies at the horizon of our achieved understanding. Thoughts dawn on us, but we can hasten this process if we keep looking in their direction and trying to find words for them. We are carried into these thoughts by pleasure, but the object of the pleasure is not what we've already seen, since this would not carry us forward but would incline us to cling to our achieved state (as in static Aristotelian contemplation). The object of the pleasure is the not-yet-wholly-appreciated elegance or revelatoriness of the thought that pleases us and elicits focused attention from us, attention bent towards the attainment of fuller appreciation or understanding. We are guided, as we search for the right words, by fidelity to what is worth saying and not by fidelity to the achieved contours of our state of mind. If an attempted formulation of a thought does not render it a good thought, then either the formulation has gone awry or the intimation that pleased us was illusory.

At the outset of the *Nicomachean Ethics*, Aristotle stridently denounces the "vulgar" equation of *eudaimonia* and pleasure as a recipe for a slavish life—the life, as he puts it, of "a grazing animal" (*EN* 1095b16–21). It comes as a bit of a surprise, then, that by the end of the book he commits himself to the claim that pleasure is essential to *eudaimonia*. Yet this conclusion clearly is implied by his claims, over the course of the book, that *eudaimonia* must be a complete good, that it must be an activity, and that no activity is complete unless it is accompanied and completed by pleasure. This surprise is mitigated when we distinguish between the sort of pleasure at which one might aim as an intended product of one's doings, and the active pleasure that accompanies and completes intrinsically valuable activities. Aristotle's claim is that the latter sort of pleasure is essential to *eudaimonia*. This claim looks plausible when we consider the way in which this sort of pleasure deepens our life activities by drawing us into them and soliciting our full and undistracted attention to their significance or value. We can admit that such pleasure is necessary for the *eudaimon* life without abandoning the guiding Aristotelian thought that *eudaimonia* is the full actualization, in the best sorts of activities, of the human capacity for practical thought. The pleasure in question is the marker of the full and unimpeded actualization of this distinctively human capacity. Nor do we need to rely upon the thought that this capacity is distinctive of human beings in order to see its value. While Aristotle sometimes seems to favor such arguments, they are obviously flawed. Human beings are the only featherless bipeds, but Daedelus does not debase himself as a human being simply in virtue of his decision to affix bird feathers to his arms. The human capacity for practical thought is different, and it would not cease to be our proper end if we encountered non-human creatures who had it in equal measure. If we embark upon a serious-minded quest for understanding of the good life for human beings, we can hardly deny the importance of our capacity to live a life informed by a worthy conception of the good. That would be tantamount to abandoning the quest. If and when we are genuinely gripped by the question how to live, and are drawn to philosophize because of this question's grip on us, we would fall into performative contradiction if we denied the value of living in the light of an understanding of the good.

PLEASURES AND PASTIMES

One pressing question about the Aristotelian account of pleasure is whether it can account for the pleasures we take in the idiosyncratic pastimes or games we happen to enjoy. These pleasures appear to consist not in agreeable sensations but in wholehearted engagement or absorption in what one is doing; that is, they seem to be prototypical attentional pleasures. Yet it might seem hard to credit the idea that those who take pleasure in a game or pastime must be gripped by a tendency to see their favored activity as intrinsically valuable.

On reflection there is considerable plausibility to the claim that the pleasures we take in games and pastimes do involve a tendency, quite possibly illusory, to see these games and pastimes as intrinsically worthwhile. Consider, for instance, the game of chess. As Alasdair MacIntyre points out, one might induce a child to play chess by offering her candy to play, and more candy if she wins.[53] This

---

[53] Alasdair MacIntyre, *After Virtue: A Study in Moral Theory* (Notre Dame, Indiana: University of Notre Dame Press, 1984 (1st edn 1981)), 188. See also Myles Burnyeat's comparison of learning to be good and learning to ski in "Aristotle on Learning to Be Good," 76.

might prompt the child to play in order to secure a sensory pleasure, but as long as she is motivated solely by the anticipated pleasure of candy, the game itself won't be pleasurable—the child won't take pleasure *in chess*. This won't happen unless she comes to see some value in the game itself—or, more precisely, in the excellences that structure and give point to the game. At that point, she would come to have a new reason not to cheat in order to secure candy.[54] Doing so would rob the game of its pleasure.

MacIntyre's observations seem correct, and they seem to indicate that chess enthusiasts do take pleasure in the game because they see the pursuit of its constitutive excellences as intrinsically worthwhile (even if not vitally important). If the pleasure that enthusiasts take in games or sports were a mere sensation caused by the activity, unrelated to any subjective sense of the activity as intrinsically worthwhile, it would come as a surprise that the pleasure is rarely produced when the rules are disregarded. It would also come as a surprise that those who enjoy particular sports or games also tend to enjoy watching others who play them surpassingly well. Finally, it would be baffling that we sometimes feel pity or even derision for those who take pleasure in what seem to us to be entirely pointless or trivial pursuits (whether shopping, or golfing, or playing solitaire, or picking up toothpicks). Such reactions would be inapt if directed at mere variations in the causal determinants of agreeable sensations; they make better sense if interpreted as responses to varying outlooks on what is good or worthwhile.

It may be that part of what we like about certain activities is simply that they seem entirely worthwhile when we engage in them, whatever we might think of them on calm reflection. Such activities might be valued as *divertissement* in the Pascalian sense—that is, as diversions of attention, valued because they take our minds off of weightier matters.[55] This "escapist" strand of pleasure might help to explain why we are so easily taken in by facile and dubious appearances of value, as when we watch soap operas or visit amusement parks or shopping malls.[56] Just as complete Aristotelian *energeiai* can involve a kind of self-collection in which one's highest capacities are fully actualized, certain mindless amusements might involve an element of self-abandonment, and might appeal to us partly because

---

[54] MacIntyre, *After Virtue*, 188.

[55] Blaise Pascal, *Pensées*, Sections 131, 139–43, 164–75.

[56] Shopping malls are, in fact, purposely designed to encourage a transformation of patterns of evaluative attention called "the Gruen transfer" (named after Victor Gruen, architect of the first shopping mall). The Gruen transfer is the metamorphosis of a goal-directed shopper with a specific errand into an undirected impulse buyer who wanders a mall, fascinated by its wares and hardly aware of passing time. The conditions that conduce to the Gruen transfer are soft and blandly comforting music, neutral color tones, uniform artificial lighting, disorienting floor plans, an isolation from the changing weather conditions, and natural lighting that provide our sense of passing time. See Douglas Rushkoff, *Coercion: Why We Listen to What "They" Say* (New York: Riverhead Books, 1999), 84–5.

they divert our evaluative gaze from matters that are genuinely important but deeply troubling. To quote from Pascal:

How does it happen that this man, so distressed at the death of his wife and his only son, or who has some great lawsuit which annoys him, is not at this moment sad, and that he seems so free from all painful and disquieting thoughts? We need not wonder; for a ball has been served him, and he must return it to his companion. He is occupied in catching it in its fall from the roof, to win a game. How can he think of his own affairs, pray, when he has this other matter in hand?[57]

We can affirm that those who take pleasure in games or pastimes must see what they are doing as intrinsically valuable without adopting the implausible view that they must see their favored games and pastimes as things that *everyone* ought to do. In the first instance, it may not be possible to engage in certain activities unless one has certain basic capacities. Thus, someone who finds long-distance running intrinsically worthwhile need not agree that the handicapped are making a mistake if they fail to give running a try. Second, there might be innumerable games and pastimes of intrinsic value—so many that no one person could possibly engage in all of them in a single lifetime, much less develop a keen appreciation of each. If so, then (since 'ought' implies 'can') it is false that everyone ought to engage in all intrinsically valuable activities.

A MISTAKENLY SUBJECTIVIST COUSIN OF THE ARISTOTELIAN CONCEPTION OF PLEASURE

The Aristotelian view of pleasure set out above has affinities with the view favored by Fred Feldman, who argues that to have a pleasure is to welcome some state of affairs, where the relevant state of affairs might or might not involve a sensation.[58] There is, however, an important difference. Feldman offers his view in service of a broader utilitarian project that grounds all value in pleasure and all disvalue in pain. The attitude of welcoming cannot, then, involve seeing that which is welcomed as in some way good or valuable without thereby being discredited as persistently illusory. By Feldman's lights, only pleasures are good. Even when the welcoming attitude is directed towards sensations, these sensations are not themselves pleasures, hence not themselves good; they are, rather, that which we are pleased about. This picture cannot make good sense of the many and varied evaluative outlooks through which we actually welcome, and actually take pleasure, in our circumstances and activities. We welcome things, and are pleased

---

[57] Blaise Pascal, *Pensées*, translated by W. F. Trotter (New York: E. P. Dutton and Co., Inc., 1931), Section 140.

[58] Feldman, *Utilitarianism, Hedonism, and Desert: Essays in Moral Philosophy*, chapters 5 and 7.

by things, under the guise of the just, the kind, the funny, the elegant, the philosophically illuminating, the ironic, the loyal, the friendly, the dignified, the gracious, the human . . . the list could be extended at length. As I will argue in the next chapter, we cannot make sense of the content of these different evaluative outlooks without irreducible reference to the different kinds of value that they seem to bring into view. We welcome through the lens of thick concepts whose meaning cannot be parsed into a descriptive component and a thin pro-attitude of "welcoming." To draw upon Frithjof Bergmann's revealing analogy, trying to make sense of value with only this generic sort of approval would be like trying to convey one's aesthetic reactions to paintings in a museum by describing their features in non-evaluative terms then holding one or two thumbs up or down to convey the directionality and intensity of one's approval or disapproval.[59] It would be a recipe for inarticulacy.

The outlooks through which we actually take pleasure in the world and in our own doings have representational content—they present their objects as good or valuable, usually in a rather specific way. This means that we cannot both take these attitudes at face value and count it as a good thing whenever they occur. We can take them at face value, and make use of them as guides to what to seek and how to act, only if we recognize (or, at least, do not explicitly deny) the reality of the independent values that they seem to bring into view. In so doing, we thereby recognize the possibility that we might mistakenly take these attitudes towards things that do not answer to them. Hence we cannot trace pleasure to the actual outlooks through which we welcome various states of affairs and activities, and also take all and only pleasures to be good.

A second difference between Feldman's view and the one set out in this chapter is that Feldman takes pleasures to have propositional objects.[60] I have argued that we ought to understand the sorts of desires that draw us into activity and towards other persons as intimations of instances of goodness rather than as attitudes towards propositions, and I have tried to show that we can account for pleasure in terms of this sort of non-propositional desire. By contrast, Feldman regards pleasure as a previously unrecognized kind of propositional attitude. It seems to me that Feldman's propositionalism gets him into trouble even in the simpler case of sensory pleasures. For Feldman, such pleasures are taken in propositionally specifiable states of affairs (e.g. that I am feeling the sun's warmth) rather than in sensations themselves (e.g. the sensation of warmth itself).[61] This would cast serious doubt on the capacity of infants and animals to feel sensory pleasures, since they presumably lack propositional representations of

[59] This analogy is due to Frithjof Bergmann, "The Experience of Values," *Inquiry* 16 (1973), 249–50.

[60] Feldman, *Utilitarianism, Hedonism, and Desert: Essays in Moral Philosophy*, 83–4, 96–104, 142–6.

[61] *Ibid.*, 99–101.

the fact that they are feeling certain sensations.[62] It would also provide a wholly implausible picture of the process through which we extend the sophistication of sensory pleasures. A connoisseur might tell us that a certain wine has a pleasant oaken flavor, imparted by the barrels used to age it. We might believe the connoisseur even before we can actually discern that element of its taste. At this point we would have the propositional belief that there is an oaken flavor to be discerned in the swirl of undifferentiated sensations that arise when we sip the wine. If pleasures were taken in propositional representations that we believe to be true, then it would seem possible at this stage for us to take pleasure in the oaken taste. In fact, though, we are not able to take pleasure in this element of its taste until we clearly discern it—that is, until we have a direct and unmediated sensation as of oak. This too indicates that we take pleasure in objects of immediate experience and not in propositional representations of them.

Chris Heathwood has attempted to build upon Feldman's view in a way that sidesteps this problem. Heathwood's proposal is that an occurrent sensation is pleasurable if and only if its subject desires intrinsically and *de re* that it be occurring.[63] I have already registered my objection to the idea that a sensation must be desired in virtue of its intrinsic properties in order to be pleasurable. But Heathwood's proposal faces a more fundamental objection. The problem is that so long as one thinks of desires as one-size-fits-all pro-attitudes towards propositionally depicted states of affairs, there is no intrinsic difference between an intrinsic and an extrinsic desire that a sensation be occurring. We do not generally desire the state of affairs consisting in a sensation's occurring in light of its intrinsic properties; rather, we are motivated by a sensation's intrinsic properties to desire the state of affairs in which it occurs. The difference between desiring intrinsically and desiring extrinsically that a sensation be occurring is a difference in etiology and not a difference in the desires themselves. Heathwood seems not to notice this, hence he leaves it entirely unclear why desires differing only in their etiology should also differ in their capacity to transform sensations into pleasures. Because he remains within the bounds of propositionalism about desire, his view leaves entirely unexplained the crucial phenomenological difference between sensations that are pleasant and those that are not. It does not help here that Heathwood requires that a sensation's occurrence must be desired *de re*—that is, that the desire must be for the occurrence of a particular sensation, picked out via one's direct awareness of it. Intuitively it seems that one could simply want that the world to be such that a particular sensation occur, as a kind of inexplicable whim, even while finding the sensation itself to

---

[62] It might be thought that my view faces similar difficulties, since sensory pleasures require that a sensation seem good to the being who feels it. I see no knockdown objection, however, to the thesis that infants and animals find certain sensations welcome, and that this can be counted as an inarticulate sense of goodness.

[63] Heathwood, "The Reduction of Sensory Pleasure to Desire," 32.

be painful. For instance, one might find oneself probing a damaged tooth with one's tongue with no further end in view than to bring it about that a mildly painful sensation occur. The favorable attitude towards the occurrence of the sensation need not imply a liking of the sensation itself, though of course it usually does. If (as I have argued) desires are evaluative outlooks that can take things such as sensations as their objects, then it is much clearer why they alter the phenomenology of any sensation they bring to conscious attention. Heathwood shows considerable sensitivity to the problems that arise when one tries to analyze pleasures in terms of propositional desires. What he does not see is that the way to surmount these problems is to scrap rather than merely to tinker with the propositional framework.

PLEASURES AND JUSTIFICATORY REASONS

It is often thought to be entirely obvious that all pleasures are good and that we have a reason, even if not a decisive reason, to pursue them.[64] By this point it will come as no surprise that I deny this. Before laying out my argument, let me distinguish my claim from another thesis with which it might be confused—a thesis that commonly goes under the name of the paradox of hedonism. The paradox of hedonism is that pleasure is most efficiently secured by aiming at ends other than pleasure—for instance, by cultivating selfless friendships, or by devoting oneself to raising children or bettering one's community. This paradox arises from keen observation of our actual dispositions to feel pleasure and pain, and it is a benefit of the Aristotelian conception of pleasure that it can explain the relevant observations. We can pursue attentional pleasure only by indirection because they require a vivid sense of the value of something else. This is true even of many sensory pleasures. For instance, the pleasures of caresses or of the taste of home cooking themselves tend to be imbued with a sense of significance that could not be sustained if we saw value only in pleasure. The paradox takes a particularly sharp form when it comes to the pleasures that accompany and complete our activities. We have to be wholeheartedly taken with some *other* picture of value of our activities in order to secure this sort of pleasure. But if we are wholeheartedly taken with some other picture of the activity's value, then presumably we would already take ourselves to have good reason to perform it. Prospective pleasure (of the sort under discussion) turns out to be the "fifth wheel" of practical reasoning: it is hardly ever anything more than a redundant reason for action.

[64] Shelly Kagan, for instance, claims that the value of pleasure and the disvalue of pain are self-evident to anyone who experiences them and hence that pleasure is one component of well-being. See Kagan, *The Limits of Morality* (Oxford: Oxford University Press, 1991), 30. See Goldstein, "Pleasure and Pain: Unconditional, Intrinsic Values," *Philosophy and Phenomenological Research* 50 (1989), 255–76.

This argument is convincing, but the Aristotelian account of pleasure has a stronger implication. It implies that sometimes the prospect of pleasure is no reason at all—not even a redundant reason—to do that which gives rise to it. On the Aristotelian view, taking pleasure in an activity amounts to engaging in the activity with a vivid running awareness of its value. Suppose I am completely convinced, after due reflection, that some activity is entirely valueless, yet I know from experience that I would tend to see it as valuable, hence take a degree of pleasure in it, if I were to engage in it. By hypothesis, I now regard the value I would see in the activity as entirely illusory. Why should I regard the activity as one whit more valuable simply because I can anticipate being tempted to mistake it as such? Indeed, the prospective pleasure would seem to be a reason to *avoid* the activity, since doing so would spare me from what I now regard as a delusion about what's worth doing. Taking a similar posture towards the evaluative outlook of other persons, whether future or present, might be objectionably paternalistic. However, it is quite proper to concern oneself with the proper shaping of one's own future evaluative outlook, rather than simply predicting one's outlook and regarding it as a fixed fact that must be honored in determining how to maximize the contentment of one's future self. The latter picture manifests too passive a posture towards the cultivation of one's character, and is inconsistent with serious engagement in the task of living a coherent, unified, and laudable life.

It might be objected that one could not really take pleasure in an activity that one judges to be valueless. This seems mistaken. As noted above, we take pleasure in activities by degrees, for we could always be more clearly focused on what we are doing and more vividly impressed with its value. Even if I am distracted by my belief that there is something wrong with what I am doing, I might still be able to take some modicum of pleasure in it. Further, there are some cases in which I can be fairly confident that if I engaged in some activity, my current conviction that it is valueless would fade. For instance, I might believe that if I took a job in the fashion industry, I would eventually become vividly attentive to what I and others are wearing, and might come to see as good—hence to take some degree of pleasure in—wearing pricy clothing in the current year's designs. This prospective pleasure would not seem to be any reason at all to work in the fashion industry, and indeed could reasonably be regarded as a reason to avoid such work. My account of pleasure vindicates this intuition and provides it with a reasonable articulation: insofar as a pleasure is justifiably regarded as delusory, its prospect lacks reason-giving force. Like desires, so too prospective attentional pleasures have justificatory authority only on the supposition that they accurately reflect independent goods or reasons.

While I am hardly the first to deny that pleasures are invariably good or reason-giving, I think that the above-elaborated Aristotelian account of pleasure helps to set this claim in its proper light. Some have followed Kant in thinking that the value of pleasure is conditioned on the moral virtue of the person experiencing it.[65] This position seems far too general, since a vicious person might sometimes catch an appreciative glimpse of a genuine value, and take at least a limited pleasure in some action precisely because it reflects that value. Other philosophers have culled forth intuitions about particular cases to try to show (as part of a larger argument for "particularism" about reasons) that some pleasures are good and others bad. For instance, the fact that some audience might take pleasure in bloody public executions counts not as a reason to perform such executions, but as reasons to avoid them.[66] This seems intuitively right, but the controversy need not remain a *mere* clash of intuitions. The Aristotelian account of attentional pleasure yields a plausible account of *why* our intuitions about the value of pleasure vary from case to case. We have reason to avoid certain pleasures, and to try to free ourselves of them, insofar as they involve distorted outlooks on value.

Another, perhaps more surprising consequence of the view is that even when prospective (attentional) pleasures *are* reason-giving, the source of their justificatory authority is not what has commonly been supposed. Such pleasures provide reasons only because, and insofar as, they indicate the presence of other, non-hedonic reasons. They are suited to figure in practical deliberation only as projected future outlooks on what one has reason to do. The mere fact that one expects to have an evaluative outlook is not itself a reason to affirm that outlook. Further, when one does accept the projected outlook, what one affirms is the value of the *activity* in which one expects to find value and take pleasure, not of the *pleasure* one expects to take.[67] This helps to explain the reaction induced in many readers by Nozick's "experience machine" thought experiment.[68] Those readers who find little appeal in the thought of hooking themselves up to a machine that would feed them a steady diet of their favorite experiential states for the rest of their lives are perhaps moved by a sense that most of what we value under the heading of pleasure is not a form of complete passivity but, quite to the contrary, a form of complete activity. The experiential element of pleasure would not be valuable when taken in isolation from the independently valuable activities that, in the best cases, it accompanies and completes.

[65] See Immanuel Kant, *Groundwork of the Metaphysics of Morals*, Ak. 393 (Kant here states the point in terms of happiness, but he has a hedonistic notion of the human pursuits whose optimal success he calls happiness).

[66] Jonathan Dancy, *Moral Reasons* (Oxford: Blackwell Publishers, 1993), 61. The same example appears in David McNaughton, *Moral Vision: An Introduction to Ethics* (Oxford: Basil Blackwell Ltd., 1998), 193.

[67] I do not think that I am departing from Aristotle here. At one point (*NE* 1175a18–22), he refuses to answer the question whether pleasure is choice-worthy for the sake of activity or activity for the sake of pleasure. But he goes on to say that bad activities can be found pleasant by those who are vicious or corrupt, and that such pleasures are shameful and bad (*NE* 1175b279; 1176a10–29). This seems to answer the question that Aristotle previously bypassed: pleasures taken in base activities are bad, hence we should choose activities for their own sake and not for the sake of the (possibly bad) pleasures they might yield.

[68] Robert Nozick, *Anarchy, State and Utopia* (New York: Basic Books, 1974), 42–5.

One might object that a life structured around illusory goods is better if one is entirely taken in by the illusion than if one is not. This seems wrong. While wholeheartedness is sometimes admirable, it can also take the reprehensible form of dogmatic and even fanatical devotion to misguided or evil causes. When it takes such forms, it does not seem to increase the goodness of a life. More fundamentally, even if dogmatic and misguided pleasures did make a life go better, this alone would not show that pleasure detached from real values is reason-giving. A theory of justificatory reasons must be acceptable from the point of view of the deliberator trying to decide what to do; not from the third-personal standpoint of those trying to assess the quality of lives they are not in a position to choose. When I deliberate, it does not count in favor of a course of action inspired by what I firmly believe to be illusory goods that if I were to engage in the course of action, I would be completely taken in by the illusion. We have standing reasons to guard against such illusions, not to induce them whenever they would be comforting. If someone has an illusory view of the value of his activities because he himself has knowingly chosen to foster the illusion, he does not have a mere comforting illusion about the value of his activities; he has a *self-delusion* about their value. Such self-delusions are to be avoided.

This is not to deny that some things we call pleasures might be intrinsically reason-giving. We use the term 'pleasure' to refer not only to pre-reflective evaluative outlooks on our own activities, but also to bare sensory pleasures. Perhaps it always counts in favor of a course of action that it would bring about some such sensation.[69] However, as argued above, many sensory pleasures are accentuated by evaluative outlooks that might be badly mistaken.[70] The importance of sensory pleasures can easily be exaggerated by inclusion, within the category, of pleasures that owe their richness to vivid appreciation of their occasions. But for this obscuring conflation, there would be little appeal to the hedonist thesis that all and only pleasures are valuable.

CONCLUDING REMARKS ON THE VALUE OF PLEASURE

Even if attentional pleasures are not intrinsically reason-giving, this does not mean that they add nothing of value to a life. They often do. Pleasure has

---

[69] This marks a striking disanalogy between desires and pleasures: bare desires or urges, shorn of any attachment to a broader system of values and projects, are the desires that most clearly lack reason-giving force; bare pleasures, similarly detached from broader values and projects, are the pleasures that most clearly have such force.

[70] I cannot accept Thomas Nagel's attempt to navigate this slippery terrain by distinguishing a class of "physical pleasures" that consist solely in "sensory experiences" and that are intrinsically reason-giving. Many of the pleasures that Nagel counts as physical—including the pleasures of food, drink, sex, and warmth—are often enhanced by keen appreciation of the value of their occasions. See Nagel, *The View from Nowhere*, 156.

roughly the same sort of relation to the good life as belief. Having a particular belief need not make one's life one whit better, and indeed some beliefs are so disorienting that one is far better off without them. Still, there is a species of belief—namely, true beliefs about important matters—whose possession is generally good. Likewise, particular pleasures need not make one's life one whit better; indeed, some pleasures manifest so thorough a disorientation about value that they count *against* the activities with which they are associated. However, there is one species of pleasure—the sort that involves vivid appreciation of important human goods—whose occurrence is generally good.

Suppose I face a choice between two activities, both of which I judge on reflection to be genuinely valuable and equally so. Suppose too that I have reason to expect that I would be more continuously and vividly aware of the value of one of these activities than of the other, hence would take greater pleasure in it. Other things equal, my life will go better if I choose this activity.[71] But what exactly *is* the extra thing of value that is appended to a good activity when one not only does it but does it with a vivid appreciation of its goodness? To begin with, it is a good thing to have a vivid appreciation of the goods that give structure and significance to one's life. Of course, no one but the most extreme devotee of theodicy could pretend that such awareness is always pleasurable. A numbness to genuine value can blunt one's pains and sufferings as well as one's pleasures. For instance, grief can be and often is blunted by failing to attend to the value of the person lost and the intimate relationship cut short. Intuitively, it seems that one's life goes worse rather than better if one's grief is blunted in this way. On a non-cognitivist theory of pleasure and pain, this intuition would seem quite surprising. But this same intuition finds a natural place in an Aristotelian account of pleasures and pains as vivid apprehensions of the goodness or badness of the activities and eventualities of a life. It is not possible to be richly aware of the good but oblivious to its loss, and it is usually good to be awake to the good.[72]

One of the great obstacles to living a good life is a kind of evaluative numbness, attested to by those moments that punctuate our lives in which we are entirely awake to the value of the people around us and to how it would be best to live. In such moments, we have the sense that we have been asleep to our

[71] Of course, other things are not always equal. We sometimes have good reason to choose an activity that we are not yet in a position to enjoy, rather than one that we already enjoy—and not just so as to maximize lifelong prospects for pleasure, but also to expand the range of goods we are able to understand. Thus it might make sense for me to choose to listen to some genre of music I don't yet appreciate, rather than one I do, simply in order to educate my ear.

[72] I do not mean to suggest that it is *always* good to be richly aware of every value and every disvalue. For instance, it seems excessively morbid to devote to the news of each tragic death, anywhere in the world, the sort of vivid attention that we devote to the death of friends and loved ones, under the name of grief. Again, such emotions seem to track real values, but we have a sharply limited capacity to appreciate the good or the tragic, and an indiscriminate grief would evidence a lack of judiciousness and balance in one's personal economy of attention.

own proper calling, together with the disturbing, inductively grounded thought that we will soon be lulled back to distracted inattention. Such lethargy can interfere with our capacity to live a life that we ourselves are able to affirm unreservedly, and can numb us to the value of other human beings (as when our everyday routines make us forgetful of the humanity of those we rely upon as instruments for attaining our own ends). A similar evaluative numbness can also dim our view of aesthetic values that bear only distantly on what we ought to do, as when we realize that we have forgotten how beautiful the natural world is.

Now, one could argue that pleasure *per se* is valuable only as a vivid awareness of the good. The difference between a life vividly aware of real goods and a life vividly aware of real evils, then, would lie in the superiority of goods over evils, and not in the intrinsic superiority of the vivid awareness of goods (i.e. pleasure) over the vivid awareness of evils. This would certainly cohere with the claim that pleasure is not intrinsically reason-giving. However, this position implies too passive a vision of our relation to the good. Among the objects of our evaluative outlook are our own activities and our character as displayed in these activities. When we are pained by our own activities, we are at odds with ourselves. That is, we are tempted by the thought that we ought to be other than we are. Such pain is good when warranted, but it would be better to avoid actions that warrant it. Conversely, when we are pleased by our activities, we achieve a certain harmony as agents, for we see our actions, and ourselves as manifest in those actions, as good. When such an outlook tracks the truth, it is good not only as an illuminating evaluative awareness but also as an essential element of a kind of active self-unification that has no corollary in the field of pain. This self-unification is the full actualization of the human capacity for activity guided by a perspicuous understanding of the good.

The self-unification in question can be and often is diachronic. As argued above, there are many intrinsically valuable activities whose value cannot be apprehended except by understanding their place in a temporally extended narrative that is valuable as a whole. To fully appreciate the value of such an activity is to bring elements of one's own past and future activities into view simultaneously and to have a running understanding of the value of that narrative whole. This sort of awareness unifies the trans-temporal self by pulling its past and future into its evolving understanding of the nature and value of its evolving activities. In the previous chapter, I argued that we can understand the undelegability of moral thinking when we see its essential role as a constituent of certain distinctively valuable human activities. We now see similar grounds for insisting upon the undelegability of all thinking oriented towards understanding of the intrinsic value of one's own doings. Such thought is valuable both as the actualization of the human capacity for self-directed activity and as a form of presence in one's own activities without which they would be emptied of their pleasure.

When we grasp the place of Aristotelian pleasure in the good life, we come face-to-face with a distinction that is both exceedingly evasive and absolutely crucial to a tenable account of the good or well-lived human life. There is a difference between stretches of time in which one is wholly present in one's life, drinking it in, fully awake to it, and other stretches in which one merely goes through the motions, skating over life or letting it slip by. This difference cannot be captured in a reductively hedonistic conception of the good, since it is not merely a matter of intensity of sensations. Indeed, there is considerable plausibility to Pascal's suggestion that sensory pleasure is valued most by those in greatest need of distraction. Nor can the difference be captured without distortion by those who think of the good solely in terms of the satisfaction of preferences or desires, since the self-unifying wakefulness in question requires that one value something other than the satisfaction of one's desires or preferences.

Nietzsche does somewhat better in bringing this element of the good into view when he suggests that one is living the best sort of life if one would gladly consent to the eternal recurrence of precisely the same life.[73] As Heidegger says of those able to pass this test, "they are the human beings who bear within themselves a great deal of time and who live to the full the time they have—a matter that is quite independent of longevity."[74] Hopefully we have brought into view what might be meant by this talk of bearing a full measure of time. Yet it would be a mistake to accept Nietzsche's test as a way of determining who is living the most exemplary life. The problem is that one's life can be marred by tragic events such as the early death of a child, and it would hardly show one to be living well if one would consent gladly to the precise eternal recurrence even of these elements of one's life. A well-lived life is marked both by attentional pleasures and attentional pains, as they are appropriate. It would be bad *not* to be pained by worldly evil and suffering, and worse still to consent gladly to their eternal recurrence.

The test of the life well lived is not whether one is pleased by all elements of one's fate but whether one is able to take pleasure in one's active mode of navigating one's fate. More precisely, the test is whether one is able to complete with attentional pleasure, rooted in actualized understanding, those stretches of one's life activities that fate has not consigned to the status of regrettable necessities. This is a test of proper and full activity and for this reason it is a more properly human aspiration than the potentially passive achievement of *amor fati*. Indeed, the English word 'activity' seems pallid and lifeless in this context, by comparison with the Greek term *energeia*. The latter term simultaneously brings into view the notions of activity as opposed to productivity, and of the actualization as opposed to the withering or malformation of one's most essential

[73] Friedrich Nietzsche, *The Gay Science*, Section 341.

[74] Martin Heidegger, *Nietzsche: Volumes I and II* (San Francisco: Harper Publishing, 1991), Volume II, 131.

capacities. It thereby highlights the fact that for human beings, these two notions are joined at the hip: one's most essential capacities are actualized in the life of complete activity. These capacities remain withered if one is wholly passive, and misused if one devotes oneself exclusively to the production of not-yet-attained states of affairs. For humans, fully actualizing one's defining potentiality—that is, fully becoming who one essentially is—requires the sort of complete and unimpeded activity whose value lies in each of its unfolding moments rather than solely in its expected product.[75]

When we have a continuous and vivid sense of the value of a genuinely good activity, this does not leave the activity unchanged. It alters the activity itself and enhances its value by making it unreserved rather than reserved; wholehearted rather than half-hearted. In Aristotle's words, such pleasures *increase* the activities in which they are taken.[76] This suggests that it would be a mistake to affirm either of the two alternative accounts of pleasure that are sometimes attributed to Aristotle. It would be wrong to maintain that pleasure is a *separate effect* of a perfect activity, since such activity would fail to be perfect without the pleasure. It would be equally mistaken to maintain that pleasure is *identical* with unimpeded activity, since pleasure can't both be identical with unimpeded activity and be necessary for the completion of such activity.[77] If the word 'pleasure' in phrases like "taking pleasure in φ-ing" or "finding pleasure in φ-ing" can be given its own referent, it would seem to refer to that element of unimpeded activity which consists in a spontaneous evaluative outlook of unreserved affirmation or approval of the activity. It would seem to refer, that is, to the reflexive grasp of value that carries the activity forward and shapes its unfolding contours.

---

[75] Perhaps this is too quick. It seems possible for *amor fati* to take the somewhat more appealing form of a basic interpretive posture towards the world, one that brings events into view as surprises whose meaning and interest is to be divined. This seems a useful antidote to that sort of concerted focus on one's own activities that can obscure the surrounding world and impede appreciative understanding by fitting new events too quickly into one's standing aims and projects, reducing them to the categories of obstacles or opportunities. It seems a proper expression of human finitude, if not gratitude, to be ready to be surprised, instructed, and filled anew with wonder by the world. Such an interpretive stance is ordinarily associated with faith in a benevolent creator towards whom gratitude might sensibly be directed and from whom illumination might sensibly be expected. But I believe there is an appealing agnostic analogue of this interpretive frame, one that bespeaks a sense of adventure, a gameness for life. Still, to adopt this interpretive frame is to take a stance towards the world and one's place in it, hence it announces the full presence of an active mind rather than of a passive receiver of experiences.

[76] Aristotle, *Nicomachean Ethics*, 1175a30–5.

[77] For a clear statement of the idea that (1) these two interpretations are exhaustive alternatives, and (2) that the choice between them has long structured the literature on Aristotle's notion of pleasure, see Gerd van Riel, "Does a Perfect Activity Necessarily Yield Pleasure?," 212.

5

The Primacy of Good

But coming, through living with a people, to see dignity in faces that had all looked alike to us, to see the full range of human expressiveness in them, to hear suffering that lacerates the soul in someone's cry or in their music, or to see it in their art, to hear all the depth of language in sounds that had seemed merely comical to us—all or any of that is quite different from coming to acknowledge that, for example, they score well on IQ tests. We do not discover the full humanity of a racially denigrated people in books by social scientists, not, at any rate, if those books merely contain knowledge of the kind that might be included in encyclopaedias.

(Raimond Gaita)[1]

THE QUARRY OF PRACTICAL THINKING

How should we characterize the proper quarry of practical thought? Where exactly must our practical thinking "bottom out" if we are to locate a genuine point or value in our doings? As we saw in Chapter 3, some hold that at bottom we must see some non-evaluative feature of our circumstances and/or of the proposed action as a reason for action. Practical thinking, on this view, is fundamentally a matter of regulating the formation of intentions (and perhaps certain other attitudes) in accordance with one's apprehension of the reason-giving force of the sort of non-evaluative facts that can be discerned by purely theoretical exercises of reason. If the arguments of Chapters 2 and 3 are correct, then practical thinking sometimes requires a different sort of endpoint to bring its task to a proper conclusion. It must sometimes apprehend the intrinsic goodness or value of the mode of activity that it is in the course of actualizing, where this cannot be reduced to the reason-giving force of non-evaluative features of one's circumstances or of the activity itself. This is arguably true in all cases, including those in which one assigns merely instrumental value to one's immediate doings, since the decision to devote oneself to a particular instrumental pursuit at a particular time itself bespeaks at least an implicit

---

[1] Raimond Gaita, "Narrative, Identity and Moral Philosophy," *Philosophical Papers* 32 (2003), 261–77; 267.

conception of what sort of life it is intrinsically best to live. But it is true at least in some cases.

The former, reason-centric view of practical thinking is common ground between Kantian constructivists and Humean non-cognitivists (to the extent, at least, that Humeans recognize the existence of a specifically practical kind of thinking). Both of these traditions seek to accommodate a supposed lesson of the modern natural sciences to the effect that there is nothing in the world for reason to apprehend except non-evaluative facts. What this means is that our talk of practical reasons or values must be tied securely to the non-evaluative facts if this talk is to manifest a discernible consistency across changing circumstances, since there is nothing else that it could consistently track. The key difference between these two traditions is that Kant and his constructivist heirs insist we can arrive at objectively valid beliefs about how best to anchor practical reasons to the non-evaluative facts, while Hume and his non-cognitivist heirs deny this. Indeed, Humeans hold that evaluative talk does not express beliefs at all, but rather expresses sentiments or conations that are occasioned by the non-evaluative facts and that give a projected appearance of significance or value to a world that is in itself evaluatively barren.

This narrowly naturalistic, reason-centric idea of practical thought was wholly foreign to Ancient philosophy. It was characteristic of the Ancients to ground the virtues in a teleological conception of human nature that transcends the bounds of the natural as those bounds come to be understood in the wake of the Scientific Revolution. Indeed, the main conceptual innovations of Humean and Kantian ethics are best understood as responses to a crisis in ethical thought brought on by the rise of modern science, whose picture of the world seems to include nothing that ethical beliefs could possibly be about. While it is still too soon to know exactly what kinds of entities might eventually be posited by physicists in a finished "theory of everything," still it has been clear at least since the time of Newton that we will not find goodness or value on the favored list. For the Ancient ethical theorist, there was no comparable problem in conceiving of the proper objects of practical thought both as real and as irreducibly evaluative. Indeed, the Ancients did not have at their disposal a well-defined notion of nature that would count by modern lights as non-evaluative, hence they were not in a position even to formulate the problem of the relation between values and (natural) facts in anything like its modern form.

The task of this chapter is to show that the Ancient conception of value-talk is in fact implicit in a great deal of our talk about value, and that we cannot consistently renounce it without accepting a very serious restriction on this talk. More particularly, we cannot consistently reduce talk of values to talk of the reason-giving force of non-evaluative properties without incurring a steep cost in the metric of *articulacy* about value. If we accept such a reduction, we cannot make good sense of most of the evaluative concepts that we actually draw upon in our efforts to understand the nature and point of many of the activities that we regard as central to a life well lived. Nor can we sequester off a subset of the things we care about, under the heading of the moral, and reduce our talk of values to talk of reasons in this more limited domain. Our actual sense of the moral value of other human beings cannot plausibly be characterized in terms of the reason-giving force of non-evaluative facts about them.

This places an important limit on what we can hope to do under the heading of moral philosophy, since it implies that we cannot point out the basis of the value of human beings to those who have absolutely no sense of it. However, it does not imply that we can do nothing to restore our confidence that human beings have moral value when our sense of that value has waned. What we call moral value is a branch of an entire arborescence of values and concerns, and we can restore our sense of this kind of value by dwelling on its connection with other ways in which human beings are lit up with significance for us—or so it will be argued below.

THE REDUCTION OF GOODNESS OR VALUE TO REASONS

The above-sketched controversy about how best to conceive of the ultimate objects of practical thought lies just beneath the surface of a discrepancy between the dialectical account of desires set out in Chapter 2 and the very similar account of desires set out by Scanlon. Scanlon thinks of desires as subjective appearances of *reasons* to act in particular ways or to bring about particular states of affairs. In many respects the dialectical view of desires takes inspiration from Scanlon's position. However, it differs from Scanlon in holding that certain desires are appearances of some kind of goodness or value, and that we can be subject to such appearances while having only the vaguest idea what course of action would answer to them. Scanlon has offered a conception of the relation between reasons and goodness or value under which this would turn out to be a distinction without a difference. On the "buck-passing" account of the good set out in Scanlon's *What We Owe to Each Other*, talk of goodness or value can be reduced without remainder to talk of reasons, while talk of reasons is basic and irreducible.[2] On this view, to say that something is good or valuable is to say that one of its natural features has the property of being a reason to pursue or promote it or to take some other relevant attitude towards it—e.g. to respect or admire it.

[2] Scanlon, *What We Owe to Each Other*, chapter 2, especially 95–100. A similar view was championed by A. C. Ewing in *The Definition of Good* (London: Macmillan, 1947), 145–55. Versions of the view can also be found in W. D. Falk, "Fact, Value and Nonnatural Predication," in *Oughts, Reasons and Morality* (Ithaca, NY: Cornell University Press, 1986), 117–18; Allan Gibbard, *Wise Choices, Apt Feelings: A Theory of Normative Judgment* (Oxford: Clarendon, 1990), 51; and Elizabeth Anderson, *Values in Ethics and Economics* (Cambridge: Harvard University Press, 1993), 1–2.

Scanlon has since endorsed a reinterpretation of his buck-passing view offered by R. Jay Wallace.[3] He still affirms the heart of the buck-passing view—i.e. that goodness is not itself a reason-giving property and that talk of goodness is reducible to talk of the reason-giving force of other properties. However, he is more permissive about the underlying properties that do provide reasons to promote, admire, or respect those things that are properly called good. These reasons need not be the sorts of facts recognized by the natural sciences, but can themselves be evaluative properties. For instance, the boldness of a musical composition might be a reason to listen to it, hence might make it good. Likewise, the generosity of an action might be reason to admire it, hence might make it good. To the best of my knowledge, Scanlon has not elaborated upon his reasons for abandoning the earlier view (call it *naturalistic buck-passing*) in favor of the later view (*non-naturalistic buck-passing*). For our purposes, it will help to see exactly why the earlier view is untenable. This will serve several purposes. First, others who have favored "passing the buck" from value-talk to reason-talk have been motivated at least in part by the thought that the buck-passing view obviates the need to posit non-natural entities as referents for our value terms, hence an argument against naturalistic buck-passing will lock horns with positions that continue to have currency in contemporary philosophy.[4] Second, the problem with naturalistic buck-passing is shared by all extant alternatives to value realism, including Humean anti-realism and thorough-going forms of Kantian constructivism, hence elaborating the case against naturalistic buck-passing will yield a more sweeping diagnosis of the costs of rejecting value realism. This will set the stage for a brief argument, set out at the end of Chapter 6, that this cost is not worth paying. Third, the discussion will solidify the case for holding that certain desires have an irreducibly evaluative representational content—a content to which we can return again and again in search of a deeper and more perspicuous understanding. Finally, it will prepare the way for a more illuminating understanding of those motivations that are commonly called moral, since it will permit us to see that such motivations have an irreducibly evaluative content that can be understood in depth, while also permitting us to see how our relations with our fellow human beings can deepen as we progress towards a more piercing understanding of this evaluative content.

Before elaborating my objection to buck-passing, it will help to mention a different and better-known objection, one that strikes me as unsuccessful. The objection, in a nutshell, is that things can have properties that give us the "wrong kind of reasons" to respect or admire them—that is to say, reasons that don't make the things in question good. Consider, for instance, a very powerful

---

[3] T. M. Scanlon, "Reasons, Responsibility and Reliance: Replies to Wallace, Dworkin, and Deigh," in *Ethics* 112 (2002), 507–28, especially 513. Wallace's suggested reinterpretation of buck-passing is set out in "Scanlon's Contractualism" *Ethics* 112 (2002), 429–70, especially 445–9.

[4] See Gibbard, *Wise Choices, Apt Feelings*, 51 and Anderson, *Values in Ethics and Economics*, 1–2.

being who threatens to inflict great harm upon me if I do not admire him. This "evil demon" has a property that gives me a reason to admire him: the property of having made and being ready to carry out the threat. This property hardly makes him good. Hence, the objection continues, we must abandon the buck-passer's claim that being good just is having properties that provide reasons for admiration.[5] The most promising way of defending the buck-passing view against this supposed counterexample is to point out that the reason to value the evil demon is purely instrumental.[6] This is not to say that the evil demon's threats cannot generate reasons to view him as having intrinsic value. He might threaten to harm me if I do not value him for his own sake, without an eye to any benefits I might accrue, precisely because he is the sort of creature who threatens harm to those who do not admire him. This modified threat would give me a genuine reason to value the evil demon for his own sake, and indeed to value him precisely for the property that constitutes the reason. Nonetheless, the reason lies not in the mere fact that the threat has been made but in the future harm that can be expected to ensue if the threat is not heeded. The reason to admire the demon is the instrumental consideration that admiring the demon will spare me from harm, even though this instrumental consideration is a reason to admire him *with a view to* another (bad or non-genuine) reason—that is, for the "nobility" of his demand. It seems, then, that a revised version of the naturalistic buck-passing view can surmount the "wrong kind of reasons" objection. On the revised version, to be good is to have natural properties that provide non-instrumental reasons for admiration, respect, pursuit, or promotion.

The "wrong kind of reasons" objection casts a wide net. If it worked, it would work not only against naturalistic buck-passing but also against all those views that equate being valuable with being a fitting object of some sort of pro-attitude. I do not think that we ought to reject all such views, but I do believe that there is a fatal problem with naturalistic buck-passing. The problem is that it cannot make good sense of the *content* of many of the most common human attitudes of approval and disapproval, including some of the attitudes that are mentioned in the buck-passing analysis itself. It is to Scanlon's credit that he recognizes, as against Moore and other consequentialists, that regarding something as good does not always boil down to regarding it as something whose existence ought to be promoted. Scanlon rightly points out that taking something to be good sometimes involves regarding it as calling for more direct modes of appreciation such as admiration or respect, and that any adequate account of goodness will have to explain how and why this is so. Scanlon attempts to do this by holding that regarding something as good sometimes boils down to regarding certain of

---

[5] See Justin D'Arms and Daniel Jacobson, "Sentiment and Value," *Ethics* 110 (2000), 722–48. See also Wlodek Rabinowicz and Toni Ronnow-Rasmussen, "The Strike of the Demon: On Fitting Pro-Attitudes and Value," *Ethics* 114 (2004), 391–424.

[6] Such a defense is set out persuasively by Philip Stratton-Lake in "How to Deal with Evil Demons: Comment on Rabinowicz and Ronnow-Rasmussen," *Ethics* 115 (2005), 788–98.

its properties as reasons to admire or respect it. The notion of admiration, then, figures centrally in his buck-passing account of value, and helps to make the view far more plausible than it would otherwise be.

Given this, it would be a serious problem if the buck-passing view were unable to make sense of the attitude of admiration. Yet the naturalistic version of the view cannot do this. To see the problem, we can begin by asking what we see when we see something as admirable. Admiring a person involves seeing certain of the person's character traits or achievements as having a very particular kind of value. We can't coherently admire another for just any property. I will be met with incomprehension if I say that I admire someone for being left-handed or for having two legs. Such a pattern of admiration is not merely unusual; without further explanation it is not so much as comprehensible that the feeling occasioned by the bare thought of someone's left-handedness or two-leggedness could count as admiration. Nor does it ordinarily make sense to admire a strawberry's color or taste, though these things are at least good (though again, it might begin to make sense if we brought in some special story, perhaps one referring to a cross-breeder or a creator). It might make sense, though, to admire an artfully composed dish of strawberries: the meritorious work of the dish's designer might be an apt object of admiration. Admiration, then, does not bring into view a generic sort of goodness but a special kind of value—call it merit. This is distinct from the kinds of value that call for respect or production.

While merit differs from other kinds of goods, still merit is a kind of goodness. Given this, the buck-passing account will tell us that we can replace talk of merit with talk about natural properties that count in favor of having certain attitudes towards those things we regard as meritorious. If these properties constitute the thing as meritorious, then the attitude they call for would itself seem to be admiration. But this means that the buck-passing account yields a viciously circular account of admiration. To admire something, on this view, is to see certain features of the thing as calling for the attitude of admiration. But what attitude is that? It is the attitude that consists in seeing them as calling for an attitude that consists in seeing them as calling for an attitude that consists in seeing them as . . . An interminable regress has begun.

The problem we've uncovered is that the naturalistic buck-passer's reductive recipe endlessly postpones the specification of the content of the attitude of admiration, yet this attitude figures centrally in that very recipe. We can bring admiration's receding object into focus only if we distinguish between seeing something as good in the way that invites admiration (rather than e.g. respect or promotion) and seeing it as something that there is reason to admire. Yet this is precisely the distinction that the buck-passer rejects.

Though this is tangential to my main argument, it is not clear that Scanlon's newly adopted position—non-naturalistic buck-passing—could escape this objection. To make sense of the new position, one would have to explain how one could "pass the buck" from value-talk to reason-talk while admitting the existence of reasons given by evaluative properties. As far as I can see, this could only be done if a grasp of the relevant evaluative properties were exhausted by a grasp of the reasons given by these properties for certain attitudes or actions, and if these attitudes and actions could themselves be specified without reference to the evaluative properties. The argument of Chapter 3 suggests that this latter condition cannot be met for certain activities called for by evaluative properties, and the argument just adduced suggests that it cannot be met for the attitudes through which we apprehend certain evaluative properties.[7]

If the fitting response to any good thing could always be spelled out solely in terms of determinate actions it makes sense to perform rather than evaluative outlooks or attitudes that it makes sense to adopt, then the buck-passing view would not be subject to the above-sketched regress. The view might work, for instance, if acknowledging something's goodness or value were simply a matter of acknowledging that one ought to choose actions that promote or produce it. It is clear, however, that this purely production-oriented conception of the proper acknowledgment of value is not adequate. Scanlon is quite right to insist that some instances of goodness or value call for a different sort of acknowledgment, such as admiration or respect. There is perhaps some plausibility to the suggestion that respect consists solely in the recognition of practical reasons (though I take issue with this suggestion below). However, it is hard to see how admiration could possibly be reduced to the recognition of reasons for action. Admiration involves a more direct, essentially phenomenological appreciation of merit or worth. The buck-passing view cannot give a non-regressive account of the phenomenology of admiration.

ARTICULACY ABOUT THE GOOD

On reflection, this same problem arises for many of the most familiar ways in which traces of goodness or value come to light for us. These experiences are often structured by evaluative concepts that constitute them as a distinctive mode of appreciation of value while simultaneously serving to bring to light a kind of value (or, at least, the appearance of a kind of value) that calls for such appreciation. To

---

[7] The problem with the buck-passer's conception of the relation between reason and value is not shared by the "sensibility theory" favored by such thinkers as John McDowell and David Wiggins. Some commentators have counted these thinkers as buck-passers. (See for instance Rabinowicz and Ronnow-Rasmussen, *Ethics*.) But this is a mistake. McDowell and Wiggins insist upon the point that the evaluative attitudes that make up a mature evaluative sensibility cannot be characterized without ineliminable reference to the values that these attitudes bring into view, hence they explicitly rule out the possibility of "passing the buck" from value-talk to reasons-talk. See David Wiggins, "A Sensible Subjectivism," reprinted as chapter 5 of *Needs, Values, Truth: Essays in the Philosophy of Value* (Oxford: Blackwell, 1987); and John McDowell, "Values and Secondary Qualities" and "Projection and Truth in Ethics," reprinted as chapters 7 and 8 of *Mind, Value and Reality* (Cambridge: Harvard University Press, 1998).

take but a few examples, we sometimes experience people or things as gracious, courageous, beautiful, majestic, humane, elegant, wise, amusing, or deserving of gratitude. To say that these are all ways of finding something good or appreciating something's value is to bring out a family resemblance among them, not to suggest that they involve a uniform attitude of appreciation or approval. It is one thing to appreciate the elegance of a mathematical proof and quite another thing to appreciate someone's wit or humanity. It seems wholly implausible to suppose that the difference between these attitudes lies solely in the fact that they happen to be occasioned by things with different non-evaluative properties, and not at all in the kind of value that we seem to see in those things that we find elegant, witty, or wise. To appreciate a proof as elegant is not to see the proof as having non-evaluative properties that call for a generic sort of appreciation; it is to apprehend the proof as calling for a more discriminating sort of appreciation, one keyed specifically to its elegance. These specialized ways of finding things to be valuable are made apt not by reasons to be gripped by them but by the values that they bring into view. The buck-passing view serves up a viciously regressive account of the content of these evaluative outlooks. For instance, appreciation of a proof's elegance will consist in seeing the proof as possessing properties that count in favor of extending a particular sort of appreciation towards the proof—an appreciation, specifically, of its elegance. The task of clarifying how the proof's value appears to the person caught up in such appreciation is endlessly postponed.

Because we are more articulate in denunciation than in praise, the same point is all the more obvious when we turn to the many specialized ways in which we can find things wanting. We sometimes view people or things as ugly, grotesque, monstrous, fearsome, filthy, debauched, rotten, graceless, clumsy, superficial, sentimental, boorish, humorless, clownish, tiresome, trivial, boring—the list could be extended *ad nauseam*. It is true that these are all ways of finding things bad, or disapproving of them. However, to point this out is merely to bring out a family resemblance among these evaluative outlooks, and not to deny that there is a great deal of variation both in the kind of badness that they bring into view and in the mode of disapproval that each of these kinds makes apt. The buck-passing conception of (dis)value cannot provide non-circular specifications of these varying modes of "finding bad" and the corresponding kinds of badness that they bring into view. It would hold, for instance, that finding a novel sentimental consists in seeing it as having properties that call for a certain kind of disapproval—namely, the sort involved in finding it to be sentimental.

One might try to salvage the thesis that reasons are fundamental by insisting that such evaluative properties as sentimentality and kindness call for generic kinds of approval and disapproval, and that these generic kinds of evaluative attitudes can be understood without reference to the particular evaluative properties that make them apt. Sentimentality, for instance, might be thought to call for aesthetic disapproval, while kindness might be thought to call for moral approval. There are two problems with this move. The first is that it is a recipe for evaluative inarticulacy to view the entire class of aesthetic evaluations, or the entire class of moral evaluations, as involving a single unvarying kind of approval or disapproval, differing only in its intensity and in the natural properties that happen to occasion it. To see the point at hand, recall the aforementioned image of walking through a museum and trying to convey one's aesthetic reactions to the works therein by describing certain of their features in purely naturalistic terms then holding one or two thumbs up or down to convey the directionality and intensity of one's approval or disapproval of that feature.[8] This is the coarse-grained picture of aesthetic evaluation to which one must retreat if one rejects the notion that specific evaluative outlooks or attitudes are fitted specially to, and made apt by, equally specific evaluative properties. Similar retreats would be required within other domains of evaluation—retreats, for instance, from talk of boredom and triviality to generic talk of prudential goodness or badness, and from talk of generosity and courage to talk of moral goodness and badness. The naturalistic buck-passing account cannot avoid circularity without accepting this sort of evaluative inarticulacy.

Indeed, it is not clear that the retreat into evaluative inarticulacy can stop even at this already disastrous point, with these generic kinds of evaluative attitudes. The naturalistic buck-passer would still have to earn the right to distinguish between different genera of value such as the prudential, the moral, and the aesthetic. It is no small task for the buck-passer to provide non-circular accounts of these kinds of approvals and disapprovals. It would probably prove unworkable, for instance, to explain aesthetic approval as approval of certain patterns of natural properties manifest in works of art, partly because aesthetic appreciation has a wider target, but more importantly because we will then be left with the vexing problem of explaining the notion of a work of art without reference to aesthetic appreciation or aesthetic merit.

Consider, in this same vein, just how difficult it has proven for philosophers to explain moral approval without reference to the sort of value that it seems to bring into view. Clearly it won't do to explicate moral approval in terms of some other range of values, such as aesthetic or prudential values. Those who do the right thing because they find it advantageous or aesthetically appealing clearly have not yet grasped the distinctively moral reasons for doing it; if this is the only sort of point they can see in acting morally, then they have not yet understood what it means to call something morally right. But how then do we explain what it is to value something morally, if not by inducing someone to bring an instance of moral value into view *qua* moral value so that they can experience it

---

[8] This analogy is due to Frithjof Bergmann, "The Experience of Values," *Inquiry* 16 (1973), 249–50.

for themselves?[9] Here again, we seem to have run into an autonomous evaluative outlook or attitude, one whose distinctive content cannot be explained without reference to the kind of goodness or value that it brings into view.

The threat of regress might be surmounted by dropping talk of attitudes and arguing that the apprehension of moral value consists solely in the apprehension of reasons for and against certain kinds of actions, and that what it is to appreciate these reasons just is to be ready to act in the ways they make appropriate. Before discussing whether this approach will work, it might help to gain a clear sense of why it would fail for other kinds of values. A full apprehension of the value of friends and lovers, or great paintings and poems, requires a direct appreciation of the value of the friend, lover, painting, or poem—an appreciation that could not be captured exhaustively in terms of an appreciation of the reasons for treating or responding to them in particular ways. Indeed, many of the actions made apt by apprehension of the value of a lover have their value as outward manifestations of this more direct and immediate apprehension of value. They are, we might say, ways of being moved by appreciation of another.

Consider, by way of illustration, the hugs, kisses, and caresses of lovers. It is hard to deny that these are properly counted among the apt responses to the goodness or value that lovers see in each other. Yet one would have to be in the grip of a theory to insist that these are actions that lovers choose to perform on the strength of their recognition of some array of reasons for action. Their aptness depends in part on their status as spontaneous expressions, or uncalculated symbols, of each lover's appreciation of the other's irreplaceable value. To have this status, there must be an overflowing of another, more direct sort of appreciation—an appreciation bordering on wonder at least in the sense that it combines speechlessness with a longing to bring something to expression.

This might seem an excessively subtle account, one suited at best only to cerebral or supersensible lovers. But on reflection it seems to cohere with widespread and uncontroversial ideas of these matters. If we thought of caresses in reductively physical terms—say, as moving patterns of pressures exerted on nerve tips—we would have no way of registering the gaping chasm of difference, in terms of meaning and pleasantness, between physically identical touches of lovers and rapists. It is only when we consider the way in which the contours of our evaluative sensibilities are expressed in outward acts such as caresses and kisses, and the way in which these expressions are taken up and appreciated as expressions of presence and of focused love by those who are touched or kissed, that we can begin to register this chasm of difference.

---

[9] One approach that has tempted some thinkers, but that seems to me quite unpromising, is to adopt a purely formal understanding of the notion of moral reasons or values. One might hold, for instance, that a person's moral values are those to which the person gives greatest stringency, or those that the person believes all human beings to be bound by. For a convincing refutation of such views, see Joseph Raz, "On the Moral Point of View," in *Engaging Reason: On the Theory of Value and Action* (Oxford: Oxford University Press, 1999), 247–72; see especially section 7.

For precisely this reason, we cannot possibly reduce the value that lovers see in each other to reasons they see for acting in particular ways. The actions that give apt expression to loving recognition of another's value are not chosen on the strength of reasons for producing them. If they were, they would be actions of a very different sort, expressive of a very different way in which one might matter to another. There is a difference in the significance of a kiss that wells up spontaneously and a kiss that is produced out of recognition that something counts in favor of producing it—e.g. that it might soften another's anger or comfort the mind of a dying person. This is not to say that the latter sorts of kisses are always inferior, but only that they have a different relation to the subjective picture of goodness from which they emerge—a justificatory rather than a symbolic or expressive relation. The spontaneous kiss of a lover emerges expressively from an intimation of a kind of value—one we might gesture towards with words like 'irreplaceability' or 'preciousness'—whose content could not be exhausted by some list of actions there is reason to avoid or perform. It could not be exhausted by such a list, one wants to say, because it gives point to avoiding or performing such actions, hence its recognition must involve something more than the recognition *that* such actions are to be performed or avoided.

If we hold fast to the conviction that wonder and wordless expressions of love can be apt responses to certain apprehensions of value—and this is a conviction I find myself unable to compromise—then we cannot replace talk of these values with talk of reasons for action. Nor could we replace talk of such value with talk of reasons for the gestures or attitudes that express our recognition of it, since this would lead directly to the sort of vicious regress outlined above.

ON THE APPREHENSION OF MORAL VALUE

It might seem, however, that the case of moral value is different, and that a full recognition of moral value really would consist entirely in the appreciation of reasons for action—in particular, reasons for acting as duty requires. Further, it might seem plausible that these reasons are provided by purely natural facts—for instance, by facts concerning what humans need if they are to be healthy, sheltered, well-fed, literate, and free of avoidable pain; or by the fact (supposing for the moment that it is a fact, and a natural one) that human beings are capable of asking for, providing, and acting on practical reasons. Indeed, on a certain modern and recognizably liberal conception of the nature and point of morality, it will seem necessary for morality to be grounded in facts that can be discerned by all people, no matter what parochial conception of the human good they might affirm, or what conceptual framework might shape their sense of the good. This will seem necessary, in particular, if we think of morality as a scheme of constraints whose point is precisely to permit stable and mutually productive cooperation within societies whose members differ irreconcilably in their religious and philosophical convictions about the good life for human beings. Given this, it might appear that the naturalistic buck-passer has the right picture of *moral* values even if her view yields an unworkable picture of other kinds of value.

I do not think that we ought to accept even this more modest and localized proposal for reducing value to reasons. In particular, I do not think that it provides a fully articulate conception of the expressive dimensions of acts that we find morally admirable. What follows is a story of what I believe to be a paradigmatic case of a morally admirable act, admirable partly because it provides so clear an expression of one human being's vivid apprehension of the preciousness of another human life. The story is found in Primo Levi's recollections of his time in Auschwitz, and it occurred during the last weeks of the war, at a time when the distant sound of Russian artillery has filled the prisoners with hope of imminent release. (This same passage is quoted by Raimond Gaita in a fine book by the name of *Good and Evil: An Absolute Conception*, and my thoughts on the passage have been very heavily influenced by Gaita's discussion of it.)

Ladmaker, in the bunk under mine, was a poor wreck of a man. He was (or had been) a Dutch Jew, seventeen years old, tall, thin and gentle. He had been in bed for three months; I had no idea how he had managed to survive the selections. He had had typhus and scarlet fever successively; at the same time a serious cardiac illness had shown itself, while he was smothered with bedsores, so much so that by now he could only lie on his stomach. Despite all this, he had a ferocious appetite. He only spoke Dutch, and none of us could understand him.

Perhaps the cause of it all was the cabbage and turnip soup, of which Ladmaker had wanted two helpings. In the middle of the night he groaned and then threw himself from his bed. He tried to reach the latrine, but he was too weak and fell to the ground crying and shouting loudly.

Charles lit the lamp . . . and we were able to ascertain the gravity of the incident. The boy's bed and the floor were filthy. The smell in the small area was rapidly becoming insupportable. We had but a minimum supply of water and neither blankets nor straw mattresses to spare. And the poor wretch, suffering as he was from typhus, formed a terrible source of infection, while he certainly could not be left all night to groan and shiver in the cold in the middle of the filth.

Charles climbed down from his bed and dressed in silence. While I held the lamp, he cut all the dirty patches from the straw mattress and the blankets with a knife. He lifted Ladmaker from the ground with the tenderness of a mother, cleaned him as best as possible with straw taken from the mattress and lifted him into the remade bed in the only position in which the unfortunate fellow could lie. He scraped the floor with a scrap of tin plate, diluted a little chloramines and finally spread disinfectant over everything, including himself.[10]

---

[10] This passage is from Primo Levi's *If This Is Man*, and is quoted by Raimond Gaita in *Good and Evil: An Absolute Conception, Second Edition* (London: Routledge, 1991 and 2004), xvi.

To my mind, this passage describes a paradigmatic case of morally admirable action. I feel confident in saying this even in advance of arriving at a clear understanding of the nature and boundaries of the moral domain. If I ask myself why the act seems morally admirable, the answer seems to be that it emerges from and expresses one human being's vivid appreciation of the preciousness of another human life, and that this vivid appreciation had sufficient depth and luminosity to survive in Auschwitz. The action's admirableness does not rest primarily on its beneficial effects—or, at least, on beneficial effects that are conceptually independent of the meaning, which is to say the expressive value, of the action itself. The act's goodness cannot exhaustively be measured, for instance, by the quantum of physical pain and suffering that Ladmaker was spared during the last days of his life. While it may be true that Charles spared Ladmaker a great deal of suffering, this is largely because he spared Ladmaker the horror of dying surrounded by human beings who show no sign of concern with his demise, and not solely or even primarily because dying from typhus and cardiac illness hurts less or is delayed a bit if one is on a bed rather than on the floor. Thus, while it may be true that Charles' action permits Ladmaker to die with an extremely valuable sort of comfort, this comfort consists largely in awareness that another human being has been moved to minister to one's dying body and to do so "with the tenderness of a mother." That is, the act comforts at least as much by what it expresses as by the tangible alterations of the world that it produces.

It is central to Charles' moral admirableness that, even in Auschwitz, and even in the face of the possibility of contracting a fatal illness on the eve of liberation, Charles helps Ladmaker and does so in a spirit of tenderness. What makes tenderness valuable is, again, not primarily the conceptually independent effects that it promises to bring about. Indeed, when we consider the tenderness of the act, it is not even clear what these effects are supposed to *be*. The answer can't be that tenderness promises to reduce the likelihood of physical pain or contusions, since this could be achieved by a detached and clinical carefulness. The value of tenderness seems to lie primarily if not entirely in what it signals, and especially in what it signals to those to whom it is extended. Like the kiss or caress of a lover, the tenderness of a touch serves to express one person's vivid appreciation of another's value. This is not to say that tenderness is produced *in order to* express such appreciation. On the contrary, when tenderness does not surge forth spontaneously but is affected for some ulterior purpose—even an extremely laudable one—this ordinarily marks some incompleteness in the appreciation from which it springs.

But what is this appreciation that tenderness expresses? Is it an apprehension of natural facts about human beings that provide reasons to act towards them in various ways? It seems not, since the actions would themselves seem to be a fully apt response to the apprehension of reasons to perform them, and any such actions might or might not be done with tenderness. Well then, does tenderness express an apprehension of natural facts that provide reasons, precisely, to be tender? No. We would fall into a now-familiar sort of vicious circularity if we analyzed the appreciation of value that is expressed by tenderness as the apprehension of a set of natural properties that provide reasons for having and expressing this same attitude of appreciation of value. Tenderness is the expression in action of an understanding of the preciousness of another human being, and not—say—of their susceptibility to pain (which, again, could be recognized in full by a detached and clinical carefulness). This preciousness provides reasons to view and treat human beings in various ways, but it is not identical with these reasons.

It will be said that it is mysterious what this value could be. It *is* mysterious, but not in the sense of 'mysterious' that prevails in contemporary writings on ontology, where calling a putative entity mysterious is a polite way of suggesting that there is no such entity and we ought to stop talking as if there were. A father holding his baby might find that his sense of the child's value and his sense of the mystery of the child's value wax and wane together, not accidentally but as inseparable parts of a properly vivid appreciation of what it is that he has in his arms. Here the mystery does not concern whether there really is anything of value in his arms. *This* fact is likely to be far more obvious to the father than the premises of any philosophical argument that might call it into question. The mystery concerns, instead, the nature and source of this glowingly obvious value—this is what remains mysterious.

There are interesting similarities between this sort of mysteriousness and the mysteriousness of material objects, whose reality assails the eye but whose nature remains as inscrutable as the contemporary physicist's references to vibrations of loops of string whose curls enfold a half-dozen more spatial dimensions than the human mind can succeed in picturing.[11] It is worth noting that while many

---

[11] That there are mysteries here seems hard to deny. To speak for myself, and at risk of betraying my limited imagination, I am unable to understand what contemporary string theorists could possibly mean when they say such things as that there are extra dimensions that are spatial yet remain "tiny and curled up" rather than "large and extended." (Brian Greene, *The Elegant Universe: Superstrings, Hidden Dimensions, and the Quest for the Ultimate Theory* (New York: Vintage Books, 1999), 204.) No doubt there are mathematical formulae that induce theorists to talk in this way. But it seems to me (and, I suspect, to many string theorists as well) that these mathematical formulae do not serve to resolve but to announce or display the mystery of matter's nature. What could it mean, after all, for these extra spatial dimensions to be extended, if not for them to be extended across our three familiar dimensions? The problem is not just that this is our operative idea of extension, and that it is obviously inadequate to give us a sense of what it would be for one of the curled up dimensions to unfurl itself. The problem is that these extra spatial dimensions cannot possibly be failing to extend across these same extra dimensions. That would be to picture them as unfurled when used to measure themselves and as furled when measured. This is one of many examples that can be cited to bring out the mysteriousness of the rival accounts of matter on offer in contemporary physics. Drawing again from Greene's popular discussion of string theory (and Greene is said to be one of the more accomplished figures in contemporary superstring theory), what sense can we make of the notion that electrons take an infinite number of different paths in traveling from one point to another? (111). What is left of the idea of "taking a path" when one says such things? Or

people acknowledge that rival accounts of matter are deeply mysterious, hence that the nature of matter is deeply mysterious, few are moved to speak of matter as "mysterious" in the tone of condescension with which that word is used by scientific naturalists in contemporary ontology. This discrepancy becomes all the more troubling when we consider that the scientific theorist who insists on her justification for believing her favored theory, and who holds that others ought to believe it as well, has thereby committed herself to the existence of a good reason for believing her theory. Having done this, she cannot consistently deny the existence of justificatory reasons, hence of normative entities. If there were no such things, those who disagreed with the theory would have no reason to change their minds, and the scientist would have no reason not to abandon her preferred theory in favor of, say, medieval astrology. This means that no extant scientific theory can consistently recommend itself as a comprehensive account of what there is, since no extant theory recognizes the existence of normative reasons to believe in the theory itself.

When it is said that the value of a human being, or indeed any putative value, is ontologically mysterious, what is normally meant is that it is not the sort of thing that is recognized by science, hence not the sort of thing that a level-headed naturalist should recognize as real. I've suggested that the level-headed scientist does not dispense with mystery and cannot dispense with normativity. If the level-headed naturalist has reason to doubt that there is such a thing as the value of a human being, this must be because it is somehow less mysterious, or more ontologically parsimonious, to acknowledge that natural facts can be normative reasons than to acknowledge values irreducible to natural facts. Yet the former acknowledgment is deeply mysterious (in the pejorative sense), since it implies that one must see purely natural facts as something other than purely natural facts in order to see reasons aright. Offhand this seems to be a recipe for ontological confusion, not ontological clarity.

It is also a recipe for evaluative confusion. The problem is that if natural facts are reasons, their status as reasons seems to be something strictly additional to their status as natural facts. But this dissociation of natural properties and reason-giving force is itself quite implausible, since it suggests that any set of natural properties could intelligibly be regarded as a reason for any attitude, including forms of appreciation that would seem on the surface to be wholly alien to them. On this view, for instance, one could mistakenly regard the natural property of being a clump of mud as a reason for respect or admiration. Yet if someone sincerely professed to feel great admiration or respect for a clump of mud, we would be as puzzled as if someone professed to find rocks riotously

how about this claim: "Thus light does not get old; a photon that emerged from the big bang is the same age today as it was then. There is no passage of time at the speed of light" (51). What could it possibly mean to speak of something as being the same age at different times, or to make tensed references to things that don't age?

witty. Without some further story, it would be natural to assume that the person in question did not understand what it is to admire or respect something. Respect is partly constituted by appearances of dignity, while admiration is partly constituted by appearances of merit. One cannot credit the person in question with respect or admiration unless one can understand how it is so much as possible for a clump of mud to appear to him to have the sort of value we have in mind when we speak of dignity or merit. It would take a very elaborate story to convince us that he has not confused whatever value he thinks he sees in the clump of mud with the very different value that we call merit or dignity.

This suggests that our apprehension of a thing's merit is not a two-stage affair, dissociable into the apprehension of the thing's purely natural properties and an apprehension of the status of these properties as reasons for the attitude of admiration—both of which could in principle take place without our actually feeling the least admiration. Rather, it is a single seamless apprehension, one that brings an instance of admirableness into view, hence implies some minimal degree of actual admiration (since admiring something just is seeing it as admirable).

It might be thought that the apprehension of the moral dignity of another human being is different, and that it involves nothing more nor less than acknowledging the overriding reasons one has to heed reciprocal limitations on one's interactions with those others. A cogent version of this broadly Kantian conception of moral respect can be found in the work of Stephen Darwall, who equates our moral obligations with reasonable second-personal demands that others have made or could make of us.[12] Darwall maintains that this view is uniquely suited to explain why moral obligations are not merely things that it would be very good to do but things that others can demand that we do, and why there is always at least one person to whom we *owe* the fulfillment of any genuine moral obligation.[13] In my view, though, Darwall's ideas of respect and dignity are simply too narrow to illuminate the importance of moral demands. The human beings we encounter over a lifetime are not merely sources of demands. They are also sources of inspiration, consolation, conversation, companionship, and love. They are our solace against existential aloneness. We are able to develop a deep and rich sense of our life projects and their value partly by seeing how others have managed to invest their lives with value. Strip away these aspects of our encounters with other human beings and you are left with a barren landscape against which a voiced demand would protrude as something absurd rather than as a compelling summons. It is only because we occupy a richer world of human relationships that we recognize the vital importance of the imperatival aspects

---

[12] Stephen Darwall, *The Second-Personal Standpoint* (Cambridge: Harvard University Press, 2006), chapter 1; see especially p. 20.

[13] *Ibid.*, 10. I have my doubts about whether these points really count in favor of Darwall's view. I do not think that Charles would have been conceptually confused, nor even mistaken, if he had affirmed that he was morally bound to help Ladmaker but denied that Ladmaker was owed such help or could reasonably demand it.

of second-personal relationships that Darwall thematizes. What he calls moral respect, then, borrows its meaning and its urgency from a broader grasp of the value of human beings—one that cannot be reduced to a readiness to perform certain actions and refrain from others.

The criticism at hand can be sharpened by looking at Darwall's case against utilitarianism. Darwall acknowledges that the utilitarian might accept what Darwall says about the second-personal nature of moral reasons, then proceed to offer up utilitarianism as a substantive answer to the question of what we can reasonably demand of each other.[14] One cannot settle the substantive confrontation between utilitarian and deontological moral theories, then, without adopting a particular understanding of the kind of value that human beings have—an understanding that goes beyond the mere insistence that we relate to each other as equal sources of authoritative demands, and that settles such questions as whether human lives can legitimately be traded against one another in pursuit of utility-maximization. It is only after we settle such questions that we will be able to determine, as a kind of afterthought, what we can legitimately demand of each other. As against this, Darwall holds—mistakenly, I believe—"that it is our second-personal authority that is most fundamental and that substantive constraints on conduct derive from this authority."[15]

The preciousness to which tenderness testifies cannot plausibly be regarded as extraneous to morality. If we are to take seriously the thought that the domain of value can usefully be carved up into categories such as the aesthetic, the moral, the prudential, and the epistemic, it seems clear that we will have to count Charles' act as *morally* exemplary or admirable. Some will insist that his act is supererogatory, though Levi portrays Charles as performing it with a matter-of-fact sense of its unshirkability that suggests that Charles himself might have refused this description, and I do not think that such a refusal should be dismissed as simply mistaken. But even if we do place Charles' act (or his tenderness) beyond the scope of moral duty, this would hardly imply that the sort of admiration called for by his act and his tenderness is beyond the scope of morality. Charles' act calls for admiration because it manifests a vivid awareness of the sort of value that calls for a moral response to our fellow human beings, and because this actualized understanding of value has not been extinguished by prolonged existence at the receiving end of the awful routinized violence of Auschwitz. If the act were not done tenderly, it would not manifest so clear and vivid a grasp of this value, though it would still be admirable.

If Chapters 1 and 2 have set out a tenable view of what it takes to bring behavior into view as action, then we must see how the world of value looks through Charles' eyes in order to make sense of Charles' action, hence of Levi's story. Here we touch on the question of the moral force of parables and of certain works of fiction or biography. To grasp the story of an action (or a life)

---

[14] Darwall, *The Second-Personal Standpoint*, 130.　　[15] *Ibid.*, 121.

requires that we appreciate the appearances of value that motivate the person performing the action (or living the life). If such stories can serve as powerful moral exemplars, this is partly because of the exemplary clarity and discernment of the outlooks on value that we must learn to inhabit, at least imaginatively, if we are to understand them. When I imagine how Ladmaker and his predicament appear to Charles, I find myself (re)called to a way of seeing my fellow human beings and their value that has a familiar and undeniable force yet also has the aspect of something easily forgotten, something that I have inexplicably failed or refused to keep steadily in view. When I imagine this sort of apprehension of value arising in the course of Charles' life, I catch a glimpse of an unfamiliar way that the moral value of another human being might enter into consciousness. In the singular moral darkness of Auschwitz, it shows forth not merely as a source of demands or limits but as an antidote for despairing detachment, a release from the encroaching sense that nothing matters. It seems to me that it is precisely our occasional intimation of the value whose recognition is expressed in Charles' tenderness that prevents us, if anything does, from becoming jaded in our relation to morality, and that permits our moral commitment to survive as something more than mere habitual pangs of conscience, something that does not merely demand but also inspires allegiance.

The most pressing moral danger facing most people is not that they might succumb to the temptations of straightforwardly malicious actions, but that they might become numb to the value of their fellow human beings. Such numbness is a calculable effect of exposure to routine brutality. This makes its utter absence in Charles all the more remarkable. Perhaps, as certain twentieth-century Marxists believed, this sort of numbness is also a calculable effect of the contemporary form of productive activity, a form in which social interactions assume an instrumental aspect that is proper only to interactions with things. Or perhaps it is a timeless feature of human life, a feature that a Hobbesian secularist might call our egoism and that an Augustinian might call our fallenness. Whatever explains it, this sort of numbness is easily overlooked. Because it consists in an absence of awareness, it is not the sort of fact that loudly announces itself. Yet it does become visible in retrospect in those moments when we attain a momentary grasp of the value to which it numbs us, often in moments that are marked by death or illness, but also in moments when we witness or read a vivid account of decency in the face of suffering or death.

This moral understanding of the value of others is not valuable merely as an instrument for increasing the likelihood that one will behave well. It is the inward concomitant and source of morally decent action, and these actions have their significance partly as tangible expressions or actualizations of this understanding. It is true of morally good relationships, as it is of intimate love and friendship, that they can bring about a great many benefits that could in principle occur in the absence of these same relationships. However, just as some goods are partly constituted by love and friendship and not merely produced by them, so too there are goods that are partly constituted by moral relationships, hence that could not in principle exist in their absence. These "internal" goods of morality consist partly in knowing oneself to be bound together with and acting in tandem with others in a living community, each member of which has an active understanding or appreciation of the value of the others.

When we engage in cooperative activities, the value of those activities cannot be assessed in isolation from the kind of regard that each party to the cooperative activity has for the others. It is a different activity, and a far more valuable one, to live and work side-by-side over a lifetime with people who affirm one's basic worth as a human being than with people who merely find it beneficial to appear as if they do. This would be true even if these cooperative activities remained outwardly indistinguishable throughout. One cannot exhaustively evaluate the cooperative activities in which one engages without reference to the motives of one's collaborators, any more than one can evaluate one's friendships or sexual liaisons without reference to the motivations of one's friends and lovers. What Charles did for Ladmaker served, among other things, to cast retrospective light on the meaning and intrinsic value of the shared life that had arisen among the prisoners even before Ladmaker took ill. The same kind of point would hold, perhaps more obviously, if one of the prisoners had betrayed the others for some minor personal gain. This too would have called for a retrospective retelling of the meaning and value of the activities in which they had already been engaged, because it would strongly suggest a defect in the motivations that lay beneath those shared activities.

By the same token, when one human being intentionally harms another, we cannot take the full measure of the harm without reference to the intrinsic badness of a breakdown of moral recognition. To use a well-trodden example, someone who accidentally steps on my toe might leave me in pain.[16] Here is a harm, one that is conceptually independent from any specifically moral concern. Someone who intentionally grinds my toe under his heel with an eye to causing me pain does me a wrong of a different order, even if he fails in his intentions and causes very little physical pain. His action expresses a refusal to recognize my value and the value of my sufferings. The action of the person I am imagining could not be explained merely by presuming that he *lacks* a sense of my value. A mere lack would not explain his zealous effort to cause me pain in a way that ordinarily serves to signal a deprecatory attitude towards another human being. His action is most naturally explained by his determination to make known to me that he is taking an active stance on a widely affirmed and recognizably moral picture of my value, making known that he is refusing to recognize it (and, by extension, refusing to recognize me). It is true that he is refusing to see my pain as a reason to stop, as the buck-passer would insist; but in doing so he is refusing,

---

[16] Darwall makes telling use of this example at various places in *The Second-Personal Standpoint*, and my comments here are heavily influenced by his discussion.

and making known that he is refusing, to see me as someone valuable, someone whose pain matters. This is a fact of a different order, and the expressive disvalue of malicious actions cannot be fully understood without bringing this fact into view. Just as the attitude expressed in tenderness involves a picture of value and not merely a picture of reasons, so too the attitude typically expressed in brutality is a refusal of a picture of the value of human beings and not merely a refusal to recognize that their natural properties are reasons not to treat them in certain ways. One cannot understand the moral badness of torture or rape if one focuses entirely on harms that are conceptually independent of the way in which these acts violently imprint upon another human being's flesh an intolerable picture of that human being's worth.

THE SCOPE OF MORAL CONCERN

The fact that the victim has certain projects and commitments that would be thwarted by injury, or that the victim would be caused great pain, are good reasons to refrain from brutality, but the victim's projects and his pain matter because he matters. Nor does it seem plausible that we can come up with a list of the victim's natural capacities or attributes that explain why he matters—though many philosophers have thought that it must be possible to do this if the special value that we accord to human beings is anything more than an arbitrary "speciesism." I have tried to bring out the shortcoming of this approach by arguing that if we try to account in this way for the sort of value expressed in tenderness, we end up with a viciously circular account. But there is a more direct and perhaps a more powerful way to see the point: if we try to explain the special value that we accord to human beings in terms of some list of their natural properties, we lose hold of any morally serious sense of that value.

The problem at hand surfaces in an acute form in contemporary literature on abortion and animal rights. It is no easy task to specify natural properties or capacities that serve to distinguish human infants from the fully developed members of many other animal species, including most of the species that are raised for their meat. This has led some philosophers to the preposterous conclusion that killing an infant is not morally worse than killing many non-human animals, and that in some cases infanticide is morally permissible. Such arguments are premised on the notion that the moral value of a being must be explicable in terms of the natural properties of that being. If this premise, combined with observations about the natural properties of infants and humans, really did imply that human infants have no more moral value than many non-human animals, I would regard this as a *reductio ad absurdum* of the premise and not as the discovery that there really is no intrinsic moral difference between killing an infant and killing cattle.

I do not believe, however, that this *reductio* goes through, because I believe that the natural capacities of infants and full-grown non-human animals do differ in morally significant ways. The problematic conclusion follows only if we adopt an implausibly punctual conception of the temporality of capacities. There is a straightforward sense in which (most) human infants are capable of language use, complex reasoning, adopting and pursuing long-term plans and projects, and so forth: if they are raised in a good-enough environment, with minimally decent levels of love and attention and training, they will eventually do these things. This is a natural fact about what might be called their "life capacities" (as opposed to their "punctual capacities"), and it distinguishes them from non-human animals in a way that has obvious moral relevance.

There is good reason to think that when we are assessing the moral standing of different beings, the capacities that matter are life capacities and not punctual capacities. To see this, consider the case of an adult human being who has fallen into a coma that has robbed him of whatever punctual capacities are thought to be essential to the moral value of normal full-grown human beings—e.g. the capacity for self-awareness, for forming and pursuing long-term plans and projects, for using language, or for theoretical reasoning. Suppose, too, that the comatose individual has been given a drug that will restore the relevant capacities in three hours' time. Presumably we would not say that this individual lacked the relevant capacities, at least not in a sense that casts in doubt his moral standing or value. Would our verdict change if the drug took three days, or three weeks, or three years to restore the relevant functionings? I don't think so. It seems to me that if we were confident that the drug would eventually restore these functionings, we would say that the comatose individual still had the capacity for these functionings, and that this requires a kind of moral concern that is arguably not required in the case of irreversible comas. This suggests that infants too have the relevant capacities in the morally important sense, since in due time and barring unforeseen tragedy they will achieve the relevant functionings. For this reason, I do not think that we should affirm the above-sketched *reductio* of the notion that moral standing must be explicable in terms of the natural properties of those beings who have it. When the natural facts are seen aright, the thesis does not lead to morally absurd consequences.

However, while the naturalistic conception of the basis of moral value might succeed in drawing a plausible line between those beings who are and those who are not owed the highest sort of moral concern, it is wholly unable to yield a plausible explanation of that concern. As Raimond Gaita has persuasively argued, this problem comes to the surface when we attempt to rephrase the deepest and most serious of our expressions of moral concern with one or another of the better-known naturalistic accounts of its basis. For instance, it could be an expression of genuine remorse to say, "What have I done? I have killed a fellow human being." But suppose we try to express our remorse by saying, "What have I done? I have killed a sentient being capable of forming and pursuing long-term projects and commitments." I set aside for the moment the question of whether the notion of a project or a commitment really does fit within the bounds of the natural sciences. The point at hand is that if these natural properties (or others in the near vicinity) really did provide the reason for moral concern, then this reformulation (or another in the near vicinity) should serve to make clearer and more palpable what has occasioned our remorse, and why remorse is precisely what is called for. But it is hard to strike upon any such reformulation that seems remotely adequate to this task. I do not doubt that the philosophers who offer these formulations are making a serious effort to shed light on the nature and source of moral concern. But (here again, *pace* Gaita) it is striking how easily their theses can be put to use in making a parody of these concerns.[17]

The most promising direction in which to look for a naturalistic specification of the properties of human beings that make them fit objects of moral concern is towards their capacity for practical rationality (again, accepting for purposes of argument that it can be captured in naturalistic terms). It is only because of this capacity that humans are capable of demanding and assessing reasons for the ways in which they are treated, and only because of this capacity that humans are able to enter into modes of interaction that all parties can see as justifiable to them, on terms they have reason to accept. Put another way, there is considerable appeal to the thought that what we care about when we care about morality is to sculpt a form of social cooperation to which no one is merely captive. I am not claiming that we ought to endorse this contractualist picture of the basis of our moral concern. I myself doubt that we can get much content from the picture without relying upon a broader and more substantive conception of the good life for human beings. For the moment I am suggesting only that this conception of the basis of our moral concern does not sound like a parody. It seems to me, though, that the picture owes its plausibility to an implicit, extra-naturalistic assumption that there are normative entities for our practical reasoning to track. If there were no such thing as a normative reason, hence no possibility that appearances of such reasons could be anything but illusory, there would be no value in a propensity to have and act on such appearances. Nor would it be a worthy or inspiring social ideal to seek a form of cooperation that all participants mistakenly believe they have reason to accept. I do not see how the capacity for practical rationality can plausibly be assigned an overriding value unless one supposes that there are normative reasons and that it is not entirely futile to seek to act on them.[18]

---

[17] Gaita, *Good and Evil*, 28–9, 36–40.
[18] A similar argument can be found in Donald H. Regan's insightful essay "The Value of Rational Nature," *Ethics* 112 (2002), 267–91.

THE VALUE OF HUMAN BEINGS

It might be thought that I took a misstep when I claimed that serious remorse can consist in a full reckoning with the fact that one has killed a human being. This might seem to be a purely natural fact, a fact about the biological species of the being one has killed. I do not think that it is. Recognizing the humanity of one's victim counts as a moral reckoning precisely because it consists in recognizing something more than the victim's species, and indeed something more than a long list of the victim's natural properties.[19] The racist who neither sees the humanity in the faces and gestures of the members of some oppressed minority nor hears it in their words need not be overlooking some commonality in the natural properties of these human beings and those whom he does regard as morally valuable. There is something about them that he does not know, but there is no way to describe this extra something except in explicitly evaluative terms. (There may be many ways to *convey* it, but that is a different matter.)

Human beings have a very distinctive kind of value, wholly unlike the value of a physical pleasure, or a pocket full of money. It can make perfect sense to trade off physical pleasures against each other, foregoing one so as to experience another that differs only in being longer and more intense. When we make such a trade-off, we don't ordinarily lament the loss of the smaller pleasure, and we are perfectly sensible not to do so. To lament the foregoing of the smaller pleasure would be almost as senseless as to lament the loss of a five dollar bill that one has traded for a twenty-dollar bill. In both cases, one's loss has been compensated in kind. The loss of a human being is not compensable in this sense by the creation or preservation of another human life. This is not to deny that it sometimes makes sense to choose a course of action that will lead to the foreseeable death of one person but will spare the lives of many others. It is only to deny that in the wake of such a choice, it would make sense to regard the lost life as compensated for without remainder—indeed, without a literally grievous remainder—by the fact that other lives have been spared. This is precisely the blindness at the heart of utilitarian conceptions of value. Utilitarians understand the value of human lives solely in terms of a kind of event (usually pleasure or preference-satisfaction) that could in principle occur in any human life, and whose loss in one human life can be compensated without remainder by its occurrence in other human

---

[19] Here again I am indebted to Raimond Gaita, who has argued persuasively that philosophers who seek a narrowly naturalistic basis for our moral concern for other human beings "constantly appeal, despite themselves, to expressions whose associations in natural language go far beyond the conceptual resources allowed by their theories. Instead of speaking only of persons or rational agents, for example, they avail themselves of the rich associations that attach to our ways of speaking of human beings and of our common humanity. Naturally one wonders what is really doing the conceptual work." Raimond Gaita, "Narrative, Identity and Moral Philosophy," 273.

lives. Hence they arrive at the unpalatable conclusion that the loss of one human life can be compensated without remainder.

It is worth pausing for a moment over the enormity of what we are referring to when we say such things as that the loss of human life cannot be compensated without remainder. Here we are ill-served by the professional philosophical commitment to concise and bloodlessly abstract jargon. This professional commitment often serves the valuable purpose of heading off an unbecoming sentimentality, but here it threatens a lucid apprehension of a genuine value in whose reality we have great confidence. It threatens, in particular, to take what we know in the moment of loss as a yawning abyss of absence and shrink it to the unimposing dimensions of a technical anomaly in decision theory. What is at issue here is that which we cannot or at any rate won't quite believe in the possibility of when we struggle to fathom the fact that someone no longer is: it is an unfillable absence, a sense of which opens like a fresh wound when we turn our thoughts to the person who has been lost.

When we reflect on what we see in these moments of loss, we gain a fresh though not easily articulated understanding of Rawls' dictum that "Utilitarianism does not take seriously the distinction between persons."[20] We feel the force of this charge when we remind ourselves of how the value of our loved ones appears to us. This is the kernel of truth in Darwall's claim that the moral value of other persons comes to light in second-personal encounters with them. Yet the most revealing encounters go well beyond the mere appreciation of another person's authority to make demands on one's actions. For example, mature grief at the death of a loved one involves an awareness, whether articulate or inarticulate, that nothing could represent a compensation for what has been lost. Consolation might be possible, but compensation is not.

When we seek to stretch ourselves towards a fuller appreciation of the badness involved in the death of strangers, we often remind ourselves that the deceased was someone's son, someone's best friend, someone's lover. We do not remind ourselves of these rather obvious facts solely in order to appreciate the damage that his death will do to *others*. After all, if we are finding it hard to muster a proper appreciation of the badness of a stranger's death, we are unlikely to find it easier to muster a proper appreciation of several strangers' grief. We remind ourselves of these obvious facts to encourage sympathetic participation in a vantage point on the value of the deceased that we regard as particularly revealing—namely, that of his parents, children, dear friends, spouse, or lover. Most of us are unable to muster a loving gaze towards a stranger except by this sort of vicarious participation in an especially intimate vantage point. This familiar discipline of vision, then, testifies to a widespread confidence that the value of human beings is seen more clearly through the eyes of love than through the aggregative arithmetic of the utilitarian or the bureaucrat.

[20] John Rawls, *A Theory of Justice* (Cambridge: Harvard University Press, 1971), 27.

Of course, there is no special guarantee that parents and spouses and brothers and sisters and those going through the daily motions of the post of "lover" can be counted on to see with the value-illuminating eyes of love. We can and do become inured to the value of those who count nominally as our "loved ones." Speaking for myself, I depend upon regular visits from loving grandparents, and on vicarious participation in their exemplary love of family, to restore to vividness my sense of the value of my own children. In the midst of a writing jag (say, about the irreplaceable value of human beings) I am all-too-often reduced to seeing them as inconveniences or distractions. We must idealize the vantage point of intimates if we are to make vicarious use of it in sustaining or restoring a vivid sense of the value of other human beings. Perhaps if we knew a single genuine virtuoso of *agape*, we could rely exclusively on the vantage point provided by that person's outlook to stretch ourselves towards a full understanding of the value of any human being.[21] But while few of us are lucky enough to know such a person, many of us have encountered exemplary lovers and parents and brothers and sisters, and their outlooks can serve as fitting exemplars when we try to gain a vivid apprehension of the value of strangers.

It is worth noting that the extra measure of understanding that we might hope to restore by straining to see things through loving eyes does not seem reducible to any particular list or array of true and sincerely held beliefs, or even justified true beliefs. Intuitively it seems as if the understanding in question could be absent even if our sincerely avowed beliefs about the value of others were impeccable and were held on as sound a set of grounds as beliefs of this sort can be founded upon. We will return in the final chapter to the significance of this seeming discrepancy between understanding the value of the human beings in our midst and having justified true beliefs about them.

The naturalistic buck-passer is methodologically ill-positioned to offer a compelling diagnosis of the value of human beings. Such a theorist thinks of the reasons for valuing human beings as given by the natural properties of those human beings. Presumably the properties in question are relatively generic, since we do not think that human beings must meet special or idiosyncratic requirements if their deaths are to count as a fit occasion for grief. But these natural properties do seem to be replaceable without remainder. If nature were so arranged that the death of one human being always occasioned the creation of another human being with whatever generic natural properties are supposed to ground the value of human life, then human deaths would seem always to be compensated without remainder.

---

[21] Here again I take direction from Raimond Gaita, who maintains that we are best able to see the value of a human being "in the light" of love, and that what we apprehend in this light might alternatively be termed the "preciousness" or the "irreplaceability" of the human being in question. See Gaita, *Good and Evil*, xiii and xxiii.

At the risk of beating a dead horse, there is another problem with the buck-passer's diagnosis of the sort of value that comes to light in grief. If the value simply consisted in the possession of natural properties that provide reasons for certain attitudes and actions, then we could make little sense of grief. Grief must be counted as a particularly vivid apprehension of the value of another human being—a retrospective hence painful kind of appreciation that we often wish we had risen to before death, when it would have constituted a kind of joy. But how are the person's natural properties seen in the retrospective light of grief? Presumably, the buck-passer must say that they are seen as calling for that keen yet painful sort of appreciation that we call grief. But we get no further in understanding what it is to feel grief if we are told that it centrally involves seeing certain natural facts as reasons for feeling grief. Here we re-encounter the vicious circularity that keeps the buck-passer from offering a coherent account of those vital forms of appreciation of value that animate our principal concerns in life—including our moral concerns—but that cannot be reduced to a readiness to act in various ways.

One has not yet attained a full understanding of the moral value of human beings, nor by extension of the kind of badness involved in killing them or causing them to suffer, if one has no inclination to grieve their loss. But grief is not just a generic pro-attitude towards an irretrievable entity with a certain set of natural properties; grief lights up its lost object as having had a very particular sort of value. Those who already have a feel for this sort of value can be induced to bring it to mind by talk of preciousness or sacredness or irreplaceability. But if someone entirely lacked a sense of this sort of value, these words would not be sufficient to convey it to them. Such talk would only raise the puzzle how there could be a species of value that is intrinsically uncapturable in an arithmetic of gains and losses. Even if the person in question had a vivid sense of the irreplaceable value of something other than a human being—for instance, of Hieronymus Bosch's painting "The Garden of Earthly Delights"—this would not be sufficient to ground an understanding of the kind of value that is grasped retrospectively by those who are stricken by grief at the loss of a lover or a child.

This latter value cannot be understood except by becoming susceptible to a mature array of the sentiments that constitute its recognition—sentiments such as love, friendly affection, loneliness, and grief. To understand in depth what these attitudes are, or to become capable of feeling them in their mature form, is to see the depth with which one human being can come to matter to another. Put another way, it is to see what the value of a human being looks like when fully and vividly recognized. If we understand these attitudes, then we will already understand their fitting occasions in terms that cannot be reduced to the language of the natural sciences. We could not first arrive at an understanding of the attitude without understanding what might be a fitting occasion for it, then attain a purely naturalistic understanding of its fitting occasions. This sequence would be possible with a more generic and less discerning pro-attitude, but not with a discerning pro-attitude such as grief. But without such discerning pro-attitudes, we would be hopelessly inarticulate about the kind of value possessed by human beings.

We are not hopelessly inarticulate about this sort of value, but we never complete the task of attaining a full and perfectly articulate understanding of it either. The struggle to attain such an understanding begins in the typical good-enough childhood as one tries to make sense of how one's value appears in the eyes of one's parents while also struggling to become more articulate about how one's parents matter to one's own life. This task is continued, and continuously deepens itself, as one gains life experience, coming to care for a broader circle of human beings and attaining a broader awareness of how other human beings have managed to care for each other. This search is deepened and extended by dwelling on stories like Levi's account of Charles and Ladmaker. It is a search that one can never sensibly regard as completed, though it might be discarded or abandoned.

We can now provide a somewhat more determinate account of at least one thing we might mean by saying that a certain racist does not see the humanity in the gestures or the faces of members of the group he despises. What we might mean, and perhaps what we ordinarily mean, is that he does not see them as having the sort of lives whose sudden end would be a loss that nothing could make good, a loss that could not be compensated without remainder. He might or might not *say* that he does not see them in this way. But it is one thing to admit that after all they must have this sort of value, and quite another thing to be disposed in general to appreciate this value as it manifests itself in them. Racism and other deep-seated moral flaws often takes the form of a failure of appreciation and not a failure in one's sincere and considered avowals.

The evaluative *gestalt* that constitutes this sort of racism does not have an easily localizable content. It ramifies itself in almost everything one sees in another. One cannot see suffering as tragic if one does not see the sufferer as having non-compensable value, since human suffering borrows its significance from the value of the life that it distorts or keeps from full fruition, and there is nothing essentially tragic in a failure of fruition if it can be compensated without remainder by the good fortune or happiness of another. Likewise, one cannot see romantic loves or family bonds as running deep, or as carrying the significance one is likely to attach to one's own loves and family bonds, unless one credits these romantic loves and family bonds as mutual non-delusory apprehensions of a kind of value whose loss cannot be compensated. Nor can one see another's experience of oppression or persecution as a genuine experience of the intolerable thing we know the oppression and persecution of human beings to be, unless one sees in their subjugation and persecution the threat of the tragic withering of something (e.g. a life, or an array of personal projects and relationships) whose loss cannot be made good by gains registered elsewhere in some aggregate utilitarian calculus. And if one cannot see others' loves and sufferings as deep or potentially tragic, then one cannot hear their words as giving witness to real love or real suffering, nor see in their facial expressions or gestures or art or music the signs of the sort of emotions with which one credits oneself, the sort that run deep.

This brings us to the quote from Raimond Gaita with which this chapter began. Gaita's point is that the sort of shift in view that makes one aware of another human being's moral value could not be sparked merely by pointing out certain non-evaluative properties of that human being. These non-evaluative properties would have to be seen in an already morally conditioned interpretive light in order to buoy our sense of another's moral value. A *gestalt* shift is required here, one that involves a comprehensive change in one's view of what is at work and at stake in another human's inner life, and that brings in its train an equally comprehensive change in the way one hears the other's words, interprets her actions and emotions, understands her relationships, and sees her gestures and facial expressions. Here we catch sight of an important feature of moral value, a feature that might be called its unlocalizability. Recognition of this sort of value undergirds our capacity to grieve the loss of our friends, to have the deepest sort of conversation with people in full trust that their words and sentiments run deep, to read literature with the sort of trust in the author's sensibility that permits us to find solace and inspiration in her work, and much else besides.

Moral value, then, is not a special and isolated kind of value, relevant only to the formulation and vindication of a range of interpersonal demands or obligations. This might seem to indicate that there is something amiss with attempting to philosophize about moral value, and in a sense it does: it suggests that reflections about morality cannot be separated entirely from broader reflections about the value of human beings and their lives. Yet in another sense it restores a conceptual framework within which it becomes possible once again to imagine that moral philosophy might be fruitful. H. A. Prichard argued in a striking and much-cited essay that moral philosophy rests upon a mistake, at least insofar as it dedicates itself to illuminating the authority of moral reasons. The gist of his argument was that the authority of moral reasons would have to be grounded either in moral reasons or in non-moral reasons. The former alternative would amount to mere table-thumping on behalf of the authority of morality. It would beg the very question it was supposed to settle. The latter alternative would trace moral reasons to some other category of reasons, such as prudential or aesthetic reasons. Yet these could not be the reasons whose authority we are morally required to recognize, since the morally admirable motive for doing one's duty is the recognition that it is morally required and not, for example, the recognition that it serves one's interests or strikes one as aesthetically appealing.

Prichard's dilemma will look like a good reason to refrain from moral philosophy only if one has an overly balkanized conception of the realm of value. The dilemma begins to dissolve when we see that the value of persons that gives rise to moral obligations can be brought to light by fully explicating the value of many of our most important interactions with other people, ranging from our intimate loves and friendships and the shared activities they make possible, to our appreciation of the literature and music of others, to our engagement in the deepest and most valuable conversations with them. All of these valuable activities require that we trust the words, significant actions, gestures, vocal play, and facial expressions of others as manifestations of an experience of the world that runs deep. Appreciation of this depth goes hand in hand with appreciation of the irreplaceable value of these others. Hence there is something, after all, for moral philosophers to do by way of vindicating the authority of moral obligations. They can begin by looking at the realm of our most valuable everyday interactions with other human beings, very far from what we intuitively think of as a confrontation with moral obligation, and proceed to unearth the picture of the value of other human beings that is implicit in our understanding of the nature and point of these everyday interactions. It is not mere table-thumping to provide this sort of philosophical clarification of the surprising and often unnoticed *scope* of our encounter with, and daily appreciation of, the irreplaceable value of other human beings. And it is no way morally objectionable to be moved to honor various moral "thou shalt nots" by a clear and cogent apprehension of this unlocalizable value, as for instance it would be morally objectionable to be moved to fulfill moral obligations only by a sense of self-interest.

DESCRIPTION, EVALUATION, AND THICK CONCEPTS

We have seen that we cannot do away with talk of goodness or value in favor of talk of reasons, on pain of being unable to make the most minimal sense of the content of the array of fine-grained evaluative attitudes through which we are able to appreciate an array of equally fine-grained values. We have also seen that we cannot make full sense of the symbolic or expressive importance of actions, nor of the importance of the manner or spirit in which actions are performed, unless we are prepared to make irreducible reference to goodness or value. To refuse to regard values as basic, then, is to accept a heavy cost in the metric of articulacy about the good and in the metric of the meaning we can impute to human actions. It is to distrust, and either to eviscerate or to renounce, what appear on the surface to be the richest and most interesting modes of human awareness of value.

Scanlon is quite right that we end up with a coarse-grained and unconvincing picture of value if we suppose, with Moore and many other consequentialists, that the fitting acknowledgment of any value always consists in a determination to multiply the number of its instantiations. As Scanlon points out, the full and proper recognition of the value of such things as friendships or works of art does not consist solely in a determination to bring it about that there are more works of art, or more aesthetic experiences, or more friendships, or more people like one's friends.[22] Friendship is partly constituted by a more direct sort of appreciation of value—namely, the appreciation by each friend of the other friend's goodness or value. The proper viewing of a good painting or the proper reading of a good poem likewise involve an active appreciation of a valuable expression of human thought and feeling that is already there in the poem or painting, and that is to be grasped and savored rather than brought about. It makes sense to strive for an increasingly clear and nuanced appreciation of such works of art, but it is essential not to lose sight of the fact that what one hopes to deepen and extend is a mode of appreciation of value, and the value that figures in the appreciation is not something to be brought about but something already wholly present. The fitting response to the value present in works of art or in friends is to delight in them, to strive for a keener and more thorough appreciation of them, and perhaps to feel a certain measure of gratitude for them.

This is not to say that it would be misguided to seek to create the social conditions within which friendships can multiply and flourish, but this counts as a worthy goal only because friends extend to each other a more basic appreciation of a goodness that each manifests to some degree, and that it makes little sense to try to produce. A similar point can be made in the case of the value of art. No doubt it is true that encounters with works of art are worth promoting, but they would be wholly worthless if they did not frequently involve a more direct appreciation of a kind of goodness already wholly present in the work of art.

It is, then, very much to Scanlon's credit that he rejects the widely accepted equation of being good and being "to be promoted." However, if my argument to this point is sound, Scanlon's early, purely naturalistic buck-passing conception of the good also stands in the way of a fully adequate account of what we have in mind when we speak of these values or believe ourselves to encounter them. This view makes room for the possibility that different kinds of value call for different kinds of actions, not all of them bent to the task of production. However, different values call not only for different kinds of actions but also for different forms of immediate appreciation, and naturalistic buck-passing cannot make sense of the many and varied forms of contemplative appreciation that different values can call for. Because it ties the experience of value too closely to the experience of reasons, it cannot make full sense of the direct apprehension of things as in various ways good or valuable. The naturalistic buck-passing conception of value could be elaborated without circularity if all values called for a single unvarying mode of appreciation, or if the proper appreciation of any value were always simply a matter of acting in some particular way. But different values call for different forms of appreciation, and these differences cannot plausibly be spelled out in terms of differences in the intentional actions that these values make apt.

Consider, for instance, the difference between the appreciation of the wittiness of a joke and the elegance of a mathematical proof, or between the goodness of

22 Scanlon, *What We Owe to Each Other*, 88–90.

a friend and the goodness of a work of art. This difference cannot be reduced to the different actions that these values make apt. It is true that it makes sense to laugh at what is witty, and perhaps to repeat it in future social situations, but the laughter is apt only as the expression of a more immediate sort of appreciation, and the repetitions are apt only as attempts to foster this more immediate appreciation in others. If all values called for a single, mono-tonal sort of appreciation, then it would be possible to explain what we appreciate under the heading of wit or elegance to someone who had no inkling of these values, but who did understand the generic idea of having a favorable attitude to things, simply by providing them with a list of natural properties in virtue of which things count as witty or elegant. Yet it seems obvious that this would not be sufficient to convey the idea of wit or elegance. A further, specifically evaluative insight is required in order to see what sort of value people find in those things they regard as witty or elegant. To see through the lens of these concepts is to see things as having a special kind of goodness or value that makes apt—that is, provides the right kinds of reasons for—a special sort of evaluative appreciation, an appreciation precisely of those values.[23] Citing the value itself plays an irreducible role in explaining the fittingness of the attitude that constitutes its proper appreciation.[24]

It is worth pausing to dwell on just how heavily we rely upon thick ethical concepts in our attempts to articulate a conception of the good life with sufficient subtlety and depth to inspire allegiance. Imagine trying to articulate a conception of the human good without speaking of the courageous and the cowardly, the fearsome and the comforting, the gracious and the ungracious, the majestic and the ridiculous, the wise and the foolish, the debauched and the noble, the superficial and the deep, the sentimental and the unsentimental, the boorish and the polite, the interesting and the boring or tiresome, the generous and the miserly, the human and the inhumane, the merciful and the merciless, the

---

[23] While I find a great deal to agree with in Jonathan Dancy's "defense" of thick ethical concepts, it seems to me that he errs in holding that the evaluative attitudes associated with these concepts are "fairly simple." Dancy's affirmation of this view goes hand-in-hand with his openness to buck-passing, but it seems to me to cut against his broader particularist enterprise. I don't see why we should expect the extension of thick concepts to resist capture in any non-circular general principle unless the associated evaluative attitude is complex enough to guide our case-by-case judgments concerning what does and what does not fall under the concept. See Dancy, "In Defense of Thick Concepts," in Peter A. French, Theodore E. Uehling Jr., and Howard K. Wettstein, eds., *Midwest Studies in Philosophy, Volume XX: Moral Concepts* (Notre Dame: University of Notre Dame Press, 1995), 263–79, especially 264. Dancy expresses his openness to the buck-passing view in the more recent book entitled *Ethics without Principles* (Oxford: Oxford University Press, 2004), 16–17.

[24] Here I am drawing upon the position set out in McDowell's "Values and Secondary Qualities" and Wiggins' "Towards a Sensible Subjectivism." We now see just how serious a mistake it is to lump the Scanlonian buck-passers together with the McDowell–Wiggins style sensibility theorists when considering the credentials of buck-passing. The most serious shortcoming of the buck-passing view is not shared by the sensibility theorists, and indeed it is precisely the sensibility theorists who have set out the most promising way to avoid this shortcoming.

modest or the conceited, the loving and the pitiless, not to mention betrayal and fidelity, kindness and unkindness, justice and injustice . . . The list could go on for pages. One would have already to be committed to a reductive theory of the human good, or a starkly scientistic ontology, to accept such self-imposed inarticulacy as a step towards genuine insight into the nature of the good life for human beings.

The core problem with naturalistic buck-passing turns out to be a version of the problem facing any theory of evaluation that insists upon a version (or perhaps it would be better, for reasons that will emerge in a moment, to call it a *cousin*) of the fact/value divide, one that I will call the description/evaluation divide. Those who believe in the description/evaluation divide believe that there is a strictly non-evaluative language of description (usually, the one required to set out the findings of the natural sciences) with which we can describe exhaustively any and all of the things that we can meaningfully evaluate. They believe that we must draw upon this language if we are to make clear what we are evaluating, and that we can draw upon this language so as to clarify the target of evaluation without already embarking upon evaluation. They believe, in other words, that all evaluation is cleanly divisible into two distinct operations, one involving the perceiving or imagining or remembering—at any rate, the representing—of the target of evaluation (e.g. a person, thing, action, event, or state of affairs) in purely descriptive terms, and the other consisting in the association of some value or disvalue with this naturalistically specifiable object of evaluation.

Among those who favor this picture, there is considerable disagreement about how best to conceive of the second operation. Some conceive of it in cognitive terms, as the discernment or apparent discernment of an extra-natural property of the state of affairs specified in the first moment—the property of being good,[25] or the property of having natural properties that provide reasons to pursue or promote or take a favorable attitude towards it,[26] or the (supposedly) ontologically suspect property of "objective prescriptivity."[27] Others conceive of this second moment in non-cognitive terms—for instance, as the expression of a conative attitude towards the thing,[28] or as an acceptance of principles that prescribe or proscribe or permit the thing.[29] Still others think of it in constructivist terms, as an assignment of value from some vantage point that has been constructed so as to render its verdicts "objectively valid" or "reasonable" though not strictly speaking true (that is, not corresponding to an independent

---

[25] G. E. Moore, *Principia Ethica* (Cambridge: Cambridge University Press, 1903), Section 13.

[26] Scanlon, *What We Owe to Each Other*, 95–100.

[27] J. L. Mackie, *Ethics: Inventing Right and Wrong* (New York: Penguin Books, 1977), 38–40, 95.

[28] Simon Blackburn, "How To Be an Ethical Antirealist," in Stephen Darwall, Allan Gibbard, and Peter Railton, eds., *Moral Discourse and Practice: Some Philosophical Approaches* (Oxford: Oxford University Press, 1996), 167–78.

[29] R. M. Hare, *Freedom and Reason* (Oxford: Oxford University Press, 1963), chapter 2. See also Allan Gibbard, *Wise Choices, Apt Feelings* (Cambridge: Harvard University Press, 1990), chapter 3.

order of evaluative facts).[30] But what all such views share is the thought that the two moments can be cleanly divided—that is, that description and evaluation are wholly separate mental activities, and that the work of evaluation always presupposes a prior and purely non-evaluative description of that which is being evaluated.

It is this latter, widely shared commitment that leads to the problems I have been trying to bring to light. Once the commitment is in place, it can seem tempting to follow Moore in positing a realm of non-natural facts that explain our reasons for seeking to produce or promote certain naturalistically specified states of affairs, yet on reflection this move does not help. The basic problem is not that this move is ontologically inflationary but that it violates the very ontological scruples that inspire it. Since normative reasons to attribute non-natural evaluative properties can only be found in the natural properties, the view's proponents must admit that nature is not denuded of normative properties after all, on pain of accepting that evaluation is wholly arbitrary. Furthermore, if they accept that goodness is a practical reason and that natural properties can give us reasons to attribute goodness, then they must admit that natural properties can be reasons to attribute a practical reason, and this seems to imply that natural properties can be practical reasons after all. The problem is that practical reasons seem to transfer their normative status to reasons for thinking that they exist, as when a reading of 120 mph on a car's speedometer gives one a (practical) reason to slow down by giving one reason to believe that one is going at an unsafe speed.

Naturalistic buck-passing will look tempting to those who hold constant to Moore's normatively denuded conception of the natural facts, reject skepticism about practical reasons, and see that Moore's invocation of non-natural evaluative properties does not help to explain the existence of these reasons. I have tried to show that we would do better to abandon the normatively denuded conception of nature, since it is not one that the natural scientist can consistently affirm, and since it yields viciously circular accounts of the content of what are ordinarily regarded as the most discerning of human evaluative attitudes. It is only in this way that we can vindicate the intelligibility of the evaluative concepts that human beings rely upon to make sense of the things that matter most to them, including their fellow human beings and their actions and lives, friendships and loves, pleasures and pains, the natural world and the works of architecture and industry, artifice and art around which their daily lives unfold.

The most pressing difficulty for those who insist upon a strict version of the description/evaluation divide is to make sense of what have come to be known, in contemporary philosophical literature, as thick evaluative concepts. Thick evaluative concepts show up as a well-defined category of concepts only

---

[30] See for instance John Rawls, "Kantian Constructivism in Moral Theory: The Dewey Lectures 1980," *Journal of Philosophy* 77 (1980), 515–72. See also Christine Korsgaard, *The Sources of Normativity* (Cambridge: Cambridge University Press, 1996), 19, 34–48 and 246–7.

if one accepts a distinction between description and evaluation. To say that an evaluative concept is thick is to say that it spans this divide. A paradigmatic example of a thick term is the concept of cruelty. To call something cruel is unmistakably to denounce it, but it also conveys a sense of the descriptive features of the action that make it bad. It indicates that the action involves an intention to inflict pain or suffering. By contrast, concepts such as good or bad, right or wrong, are regarded as thin because they seem to have little or no descriptive content. When we are told that something is good or right, this gives us little or no indication of its descriptive features.

If there is a clear distinction to be drawn here, and not a mere continuum, then presumably it can be drawn as follows: one can betray a failure to grasp a thick concept simply by sincerely applying it to certain descriptively specifiable objects, but one cannot display a failure to understand a thin concept in this way. Thus, for instance, one might show that one has failed to grasp the concept of cruelty by insisting, without special explanation or qualification, that it is cruel for parents to hug their children or see to it that their children have enough food to remain healthy. Common usage sets decisive limits on which naturalistically specified acts can coherently be counted as cruel. By contrast, one would not necessarily show a failure to understand the concept of the good or the right if one insisted, as against the view of the many, that it is good or right for parents who face no particular hardship to refuse to feed their children. One would simply show oneself to have an outrageous and perhaps despicable view about what is good or right.

As soon as we set out the distinction in this way, worries begin to arise. If someone said with apparent sincerity that it is wrong for rocks to roll down hills, or that the electrical charge of protons is intrinsically bad, it would be hard to know what to think. There are some things that, absent some very special explanation, cannot coherently be called good or bad, right or wrong. It might be held that within the range of things that can coherently be counted as good or bad (or right or wrong), one cannot show a misunderstanding of these concepts simply by professing non-standard views about which things are good or bad (or right or wrong). But even this seems dubious. Actions seem to fall within the range of applicability of all of these concepts. Yet if someone were to assert that randomly torturing strangers is right and refusing to do so is a grievous wrong, we might well conclude that he had not yet grasped the concept of rightness or wrongness (or perhaps of torture, or strangers, or randomness), or that by rightness and wrongness he did not mean *moral* rightness and *moral* wrongness (raising the question what else he might possibly mean). We cannot announce allegiance to just any set of prohibitions and obligations and call this our moral view. Understanding moral wrongness seems to involve understanding how intentional actions can constitute a special kind of affront to the *dignity* of other human beings. Torturing randomly selected human beings is a paradigmatic affront to human dignity. This is why one can show oneself to lack an understanding of moral wrongness by denying that such torture is ever morally wrong. It seems, then, that even the putatively thin concepts of moral rightness and wrongness span the description/evaluation divide.

This still leaves open the possibility that the concepts of goodness and badness might be genuinely thin. To test this hypothesis, we might ask what we would make of someone who uttered the phrase "The electrical charge of protons is intrinsically bad" or "The number 23 is intrinsically bad." Upon hearing such utterances, it would be natural to seek clarification by asking, "What in the world do you mean?" The obstacle to understanding is not that one cannot see what would induce a person to affirm a proposition whose meaning one understands. The problem is that one cannot see how to bring the notion of intrinsic badness to bear on such a thing as an electrical charge or a number. Such things can no more be bad or good than they can be green or blue. Some might be tempted to suppose that the problem is that goodness and badness can only be attributed to some more limited ontological category of things, such as e.g. states of affairs. But it is a state of affairs that protons have positive electrical charge, yet intrinsic goodness or badness cannot intelligibly be predicated of this state of affairs.

Perhaps these ruminations are evidence for the thesis that all attributions of goodness are at least implicitly attributive—that is, that there is no such thing as goodness full-stop, but only goodness *qua* this or that sort of thing. If this attributive conception of the good were combined with the thesis that not all kinds of things can be good or bad *qua* instances of the kinds of things they are, then it would explain why we might expect to find cases of things that cannot intelligibly be said to be intrinsically good or bad.[31] Whatever the explanation, we do seem to find such cases, and their existence is evidence that 'good' and 'bad' are not thin evaluative terms after all—that is, they do not function as moveable labels that can intelligibly be affixed to anything at all.[32]

It is not clear, then, that there really are any instances of genuinely thin evaluative concepts, concepts that could intelligibly be predicated of anything.

---

[31] Philippa Foot, a well-known proponent of the view that 'good' and 'bad' are attributive adjectives, hints at this possibility when she writes that "in most contexts, 'good' requires to be complemented by a noun that plays an essential role in determining whether we are able to speak of goodness rather than badness, or indeed of goodness or badness at all." See Foot, *Natural Goodness* (Oxford: Oxford University Press, 2001), 2.

[32] To make the point more credible, perhaps it will help to turn to a concrete case in which one of these predicates is used in a way that many people find exceedingly surprising. I have in mind Nietzsche's claim that morality is bad. How does Nietzsche make this claim intelligible? He does this by re-describing the moral conscience as a kind of self-directed cruelty that erodes our capacity for joy and threatens to sap our interest in life itself. It is because he portrays the soul of the morally conscientious person as masochistic, servile, and crawling with covert shades of the same vices that such people denounce in others, that we understand what Nietzsche means by his claim that morality is bad. He tells us what sort of badness he believes himself to see in it, and in doing this he makes ineliminable use of thicker and more specialized evaluative concepts. He also uses thick evaluative concepts to make clear what we are deprived of when we are bitten with moral guilt. We are deprived of joy, playfulness, and harmony of soul. (See Friedrich Nietzsche, *On the Genealogy of Morals*, Essay II.)

There is instead a continuum between those relatively thin evaluative concepts that give us very little help in picturing how things are and those relatively thick concepts that convey a more determinate picture of how things are. I know very little about what to expect if I am told by a reliable source that I should expect something good; I have a more determinate idea if I am told to expect something generous or cruel. Yet the existence of this continuum does not show that description and evaluation are wholly separate activities.

Some have held that we can make sense of our actual use of thick evaluative concepts only on the supposition that they can be decomposed into purely descriptive and evaluative semantic components. The strongest argument for this claim is due to Simon Blackburn, who grounds it in the observation that we sometimes use thick terms while canceling or even explicitly reversing the evaluative valence ordinarily associated with them.[33] This, he claims, could not be done if the evaluative connotation of a thick term were not separable from its descriptive meaning. Blackburn is quite right to insist that we sometimes denounce things under thick terms that are ordinarily commendatory, and vice versa. For instance, we might aptly criticize someone for being tactful in a situation that calls for blunt speech. This, however, does not show that the evaluative component of tact is a separable semantic element, and that one could become expert in using the term simply by mastering its descriptive extension. What it shows, instead, is that a full understanding of tact includes an understanding of its point and hence of its apt occasions. We form and revise our understanding of thick concepts such as tact as part of a more comprehensive quest to understand certain valuable human activities, including the comprehensive activity of living a good life in a community of fellow human beings. The value of tact comes into view against an emerging understanding of the importance, in a well-lived life, of an appropriate sensitivity to the opinions of others. Without any such sensitivity, we would have little hope of sustaining an accurate assessent of our own actions or of responding in real time to the needs and interests of others. Yet this sensitivity is susceptible to a range of perversions and malformations, ranging from a shame-ridden and paralyzing self-consciousness, to a base tendency towards conformism, to vanity and thirst for adulation. We regulate our sense of what calls for tact and what does not in light of a more comprehensive understanding of these perversions and malformations. We see, for instance, that we ought to be tactful when bluntness would serve only to feed an exaggerated and paralyzing shame, but that we need not attempt to be tactful when doing so would slake another's thirst for adulation or make us complicit in another's self-congratulatory fantasies or evil designs. In these latter cases, one might well be appropriately praised for dispensing with any attempt to be tactful, or even for mustering an appropriate tactlessness. But this variability in the evaluative

---

[33] Simon Blackburn, "Through Thick and Thin," *Proceedings of the Aristotelian Society*, Supplementary Volume 66 (1992), 285–99.

valence of the tactful and the tactless does not show that one can grasp the descriptive content of these concepts without understanding their evaluative dimensions. It shows, instead, that tact has a place—one whose bounds cannot fully be understood absent a comprehensive understanding of human flourishing in its individual and communal dimensions.

It is not a new idea that thick ethical concepts pose a serious problem for prescriptivists, emotivists, projectivists, and other non-cognitivists about value. The nub of the problem is that one cannot provide a phenomenologically adequate account of the full range of human evaluative attitudes without ineliminable reference to the values that these attitudes seem to bring into view. This bars the way to a narrowly naturalistic (i.e. purely descriptive or non-evaluative) explanation of these attitudes.[34] Non-cognitivists are forced to model our apprehension of thick concepts as an apprehension of some range of non-evaluative properties conjoined with a generic sense of approval or disapproval, yet this does not do justice to the way in which specific evaluative attitudes are mated with what appear, when we are subject to them, to be quite specific evaluative properties.[35]

If thick concepts really were dissociable into descriptive and evaluative semantic components, there would be no obvious way of crediting the thought that we might be going on in the same way—i.e. carrying forward with the application of a single concept—when moral maturation alters our sense of which (descriptively specified) entities fall under these concepts.[36] The continuity cannot be traced to the descriptive component of the concept, since this element has simply changed. Nor can it be grounded in the conjoined feelings of approval or disapproval, since they lack the internal complexity needed to function as guides to their own proper deployment. After all, these alleged sentimental or conative components are supposed to be purely evaluative, which is to say that they are supposed to be stripped of all descriptive or "world-guided" content. This is why we can get no sense of how to carry forward with them consistently if we turn our gaze to them in an effort to discern what they mean, or what features of the world make them apt. But this means that we can think of what appears to be progress in the discernment with which we use thick ethical concepts only as change and not as moral maturation or as the progressive attainment of insight.

[34] See Wiggins, "A Sensible Subjectivism," and McDowell, "Values and Secondary Qualities" and "Projection and Truth in Ethics."

[35] For example, the prominent ethical non-cognitivist Simon Blackburn constructs what he believes to be a representative thick evaluative concept from the descriptive term 'fat' conjoined with a downward arrow symbolizing generic disapproval to form the thick concept 'fat ↓.' By the lights of those who are realists about thick evaluative properties, this representation of the subject matter will appear altogether misleading. What is at issue between Blackburn and these realists is whether thick concepts really can be represented as amalgams of two separate semantic components, one descriptive and one evaluative. See Blackburn, "Through Thick and Thin," *Proceedings of the Aristotelian Society*, Supplement 66 (1992), 285–99.

[36] Jonathan Dancy makes a similar point in "In Defense of Thick Concepts," 272.

Of course, the non-cognitivist can happily admit that one might find all sorts of reasons *external* to one's understanding of a particular thick concept to alter one's way of using that concept. For instance, if one suddenly fell under the thumb of a brutal tyrant, it might be deemed "prudent" (in a mean and feckless sort of way) to make over one's sense of the courageous so as to reduce the likelihood of the kind of public defiance that would likely lead to jail if not to an early grave. Someone might claim that such a change is rational, or at least that it has an obvious rationale. Yet this sort of case does not count as going on in the same way, precisely because the modification is recommended by a consideration that is wholly external to one's sense of the value that the thick concept in question (that is, courage) is supposed to track.

The lesson here is that if thick terms really were dissociable into description and evaluation (as the non-cognitivist must suppose), they would be wholly unsuited to play the role they are commonly believed to play in the attainment of a mature evaluative outlook. It seems that one of the central ways that we arrive at a deeper and more finely articulated picture of how to live is by gaining a more discerning understanding of the meaning and proper application of the array of thick evaluative concepts on which we have been nurtured. Yet if the non-cognitivist were right, thick ethical concepts could not play a central role in any process deserving to be called learning or maturation. To return to a refrain from Chapter 2, here again we see how certain prevailing philosophical ideas require that we demote what seems to be growth to the less exalted status of mere change.

More specifically, non-cognitivism does violence to our conviction that there is a vast difference between a clever child's understanding of key ethical concepts such as justice, generosity, or courage and a wise elder's understanding of those same concepts. By non-cognitivist lights, this difference is rather slight. After all, a clever child is perfectly capable of primitive and internally unstructured feelings of approval and disapproval, and is also capable of grasping relatively complicated descriptive predicates. If a wise understanding of a particular thick ethical concept were simply a matter of conjoining a primitive feeling with the right descriptive predicate, there would be no reason in principle why a sufficiently lucky or clever child could not immediately come to share this understanding. Life experience would be no more essential to grasping the concept of courage than to grasping straightforward descriptive concepts such as 'red' or 'tree.' Yet it seems not just unlikely but impossible for a child to attain a full grasp of the thick evaluative concepts that are central to full moral articulacy.[37] If this does not qualify as a *reductio* of non-cognitivism, it does at least serve to show that the view carries a

---

[37] I draw this argument from Cora Diamond's illuminating article on Iris Murdoch's critique of the fact–value divide. See Diamond, "We Are Perpetually Moralists: Iris Murdoch, Fact, and Value," in Maria Antonaccio and William Shweiker, eds., *Iris Murdoch and the Search for Human Goodness* (Chicago: University of Chicago Press, 1996), 79–109, especially 98–100.

higher price in the metric of self-understanding than is usually supposed. The acceptance of non-cognitivism entails the rejection of any intuitively appealing notion of wisdom, and the consequent renunciation of the narrative forms through which we make sense of the best sorts of human lives—the ones we ought to take as models for our own—as informed by continuous progression towards a deeper and more illuminating sense of how best to live.

Thick concepts, then, cause serious problems for non-cognitivists. What is not generally noticed is that they also pose serious problems for those who seek to reduce talk of value to talk of the reason-giving force of non-evaluative properties. While these latter figures recognize the real existence of practical reasons and the possibility of true beliefs about them, they cannot avail themselves of the full palette of evaluative concepts with which actual human beings actually strive to make sense of their lives. If they took to heart the full implications of their view and put these implications into practice, they would be unable to make good sense of their own most cherished values or of the unity of the most exemplary human lives. The naturalistic buck-passer's view is very nearly as unlivable as non-cognitivism.

THE CRITICAL ASSESSMENT AND REVISION OF THICK EVALUATIVE CONCEPTS

It might seem that if we insist upon the irreducibility of thick evaluative concepts, we threaten our ability to think critically about the putative goods they bring into view. If they could be divided into a descriptive and an evaluative component, we could raise the question whether the entities answering to the description merited the evaluation. If they cannot be so divided, then we cannot take this direct approach to critical assessment of the concept. On reflection, however, insisting upon the irreducibility of thick evaluative concepts does not rule out the possibility of critical appraisal of them. It simply alters the form that such critical assessments must take.

To see this, it will help to have some working examples of seemingly thick evaluative concepts that many have come to regard as a source of sham evaluations, such as the *uppity* or the *ladylike*. What would it take to vindicate the widespread sense that these concepts do not track real values but sham values, and that they ought to be discarded? As I see it, this sense could be vindicated by a debunking explanation of the rise and staying power of these concepts. A successful debunking explanation would offer an account of the evaluative outlook that gains expression through the concept without irreducible reference to the putative value that the evaluative outlook brings into view. That is, it would show the concept to have precisely the structure that proponents of the description/evaluation divide take all thick evaluative concepts to have. It would then have to show that this disposition is in some specific way bad, and this would seem to require the invocation of other thick evaluative concepts.

For instance, the male tendency to find the ladylike appealing might be traced to the way in which it bolsters a dominant social role for males, flatters the male ego, and gratifies male sexual fantasies. The female tendency to find the ladylike appealing might be traced to the tendency of ladylike behavior to win social approval and favorable treatment from an ascendant gender-defined class, to incite male sexual desires, and to provide a degree of control over males via the incitement and manipulation of their sexual desires. If the rise and the characteristic patterns of use of the concept of the ladylike can be explained by reference to these sorts of considerations, then it can be explained without irreducible reference to the property of ladylikeness. The appeal of the concept might then be traced largely to the appeal of such properties as the power-enhancing, the flattering, the sexually gratifying, and the wealth-promoting. We can then ask whether it is good to make use of a way of talking that shapes people's characters in ways that empower and gratify some human beings while providing residual rewards to those who are most adept in resculpting their mode of being so as to confer such gratification. If we conclude that making use of such a concept is unjust, or that it promotes alienation or inauthenticity or heteronomy or superficiality, then we might well have good reason to stop talking in this way.

Even if one believes, as I do, that it would be best for us to stop talking of the ladylike, it seems dubious to suppose that there is nothing of genuine value captured by talk of the ladylike. It seems far more plausible to suppose that there are aspects of the behavior we call ladylike that are genuinely good, but that their goodness does not depend upon their being instantiated by women. These genuine goods might more aptly be specified and encouraged by using such concepts as the gentle, the tender, the accommodating, or the consoling.[38]

A similar point might be me about many other suspect evaluative concepts, including for instance the concept of the lewd. This is the concept that Blackburn uses as his primary example in attempting to show that the evaluative and descriptive elements of thick evaluative concepts can be cleaved apart.[39] I think Blackburn is right that the lewdness of a performance can be the very thing that makes it good. But this, I think, is because the term 'lewd' tends to function as a tool for policing the boundaries of bourgeois taste rather than as the name of a genuine kind of badness. That is, calling something lewd often serves only to locate it beyond the bounds of *de facto* public approval, in the direction of the crassly sexual, while conveying the unearned implication that it is to be denounced simply on that score. One can call this practice into question, or express frustration at the constrictions on personal behavior that it

---

[38] I owe this point to Ty Landrum, who raised it during a recent seminar discussion.
[39] Blackburn, "Through Thick and Thin."

seeks to enforce, by commending something under the term 'lewd.' This does not mean that there is no genuine thick evaluative property that the term could conceivably be used to track. It means only that accepted usage of the term tracks a non-evaluative property as if it were an evaluative property. This is why this particular term's evaluative connotations can easily seem like an unearned afterthought.

CONCLUDING REMARKS ON MORAL REASONS AND MORAL VALUE

We have seen that we cannot do away with talk of goodness or value in favor of talk of reasons, on pain of evaluative inarticulacy and forfeiture of our ordinary sense of moral maturation and growth. Appearances of value are essential to the rationalizing explanation of human actions and also to our sense of the point and value—including the expressive value—of many of the actions that we find morally exemplary. These findings suggest that if we are to vindicate the notion that human actions can have point or value, we will have to credit the idea that appearances of value are not bound to be delusory but might sometimes track genuine values. Further, if we are to vindicate the idea that human actions sometimes have moral point or moral value, we cannot dismiss as delusory the appearances of value that are expressed in those actions that we find particularly morally laudable. This will require that we credit the idea that human beings have a special sort of value, and hence fall within the proper scope of that sort of concern we call moral.

6

Against Modern Dualism about the Good

Those who make self-love a matter for reproach ascribe it to those who award the biggest share in money, honours and bodily pleasures to themselves . . . Those who are greedy for these goods gratify their appetites and in general their feelings and the non-rational part of the soul; and since this is the character of the many, the application of the term ['self-love'] is derived from the most frequent [kind of self-love], which is base. This type of self-lover, then, is justifiably reproached. And plainly it is the person who awards himself these goods whom the many habitually call a self-lover. For if someone is always eager to excel everyone in doing just or temperate actions or any others expressing the virtues, and in general always gains for himself what is fine, no one will call him a self-lover or blame him for it. However, it is this more than the other sort of person who seems to be a self-lover. At any rate he awards himself what is finest and best of all, and gratifies the most controlling part of himself, obeying it in everything.

(Aristotle)[1]

QUESTIONING MODERN DUALISM ABOUT THE GOOD

It is very nearly a fixed point within contemporary analytic philosophy that practical rationality calls for the efficient pursuit of that which is good for oneself. By contrast, it is a hotly disputed question whether practical reason demands anything more—for instance, whether it demands pursuit of what is good impersonally, or observance of moral limitations on the pursuit of prudential goods. This dispute takes its shape from a deeper background agreement that there is a fundamental schism within the domain of the good—a deep distinction between one kind of goodness (sometimes called "prudential goodness") that is in some sense indexed to those particular persons whose good it is, and another kind of goodness that is not indexed to particular persons. The sort of goodness possessed by morally exemplary actions is generally taken to fall under the latter category.

---

[1] Aristotle, *Nicomachean Ethics*, translated by Terence Irwin (Indianapolis: Hackett Publishing Company, 1985), 1168b16–33.

This way of understanding the realm of the good raises a serious question about the deliberative authority of moral considerations. Since moral goodness seems to fall within the category of the impersonally good, one cannot infer from the fact that an action would be morally good that it would be the least bit good *for* the person in a position to do it. Indeed, we are intuitively inclined to think that in some cases morality requires us to do things that are downright bad for ourselves. If the normative authority of the good-for-oneself is clearer and more obvious than that of the impersonally good, then these cases pose a threat to the normative authority of morality. And if a proper acknowledgment of our moral duty always requires that we acknowledge that we are bound by it whether or not it conflicts with our own good, then this threat to the authority of morality will not be confined to circumstances that call for self-sacrifice. It will be omnipresent. Modern moral philosophy has been riveted by this sort of conflict between self-interest and morality, and has returned again and again to the question of whether the normativity of morality can be defended in the face of this threat.

Some think that there is no possibility of a reasoned conclusion of conflicts between the demands of prudence and the demands of morality, and that any attempt to effect such a resolution will inevitably result in mere table-thumping. They think, in other words, that norms of self-love can be defended only on grounds that already presuppose the authority of prudential considerations, and that moral norms can be defended only by invoking convictions that are at least implicitly moral. This idea that practical reason is irrecoverably riven between personal and impersonal goods, and that this poses an intractable threat to the authority of morality, is associated in particular with Henry Sidgwick. In his seminal late nineteenth-century work *The Methods of Ethics*, Sidgwick asserts a fundamental principle of practical reason to the effect that one ought to aim at one's own maximal happiness, conceived along hedonistic lines.[2] He also maintains that we cannot reasonably regard our own happiness as good unless we recognize the equal value of the happiness of other persons.[3] This leads him to put forward a second principle of practical reason requiring that we do what we believe to be maximally conducive to universal happiness. Sidgwick regards both principles as equally fundamental, and he recognizes that unless we posit a divine dispensation of justice in the afterlife, they sometimes conflict. In such cases, Sidgwick claims, practical reason is divided against itself and there is no higher-level principle of rationality to which the conflict can be referred for resolution.

Sidgwick calls this schism between the rational demands of impersonal and personal reasons *the dualism of practical reason*, and he regards it as a

---

[2] Henry Sidgwick, *The Methods of Ethics*, 7th edn (Indianapolis: Hackett Publishing Company, 1981; first published 1907), 120–1.

[3] *Ibid.*, 403.

genuine discovery of modern philosophy. Sidgwick attributes this discovery to Bishop Joseph Butler, but he claims that it was anticipated in William Wollaston's *Religion of Nature Delineated* (1722), where for the first time we find a recognition that moral goodness and individual happiness are "two essentially distinct objects of rational pursuit and investigation."[4] In virtue of this discovery, Sidgwick maintains, modern philosophical ethics was able to see its way past a basic confusion that haunted "the earlier age of ethical thought which Greek philosophy represents."[5] According to Sidgwick, the Greeks (by which he seems to have meant: Plato and Aristotle) mistakenly believed that virtuous acts were "good *for the agent*" (Sidgwick's emphasis) even when their consequences "would be on the whole painful to him—as (*e.g.*) a heroic exchange of a life full of happiness for a painful death at the call of duty."[6] This belief was due to "a confusion of thought between what it is reasonable for an individual to desire, when he considers his own existence alone, and what he must recognize as reasonably to be desired, when he takes the point of view of a larger whole."[7] For Sidgwick, this means that it is due to a confusion about the good, since he defines the good as that which there is reason to desire.[8] Thus he maintains that to modern readers, Socrates' attempt to vindicate the virtues is aptly seen as "a more or less dexterous sophistry, playing on a confusion of thought latent in the common notion of good."[9] This is a particularly direct and biting criticism, given that Socrates was a strident critic of sophistical speech, regarding it as vicious and as antithetical to the philosophical life.

There can be little doubt that Sidgwick has located a sea change of some sort in Western conceptions of the good and its bearing on action. The rise of some form or another of dualism about the good has been pivotal in providing modern moral philosophy with a working sense of its subject matter. Its task is widely thought to be that of vindicating or debunking the notion that there is a distinct, impersonal kind of goodness in limiting one's pursuit of one's own good so as to accommodate and perhaps even to promote the similar self-interested pursuits of others. Because of this background idea, the morally good or right appears to protrude as a subject matter of its own, and many theorists have believed that it can be theorized in isolation from a broader inquiry into the good life for individual human beings. This dualistic idea of the good shows up in the Kantian idea of the will as torn between allegiance to two highest-level principles: the moral law, adherence to which makes for a good will; and the principle of self-love, which calls for the efficient pursuit of that which is good for oneself in the sense of satisfying one's desires and hence augmenting one's happiness. This same dualistic notion of the good conditions the contemporary theory and

---

[4] See Henry Sidgwick, *Outlines of the History of Ethics*, 197.

[5] Sidgwick, *The Methods of Ethics*, 404.   [6] *Ibid.*, 404.   [7] *Ibid.*, 405.

[8] *Ibid.*, 112–13 and Thomas Hurka, "Moore in the Middle" in *Ethics* 113 (April 2003), 599–628, esp. 603.

[9] Sidgwick, *The Methods of Ethics*, 405n.

practice of liberal-democratic politics in the form of a distinction between the public realm governed by the impersonal dictates of justice and a private realm within which citizens are free to pursue their personal conceptions of the good. A similar dualism surfaces in utilitarian thought in the form of a residual doubt about whether human beings could really direct all of their efforts at aggregate utility maximization without eclipsing the personal projects and commitments that make human life valuable in the first place. This latter sort of dualism can be seen, too, in the many offspring of utilitarianism that have sprouted up around the contemporary academy, including the "law and economics" movement in legal theory and cost–benefit analysis in public policy.

Despite the vast historical influence and growing contemporary prestige of broadly dualistic conceptions of the good, their rise is not a simple story of progress or discovery. Indeed, to the extent that so complex and multi-faceted a historical change can be discussed as a unity, it ought to be regarded instead as a story of encroaching confusion. Plato and Aristotle can be read as having offered a diagnosis of our propensity to fall into precisely this sort of confusion, but only if we cease to read their main claims through the lens of this confusion itself.

MODERN DUALISM VERSUS ANCIENT MONISM

It is not easy to put one's finger on the blind spot in Greek ethics that Sidgwick thinks we moderns have overcome. Sidgwick's remarks make little sense unless the Greeks are credited with having had some sort of grasp—even if not a perfectly clear and unwavering one—of the distinction between what is good *for* a person and what it is good in a more impersonal sense for that person to do or to be. After all, both Plato and Aristotle held that the virtues were fine or admirable (*kalos*), and this seems to mean that the virtues are properly regarded as good or valuable from an impersonal point of view. If the Greeks also affirmed the thesis that the virtues are invariably good for their possessors, then they must have had a grasp of both of the kinds of goodness that Sidgwick distinguishes, hence the modern achievement cannot consist merely in distinguishing these kinds of goodness. It must consist, instead, in seeing what follows from the distinction, or in taking care not to trade on it. Perhaps this is what induces Sidgwick to accuse Socrates (and presumably by extension Plato) of *sophistry* rather than mere blindness or innocent confusion.

At one point, Sidgwick claims that "in the whole ethical controversy of ancient Greece . . . it was assumed on all sides that a rational individual would make the pursuit of his own good his supreme aim: the controverted question was whether this Good was rightly conceived as Pleasure or Virtue, or any *tertium quid*."[10]

---

[10] *Ibid.*, 92 (see also 172).

This passage suggests a somewhat more coherent picture of the putative blind spot in Greek ethics. On this reading, Sidgwick's claim is that the Greeks failed to see that there are two different standards—one impersonal and altruistic, the other person-relative and egoistic—by which we might establish the rational credentials of a course of action, character trait, or way of life. For this reason, the Greeks sought to vindicate the virtues by showing that their possession is invariably *good for* their possessors. What Wollaston and Butler discovered was that the virtues might be vindicated by showing that they are good in an impersonal sense, even if they are not invariably good for their possessors.

The same interpretation of the Greeks, if not the same criticism, is favored today by the prominent historian of philosophy Terence Irwin. Irwin agrees with Sidgwick that dualism about the good is a distinctively modern notion, wholly foreign to the work of Plato and Aristotle, and that the Greeks attempted to vindicate the choice-worthiness of the virtues by showing them to be good for their possessors. "They encourage us to reason about what promotes our happiness; in reasoning about this we reason about what achieves our own interest; and so our reasoning is prudential."[11]

If this is Sidgwick's criticism of the Greeks, it must be admitted that it has a certain *prima-facie* appeal, especially in the case of Aristotle. When we read *Nicomachean Ethics* through modern eyes, we are likely to be struck by just how motley an array of character traits are listed among the ethical virtues. We moderns tend to think of justice and truthfulness as morally required whether or not they make their possessor happy, while we tend to think of wit and friendliness as morally optional traits whose value lies in the pleasure they give to their possessors and a small circle of intimates. Yet Aristotle counts all of these traits as ethical virtues, and he offers a unified theoretical account of their value—an account that portrays all of them as necessary for, and properly actualized in, the flourishing of their possessor. He does not recognize a realm of person-relative or prudential goods whose pursuit must be limited if one is to exemplify seemingly moral virtues such as justice, kindness, and truthfulness. For this reason, he seems both to be doing and not to be doing what we moderns think of as moral philosophy. This conceptual misalignment is what lies beneath Elizabeth Anscombe's comment that those who mouth words about Aristotle's "moral" views "must be very imperceptive" if they do not constantly feel as if "the teeth don't come together in a proper bite."[12]

---

[11] Terence Irwin, "Prudence and Morality in Greek Ethics," *Ethics* 105 (1995), 284–95; quote 286. This quote sets out a core element of what Irwin calls the "traditional" reading of Plato and Aristotle. Irwin makes clear that he favors this interpretation. He also makes clear that on this interpretation, one cannot vindicate the virtues by showing them to be good or valuable from an impersonal point of view. As he puts it at the outset of the article (284): "there is no reason to assume that whatever is good and valuable from some point of view is thereby good for the agent who possesses it."

[12] Elizabeth Anscombe, "Modern Moral Philosophy," in *The Collected Philosophical Papers of G.E.M. Anscombe, Volume Three: Ethics, Religion and Politics* (Oxford: Basil Blackwell, 1981), 26–42; 26.

On this interpretation, Sidgwick's pocket history of ethics can be put as follows. The Greeks were feeling their way to a proper specification of the subject matter of moral theory but had not yet drawn the field's boundaries in a way that would permit the unified theoretical account to which they aspired. This conceptual confusion is overcome in the modern era, and this reframes the subject matter of moral philosophy in a way that conduces to greater philosophical insight. The boundary lines are redrawn in such a way as to permit separate inquiries into one's own good and the impersonally good, including in particular that portion of the impersonally good that we call the morally good. This, in turn, is said to afford more illuminating accounts of these distinct practical concerns and the relation between them. It might be thought to count in favor of this diagnosis that Ancient Greek lacked any straightforward equivalent for the modern English term 'morality.'

Before we settle upon this decidedly self-congratulatory outline of the history of ethics, we might ask whether an equally convincing account of progress in ethical thought might not have been available if this history had unfolded in reverse chronological order, beginning with Sidgwickian dualism and ending with Greek monism. The question, at heart, is whether we can see Greek monism as resulting from clear-headed philosophical insight into the pitfalls of one or both of the poles of Sidgwickian dualism. No sooner have we framed this question than we are likely to be struck by a similarity between the outlook of the two great anti-moralists in Plato's dialogues, Callicles and Thrasymachus, and the modern proponents of the dualism of practical reason. Callicles and Thrasymachus both claim that the conventional virtues often undermine the interests of their possessors while serving the interests of the many. This is hardly to say that they affirm Sidgwickian dualism, since they do not assign normative authority to the interests of the many and consequently they denounce the conventional virtues as mere markers of gullibility or servility. However, they do purport to have exposed a hidden dualism in popular *beliefs* about the good, some of which are keyed to genuine self-interest while others are the covert agents of the interests of the many.

The Sidgwickian response to this sort of challenge to the conventional virtues would be to accept the truth of the charge that the virtues serve the aggregated interests of the many rather than the particular interests of their possessors, but to insist that this does not undermine their normative authority since we all have good reason to further the interests of the many. This clearly is not the response offered by Socrates. But then, what sort of response *does* Socrates offer? Sidgwick suggests an answer in the above-quoted passage when he claims that in Greek ethics, "it was assumed on all sides that a rational individual would make the pursuit of his own good his supreme aim." As noted above, Irwin regards this as the traditional reading of Plato and Aristotle, and as the correct one.[13] On this reading, Socrates and his interlocutors agreed about the rules of the

---

[13] Irwin, "Prudence and Morality in Greek Ethics," 284.

game for vindicating the virtues: what has to be shown is that the virtues serve the self-interest of their possessors. Their disagreement centers on whether the virtues pass this test. Socrates attempts to answer Callicles and Thrasymachus by showing that they do.

This way of portraying the main arguments of the *Gorgias* and *Republic* is misleading. It threatens to lose track of a fundamental difference between the subjective pole of the modern dualistic conception of the good and the kind of goodness that Socrates purports to find in the virtues. This latter sort of goodness does not align neatly with either pole of the dualistic conception of the good. It represents a wholesale alternative to modern dualism rather than a mere failure to notice one of its poles. What is at stake in these dialogues is how best to understand the human self, its internal structure, its boundaries, its proper function, and its genuine interests. About these matters, Socrates disagrees in the most radical way with Callicles and Thrasymachus. Both Callicles and Thrasymachus think that there is such a thing as a self that might be vicious or virtuous, and that we can intelligibly ask whether the interests of a given self are better promoted by conventionally virtuous action or conventionally vicious action. Socrates argues, by contrast, that the virtues are good in the sense that they actualize the proper potentiality of their possessors, pulling them together as full-fledged instances of the human kind. Vice, by contrast, is dissolution. To the degree that one becomes vicious, to that degree one comes undone as a coherently unified agent to whom interests can intelligibly be attributed.

The virtues order the human psyche so that its distinguishing capacity for *logos*—that is, for thought and speech—is actualized according to its own internal standards rather than serving, and ultimately being dissipated by, an array of alien psychological drives. This is the heart of Socrates' critique, in the Gorgias, of rhetoric as practiced by his contemporaries.[14] The rhetorician makes use of the distinctively human capacity for thought and speech as a mere means of persuasion, which in turn is bent to the task of satisfying desires for pleasure or wealth or power. This alters the proper relation between the rhetorician and his own tongue, since he views his words as calculated instruments for re-making the world, and thereby cannot make use of them as the medium of the continuous effort of self-expression through which humans can lend clarity and articulacy to their evolving thoughts and the life activities conjoined with these thoughts. The practice of rhetoric effectively subverts a capacity whose proper use is essential to the highest human activities, including the activity of self-formation through careful reflection, with the effect that one is continuously shaped by one's sense

---

[14] I say "as practiced by his contemporaries" because, as my colleague Dan Devereux has pointed out to me, Socrates refers at several points in the *Gorgias* to a "true art of rhetoric" that is guided by an understanding of the soul and its real needs, and that consequently can provide sound reasons for the oratory it produces. The relevant passages of the *Gorgias*, as cited in an unpublished manuscript by Devereux, include 502e–503b, 504d–e, 517a, and 522d–e.

of what others would find flattering. In trying to become the master of others, the rhetorician becomes their puppet.[15]

The equation between vice and dissolution is developed in a slightly different and somewhat more picturesque way in Books VIII and IX of the *Republic*, where Socrates portrays a series of increasingly vicious kinds of psyches, each marked by increasing levels of intra-psychic conflict and disorder. This elaborate foray into moral psychology is supposed to help us see that the more vicious one becomes, the less sense it will make to call the utterances and motions emanating from one's body *one's own*. Plato offers a metaphorical portrayal of the tyrannical soul as a fusion of three warring parts: a multi-colored beast with a ring of heads (representing an undisciplined array of competing desires), an outsized and well-fed lion (representing an unreasoned *thumos*—that is, an anger-tinged thirst for triumph and public honor) and a starved and weakened human being (representing the capacity for reasoned thought and action). The reasoned capacity is dragged about and bitten ceaselessly by a menagerie of bestial "soul-mates," and this keeps it in a wholly passive form, unable to express itself even by mounting an active resistance to the psychological forces that master it.[16] These three inseparably fused parts of the vicious psyche are enclosed in the outward form of a human being, giving the illusion of a single unified self rather than a chaotic multiplicity. But the interests that we are tempted to assign to this seemingly unified self are in fact the interests of no single agent or self, and the interests of the (potential) self lie in the sort of wholesale reordering of the entire psyche that would constitute it as a locus of self-initiated activity—that is, as an agent. Hence it is true only in an abstract and potentially misleading sense that all parties to these dialogues agree that the virtues can be vindicated only if they can be shown to serve the self-interest of their possessors. The virtues are not possessed, if by a possession we mean something that one might possibly be wholly without. They are structural constituents of selves, in whose utter absence we cannot bring into view a self but only a chaotic array of drives. Hence in the utter absence of the virtues we cannot speak straightforwardly of a self whose interest lies in their possession.

It is tempting to think of the remnant of humanity in the Platonic picture of the vicious psyche as itself a fully constituted human self to whom interests can unproblematically be assigned. This would be a mistake. Plato's point in crafting this image is to help us see the radically dissolute constitution of the tyrant, not to suggest that the tyrant's true self is an inner homunculus that might itself be perfectly well-constituted but that has the misfortune of being fused to a bevy of ravenous beasts. If we misread Plato's metaphor in that way, this would open the possibility that the tyrant's true self could be as well-constituted and

---

[15] Plato, *Gorgias*, 481c–e.
[16] Plato, *Republic*, 588b–589a. A similar if far less vivid idea of the connection between virtue and psychic unity or order can be found in the *Gorgias*, 506d–507c.

as impervious to harm from his hidden tormentors as the virtuous man on the rack from his visible tormentors. But the whole point of the metaphor is to picture the tyrant as badly constituted. The tyrant's predicament is not that he has been abducted by wholly alien forces that are subjecting him to a kind of covert torture—a fate consistent with a greatly admirable character. The tyrant's problem is that he (a singular pronoun that, at the limiting case of evil, singles out only an aspiration) has come undone; he has fractured into a multiplicity of warring drives, and consequently has lost—or at least very nearly lost—the capacity for self-initiated activity.

It is not flatly wrong to say that Plato attempts to meet the challenge of showing that the virtues are good for their possessors, but it is potentially misleading, since he tries to meet this challenge precisely by overturning a widespread understanding of its meaning. He does not seek to meet this challenge in the form in which it is understood by such figures as Callicles and Thrasymachus, or even by less hostile and more philosophically inclined interlocutors such as Gorgias, Glaucon, and Adeimantus. Plato tries to show that the virtues are "good for their possessors" in a sense that relies upon and vindicates their impersonal goodness. He tries to show that the virtues are good because they bring the human soul into closer proximity to its ideal state, the state that permits it to perform its proper function of leading a deliberate life, directed by reason.[17] This sort of goodness will be discernible as goodness by anyone who has a proper understanding of the kind of creature that human beings are, since the human form, like all forms, is grasped in light of the good, and exhibits all excellences proper to the human kind. Such goodness, then, is not associated with a particular personal outlook or standpoint. Nor does this sort of goodness have the character of a detachable possession that could be transferred to others, or a zero-sum benefit that imposes tangible costs on others. On the contrary, those who are good are inclined by their love of the good to engage in exchanges with others that conduce to the good of others, and to avoid actions that will make others less good. The virtues of any given person are properly acknowledged as good from all social standpoints.

The Platonic view, then, vindicates the impersonal goodness of the virtues, yet preserves the idea that one has a highly personal stake in sustaining and deepening one's own virtues, since one thereby sustains or deepens one's coherence as a self capable of harmonious and unreserved activity. This highly personal stake, though, does not imply that the virtues have two kinds of goodness or value, one personal and the other impersonal. To say that one's own virtues are especially good for oneself is not to say that one properly regards them as having a special kind of *goodness* that the virtues of others do not have, but rather that one has an especially intimate *relation* to their goodness. One's virtues are good because they are essential to *one's own* constitution as a human being capable of harmonious and unreserved activity, and by extension capable of leading a

---

[17] Plato, *Republic*, 353d–e.

coherent life. The virtues of others have the same kind of *goodness*: they are essential to constituting others as human beings with these capacities. Hence anything that counts as my own good, or as good for me, is also properly seen as good from an impersonal perspective. There is no deep distinction between personal and impersonal goods.

The same point can be approached via some broad-brush observations concerning the role of apprehending the form of the good in the Platonic idea of the perfected human psyche. For Plato, one cannot see the good except perhaps in veiling shadows unless and until one has undergone a long training aimed at harmonizing the various parts of one's soul under the control of one's reason. But likewise, one cannot fully perfect one's constitution except by attaining progressively clearer intimations of the good, since it is by the light of the form of the good that one sees how one ought to be and to live. Apprehending the good is essential not only to what we would call practical understanding but also to theoretical understanding, since theoretical understanding involves a grasp of the forms, and the genuine contours of each form are lit up by the good.[18] A full apprehension of the form of the good goes hand-in-hand with apprehension of the contours of all other forms, including that of the true or properly constituted city and of the true or properly constituted soul. Nor can one's soul be perfect before one has attained understanding of this objective and unvarying sort of goodness. Just as the city is not perfect if its leaders lack understanding of the good but happen by good fortune to make good decisions anyway, so too a soul is not perfect unless its proper leader (that is, its reasoned part) has attained genuine understanding of the good.

There is, then, a pleasingly reciprocal relation between the form or idea of the good and one's own attainment of goodness. The good is that in the light of which all things are known, including one's proper form. And one's own proper form is precisely the form that permits one to see clearly and act reliably by the light of the good, since it places the reasoned part of the soul firmly in control of one's thoughts and other activities, while removing various psychic distractions that might interfere with apprehension of the good. The deepening of one's grasp of the good is one side of a two-sided coin; the other side is a progressive harmonization of one's psyche, consisting in an expansion of one's capacity to know and delight in the goodness manifest in one's unfolding activities, thereby making possible a full and unimpeded presence in those activities. Yet it is a timeless, objective, and impersonal good by whose light one's constitution is harmonized. It is not perspectival, nor is it relative to one's own desires, pleasures, or idiosyncratic pursuits. It is through our grasp of it that we determine whether the characters of particular persons are well-constituted and whether their lives are going well or badly. Once again, we see that Platonic talk of a person's

---

[18] This is the point of Plato's famous analogy between the sun in the visible world and the form of the good in the world of thought. See the *Republic*, 508–9.

own good, or of what is good for a person, does not pick out a special *kind* of goodness. Rather, it picks out a special *relation* that a person has to the human good when that person apprehends the good and is brought into a unity, hence made to instantiate the good, as a concomitant of that very apprehension.

If the Platonic and Aristotelian justifications of the virtues were really prudential, as Sidgwick and Irwin suppose, then we would expect the Platonic philosopher and the Aristotelian *phronimos* always to reason prudentially about what to do. This expectation would be misplaced if the virtues were seen as traits that are valuable on the whole yet sometimes manifest themselves in actions that lack whatever sort of goodness it is that makes the virtues valuable. It would also be misplaced if the virtues were traits that yielded good actions without imparting an appreciation of what it is that makes these actions good. There is, however, no sign of either view in Plato or Aristotle. They seem to have held that the virtues conduce to a clear apprehension of the good and that the distinctive value associated with the virtues is realized in each and every virtuous action. What this means is that if Sidgwick and Irwin were right to suppose that Plato and Aristotle assigned a purely prudential value to the virtues, we should expect them to portray the virtuous person as someone who invariably chooses actions under the aspect of the prudentially good. It is clear, however, that neither philosopher portrays the deliberation of the virtuous in this way.

Consider, for instance, Socrates' portrayal of the true philosopher's reasoning about political rule—both about whether to accept such rule when told to do so, and about how to discharge the responsibilities associated with such rule once he has assumed office. If the wise philosopher owes his grasp of the forms to the education and training that has been bestowed upon him by a well-constituted state, then it can justly be demanded of him that he rule the city. Since this just demand is directed to a person who is just, the demand will be accepted.[19] But when he accepts the demand, he does not do this in the name of his own good. He does it for the good of the city, and in a sense (one that we will have to qualify carefully) he acts against his personal preferences.[20] If he accepted eagerly, out of a positive desire to rule, he would not be a fit ruler. He is a fit ruler only if he would prefer to have been left alone to spend his time in pure contemplation, and agrees to rule only because the city has demanded this of him and he cannot refuse this demand without manifesting ingratitude to the city for having made him what he is.[21] His grasp of the form of the good is put to use in seeing that he must do this, but what he grasps—at least in the first instance—is a fact about

[19] Plato, *Republic*, 520a–e.

[20] See Plato, *Republic*, 519e–520a for textual confirmation that the demand conduces to the good of the city yet does not maximize the happiness of the rulers (or any other class of citizens). Further on, at 521a–b, Plato makes clear that the ideal ruler would prefer to be permitted to spend his time in pure philosophical contemplation.

[21] Plato, *Republic*, 521a–b.

justice in the city. This is what convinces him that he would be ungrateful and vicious to refuse to rule.

Once he sees this, something further becomes true of him. It becomes true of him that his own good no longer lies in refusing to rule and spending his time instead in contemplation of or dialectical conversation about the forms. Given that the city has demanded that he serve as ruler, it is no longer possible for him to choose the perfect life of innocent and pure contemplation, but only the shameful life of ungrateful and defiant insistence upon contemplation. He might sensibly regret that the former life is no longer available to him, and he might wish that the demand to rule had not been made. But once it has been made, it is no longer true of him that his life will go better if he refuses it. To refuse the demand would be to lead a shamefully irresponsible life. Once he sees this, it is no longer good *for him* to refuse to rule, since this would be tantamount to refusing the verdict of the reasoned part of his psyche, hence would disorder his psyche by deposing his reasoned part from its proper position of leadership. It is crucial to notice, however, that this act would count as the disordering of his psyche only because he has judged that it would be wrong for other reasons. The ground-level practical judgment here is not about the proper ordering of his psyche but the proper ordering of the city. In particular, it is a judgment about what citizens can demand of each other and about when these demands cannot justly be refused. The proper ordering of the psyche conduces to this judgment, and is perpetuated by making and acting on it, but it is not the subject matter of this judgment.

The same pattern of practical reasoning surfaces in the *Crito*, where Socrates explains his decision to accept his death sentence rather than to flee to another city. Had he not been convicted by the citizens of Athens, a life of innocent philosophical contemplation in another city would presumably have been far better for him than death. However, given that he has been convicted, Socrates concludes that fleeing to another city would be a recipe for ending his life in shame rather than in dignified exile. Here again, the conclusion about what sort of life it would be best for him to live is parasitic upon a prior conclusion about what he owes to his native city. It is because he regards fleeing as unjust that he concludes that it would be a recipe for a life that is not worth living. If the value of virtuous actions were grounded in purely prudential considerations, Socrates' reasoning in the *Crito* would be wholly misguided. Yet clearly Plato seeks here to draw the portrait of an exemplary human being, one worthy of imitation.

We now see why it is easy to misread Plato as a proponent of a purely prudential kind of practical reasoning. His picture of the psyche's proper constitution implies that whenever the reasoned part of the psyche concludes that some action is best, failing to do that action would be bad for oneself. Given this correlation, it is easy to get the mistaken impression that what *makes* an action the best thing to do is that it is best for oneself. But this inference does not fit Socrates' account of his own reasoning about whether to go into exile, nor does it fit his portrayal of the reasoning of the philosopher-king. Likewise, it fits uneasily with Socrates' claim, both in the *Apology* and the *Gorgias*, that he has chosen the life of continuous dialectical engagement with his fellow citizens partly in order to do what he could, under non-ideal political circumstances, to contribute to their improvement.[22] Here again, Socrates is portrayed as choosing actions under the guise of the good, but not in the first instance under the guise of the prudentially good.

In conclusion, we can say that for Plato the difference between "goodness *simpliciter*" and "goodness for" does not run deep. What is good for a particular person must also be good in an impersonal sense. The good can be equated with the admirable rather than with the advantageous, and the bad with the contemptible rather than the disadvantageous. This is precisely the equation that Socrates favors in the *Gorgias*.[23] If an action is the best or most admirable thing for an agent to do, then things cannot go ideally well for the agent by not doing it, but this is only because a failure to perform the action would imply either that the agent has a defective belief about the good or that her reasoned verdicts have been displaced from their proper position of leadership within the psyche.

This might perhaps seem like a wholly inapt thing to say about those actions in which one puts one's life at grave risk or sacrifices it entirely for the good of others or for the good of the city. Don't we lose sight of their admirableness if we refuse to see people who do such things as having sacrificed a good life for themselves? I don't think so. There is another way of understanding what is admirable about such people, and on reflection it seems quite plausible. In cases of this sort, fortune has closed off the possibility of a long and fully honorable life. That this is a personal tragedy can readily be admitted. It is a loss in the metric of what is good for oneself, but the tragedy does not consist in having to forego a wholly good future that is still available. Those who are most admirable will not be taken in by the thought that there is a fully valuable future they could still have. They recognize that the valuable future that might have been available in happier circumstances is no longer open to them, and that it could only seem to be open, or seem in the future to be theirs, thanks to an opacity or forgetfulness in their apprehension of their own life and its significance. They could have a simulacrum of happiness in the future only if they lived without lucidity, with a permanent inner squint. They are most admirable if they are immune from the illusions about the value of their own lives that might have made it possible for them to enjoy an extra measure of wealth or longevity secured by an objectively base or despicable act. Someone who could easily enjoy those benefits yet refuses to choose them might still be admirable, but less so. And even in this latter case, the voluntary forbearance would not really be self-sacrificial, though it would appear that way in the eyes of the deliberator. On this approach, then, what is

---

[22] Plato, *Apology*, paragraph 66 and *Gorgias*, 521d–e.   [23] Plato, *Gorgias*, 474c–d.

noble about what we call self-sacrifice is not that one shows oneself to care more about the good of others than about one's own good; it is that one manifests an unshakeable clarity about what is really good even in the face of temptations that would overcome the evaluative outlook of many other human beings.

This account would be far less plausible if goodness figured in practical deliberation solely as a product or outcome to be maximized, and not as an ideal to be exemplified in all of one's doings. I've argued against this restrictive conception of the role of the good in practical deliberation, and there are textual indications that Plato would have rejected it as well. For instance, Socrates says in his trial that ". . . a man who is good for anything ought not to calculate the chance of living or dying; he ought only to consider whether in doing anything he is doing right or wrong—acting the part of a good man or of a bad."[24] It would be absurd to regard the probability of death as irrelevant to the efficient promotion of valuable states of affairs, some of which presumably depend upon one's continued existence. It makes perfect sense to regard it as irrelevant to the question whether one's current actions are or are not exemplifying an objective standard of goodness in which one is called to participate in all of one's activities.

I believe that Aristotle follows Plato in the main particulars that I have just emphasized. He too sees the virtues as constituents of a well-ordered psyche, without which the human self dissipates into a disordered multiplicity. The vicious, he maintains, are at war with themselves, and the combatants tug against each other as if tearing the psyche to pieces.[25] There is a recognizable strain of Platonism, too, in Aristotle's insistence that genuine self-love does not consist in a determination to get as large as possible a share of what one desires or finds pleasurable, but rather in an abiding concern to act in accordance with the dictates of right reason.[26] This counts as self-love because the reasoned part of the psyche is the part that is most truly and properly one's own, and because this part must be ascendant if one is to pull oneself together into a unified and coherent self. Hence the true self-lover is the person who loves himself because and to the extent that he thinks and acts as he should, and not merely out of a kind of brute self-preference. This sort of self-love leads one to do nothing but what is objectively fine and hence properly praised by all. That is, it wholly defangs the potential for conflict between self-love and the impersonally good—or so I will argue in Chapter 7.

---

[24] Plato, *Apology* (translated by Benjamin Jowett), paragraph 55. See also paragraph 69. Similar passages can be found in the *Crito* (e.g. paragraphs 28 and 34)

[25] Aristotle, *Nicomachean Ethics*, 1166b19–23. I do not think that this passage contradicts Aristotle's earlier claim, in Book VII, that the *akratic* agent is at odds with his own actions while the vicious person is not. I take this to mean only that the *akratic's* actions are at odds with his considered judgments, and not that the vicious person has an unified and harmonious attachment to his misguided pursuits. I try to vindicate this suggestion in Chapter 7.

[26] These convictions surface in the passages quoted at the outset of this chapter and found in Aristotle, *Nicomachean Ethics*, 1168b16–33.

Aristotle argues from the outset of the *Nicomachean Ethics* that the human good must lie in the actualization of the characteristically human function, and that this function is the continuous surging forth of reasoned thought in a life of activity. It follows from the fact that the highest human good is a lifelong activity that its instances will always be the good of someone in particular, since it can only be realized by somebody's active engagement in the leading of a life. Yet the claim that human goodness pertains to particular people in this sense does not suggest what we moderns would call a prudential conception of the good. The goodness of even the most altruistic acts will belong in this sense to the agents of those acts.

If these interpretive suggestions are on target, then Sidgwick's characterization of what was "assumed on all sides" in Greek philosophy does not aptly characterize either Plato or Aristotle. Plato and Aristotle both seek to refute the charge of certain sophists that it is against one's interests to be virtuous in the conventional sense. However, they seek to refute this charge by refiguring the idea of self-interest on which it is premised. Their concern is to show that goodness cannot be relativized to persons in a way that makes "Well, who exactly is it good *for?*" a pointed question, one that points in particular towards possible doubts about whether the virtues are worth having. This is not to suggest that Plato or Aristotle would deny that the virtues are good for their possessors. They would insist upon this thesis as crucial to the vindication of the virtues, but not under any interpretation of 'goodness for' that is suited to serve as the personal pole of a Sidgwickian dualism about the good. Hence it would be a distortion to interpret them as having been concerned only to show that the virtues have what we moderns would think of as personal or agent-relative goodness.

A NARRATIVE OF DECLINE

Here we have all of the elements of a Hegelian narrative in progressive intellectual history . . . provided only that we tell the story in reverse chronological order. Looking back over our shoulder, we see in the foreground two stridently opposed theses about the value of those virtues we call moral. The first thesis is that the virtues are good because they yield actions that accommodate the equal standing of others or that promote the interests of others. The second thesis is that the virtues are bad because they often induce their possessors to sacrifice their own good for the sake of others. In order to avoid blatant contradiction, those gripped by these two thoughts invent two kinds of goodness and two corresponding senses of the term 'good,' one personal and the other impersonal. The bulge in the carpet is thereby transferred to their theory of practical rationality. Since both kinds of goodness appear to make rational demands, these demands can come into conflict, and there seems to be no argument for regarding one conception of the good as supreme that does not beg the question by covertly presupposing the supremacy of precisely that conception. The authoritative norms of practical reason are irrevocably at odds with each other. *Geist* has reached an impasse in its self-formative reflection.

If one peers back further to the Ancient Greek origins of Western philosophy, one sees how to overcome this impasse. The resolution lies in an alternative understanding of the self and its relation to the virtues. With this understanding in hand, it appears to be a false dichotomy to suppose that the value of the virtues must be traced either to one's personal aims and desires or to the value of other people and their ends. The virtues are valuable because they bring selves into closer approximation to an objective standard of proper constitution, specified by the soul's proper form or *telos*. This alternative yields a single answer to the question whether it is good to be virtuous—an answer that can properly be affirmed from a maximally personal and a maximally impersonal point of view.

In this synthesis, each of the initially opposed theses can be regarded as *aufgehoben* in the complicated Hegelian sense: each is discarded as it stands, but the kernel of insight present in each is lifted up and preserved in the synthesis. The idea that one's own virtues are of particular value to oneself is preserved, not because one's virtues fulfill interests that could be assigned to oneself in their absence but because it is one's own agency and life that one's virtues partially constitute and not the agency and life of a stranger. The idea that virtues are impersonally admirable is also preserved, not because they conduce to the satisfaction or pleasure of all comers (they don't: an accused criminal might be pained to find that the judge cannot be bribed) but because they bring their possessors closer to a standpoint-neutral, objectively fitting standard for a properly human and hence fully active life. The appeal of the Greek view is wholly lost if one thinks of it, *à la* Sidgwick, as a one-sided deployment of the personal or subjective pole of the modern dualist conception of the good. Its appeal is restored to view when one sees it as a synthesis that overcomes the putative opposition between these poles. It then shows forth as the culmination of a reverse-chronological history of dialectical progression rather than of mere forgetfulness. Or—to return to history told in properly chronological order—it is lit up as a forgotten alternative whose retrieval might resolve certain otherwise intractable puzzles in contemporary normative philosophy.

It might seem bizarre to suppose that intellectual history would be susceptible to "reverse Hegelian" regression. What could possibly induce thinkers to decompose a coherently unified outlook into two partial and irrevocably conflicting poles? As it happens, both Plato and Aristotle offer elaborate accounts of the persistent temptation to misconceive of the good as relative to subjective desires or appetitive pleasures. Given Plato's conception of the soul and its fate in non-ideal political circumstances, he has every reason to expect that actual human beings, raised in actual and deeply corrupt polities, will tend to view the good through the distorting lens of over-indulged appetites and/or an overweening *thumos*. Long stretches of the Socratic dialogues are devoted to the therapeutic task of unseating appetite-relative and honor-based conceptions of the good so that the human good can come into clearer view. In the course of the *Gorgias*, for instance, Socrates is principally concerned to convince Callicles and other participants that to devote one's life to the quest for public esteem and power is effectively to surrender to the *demos* effective control over one's own best and highest capacity—the capacity for *logos*, or thought and speech. He also attempts to show that a life devoted to the pursuit of pleasures or the satisfactions of desires is a slavish and ridiculous one, akin to a life devoted to scratching itches or filling a leaky jar with water.[27] Plato as dramatist, and to a lesser extent Socrates as character, suggest that the same deformations of the psyche that lead to errors about the good also limit the therapeutic power of philosophical reflection to correct these errors. For instance, those with a thirst for power or public approval will have too calculating a relation to their own words and thoughts, and too indignant a reaction to illuminating objections, to learn readily from philosophical dialogue.[28]

Aristotle, for his part, offers an explicit account of the role of desires and pleasures in structuring the images or appearances (*phantasmata*) of goodness and badness that provide initial guidance to practical thinking.[29] If one's characteristic desires and pleasures have been misshapen by a bad upbringing, one will lack a reasoned appreciation of virtuous action, and philosophical inquiry will be powerless to set things aright. The therapeutic powers of philosophy extend only to stabilizing and deepening evaluative outlooks that are already tolerably virtuous.[30] Those who have been badly brought up will see goodness in what they desire or what pleases them, but there will be no deeper illuminating commonality in these appearances of goodness that might be articulated by sustained philosophical reflection. If such people attempt to put their conceptions of the good into words, their efforts might be expected to come to a rapid end with the general claim that those things that are desired and/or pleasant are good. In Aristotle's view, one's conception of the good can be harmonious and reliable only if one's pleasures and desires are made over in accordance with an independent and fully objective conception of how it is fitting for human beings to act and to live.[31]

---

[27] Plato, *Gorgias*, 493a–494d.

[28] According to Socrates, for instance, Callicles' love of the Athenian demos, and his related concern to avoid getting bested by Socrates in front of others in the course of what is and is not a philosophical dialogue (the love of wisdom being represented by only one of the parties to it), keep him from being won over by Socrates' arguments concerning the proper use of the human capacity for reasoned thought and action. See Plato, *Gorgias*, 513c–d.

[29] Aristotle, *De Anima*, Book III, chapters 7 and 10.

[30] Aristotle, *Nicomachean Ethics*, 1179b5–18.

[31] In trying to articulate common ground between Plato and Aristotle, I have inevitably passed over the considerable differences in the general tenor of their views of these matters. Among the most important of these differences is a difference in the degree of cultural pessimism displayed by

We see, then, that both Plato and Aristotle hold open the possibility of cultural forms that impede philosophical insight into the human good by fostering errant desires and pleasures, or by encouraging too uncritical a stance towards the sense of value delivered up by one's pleasures and desires. Within a culture whose members are continuously exhorted to indulge their desires or to pursue purely sensory pleasures, Plato and Aristotle would expect the good to be confused with the pleasurable or the desired. Since we cannot say which things are pleasing or desired *simpliciter*, but only which things are pleasing to or desired by particular people, this will lead in turn to a brutely person-relative conception of goodness. Hence Plato and Aristotle offer the seeds of a psycho-social explanation of the persistent appeal of the subjective pole of Sidgwickian dualism.

With this explanation in place, it is not hard to see how a brutely dualistic picture of the good might take hold. If one were tempted by a subjectivist conception of the good, one might well encounter phenomena that resist explanation within its parameters. For instance, we often have arguments about the good, and it seems evasive to suggest that all of these apparent disagreements can be defused by relativizing the opposing claims to the differing desires or pleasures of the antagonists. Likewise, in the course of deliberation we often wonder what *should* please us or what we *should* desire, and the answer seems to require a conception of the good that is not anchored directly in our actual pleasures or desires. These recalcitrant phenomena might induce us to reconsider subjectivism (as I believe they should), but they might also induce us to supplement it with a second, more objective conception of goodness—one that might be composed by aggregating across subjective goods (*à la* utilitarianism) or by elaborating transcendental conditions for the possibility of coherently valuing subjective goods (*à la* Kantianism). We would then have arrived at full-fledged modern dualism.

AGAINST THE MODERN INTERPRETATION OF "GOODNESS FOR"

We are faced, then, with two broad-brush stories of a sea-change in Western understandings of the good, one a story of discovery and the other of decline. How are we to decide between them? One possibility is to turn from intellectual history to the philosophical assessment of the modern dualistic conception of the

---

each. Plato's understanding of the social and political conditions for a proper upbringing is deeply utopian (or, some would say, dystopian), while Aristotle's seem to fit within a feasibly idealistic republicanism. There is a related difference in their respective understandings of the role that desires and emotions might play in a properly constituted human being. Plato seems to think of the desires that incite our daily interactions and civic engagement as sources of blinding illusions, while Aristotle thought of them as more thoroughly redeemable.

good. If this dualism is fundamentally mistaken, its historic rise can hardly be hailed as a discovery.

Yet if we ask whether *the* modern dualistic conception of the good is fundamentally flawed, the answer seems to be that the question is "void for vagueness" (as lawyers are wont to say). While Sidgwick clearly has drawn attention to a sweeping change of considerable importance in the history of Western ethical thought, there is no single dualistic thesis about the good to which the term 'modern dualism' can uncontroversially be affixed. We moderns do see an important difference between goods that are in some sense assignable to particular people and goods that are in some sense impersonal. But we disagree about how best to characterize this distinction. Furthermore, there is nothing distinctively modern about the mere thought that there is *some* important distinction in this vicinity. As noted above, Plato and Aristotle have the conceptual resources to offer an account of the distinction between that which is good *simpliciter* and that which is good *for* this or that person. They can explain it as nothing less than the difference between those things that make my life good *simpliciter* and those that make anything else good *simpliciter*. This approach has few friends in modern philosophy, but it was affirmed in the following passage from G. E. Moore:

What, then, is meant by "my own good"? In what sense can a thing be good *for me?* It is obvious, if we reflect, that the only thing which can belong to me, which can be *mine*, is something which is good, and not the fact that it is good. When, therefore, I talk of anything I get as "my own good," I must mean either that the thing I get is good, or that my possessing it is good. In both cases it is only the thing or the possession of it which is *mine*, and not *the goodness* of that thing or that possession . . . In short, when I talk of a thing as "my own good" all that I can mean is that something which will be exclusively mine, as my own pleasure is mine (whatever be the various senses of this relation denoted by "possession"), is also *good absolutely*; or rather that my possession of it is *good absolutely*.[32]

If we were to accept Moore's analysis of talk of "goodness for," there would be no point in the extended philosophical analysis of this sort of goodness.[33] A footnote would do. Yet in contemporary philosophy, a specialized literature has emerged that focuses on the nature of this special sort of goodness, usually under the name of 'welfare' or 'well-being.' Not surprisingly, proponents of this

---

[32] G. E. Moore, *Principia Ethica* (Cambridge: Cambridge University Press, 1903), chapter 3, section 59, paragraph 4.

[33] Richard Kraut reads Moore as holding that ordinary talk about what is good for this or that person is nonsense. I do not think that this is Moore's view. As I read him, he thinks it nonsensical to understand such talk as referring to a brutely person-relative property—one that can be attributed to a thing without implying that the thing is good *simpliciter*. He proposes instead that talk of 'goodness for X' is talk of goodness *simpliciter* that has a certain relation to X. At any rate, this is the view that I seek to defend, whether or not it is Moore's view. See Richard Kraut, *What is Good and Why? The Ethics of Well-Being* (Cambridge: Harvard University Press, 2007), 70.

theoretical enterprise have maintained, as against Moore, that what contributes to the impersonal goodness of a person's life need not be good for that person. Many have also held that what is good for a particular person need not have the least impersonal or objective goodness. It is not easy to formulate the view of these theorists. It is tempting to say that they insist upon a sense of 'goodness for' that picks out an essentially person-relative or perspectival kind of goodness. Yet this formulation misleadingly suggests that what is picked out by the relevant sense of 'goodness for' is after all a kind of goodness *simpliciter*, and this cannot be right. If it were, then nothing could make a person's life better for that person unless it also made that life better *simpliciter*, and this is precisely what these theorists deny. Their position, then, is that *goodness for* is not a species of goodness *simpliciter* but a *sui generis* and essentially person-relative evaluative property.

I propose to focus critical attention on *this* version of the subjective pole of modern dualism about the good, because it is at once intuitively plausible, widely accepted, and a direct and serious impediment to the retrieval of a truly plausible Aristotelian (or Platonic) conception of the virtues and their value. I should perhaps add that in calling this an interpretation of the *subjective pole* of modern dualism, I mean to leave open the possibility that it might also form the centerpiece of a monistic conception of the good—one that takes all goodness to be person-relative.[34] I hope to show that it is untenable whether taken as part of a dualistic doctrine or as the centerpiece of a monistic doctrine.

An admirably clear affirmation of this sort of dualism can be found in the following passage from L. W. Sumner's influential book on welfare:

. . . you can easily imagine yourself at the end of your life, taking pride in your high level of self-development but none the less wishing that you had got more out of your life, that it had been more rewarding or fulfilling, and thinking that it might have gone better for you had you devoted less energy to perfecting your talents and more to just hanging out or diversifying your interests. Whatever we are to count as excellences for creatures of our nature, they will raise the perfectionist value of our lives regardless of the extent of their payoff for us. There is therefore no logical guarantee that the best human specimens will also be the best off, or that their underdeveloped rivals will not be faring better.[35]

Sumner is undoubtedly right that it is possible for a person to be unable to appreciate certain respects in which his own life has been good, and to wish that his life had been different even in ways that would in fact have made it worse. But if we turn to this passage after a fresh reading of Plato and Aristotle, we will find it natural to ask why this detracts only from the value of the person's life *for him*

---

[34] Such a view is elaborated in the following contemporary works: Michael Smith, "Neutral and Relative Value after Moore," *Ethics* 113 (April 2003), 576–98; Judith Jarvis Thomson, "The Right and the Good," *Journal of Philosophy* 94 (1997), 273–98; Jamie Dreier, "The Structure of Normative Theories," *Monist* 76 (1993), 22–40; Richard Kraut, *What is Good and Why*, chapter 2, especially 81–91.

[35] Sumner, *Welfare, Happiness and Ethics*, 24.

and not also from its goodness in what Sumner calls the "perfectionist" sense? An inability to appreciate the defining activities of one's life must necessarily imply either that those activities are unworthy of appreciation, or that one is unable to appreciate that which is worthy of appreciation. In other words, it implies either a deficiency in one's activities or in one's running apprehension of the value of those activities. Either way, it implies that one's life has not been ideally good from an impersonal perspective. Hence, those who really measure up fully to the standards of perfection proper to human lives, including those standards that apply to evaluative thought itself, cannot at the same time regret this accomplishment.

This is not to say that those who have done ideally well at their life activities—including that central life activity by which we apprehend and appreciate the goodness manifest in our own lives and in the world around us—must think of their lives as having been ideally good. The monist can side with Aristotle and with common sense in recognizing that the lives of such people might be marred by ill health, the tragic and untimely death of loved ones, war and mayhem, and other forms of bad fortune. The monist can also accept that the same event can be bad fortune for one person and good fortune for another. Furthermore, the monist can accept the truism that there is an important difference, for me, between my bad fortune and that of a stranger, or my life going well and a stranger's life going equally well. Only one of these lives is mine, and I must be actualized in this life if I am to be actualized at all. The difference here lies in how we are related to various goods and not in what sorts of goods they are. It is at heart nothing less than the difference between persons. This difference can shrink almost to an irrelevance in the context of intimate love or family bonds. Yet in many cases it appears to loom large, and we can accept this appearance at face value without committing ourselves to the existence of an irreducibly person-relative kind of goodness.

On the Moorean approach, we cannot say which goods are good for X unless we can say which goods X possesses. Sumner suggests that there is no plausible way for the Moorean to spell out what it means for someone to possess a good, such that each person possesses all and only those goods that conduce to that person's well-being. The most plausible approach would be to hold that intrinsically valuable experiences or activities are good for those who experience or engage in them. Sumner thinks that this sort of approach reverses the order of explanation between intrinsic value and well-being. "It is believable," Sumner writes, "that intimate connections with others make the world a better place by virtue of enriching our lives, but it is not believable that they enrich our lives by making the world a better place."[36] This objection misses the mark. What the Moorean must accept is that our lives are made richer by experiences or activities that are intrinsically good. We can affirm this plausible-sounding claim without

---

[36] Sumner, *Welfare, Happiness and Ethics*, 51.

settling the question whether a clear sense can be attached to talk of the value of the world. Reticence about the intelligibility of this latter sort of talk will be particularly natural if we accept the Aristotelian thought that the goodness of a thing is a matter of its approximation to the *telos* by reference to which we grasp the kind of thing it is. It is not clear that the world has a *telos*, nor that a world is made better whenever the entities found in it more closely answer to their *telos*—as for instance when all knives are sharp and all chicken eggs are fertile.

It might seem that there must be a difference between "perfectionist value" and welfare because a person can have any array of excellences of character without having a life that is ideally good for her. Even if the Platonic thought that the good person cannot be harmed is not absurd on its face, still it is a substantive and controversial claim about the coincidence of two conceptually distinct kinds of value, not a straightforward conceptual truth. But while this point seems extremely plausible, it implies only that one's welfare is conceptually distinct from the impersonal goodness of one's *character*, not from the impersonal goodness of one's *life*. In my view, we should follow Aristotle in holding that a good character is necessary but not remotely sufficient for an ideally good life. Such a life requires many other goods, including health, fulfilling loves and friendships, engagement with the arts and sciences, and the good fortune not to be laid low by oppression, abuse, hunger, or physical or psychological illness, not to mention earthquakes, tidal waves, land mines, military invasions, or oversized asteroids. Without such good fortune, a good character cannot express itself in a full life of valuable activities. Hence we can accept the common-sense thought that being an ideally good person is no guarantee of living an ideally good life without insisting upon the existence of a special, essentially perspectival kind of goodness that a life can have for the person leading it.

This point is sometimes lost on those who seek to frame the subject matter of theories of welfare. We see such an error in Sumner's criticism of Aristotle. After claiming that Aristotle mistakenly equates the goodness of a person's character and the prudential value or welfare enjoyed by that person, Sumner goes on to say:

> Where human beings are concerned, it is a contingent matter whether the possession of some particular excellence makes us better off. There may, of course, be a strong empirical correlation between the excellences of mind and body and the well-being of their owners; it would be surprising if there were not. But as a conceptual matter the inference for any agent from perfectionist to prudential value is never guaranteed; there is always a logically open question. The gap between the two is opened by the agent's own hierarchy of projects and concerns, which is but one manifestation of her subjectivity.
>
> (79)

This is a rather bald misreading of Aristotle, since Aristotle denies that the virtues are sufficient for *eudaimonia*.[37] Still, there is a revealing difference

---

[37] Aristotle, *Nicomachean Ethics*, 1099a30–b8.

between Aristotle's grounds for insisting that there is a gap between virtue and *eudaimonia*, and Sumner's grounds for insisting upon a gap between excellence of character and well-being. For Aristotle, it is fortune that opens the gap. For Sumner, the gap exists because what is good for us is a function of our subjective projects and concerns. If there are objectively excellent ways to be or to live, there is no guarantee that they will answer to our subjective projects and concerns, hence no guarantee that they will be good for us.

This fits nicely with the diagnosis set out above of the appeal of subjective or person-relative conceptions of goodness. On this diagnosis, the conception goes hand-in-hand with a powerful intuition to the effect that it would be good in some sense for one's life to unfold in ways that fulfill one's desires. Yet on reflection, it is not easy to clarify the content of this intuition in a way that sustains its credibility. Is desire-satisfaction supposed to be good *simpliciter* or is it supposed to be good in a purely person-relative sense—good, as it is said, merely for the person whose desires are satisfied? Clearly the latter, since the value of desire-satisfaction is supposed to force us to acknowledge the existence of a special sort of goodness not already compassed by the person-neutral notion. But this means that the content of the intuition can be clarified only if we can first make independent sense of the special sort of goodness that the intuition itself is supposed to help us to understand. We are no further along.

Moore's deepest reason for analyzing talk of "goodness for" in terms of goodness *simpliciter* is that otherwise the concept becomes unintelligibly speaker-relative. When I speak of that which is good *for me*, Moore writes, "The *good* of it can in no possible sense be "private" or belong to me; any more than a thing can *exist* privately or *for* one person only . . ."[38] I believe that Moore is right about this. His argument might be reconstructed as follows. If something is good for me, this implies that I would be right to regard it as good. But the proposition that the thing is good can't very well be true when I entertain it and false when other people entertain it. The proposition is either true or it isn't. Hence anything that really is good for me must be objectively and impersonally good. This is not to say that it must be good for everyone. It could, after all, be good for me in the sense favored by Moore—i.e. an objectively good occurrence arising in my life rather than in the lives of others. Nor is it to say that anything that is good for a particular person must be good on balance or overall, since something can make one life better while making hundreds of lives far worse.[39] It is only to disown the thought that its *goodness* is mine in the more radical sense of being something that I can affirm and others can deny without someone being mistaken.

We might try to preserve a distinctive realm of person-relative goodness by denying that when something is good *for me*, I would be correct in regarding it

---

[38] G. E. Moore, *Principia Ethica*, chapter 3, section 59, paragraph 4.
[39] I thank Brad Hooker for this point.

as good *simpliciter*. But how then am I supposed to see those things that are good for me, if not as good? Presumably I see them aright when I see them simply and irreducibly as good-for-me. If this is an intelligible way of seeing them, then we sidestep the threat of person-relative truth. Others can agree that things that are good-for-me are indeed good-for-Tal-Brewer—provided that they have some way of understanding what they are agreeing to. Yet if *goodness for* is not a kind of goodness, they will be unable to bring their understanding of *goodness* to bear on the task of understanding what this phrase means. But how, then, are they to cotton on to its meaning?

No concept can be *brutely* person-indexed. If I attempt to introduce a new person-indexed concept with the phrase 'nose-for-X,' and tell you that what is a nose-for-me need not be a nose-for-you, you might suppose that this new phrase names the particular nose among all noses that is found on the face of the speaker. But suppose I go on to say that a nose-for-X need not be a nose at all. I will have to tell you what something must be and how it must be related to a particular person if it is to be a nose-for-that-person. If I can't do that, I will have succeeded in introducing only a meaningless string of vocables.

The question, then, is what non-indexical anchoring relation is supposed to give sense to 'goodness for X' if this phrase does not pick out a kind of goodness with a certain relation to X. Sumner holds that it must be some subjective pro-attitude, and this does seem like the most appealing candidate. (It is also just the sort of view that we are led to expect by the Platonic and/or Aristotelian diagnosis of the appeal of subjectivist understandings of goodness.) However, Sumner doubts that traditional candidates such as preferences or desires can do the trick. His own favored candidate is a pro-attitude that he calls personal life-satisfaction, where this involves "an endorsement or affirmation of the conditions of one's life."[40] If it is supposed to be a substantive claim that there is a congruence between those things that I affirm (or desire or prefer) and those things that are good for me, then we've simply postponed the puzzle. We still haven't seen what it could mean for something to have the irreducibly indexical property of goodness-for-me. The "subjective pro-attitude" approach will help us to get a grip on this strange property only if what it *means* for something to be good-for-me is for it to be authentically affirmed by me (or desired by me, or preferred by me). Yet those who deny that it is invariably good for me to perform those actions that I authentically affirm (or desire, or prefer) do not seem simply to be ignorant of the meaning of the phrase 'good for X.' If there is an objection to what they are saying, the objection is not that it is self-contradictory but that it is false.

On reflection, there are strong reasons for supposing that what they are saying is true. This is perhaps easiest to see in the case of Sumner's proposal. The fundamental problem with this proposal is that one begins to fall into circularity

---

[40] Sumner, *Welfare, Happiness and Ethics*, 159.

as soon as one tries to say what it is to affirm or endorse the conditions of one's life. Presumably this is a matter of seeing something good or valuable about them. This raises the question what sort of value we see in our life conditions when we affirm or endorse them. If the answer is goodness *simpliciter*, then it would be surprising in the extreme to suppose that our lives go better for us whenever we affirm or endorse them. After all, we can presumably be mistaken about the goodness *simpliciter* of our lives. It is hard to believe that things go well for us when we perform bad activities under the mistaken idea that they are good, and that they begin to go worse for us as soon as we gain an inkling of their badness. We might well say of people who are blissfully ignorant of their own badness that for *them*—that is, *according* to them—their lives are going perfectly well. But it would be a mistake to regard this manner of speaking as an indication that there is some genuine yet essentially perspectival form of goodness that they currently enjoy but would lose if they were suddenly made aware of the badness of their lives. (It would also raise formulation problems, since 'form of goodness' cannot here mean 'kind of goodness' and it is unclear what else it could mean.)

Presumably, then, when we endorse our activities in Sumner's sense, we see them as good-for-us rather than as good *simpliciter*. But if goodness-for-us just is the property that our activities have when we affirm or endorse them, then to affirm or endorse an activity is to view it as something that one affirms or endorses, and to ponder whether to affirm or endorse an activity is to ponder whether it makes sense to see it as an activity one affirms or endorses. This is, of course, nonsense. But it is just the sort of nonsense we ought to expect when we try to ground the value of some array of our life activities in our subjective approbation of them rather than understanding our approbation as answerable to their value. The former alternative leaves nothing for approbation to be—or, at least, nothing that could sensibly be seen as an apt lodestone for key life decisions.

The same fundamental objection arises for other, more familiar subjectivist analyses of 'goodness for,' including those that hold that what it means for something to be good-for-me is for it to be desired or preferred by me. In the course of deliberation, we ordinarily take great pains to formulate our preferences, even in cases where nothing but our own interests are at stake. This would make little sense if our preferences had the power to confer value upon their objects. We take pains to strike upon the right preferences because we seek to prefer that which is worth preferring. To prefer one thing to another is not merely to have a brute behavioral tendency to "go for" one thing rather than another. Preferences are not mere behavioral obsessions. To prefer one thing to another is to see it as better or more worthy than the other, and to stand ready to act in accordance with this assessment. Here again, we must ask: Better in what sense? And here again, the subjectivist analysis faces a dilemma: if the answer is "better *simpliciter*" then the view is deeply implausible; if the answer is "better for us" then we are no further along in our efforts to understand this puzzling phrase.

Unlike the term 'preference,' the word 'desire' might perhaps be used without infelicity to refer to mere urges, or obsessions, or other dispositions to move one's body in certain goal-directed ways. However, if we count such things as desires, then it is wholly implausible to suppose that whenever a desire is satisfied, our lives go better in any sense. Consider, for instance, obsessive urges that seem entirely pointless—urges, for instance, to wash hands or collect saucers of mud. If it makes our lives better to act on such urges, this is not because the action satisfies a desire but only because it rids of us the urge and frees us to do something genuinely worthwhile. The equation of what is good for us and what we desire becomes remotely plausible only if we assume that having a desire to do something involves having at least an inchoate sense that there is some point or value in doing that thing. This is the conception of desire elaborated in Chapters 1 and 2. It does guarantee an important connection between desire and value, but the connection is not one that will suit the purposes of those who equate what is good for a person with what satisfies that person's desires. Indeed, this equation will confront what will now begin to sound like a familiar dilemma. If desires involve the appearance of objective or impersonal values or reasons, then presumably it is possible for these appearances to be misleading, and it would be highly implausible to suppose that our doings can be made good-for-us (rather than merely good according to us) by the mistaken sense that they have another, more objective sort of value. On the other hand, if desires involve appearances of goodness-for-the-desirer, then it would be strange to suppose that this appearance is self-vindicating, and viciously circular to attempt to explain the very idea of person-relative value by holding that it is possessed by those things that we desire.

It would be somewhat more plausible to hold that what is good for a particular person is what that person *ought* to affirm or prefer or desire, or has *reason* to affirm or prefer or desire, rather than what the person actually *does* affirm or prefer or desire. Yet it is not clear how such an approach is to provide us with insight into the nature of a special, person-relative kind of goodness. After all, if there are impersonally good states of affairs, then presumably we all have reason to affirm them and to desire that they obtain.[41] Likewise, if there are impersonally valuable virtues or impersonally moral principles, then presumably we all have reason to desire to exemplify those virtues or to conform to those moral principles, to prefer to do so, and to affirm ourselves when and only when we do.

A second problem with this sort of view is that there are cases in which one ought to have a desire for something, but only for instrumental reasons and not

---

[41] This is a sensible posture towards the good as a property of states of affairs, but as I have stressed, it is not the only fitting posture towards the good, nor the most central to a life well lived.

because the thing in question is at all good. An insanely insecure ex-lover might threaten to kill his ex-mate if she does not work up a burning desire to marry him, yet not have the slightest interest in actually tying the knot. The ex-mate would then have a very powerful reason to desire to do something that would be very bad for her.[42] We can make the position plausible only if we refine it so as to rule out such cases, presumably by equating that which is good for oneself with that which one ought to desire for its own sake.[43] But if we accept the arguments of Chapters 1 and 2 for the "evaluative outlook" account of desire, then we must reject this revised version as well. According to the "evaluative outlook" account, to desire something for its own sake is to see it as intrinsically good or valuable. If this is right, then it will not do to define the good for X as that which X ought to desire, since this would be tantamount to defining it as that which X ought to see as good in some way—either for himself, or *simpliciter*. The latter alternative would effectively eliminate goodness-for-X as a distinctive category of goodness. But the former alternative would give rise to a vicious regress. The good for X would be equated, on this view, with what X ought to see as something that X ought to see as something that X ought to see . . . The specification of the apt outlook is forever postponed.

The same objection can be pressed against Michael Smith's suggestion that to be good for X is to be something that X would desire if his desires were maximally informed, coherent, and unified.[44] If desires are appearances of goodness, then it is true that there will be a constant correlation between that which is good for someone and that which the person would desire (i.e. see as good) under epistemically ideal circumstances. However, this correlation merely marks the fact that under epistemically ideal circumstances, subjective appearances of goodness will track objective facts about goodness. Otherwise these appearances, hence the desires they constitute, would not be maximally informed. If this mere correlation is seized upon to formulate an analysis of talk of goodness-for-X, then the above-sketched regress looms.

THE ILLUSION OF PERSON-RELATIVE GOODNESS

What we have, then, is a powerful intuition that seems at first blush to support the existence of an essentially person-relative or perspectival goodness, but that

---

[42] This is a straightforward adaptation of the "wrong kind of reasons" objection to Scanlon's buck-passing conception of the good, as found in Justin D'Arms and Daniel Jacobson, "Sentiment and Value," *Ethics* 114 (2004), 391–424 and in Wlodek Rabinowicz and Toni Ronnow-Rasmussen, "The Strike of the Demon: On Fitting Pro-Attitudes and Value," *Ethics* 114 (2004), 391–424.

[43] I borrow here from Stratton-Lake, "How to Deal with Evil Demons: Comment on Rabinowicz and Ronnow-Rasmussen."

[44] Michael Smith, "Neutral and Relative Value after Moore," 591.

cannot be disambiguated in any way that sustains this first impression.[45] Theories of well-being or welfare that seek to make sense of this intuition at "face value" amount to attempts to shed light on a kind of thing that could not exist—or, at least, that could not exist while also having the normative status intuitively assigned to it. These theories tend to trace welfare to the satisfaction of desires or to the fulfillment of chosen projects. Because of this, they suffer from a single recurring defect: they are reflectively unstable from the point of view of the first-person deliberator. This is because these theories relativize reasons or goods to subjective states that appear, in the course of deliberation, to be wholly unsuited to the task of determining what it would be good for us to do, because they themselves are subjective outlooks on what is good and their dependability is itself fair game for deliberative review. These kinds of theories might perhaps provide us with a sensible way of thinking about individual advantage for purposes of helping those we care about or making public policy decisions. From these second- and third-personal perspectives, it might well make sense to promote the chosen projects of others or to see to it that they have more rather than less of what they want. However, they are unfit to serve as guides for first-person deliberation.

If welcoming or liking one's life always made one's life better, then perhaps there would be a distinctive and interesting subject matter for theories of welfare to illuminate. Yet it seems quite dubious that welcoming or liking one's life does invariably make it go better. When we consider people who are living in a way that is objectively bad, it seems offhand that it makes things worse for them, not better, if they have so badly deficient an outlook on what it is for a life to go well that they are blissfully ignorant of their own badness. We might very well say of such people that for *them*—that is, *according* to them—their lives are going perfectly well. But this does not show that their opinion corresponds to any genuine realm of values. It does not show that there is some genuine yet essentially perspectival form of goodness that they currently enjoy but would lose if they were suddenly made aware of the objective badness of their own lives.

---

[45] The Moorean argument for this conclusion that I have set out in the previous section has affinities with the very interesting arguments put forward by Mark Schroeder in two recent articles: "Teleology, Agent-Relative Value, and 'Good,'" *Ethics* 117 (2007), 265–95; and "Not So Promising After All: Evaluator-Relative Teleology and Common-Sense Morality," *Pacific Philosophical Quarterly* 87 (2006), 348–56. Schroeder's main concern in these essays is to refute an evaluator-relative version of consequentialism that is supposed to be capable of capturing the common-sense idea that agents are morally required to refrain from certain acts (e.g. murder) even when they can foresee that this will increase the overall incidence of equally bad acts. The evaluator-relative consequentialist seeks to accommodate this idea by holding that right actions are those that maximize the good-relative-to their agents, and that performing certain acts (e.g. murders) is worse-relative-to the agent than the performance by others of many such acts. Schroeder's objection to this view is that we have no pre-theoretical notion of good-relative-to, and hence that the evaluator-relative consequentialist cannot claim to be capturing the common-sense thought about the importance of promoting good consequences that makes consequentialism appealing to begin with. Schroeder's semantic arguments for this conclusion strike me as quite forceful.

This is not to deny that a palpable appreciation of the value of one's life is an essential part of the best life for humans. It is. But 'appreciation' is a success term—it involves palpable awareness of a genuine goodness or value. Being subjectively impressed by the cogency or elegance of a transparently fallacious math "proof" is not appreciation of good mathematical argument. Indeed, it indicates an incapacity for such appreciation. Likewise, being subjectively impressed by what appears, in one's eyes, to be the goodness of one's own transparently bad life activities is not appreciation of the goodness of one's life. Indeed, it suggests an incapacity to appreciate the goods that are proper to human lives. Hence one can insist upon the value of the vivid appreciation of one's own intrinsically valuable doings (as I did in Chapter 4) without committing oneself to the existence of an essentially perspectival or person-relative kind of goodness. Furthermore, one can insist that the value of genuinely good activities is accentuated when one is appreciatively absorbed in them, and that some degree of appreciative absorption is a necessary condition for actually succeeding in engaging in certain valuable human activities, without admitting the existence of a special kind of goodness that is essentially perspectival.

The conclusion that there is no such kind of goodness is at odds with deep-seated contemporary beliefs about value, both among philosophers and (in somewhat less articulate form) within the culture at large. We might diagnose the temptation to affirm the existence of such goods as follows. Since desires just are vivid appearances of value, it appears to us that those things we desire are objectively good or valuable. But even as this intuition announces itself, it invokes the embarrassed concession that of course others have no reason to recognize the sovereign capacity of our desires to confer value upon their objects. In conceding this, we have the mistaken sense that we have simply qualified the original intuition and not disowned it entirely. Yet when we attempt to formulate the qualified version of the intuition, we are reduced to a mere form of words that picks out no clear thought. The subjective pole of the dualist view is essentially unclarifiable, then, because it consists in an appealing illusion and not a clear thought.

It might seem that we must affirm a dualist conception of the good if we are to have sufficient reason to further our personal projects and commitments. Given our technologically enhanced capacity to do good for those in far-flung locations, those who are not in need can usually bring about more good in the lives of others than in their own lives. If all reasons for action were grounded in impersonal goods, this might seem to imply that it would be unreasonable for those not in need ever to act in the name of merely personal projects and commitments. This, however, would be tantamount to saying that they could not reasonably have such projects or commitments, since there is no such thing as a project or commitment upon which one never acts. Only dualism, it might seem, can explain the rational priority of one's own projects and commitments.

This objection represents an attempt to generalize a potent criticism of utilitarianism first set out by Bernard Williams. Williams plausibly argues that universal adherence to the act-utilitarian goal of maximizing the aggregate good with each and every action would have the self-defeating effect of undermining the idiosyncratic projects, relationships, and commitments that give unity to our lives over time, make them worth living, and serve as invaluable sources of the sort of utility that the utilitarian seeks to promote.[46] In other words, the universal adoption of selflessness would result in universal banality, and this is a consequence that ought to be deplored even by those who are perfectly selfless.

It might look as if Williams' criticism applies to any conception of the good that refuses to recognize a category of person-relative goods whose reason-giving force often outweighs whatever reasons might be associated with impersonal goods. It does not. If we accept the non-production-based conception of value set out in the first three chapters of this book, we have a decisive answer to the criticism at hand. On the production-based view, the practical upshot of recognizing that a thing is good or valuable is recognizing that it is to be promoted. It is this conception of the good that makes it tempting to suppose that we should respond in the same way to all prospective goods, whether they would occur in our own life, in the lives of others, or in events or states of affairs that are not plausibly placed "in" any life at all. We should promote them. By contrast, if we locate intrinsic value in certain kinds of activities and if we hold that the proper recognition of this intrinsic value consists in appreciative absorption in those activities rather than in a determination to bring about such engagement, then the problem at hand does not arise. Appreciative absorption is essential to many of the best life activities and to many of the best modes of interaction with other persons, including many of those to which we assign moral value. Yet it essentially requires a different relation to goodness than being determined to produce or promote that goodness. While we can and perhaps should seek to promote engagement in such activities, it is not possible to complete someone else's activities with active appreciation, any more than it is possible to do another's loving or another's living. Likewise, if we think that the intrinsic value of other human beings is not the sort of thing that we could intelligibly seek to bring about, but is instead to be respected or savored, then the problem at hand does not arise. We cannot bring about human dignity. While we might well have reason to do our part in promoting respect for it, we are also called upon to extend a more direct acknowledgment of its value, and this is something that can only be done in the first person.

In Chapter 3, I argued that we bring value into view largely through the lens of thick or specialized evaluative concepts rather than with thin concepts like goodness or badness. We find various actions appealing or unappealing under

---

[46] Bernard Williams, "A Critique of Utilitarianism," 108–18 and 129–35.

the guise of the just or unjust, the gracious or ungracious, the kind or unkind, the courageous or cowardly, and so on. When the goodness of possible future acts is lit up through the lens of these evaluative concepts rather than through the lens of thinner concepts, there is far less temptation to suppose that we must categorize the goodness in question either as "for ourselves" or "for others." We seek to use these evaluative concepts in a uniform way whether we are considering our own future acts or those of others, and we think that they provide us with guidance in determining what is fitting for human beings in general, and not merely what is fitting for us or what is fitting for others. The serious use of these concepts is itself a bulwark against the confused partition of the realm of the good into subjective and objective kinds or poles. Nor does this partition seem appealing when we think about the upbringing of our children. Most of us want our children to be generous, brave, kind, and just. We do not want this merely for others—that is, because we care about the welfare of those who will have daily dealings with our children. Nor do we want this because we believe that this will have the indirect effect of serving the good of our children—perhaps by ensuring that they will enjoy the benefits that tend to accompany a reputation for decency. We would think that we had done a disservice to *them* if we raised them in such a way as to make them vicious, even if they never paid any (further) price for this outcome. This rather ordinary observation fits uneasily, if at all, with the dualistic conception of the good. It makes perfect sense, though, on the view shared by Moore, Plato, and Aristotle, since this view implies that wanting what is good for our children just is wanting them to lead lives that are long, fortunate, and objectively good. This indicates that our pre-theoretical intuitions have not been made over entirely in accordance with the dualism that Sidgwick takes to be characteristic of modernity, hence that we can find intuitive grounds as well as more abstruse theoretical grounds for retrieving some variant or another of the monism favored by the Ancients.

One further source of the intuitive appeal of subjectivism about the good is that idiosyncratic variations in objective goodness often correspond with subjective desires and pleasures. For instance, if one fervently desires to do philosophy, this puts one in a position to engage in it in the proper spirit—the spirit that constitutes it as philosophy rather than as some other activity. This is a reason to engage in philosophy rather than trying to engage in some other intrinsically valuable activity for which one might lack a running activity-constituting or activity-deepening appreciation. But the reason lies in the quality of the activity made possible by one's desires, not in some mysterious power of desire to confer value upon whatever otherwise pointless bodily motions it might dispose us to produce.

Yet another source of the intuitive appeal of subjectivism is that a significant degree of continuity in one's projects and commitments is a precondition for leading a coherent and unified life. This means that other things equal, it is good to carry through with those projects, commitments, and relationships that one has already undertaken. But this does not show that the value of our projects, commitments, and relationships is conferred upon them by the mere fact that they are ours. It remains possible—and I think overwhelmingly plausible—that we ought to abandon any project, commitment, or relationship whose perpetuation we correctly see as having no value apart from the dogged persistence that we would display if we stuck with it.

The monistic understanding of *goodness for X* should not be mistaken for a proposal about the invariant meaning of phrases such as "good for X" or "goodness for X." These phrases are used to mean many different things in many different contexts. I might use the words, "For me, what is good is . . ." to make known that I am merely conveying an *opinion* about what is good, or in order to call attention to the nub of disagreement between my beliefs about the good and those of another. I might also be taking note of variations in what exactly makes different lives go better rather than worse. I might say, for instance, "For me, a daily run is good, but for someone with a broken ankle it is not." But we can affirm that not every sort of good activity is available to every person without affirming a subjective or perspective-relative kind of goodness.

SUBJECTIVE GOODNESS AND INTERNALISM ABOUT REASONS

There is another tempting route to the claim that what one ought to recognize as good is relative to one's desires. One might affirm this thesis on the basis of an internalist view about justificatory reasons. This is a potentially confusing subject, since there are (at least) two different theses about justificatory reasons that sometimes go under the name of "internalism about reasons," and it is only a particularly dubious (though nonetheless quite influential) version of internalism that supports the relativization of goodness to desires.

One relatively uncontroversial internalist thesis is that judgments about what it would be good or right to do, or about what one has reason to do, can give rise to action even in the absence of some further desire or motivational state. This thesis seems right. When conjoined with a moral psychology that strictly separates conations from cognitions in accordance with their different direction of fit with the world, it lends support to the conclusion that what we call moral judgments are not cognitions at all but expressions of conative states, since otherwise they would be motivationally inert. This non-cognitivist conclusion does not follow if we adopt the alternative moral psychology elaborated in Chapters 1 and 2. On that view, desires are spontaneous and vivid appearances of goodness or value. While they are not themselves judgments, their presence is implied by any judgment to the effect that some available action would be good or valuable, provided that the judgment amounts to a vivid conviction rather than to a tepid or begrudging conclusion. This leaves room for cases in which one is left cold by one's own (tepid or begrudging) conclusions about what it would be best to do. But it also leaves open the possibility that one might be motivated to do what one has no desire to do, since a conception of value can motivate even if it does not recur spontaneously but remains in place only when one concentrates upon the grounds for affirming it. This seems like the right degree of "internal" connection between practical judgment and motivation, since it leaves room for the possibility of doing what one has no desire to do and of failing to do what one judges to be best.

Some have thought that this first sort of internalism supports a second, stronger, and far less plausible view—one that also goes under the name of 'internalism.' Their line of thought can be reconstructed as follows. Reasons must be capable of motivating actions when one thinks about them aright. But one's idiosyncratic subjective motivations place limits on what lines of thought one could possibly be moved by. Hence reasons are relative to subjective motivations. This subjectivist conception of reasons can readily be extended to yield a similarly subjectivist conception of goodness. After all, it is widely thought that the fact that some action or state of affairs or person is good implies the existence of a practical reason (e.g. to perform it, or promote it, or praise it). But if goodness implies reasons, and if reasons are relative to subjective motivational sets, then goodness too must always at heart be "goodness for" in the sense that it must be relative to subjective motivations.

This sort of internalism has wide popularity and philosophical appeal, but on reflection it is fundamentally misguided. The basic problem will by now sound familiar: it reverses the "direction of gaze" appropriate to practical thinking, mistaking the psychological states that shape our view of how best to act for reasons to act in accordance with that view.[47]

The contemporary debate about internal and external reasons takes its shape, to a large degree, from Bernard Williams' highly influential essays on the topic.[48] Williams first characterizes internalism "very roughly" as the view that we have reason to do only that which will *serve* or *further* one or more of our own occurrent motivations.[49] While Williams sometimes calls the relevant motivations "desires," he makes clear that he is using the term 'desire' in a formal sense to encompass a broad array of psychological states and dispositions, including "dispositions of evaluation, patterns of emotional reaction, personal loyalties, and various projects, as they may be abstractly called, embodying

[47] I borrow the term "direction of gaze" from Richard Moran's "Self-Knowledge: Discovery, Resolution and Undoing," *European Journal of Philosophy* 5, (2) (1997), pp. 141–61. My argument has clear affinities with Moran's, though he is primarily concerned with making up one's mind about what to *believe*, not what to *do*.

[48] Bernard Williams, "Internal and External Reasons," in *Moral Luck: Philosophical Papers 1973–1980* (Cambridge: Cambridge University Press, 1981), 101–13; Williams, "Internal Reasons and the Obscurity of Blame," in *Making Sense of Humanity and Other Philosophical Papers, 1982–1993* (Cambridge: Cambridge University Press, 1995), 35–45.

[49] Williams, "Internal and External Reasons," 101.

commitments of the agent."[50] The range of a person's reasons for action is a function of the "subjective motivational set" (S) composed of that person's "desires" in this broad sense. An action will have the relevant relation to some desire if there is a "sound deliberative route" that begins "from" that desire and culminates in the conclusion that one has a reason to perform the action.

Williams is not altogether clear about what exactly it means for deliberation to begin "from" a desire. He oscillates between two strikingly different understandings of this relationship, each pointing towards a very different sort of internalism. On one interpretation, to deliberate *from* a desire is to deliberate from *the fact that one has* that desire, to whatever that fact implies about what one has reason to do. Internalism would then be the claim that we have a (justificatory) reason to φ only if we have some desire, and the fact that we have this desire implies (i.e. leads, via some sound deliberative route, to the conclusion) that we have a reason to φ. Let's call this reading of Williams' position "inferential internalism." On a second interpretation, deliberation begins *from* desires in the sense that they spark the deliberation and shape its route. Internalism would then be the view that one has a justificatory reason to φ only if one's desires can spark and shape an episode of sound deliberation resulting in the conclusion that one has reason to φ. Let's call this position "causal internalism." If Williams is a causal internalist, the externalist thesis he rejects is that claims of the form "A has a reason to φ" can be true even if A's desires leave her causally unable to appreciate and be moved by the conclusion that she has a reason to φ except by some extra-deliberative or deliberatively infirm route (e.g. shock therapy, misinformation, propaganda, rhetorical manipulation).

There is strong textual evidence that Williams was an inferential internalist: his most compelling argument for internalism supports only that view. Here is the argument:

If it is true that A has a reason to φ, then it must be possible that he should φ for that reason; and if he does act for that reason, then that reason will be the explanation of his acting . . . When the reason is the explanation of his action, then of course it will be, in some form, in his S, because certainly—and nobody denies this—what he actually does has to be explained by his S.[51]

According to Williams, one of the two "fundamental motivations" for the internalist view is that it correctly represents this connection while externalism does not.[52] On the justificatory reading, we can perhaps see what Williams has in mind. If we deliberate "from" some element of our S to the conclusion that

50 *Ibid.*, 105.

51 Williams, "Internal Reasons and the Obscurity of Blame," 39.

52 Williams' second fundamental argument is that the externalist insists upon saying of people who fail to do what the externalist thinks they have reason to do that they are irrational, while internalism restricts itself to "thick" descriptions of their shortcomings. For instance, the internalist might say of a man who is not nice to his wife, and who professes to see no reason to be nicer, that he is "ungrateful, inconsiderate, hard, sexist, nasty, selfish, [or] brutal," while the externalist

we ought to φ, and then proceed to φ, the initial element of our S might seem to be both a cause of and a justification for our φ-ing. On the causal reading, however, the argument makes little sense, since the element of our S from which we deliberate need not figure in the deliberative foreground of our justification for φ-ing. This suggests that Williams means to argue for inferential internalism. Still, since both kinds of internalism have their proponents, and since my aim is to show that internalism is wrong and not just that Williams is wrong, I hope to show that there are decisive objections to both.

Before we can bring either sort of internalism into focus, we need to understand the notion of a sound deliberative route. The simplest cases of sound deliberative routes begin with some desire and ground the conclusion that there is reason to φ on evidence that φ-ing will conduce to the satisfaction of the desire. But as Williams notes, sound deliberation need not always fit this restrictive mold. We often *assess alternatives* for fulfilling a desire in order to determine which is most convenient or pleasant. We also *schedule* the fulfillment of different desires, and resolve conflicts among them by *weighing* desires against each other and determining their relative importance. In other cases, we extend our desires to new activities by *noticing similarities* between these new activities and others that we already desire to perform.[53] Finally, we sometimes deliberate by *specifying* the object of a general desire.

What is essential to Williams' view, at least on the inferential internalist reading, is that sound deliberative routes must establish a *rational relation* between some element of one's S and some conclusion about what one has reason to do.[54] This sets a limit, though a rather hazy one, on what can count as a sound deliberative route. For instance, one might begin with the generic desire to have a fulfilling career and, after vividly imagining different career possibilities, come to have a desire to be a film director. This will be a case of sound deliberation only if there is a rational link between the generic desire from which one began and the specific desire with which one ends—i.e. if one's

insists upon saying one further thing—that the man is irrational. Williams doubts that the externalist can assign any meaning to this extra charge. (Williams, "Internal Reasons and the Obscurity of Blame," 39–40.) This argument seems to me to be entirely without force. In the first instance, the externalist need not say that the person in question is irrational, but only that he has a reason to be nicer. T. M. Scanlon has argued convincingly, in response to Williams, that the latter claim does not entail the former (T. M. Scanlon, *What We Owe to Each Other* (Cambridge: Harvard University Press, 1998: 27)). Second, it seems clear that if someone is inconsiderate, nasty, brutal, selfish, etc. (or "cruel" or "imprudent"—for Williams makes the same claim about these charges in "Internal and External Reasons," p. 110), then they *do* have a reason to be different. These are terms of condemnation, not dispassionate descriptions. To condemn a person in any of these terms is to imply that they ought to act differently, and this in turn is to imply that they have a reason to act differently. Williams' internalism is inconsistent with the full-throated use of these terms of condemnation in the cases he describes.

53 Williams, "Internal Reasons and the Obscurity of Blame," 38.
54 Williams, "Internal and External Reasons," 103.

justification for wanting to be a film director is partly to have a fulfilling career.[55] If practical thinking leads to a new desire that has no such rational link to prior desires, then it induces a non-deliberative transformation in what one has reason to do. It would then be wrong to say that one had the reason in question prior to the transformation.

Williams departs from orthodox Humeanism not only in his expansive notion of sound deliberation but also in his expansive notion of desire. He counts as desires, hence as potential starting points for sound deliberation, such disparate things as "personal loyalties," "patterns of emotional reaction," "dispositions of evaluation," and the "various projects" that embody an agent's "commitments." While this breadth makes Williams' view more plausible than orthodox Humeanism, it raises perplexing questions about what it might mean for deliberation to begin *from* the different sorts of states compassed under the term 'desire.'

What might it mean, for instance, to deliberate *from* a "disposition of evaluation"? We can attempt to answer this question by examining Williams' discussion of those who are disposed to evaluate possible actions in terms of some "thick" ethical concept such as 'cruelty,' 'cowardice,' or 'chastity.' Those who make serious use of the concept of cruelty might sensibly regard *the fact that an action would be cruel* as a weighty reason not to perform it. The inferential internalist abandons this compelling picture of the deliberative role of thick ethical concepts. On this view, the justificatory reason one might have to avoid cruel actions is not *the fact that the actions would be cruel* but rather *the fact that one is disposed to count the actions as cruel.* Since the reason is premised on the disposition, it need not apply to those who lack the disposition. This might perhaps explain why Williams insists that those who do not care about cruelty have no reason to avoid it. Yet here he manages to relativize the reach of a widely recognized value only by reversing the "direction of gaze" appropriate to practical thinking. When we try in earnestness to discern how it would be best to act, we do not and ought not to look *inward* at our dispositions to evaluate actions in various ways, but rather *outward* at the values we are disposed to find in proposed actions or their expected outcomes. It is obvious that our dispositions of evaluation *shape* this gaze, but they generally do not *fall within* our gaze.

When engaged in deliberation I cannot coherently take my own disposition to evaluate actions in terms of some thick concept to count in favor of guiding my action in the way suggested by that very evaluation. As a piece of justificatory reasoning, that would be viciously circular. The problem is not simply that this so-called "justification" won't satisfy *other people.* If I am genuinely concerned about the justifiability of some proposed action, the mere psychological fact that

---

[55] Here we catch sight of another reason to read Williams as an inferential internalist: it is hard to know what to make of talk of "rational links" between desires that *shape* deliberation and conclusions reached via deliberation.

I have a tendency to bring it under some action-guiding concept ought not to satisfy even *me*. What I want to know is whether the action really does fall under that concept, and perhaps also whether and how I ought to make use of that concept.

This is not to deny that justifications might run out with certain basic propositions like: It's simply cruel to intentionally cause needless suffering. If asked why one believes such a thing, one might have nothing more to say than, "I just do." But we must be careful about how we understand this utterance. It might be a way of recording that one is simply unable to imagine anything *more* basic or obvious that could be offered by way of justification. If we understand the comment in this light, it can play a perfectly coherent part in justification. But if the remark were forwarded as a mere description of one's own psychological tendencies, it would play no direct role in justifying the proposition under dispute, since tendencies to think things are not themselves good justifications for thinking those things.[56]

This basic problem arises not only for dispositions of evaluation but for many of the other subjective motivational states that Williams counts as possible starting points for deliberation, including personal loyalties, ideals, and commitments. It is true that we do sometimes cite our loyalties and commitments as justifications for our actions. However, such utterances are not mere descriptions of our psychological dispositions to count certain things as reasons and to act on those reasons. For instance, when I announce my loyalty to my country or my commitment to world peace, I am usually not merely claiming that I am psychologically disposed to assign deliberative priority to my country's interests or to the pursuit of world peace. I am also expressing my conviction that I ought to assign these deliberative priorities. Since the content of the conviction is (or at least implies) that there is good reason to perform actions reflecting

---

[56] It might also be objected that my refutation of inferential internalism rests on a mistaken understanding of internalism. Williams claims that propositions of the form 'A has a reason to φ' are false unless they are related, via a sound deliberative route, to true propositions about A's desires. Internalism claims only that the existence of such a deliberative connection is necessary to such a reason claim. Williams says that he is tempted by, but not committed to, the further claim that a deliberative connection is sufficient for having a reason. ("Internal Reasons and the Obscurity of Blame," 35–6). Have I mistakenly imputed to Williams the claim that the existence of a deliberative connection is sufficient for having a reason, then refuted this claim rather than his actual view? I don't think so—at least not if Williams is properly interpreted as an inferential internalist. If one has a desire from which there is a sound deliberative route to the conclusion that one has reason to φ, then presumably one would be fully justified in following the deliberative route and drawing the conclusion. It would be odd to think otherwise, since this would be tantamount to admitting the possibility of a sound deliberative route whose conclusion is false. At any rate, Williams must accept this point on pain of losing the right to one of his two main arguments for internalism—namely, that internalists have a straightforward way of justifying the reason-claims they countenance, while externalists do not. But if Williams does accept this point, then his position falls subject to my criticism. What he must affirm, and I have denied, is that the mere existence of a psychological disposition to make certain evaluations, or to be loyal, or to give weight to certain projects, can provide a sufficient warrant for affirming the reasons that said disposition disposes us to affirm.

these deliberative priorities, it would be viciously circular to cite the fact that one *has* the conviction as one's justification for performing these same actions. To think otherwise would be to think of practical convictions as self-justifying. That would make the search for reasons too easy in one sense and too hard in another sense: too easy because convictions about what it would be best to do would be self-justifying, hence infallible; too hard because nothing could tell us which convictions to adopt. The upshot would be to render it entirely obscure why so many of us care so much about getting the content of our action-guiding convictions *right*.

There is an insuperable tension between the actual implications of Williams' internalism and his efforts, in other writings, to defend the normativity of individual projects and commitments, and of the culture-specific norms and ideals expressed in "thick" ethical concepts.[57] If Williams is right that a certain Enlightenment-inspired, universalistic brand of ethical reflection tends to undermine the authority of thick ethical concepts and idiosyncratic projects and commitments, he is wrong to suppose that his approach is more friendly to them. Williams' fondness for Humean conceptions of practical rationality undermines his efforts to question certain fixed ideas of modern moral philosophy and to retrieve key themes of Ancient ethical thought.

It might be objected that the problem lies not in internalism but in Williams' over-inclusiveness about the motivational states from which deliberation might begin. However, the problem will arise for any deliberative starting point that involves an appearance of reasons or values. On the picture of desires set out in the first two chapters of this book, this will include any desire that is actually capable of rationalizing action.

Some interpreters have understood Williams' idea that we deliberate "from" elements of S in a way that might seem to sidestep the objection I have been developing. According to these interpreters, one deliberates from the subjective motivations in one's S in the sense that these motivations control the course of one's deliberation, determining which considerations one finds weighty or compelling, hence what conclusions one is able to reach and be moved by in the course of practical deliberation. Thus, Thomas Scanlon characterizes Williams' view as follows:

An externalist, according to Williams, wants to claim that it can be true that a person has a reason even if, because of deficiencies in that person's dispositions to respond to considerations of the relevant kind, he or she would never come to be moved by those considerations even after the most complete and careful process of reflection and deliberation. An internalist denies this.[58]

---

[57] See Williams, "Persons, Character and Morality," in *Moral Luck*, 1–19; or *Ethics and the Limits of Philosophy* (Cambridge: Harvard University Press, 1985), especially chapters 7–10.

[58] T. M. Scanlon, *What We Owe to Each Other*, 369. A similar reading is found in John McDowell, "Might There Be External Reasons?" in J. E. J. Altham and Ross Harrison, eds., *World,*

On this reading, Williams is a proponent of causal internalism—i.e. the view that we can be said to have a justificatory reason only if our subjective motivational set (including especially our dispositions of evaluation) makes it causally possible for us to find subjectively compelling some line of reasoning that yields the conclusion that we have that reason. Causal internalism neatly accommodates the point that many components of one's S shape one's evaluative gaze during deliberation. Yet causal internalism is not just an innocuous thesis about the role of desires in shaping deliberation; it is a controversial thesis about the scope of claims about justificatory reasons. If we think that some fact about person A's situation implies that A has a reason to φ, and A accepts the relevant facts about his situation but is not at all tempted to conclude that he has a reason to φ, causal internalism tells us that A does not have a reason to φ. To use one of Williams' examples, if we think that some man has a reason to be nicer to his wife, we might mention to him the facts about his situation that *we* would take as a reason to be nicer—e.g. his behavior is undermining his wife's happiness. Many of *us* would have reason to be nicer if we were in his shoes, but if he is unmoved by all of our arguments, we must eventually admit that in fact *he* has no reason to be nicer to his wife.[59]

To see more clearly what is at issue, let 'D' represent one of the sound deliberative routes whose availability would give some people reason to be nicer if they were in the hard-hearted husband's shoes. For illustrative purposes, we can stipulate that D is the deliberative route from the fact that some action would make one's spouse unhappy, to the conclusion that one has a reason (though perhaps not an all-things-considered reason) to avoid that action. The causal internalist must hold that D, which is sound for some deliberators, is not *sound for* the hard-hearted husband, or that D's conclusion is not binding upon him because the deliberative route to it is not *available to* him.

From the first-person point of view to which Williams' theory is explicitly addressed, it won't do to claim that D's conclusion is not binding on the hard-hearted husband because D is unavailable to him. He cannot regard its unavailability as a justification for not following it. His desires might shape his thought so that he finds the deliberative route misguided or mistaken, but then his justification for refusing to follow the deliberative route will be that it is misguided or mistaken, and not that his desires cause him to view it as misguided or mistaken. He can only think of himself as *justified* in refusing the deliberative route's conclusion if he thinks of his refusal to follow it as an appropriate reaction to the argument's unsoundness rather than as the manifestation of a psychological obstacle.

Mind, and Ethics: Essays on the Ethical Philosophy of Bernard Williams (Cambridge: Cambridge University Press, 1995), 71–2.

[59] Williams, "Internal Reasons and the Obscurity of Blame," 39.

Might the causal internalist relativize the applicability of deliberative conclusions by relativizing the soundness of the arguments for them? The proposal, in the case at hand, would be that D is sound for those people (call them soft-hearted spouses) who find themselves disposed to accept it, but not for the hard-hearted husband and others who find themselves unmoved by it. This psychologistic picture of soundness fails for the same reason that inferential internalism fails. It reverses the direction of gaze appropriate to deliberation, locating normativity in our psychological dispositions to find things (here, patterns of deliberation) normative, and not in the things (patterns of deliberation) we are disposed to think normative. When we worry about the soundness of some deliberative route we are inclined to follow, we don't want to know whether we are psychologically disposed to find the route convincing. What we want to know is whether we have good reason to find it convincing. Causal internalism fails to make good sense of this ubiquitous and deep-seated concern.

Causal internalism might seem at first blush like an unproblematic consequence of the dictum that 'ought' (or at least 'has reason to') implies 'can.' How, one might ask, could one have a reason to do something if one *cannot* follow a sound deliberative route to the conclusion that one does indeed have that reason? If we have a reason to do something, doesn't this imply not only that we *can* do it but also that we *can* do it for that very reason? Such rhetorical questions help to account for the *prima-facie* appeal of internalism, but in fact they support internalism only given a highly controversial understanding of what we can and cannot do in the course of deliberation. On the causal internalist view, our own decisive rejection of a proposed deliberative route sometimes has the status of a psychological barrier or incapacity that prevents us from affirming the conclusion of the deliberative route. From the inside, things look quite different. Rejected deliberative routes do not appear as incapacities but as errors. Our rejection of them appears not as a limit on what we are *capable* of thinking but as a limit on what we *ought* to think. When we refuse to think them, what we are doing is a paradigmatic instance of the sort of practical thought for whose course we take ourselves and others to be answerable.

Another source of internalism's appeal is that it seems to cohere with, and indeed to provide intellectual foundations for, an appealingly anti-paternalistic humility about our capacity to pass judgment on the reasoning of others. One might be drawn to internalism in *ethical* recoil from the potentially paternalistic claim that others have reasons whose force they persistently refuse to recognize. However, internalism itself—at least on the causal reading—involves a picture of the relation between reasons and deliberative processes that is incoherent when applied to oneself, and both demeaning and potentially paternalistic when applied to others. What looks from the inside like a reasoned rejection of available actions is pictured by the causal internalist as the operation of a brute psychological mechanism that bars one from affirming the alternatives one takes oneself to have reason to reject. From the inside, one might think that one is off the hook, ethically speaking, because one has chosen well; the causal internalist lets one off the hook on the different and far less gratifying ground that one had no real choice. This view of practical reasons does not itself provide a dependable bulwark against paternalism. It would only supply such a bulwark if supplemented by the controversial and already deeply anti-paternalistic claim that it is never right, or hardly ever right, to force others to do that which they are causally debarred from concluding that they have reason to do. It makes no sense, then, to adopt internalism because of its association with the rejection of paternalism. Indeed, this ought to be obvious, given that the internalist relativization of reasons will extend to anti-paternalism as well. The internalist cannot consistently embrace any form of anti-paternalism that purports to bind those who are unmoved by whatever case might be made in favor of anti-paternalism.

Williams sets out to illuminate the nature of the reasons we are in search of when we deliberate about what to do, or offer advice about what others ought to do. His theory fails as an account of reasons as they appear in the course of deliberation. In his critique of internalism, Scanlon suggests that the position works better as an account of the sorts of reasons we are in search of when we offer advice, presumably because this sometimes requires us to imaginatively occupy the standpoint, and even presumably to mimic the blind spots, of our advisee.[60] I don't think that this suggestion holds water. Suppose, for instance, that we come to believe that Williams' hard-hearted spouse is unable to appreciate the soundness of the deliberative route that we would follow, in his shoes, to the conclusion that he ought to be nicer to his wife. Should we then cease to advise him to be nicer, or perhaps advise him that he has no reason to be nicer? I'm not inclined to think so. To see why, consider that if he asked us to explain such advice, and if we responded honestly, we would have to tell him that we offer it only because he is unable to appreciate the force of the deliberative route that would convince us to be nicer if we were in his circumstances. This explanation would display an objectionably condescending view of another's deliberative faculties. Perhaps such an approach would silence the sort of strident scolding that Williams objects to, variously, under the names of "bluff" and "moralism."[61] However, this respite from brow-beating seems unwelcome when it emerges not from *respect* for one's deliberative capacities but from *despair* at their sorry state.

In my view, the appeal of internalism owes in part to a failure to notice a crucial ambiguity in the notion of a justificatory reason. There are two different standpoints from which we might take an interest in justificatory reasons. On the one hand, we can raise live deliberative questions concerning what we ourselves should do, or what should be done by others whom we are in a position to advise.

[60] Scanlon, *What We Owe to Each Other*, 372.

[61] Williams, "Internal Reasons and the Obscurity of Blame," 44; "Internal and External Reasons," 111; see also Scanlon, *What We Owe to Each Other*, 371–2.

On the other hand, we can assess the rationality of actions that we are not in a position to choose or to influence. There is considerable appeal to the idea that actions are irrational if performed by people who are constitutionally unable to see any reason for them, even if there is a good reason—a reason that one would hope to have found if one had been in their shoes, and that one would have tried to point out to them if one had been asked for advice. Internalism, then, might be recast as a plausible guide for assessing the rationality of deliberative episodes that one is not in a position to influence. Internalism mistakes this fact about rationality as an insight into the existence conditions for justificatory reasons. If an agent has a good reason to do something but cannot see the reason, she would be irrational to do it, but this does not imply that the reason will cease to exist. Williams-style internalism holds that it does.

Nearly all contributors to the contemporary debate have assumed that there are many internal reasons.[62] The controversy has centered almost exclusively on whether there are or might be external reasons as well. In my view, the burden ought to be placed squarely on the shoulders of the internalist to show that some important class of reasons are indeed binding only in virtue of their relation to the subjective motivational states of the agents they bind. On the conception of desires set out in this book, the prospects for discharging this burden are bleak. On this view, desires are capable of giving point to action only because and insofar as they provide us with windows upon an independent realm of values. The justificatory force of these reasons cannot plausibly be conditioned on the desires that bring them into view.

It might be thought that even if I have succeeded in showing that there are no internal reasons, I have said nothing that would support the existence of external reasons. I have shown, at most, that we must choose between externalism and nihilism. I think that my argument has a stronger consequence than this. Thus far I have concluded that if we have reason to do one thing rather than another, this is only because there are external reasons. If there are no external reasons, then we cannot go wrong no matter what we do. If we commit ourselves to making the best effort we can make to discern any external reasons that might be in play in our circumstances, what then? Well, if there are no external reasons, then by hypothesis we will not have done anything that we ought not to have done. But what if there are external reasons? Then it seems clear that one of these reasons is a reason to try to discern and act on these reasons. After all, a reason just is a consideration on which we ought to act, and we cannot act on those reasons we have not yet discerned. Hence we should deliberate and act on the supposition that externalism is true, for we either have reason to do so or no

---

[62] The notable exception is T. M. Scanlon, whose discussion of desire forthrightly broaches the question whether our psychological states are ever themselves sources of reasons for action. Still, I do not think that Scanlon has succeeded in spelling out the implications of this point for the debate between internalists and externalists. See Scanlon, *What We Owe to Each Other*, 33–55 and 363–73.

reason not to do so. If the arguments of Chapter 5 are right, this commitment will not involve us in indefensible ontological commitments, and it will require us to take seriously the existence of an array of different values on pain of lapsing into inarticulacy about the point of our life activities.

It might be objected, at this stage, that if there are no practical reasons, then we have theoretical reasons not to deliberate under the false supposition that there are. I believe that this objection fails. As I will argue in Chapter 8, we cannot sequester off a purely theoretical category of reasons for believing truly without depriving ourselves of the broader evaluative resources we need to illuminate our theoretical reasoning as important or worth doing well. If this is right, then theoretical and practical reasons stand or fall together.

CONCLUDING REMARKS ON THE PURSUIT OF PERSONAL PROJECTS

We should be worried by those who seek to reshape the culture's self-image in accordance with their own political or pecuniary interests. But we should be almost equally worried by those well-meaning souls who, under the banner of unsentimental and sober realism, offer human beings a reductively egoistic and instrumentalist image of their thoughts and actions. This dispiriting picture is ascendant in economics and its influence is growing in the study of politics, law, and business. Outside the Academy too, this projected shadow of our suspicions and distrust is increasingly mistaken for a true outline of our psyches. Few are ready to make peace with it, but humorists ceaselessly caricature it (it is the common theme of almost every laugh line in "Seinfeld"), advertisers ceaselessly bank on it, preachers ceaselessly denounce it, and New Age spiritualists ceaselessly invent new cures for it. The more we become convinced that it correctly describes the motivational wellsprings of the actions of others, the more we permit ourselves to be made over in its image—if for nothing else than to avoid being everybody else's fool. This vicious cycle cannot be arrested by romantic allusions to noble savages. Perhaps it can be combated more successfully by sober examination of the conceptual confusions upon which it rests.

The dualistic conception of the good appeals to philosophers because it already structures the thoughts (or the *confusions*) of the contemporary Western culture from which their reflections emerge. It also plays an indirect role in structuring the prevailing interpretations of the historic works to which philosophers might naturally turn in the hope of retrieving a more coherent conception of the good. These works are all too often read as if their notion of the good corresponds with the subjective pole of the dualistic conception. I have tried to show that we can find in these texts the seeds of a monistic conception of the good that corresponds with neither pole of the contemporary dualistic conception. By retrieving this prior conception of the good, we might hope to free ourselves from the perplexities and paradoxes associated with modern dualism and from the sort of monism that affirms only the subjective pole of this dualism.

This interpretive exercise can succeed in retrieving a plausible alternative view only if it is accompanied by a reconsideration of the prevailing idea that the proper practical response to the good is always to promote it, and where possible to bring about more rather than less of it. If we retain this production-based conception of the practical import of the good, then it is particularly tempting to suppose that there *must* be a realm of specifically personal goods that supply particularly strong practical reasons for those to whom they apply. Otherwise we would rarely have good reason to pursue our own distinctive projects, hence we could not reasonably have any such projects. The only reasonable project would be the mandatory group project of efficiently producing impersonal goodness. If everyone were reasonable, the impersonally good would itself become colorless, and human life insipid.

This problem evaporates if we re-conceive of various kinds of intrinsic goodness or value as properties of ongoing activities to which practical thought is to lend a motivationally efficacious and appreciative attention. On this view, proper responsiveness to the impersonally good does not alienate us from our own distinctive projects and commitments, nor does it stand as a barrier to their reasonable development. Rather it draws us into our own activities and renders them complete and unreserved, hence fully enjoyable.

As noted at the outset of this chapter, modern moral theorists have conceived of moral goodness as an impersonal species of goodness that can and often does come into conflict with the pursuit of what is good for oneself. If the arguments of this chapter are right, then this way of conceiving of morality, and of one of the central tasks of philosophical ethics, is fundamentally misguided. The proper task of ethical philosophy is not to show that moral norms provide sound reasons for self-sacrifice but instead to shed light on the sort of self-realization, or individual flourishing, that goes hand-in-hand with a growing appreciation of the value of morally decent relations with one's fellow human beings. While I have touched upon this topic in prior chapters, I turn to it in earnest in the next chapter.

7

Virtues and Other Selves

I ought to be equal to every relation. It makes no difference how many friends I have and what content I can find in conversing with each, if there be one to whom I am not equal. If I have shrunk unequal from one contest, the joy I find in all the rest becomes mean and cowardly. I should hate myself, if then I made my other friends my asylum . . .

(Ralph Waldo Emerson)[1]

. . . now we are not able to see what we are from ourselves (and that we cannot do this is plain from the way in which we blame others without being aware that we do the same things ourselves; and this is the effect of favor or passion, and there are many of us who are blinded by these things so that we judge not aright); as when we wish to see our own face, we do so by looking into the mirror, in the same way when we wish to know ourselves we can obtain that knowledge by looking at our friend.

(Aristotle?)[2]

MAKING SENSE OF *EUDAIMONISTIC* ETHICS

Aristotle portrays the virtues as necessary conditions for a life-long good that he calls *eudaimonia*. While there are perennial debates about how best to capture this Aristotelian notion in English, still 'happiness' remains the preferred translation. This has given rise to an enduring interpretive puzzle. The problem is that Aristotle's list of virtues includes a number of traits that we moderns would categorize as moral, including generosity, truthfulness, and justice. To modern eyes, it seems all but preposterous to suppose that one can never do better

---

[1] Ralph Waldo Emerson, "Friendship," reprinted in Michael Pakaluk, ed., *Other Selves: Philosophers on Friendship* (Indianapolis: Hackett Publishing Company, Inc., 1991), 218–32; quote from 224.

[2] *Magna Moralia* 1213a15–22. The authorship of *Magna Moralia* is in dispute, but if the author was not Aristotle it was at least a near contemporary with considerable insight into and sympathy for his ideas, hence I occasionally help myself to quotes from it in my attempts to explicate Aristotle's ideas.

in the metric of happiness by lying, hoarding possessions, stealing, breaking promises, or performing other injustices—especially if these acts are undetected. Yet Aristotle quite clearly held that one can never enhance one's *eudaimonia* by acting viciously. Furthermore, while we recognize that just actions do sometimes serve to enhance the happiness of those who perform them, we generally think that this is incidental to their value. Aristotle holds, by contrast, that the value of the virtues lies precisely in their constitutive role in the *eudaimon* life.

As we saw in the previous chapter, this is the sort of puzzle that prompted Sidgwick to claim that Greek ethics foundered on "a confusion of thought latent in the common notion of good"[3]—a confusion, more precisely, between what is good for oneself and what is good impersonally. We moderns tend to think that to "do" moral philosophy is to inquire into the nature, source, and content of a cluster of putative norms that limit our self-interested pursuits in recognition of the value of others and their pursuits. Moral virtues seem, on this account, to be states of character that limit the pretensions of self-love in such a way as to manifest a proper recognition of the value of others. From this perspective, it seems like an obvious category error to seek to illuminate the nature or distinctive value of the moral virtues by shedding light on their contribution to the happiness of their possessor. This is what lies behind Anscombe's wry observation that someone who attempts to incorporate Aristotle's views on the virtues into the subject matter of modern moral philosophy "must be very imperceptible if he doesn't constantly feel like someone whose jaws have somehow got out of alignment."[4]

Those who find their jaws "out of alignment" in this rather esoteric way might perhaps be inspired to follow Sidgwick in dismissing Greek ethics as a confused prelude to modern moral philosophy. Yet it would be uncharitable in the extreme to dismiss Aristotelian *eudaimonism* as the manifestation of a simple confusion between prudential and moral goodness, especially given the enormous influence exercised by Aristotle's writings on ethics in twelfth and thirteenth-century Europe, and through Aquinas on the subsequent development of Western thought about ethics and religion. Before we adopt this alternative, we ought to take all available steps to see whether the "misalignment" that we feel when discussing "Aristotelian moral theory" might not mark confusions in the evaluative outlook upon which we have been suckled. The first such step is to note the conceptual strain involved in attempting to capture Aristotle's notion of *eudaimonia* with the reigning modern notion of happiness. Aristotle regards *eudaimonia* as a lifelong *energeia*, or activity. As we saw in Chapter 4, this is tantamount to characterizing it as the sort of human doing that has no end beyond itself, and that actualizes the distinctively human capacity for self-directed movement emerging from and according with right reason. We moderns, by contrast, tend to think of happiness not as an

---

[3] Sidgwick, *The Methods of Ethics*, 405n.   [4] Anscombe, "Modern Moral Philosophy," 26.

activity but as a passive experience that we might seek to produce. We cannot convict Aristotle of a confused conception of the relation between virtue and happiness before we have figured out whether he really is making claims about what we call 'happiness,' and if so, how exactly we are to understand these unfamiliar claims.

Aristotelian ethics also fits uneasily into prevailing conceptions of moral theory because of its non-standard conception of the proprieties of practical thinking. As noted in Chapter 3, it is commonly supposed that a complete ethical theory would be a system of general principles that would tell us which actions are required and which are forbidden in which circumstances. I have argued that moral excellence in practical thinking cannot be captured in principles of this sort. On this question (as on many others) I have followed Aristotle, who insisted upon the uncodifiability of practical wisdom.[5] This stance has a great deal of common-sense appeal, since it seems vaguely ridiculous to suppose that we could become wise by reading a properly elaborated instruction manual, committing it to memory and applying it conscientiously, and worse than ridiculous to put forward the academic philosopher as the ideal candidate for dictating such a manual.

If we accept the thesis of uncodifiability, this raises two closely related methodological questions. First, it raises the question of whether there is anything sensible that can be done under the heading of moral *theorizing*. After all, to accept the thesis of uncodifiability is to disavow the possibility of providing a clear and determinate account, applicable in the course of deliberation, of what morality requires. Once we've abandoned this clearly theoretical aspiration, it remains unclear what other form of normative inquiry might be systematic enough to deserve the honorific title of "theory." Second, it raises the question of whether we can understand ourselves as engaged in *moral* theorizing. Morality, after all, is concerned in large part with articulating and abiding by fair terms of cooperation with others, and it is hard to see how a proper pattern of cooperation could possibly be developed and sustained if its terms cannot be captured in a communicable set of principles. Without such principles, it might seem that we will have no way of letting each other know what we are prepared to count as a proper form of interaction, and this might seem to rule out the development of a mutually acceptable pattern of social cooperation. The Aristotelian must either reject this background picture of the subject matter of moral theory or provide an alternative account of the genesis of mutually affirmable patterns of social cooperation—one that explains how an uncodifiable moral outlook can come to be shared.

The task of this chapter is to retrieve a recognizably Aristotelian view that is capable of meeting this nest of challenges. On the view elaborated below, we learn to be virtuous not by tacitly internalizing or explicitly memorizing

---

5 See Aristotle, *Nicomachean Ethics*, 1094b14–16; 1104a2–11; 1137b13–32; and 1165a12–14.

some list of authoritative principles of action but by developing an uncodifiable evaluative outlook—a sensibility, as it might be called. If we are to develop a virtuous rather than a vicious sensibility, the relationships in which we are engaged must have a very particular sort of structure. They must be sustained by continuously deepening approval by each participant of the other participant's evaluative outlook considered in itself rather than in light of its tendency to serve or further interests of the other person that are conceptually independent of the relationship. Such relationships are wholly different from those symbiotic attachments that are pursued because of their tendency to produce external benefits, such as sensory pleasure or wealth or fame, that could in principle be enjoyed even without the relationship. They differ from these latter relationships in that they require that each participant grasp the other as valuable in himself or herself rather than as a contingent source of personal advantage. For precisely this reason, they provide participants with an external validation of their status as valuable in themselves rather than merely as an instrument for bringing about valuable states of affairs.

The seeds of this view can be found in Aristotle's discussion of friendship (*philia*)—a topic to which he chose to devote two of the ten books of *Nicomachean Ethics* and nearly a third of *Eudemian Ethics*.[6] Drawing upon these writings, I hope to show that Aristotelian character friendship both fosters, and requires for its flourishing, an uncodifiable evaluative outlook whose verdicts meet a stringent standard of affirmability from all relevant social perspectives. The practical demands associated with this standard include many of the demands that we moderns think of as moral obligations. Yet to approach this standard is to enjoy a good that compasses a great deal of what we care about under the heading of happiness. By exploring this standard, then, we might hope to give flesh to the still rather abstract suggestion, put forward in the last chapter, that we moderns have come to accept a misleading dichotomy between personal value of the sort possessed by happiness and impersonal value of the sort possessed by the moral virtues. As we come to see this, we simultaneously bring into view a different way of vindicating the value of the virtues. On this characteristically Ancient conception, the virtues are valuable as necessary constituents of a kind of flourishing whose appeal is not itself merely moral nor merely prudential.

---

[6] Once largely ignored, these writings have recently received a great deal of scholarly attention. The best of this scholarship has helped to dispel the impression that Aristotle (mis)understands friendship as a mutual admiration society, available only to those who are already fully virtuous and sustained by the mutual fascination of such persons with external likenesses of themselves. What has become clear is that Aristotelian friendship is open to imperfect though not to irrevocably vicious human beings, and that it can play an important role in refining the character of those flawed humans who participate in it. For exemplary discussions of these matters, see John Cooper, "Friendship and the Good," in *Reason and Emotion: Essays on Ancient Moral Psychology and Ethical Theory* (Princeton: Princeton University Press, 1999), 336–55; and Nancy Sherman, "Aristotle on Friendship and the Shared Life," *Philosophy and Phenomenological Research* 47 (June 1987), 589–613.

The key aim of this chapter is to shed light on this sort of flourishing and thereby to vindicate the value of the virtues in a way that does not amount to moralistic table-thumping nor to the misguided reduction of moral decency to self-interest.

There is a dialectical relationship between the attainment of virtue and participation in these particularly valuable sorts of human relationships. We cannot enter into the relevant sort of friendship unless we already have a glimmer of appreciation for fine action. Yet as we kindle and deepen human relationships of this ubiquitous sort, our evaluative outlooks are reshaped so as increasingly to be affirmable as good from all relevant social perspectives. Indeed, such relationships cannot move into close approximation to their own defining *telos* unless participants become more virtuous. Hence it can be said both that these relationships are schools of virtue and that they are rewards of virtue. Virtue, then, emerges as a concomitant of an exceedingly valuable kind of human relationship that is not possible in its absence. It also makes possible a valuable sort of wholeheartedness in one's activities.

This is not to suggest that the *point* of Aristotelian friendship is to make people virtuous. Such friendship is *intrinsically* valuable, and ought to be pursued as such. Indeed, neither genuine Aristotelian friendship nor its attendant benefits can be attained by those who value human relationships merely as a means to some further good, including the good of self-improvement.[7] I am suggesting only that when intimate human relationships arise in something approaching their proper form, they are valuable not only for their immediate delights but also for their beneficial influence on one's character and on one's prospects for happiness. This is a marked departure from the philosophically ascendant conception of the relation between friendship and morality, which holds that the demands of friendship and morality are fundamentally antagonistic, and that our friendships might at any time place personal demands upon us that directly conflict with the impersonal demands of morality, yet that can have a similarly uncompromising claim on our allegiance.

WHAT IS ARISTOTELIAN FRIENDSHIP?

There is significant potential for confusion in talk of Aristotelian *friendship*, since Aristotle uses the term '*philia*' to pick out a much broader array of

---

[7] Some interpreters seem to think that Aristotelian friends are engaged in the self-conscious pursuit of mutual moral improvement. For instance, this view is approvingly developed by Dale Jacquette in "Aristotle on the Value of Friendship as a Motivation for Morality," *Journal of Value Inquiry* 35 (2001), 371–89, especially 382. Ferdinand Schoeman also sees traces of this view in Aristotle, though unlike Jacquette he regards this as a serious problem with Aristotle's position. I do not think that Aristotle held this view, but I agree with Schoeman that it is a bad view. See Ferdinand Schoeman, "Aristotle on the Good of Friendship," *Australasian Journal of Philosophy* 63 (1985), 271.

human relationships than speakers of English tend to compass under the term 'friendship.' We distinguish those who are "just friends" from those who are lovers or family members. It would make little sense, by contrast, to say of two people that they were "just *philoi*."[8] The latter term can refer even to the most intimate relationships between lovers, and to the familial relationships between husbands and wives or parents and children. Yet the term can also refer to many relationships that we regard as more impersonal than friendships, including relationships between business associates or fellow citizens. English does not offer an exact synonym for '*philia*.'[9]

What genuine forms of *philia* have in common, according to Aristotle, is that all of them involve reciprocated goodwill (*eunoia*) between two persons, each of whom is aware of the other's goodwill.[10] Aristotle maintains that the best sort of *philia* arises between two people when they choose to seek each other's company and aim to benefit each other out of mutual appreciation of each other's character, and not merely in hope of securing pleasures or other benefits from the other.[11] I will follow the practice of calling these central and particularly valuable sorts of friendships *character friendships*.[12]

In order for a character friendship to take shape between two people, they must spend a great deal of time together, sharing in conversation and other activities.[13] The most basic activity of friendship—the one that accompanies and deepens all the others—is *theorein*. This term is used by Aristotle to refer to focused contemplation of an object of understanding. In other words, it denotes understanding considered as active and attentive appreciation rather than as a mere capacity for recognition of truths.[14] Aristotle uses this term to denote the solitary contemplative activity that stands as the consummation of

[8] Martha Nussbaum makes this point, and the other points rehearsed in this paragraph, in *The Fragility of Goodness: Luck and Ethics in Greek Tragedy and Philosophy* (Cambridge: Cambridge University Press, 1986), 354.

[9] Gregory Vlastos suggests 'love' as "the only English word that is robust and versatile enough" to translate '*philia*.' To my ear, it is odd to use 'love' for the more casual sorts of *philia*, including the relations of fellow citizens in a well-constituted state. See Vlastos, "The Individual as an Object of Love in Plato," in *Platonic Studies* (Princeton: Princeton University Press, 1973), 3–42; quote from 4.

[10] *EN* 1155b32–5

[11] Aristotle makes clear that friendship involves a choice (*prohairesis*) on the part of each to devote active attention to the other, and mutual awareness of having been chosen in this way (*EN* 1158a30–2; *EE* 1236b3–6 and 1237a30–4). See Nancy Sherman, "Aristotle on Friendship and the Shared Life," 589–613, especially 597–8; see also Sherman, "Character, Planning and Choice in Aristotle," *Review of Metaphysics* 39 (1985), 83–106.

[12] I believe this practice was initiated by John Cooper, who finds precedent for it in the following passages: *Eudemian Ethics* 1241a10, 1242b36, and 1243a8, 32 and 35; and *Nicomachean Ethics* 1157a11, 1162b21–3, 1164a12, and 1165b8–9. See Cooper, "Aristotle on the Forms of Friendship," in *Reason and Emotion* (Princeton: Princeton University Press, 1998), 312–35, especially 319–20.

[13] *EN* 1156b25–33 and 1170b11–13.

[14] I owe these points about the meaning of '*theorein*' to Terence Irwin. See the entry under 'study' in Irwin's glossary to the Hackett edition of *Nicomachean Ethics*, 427.

philosophical inquiry and that provides the central activity of the most divine human life. Somewhat surprisingly, Aristotle uses this same term to characterize the sort of appreciative attention that friends direct at each other in a properly constituted friendship.[15] In using this term, Aristotle is not suggesting that explicit philosophical conversation or thought is essential to a good friendship. What he says, instead, is that proper friendship makes possible an immediate appreciation of the nature and goodness of another's character and activity, and that this amplifies one's life by expanding the range of activities that one is able to accompany and complete with appreciative attention.[16] The *theôria* central to character friendship, then, is a natural extension of the *eunoia* that draws us into such friendship—it is the form that a mutual approving regard takes when it becomes confident of the goodness of its object. Given the Aristotelian thesis that the substantive practical implications of virtuous character cannot be codified in a surveyable set of principles, it is hard to see what other form could be taken by the contemplation of human excellence. Since the excellence in question is partly definitive of the human kind, it is hard to see what other form could possibly be taken by a full contemplative awareness of the kind of beings we ourselves are.

It is true that those who have a virtuous ethical disposition have a certain *kind* of knowledge of the verdicts of right reason, yet (at least by the lights of the Aristotelian particularist) they have no way of capturing this knowledge in the form of tractable principles, hence no way of bringing more than selective portions of it before their cognitive gaze at any one time. Their knowledge permits them to see what must be done in whatever circumstances they find themselves or vividly imagine themselves to be. However, this practical mastery of the participant perspective would not itself provide them with a fully substantive and perspicuously surveyable representation of the human *telos*. If this were the only sort of understanding of ethical excellence they had, they would be in the position of the accomplished ballet dancer who has never actually watched a ballet: they would lack full appreciation of the nature and point of the activity at which they excelled. (Though of course it strains credulity to imagine that there could be an accomplished dancer who had never seen others dance well, just as it strains credulity to imagine that anyone could become a consistently praiseworthy agent without having attended to, and developed an appreciation for, the way in which other praiseworthy persons navigate their changing circumstances.) The *theôria* that sustains friendships, then, is arguably essential to genuine insight into the human *telos*. If it is, then it provides an undeveloped Aristotelian ground for denying that the best life for human beings could consist solely in the sort of isolated contemplation described by Aristotle in Book X of the *Nicomachean Ethics*: human beings must enter into active intimate relations with each other if they are to understand what sort of beings they themselves are and what

---

[15] *EN* 1169b34–1170a4.   [16] *EN* 1170a2–1170b18.

aspirations are fitting for them.[17] Hence they must recognize that friendship must be recognized among the things that are fitting for them—and not only fitting, but necessary to any human life well lived.

Aristotle is sometimes taken to have maintained that character friendship is available only to those who are completely virtuous.[18] This interpretation seems to be licensed by Aristotle's claim that such friendship obtains only between "good people similar in virtue"—indeed, between people who are "good unconditionally"—and hence that such friendship is quite rare, since such people are few.[19] However, it would fly in the face of many other things that Aristotle says about character friendship to suppose that less than fully virtuous people cannot engage in it.[20] For instance, Aristotle makes clear that friendship built on mutual love of character can arise between people who are unequal in virtue, though such love should also be unequal so as to remain properly proportioned to the goodness of its object.[21] Further, Aristotle regards character friendships as important schools of virtue, capable of keeping participants from error and deepening their attachment to the good.[22] Clearly character friendship could not play this role if participation required perfect virtue.

It seems, then, that we should follow John Cooper in attributing those passages in which Aristotle seems to suggest that character friendship is the exclusive provenance of the virtuous to "the pervasive teleological bias of [Aristotle's] thinking, which causes him always to search out the best and most fully realized instance when attempting to define a kind of thing."[23] This interpretation permits us to set aside the objection that Aristotelian character friendship is a

---

[17] As is well known, Aristotle concludes the *Nicomachean Ethics* by identifying the life devoted to contemplation (*theorein*) of invariant truths as the best and happiest human life. One of the most perplexing questions in the interpretation of Aristotle is how this account of human happiness can be squared with Aristotle's discussion of the life of virtuous cooperative activity, which occupies the bulk of the *Nicomachean Ethics*. Part of the answer is that humans cannot spend their entire lives engaged in philosophical contemplation. Unlike the Gods, humans need food, shelter, clothing, and much else in order to survive and flourish, and they depend upon productive cooperation with other humans in order to meet these needs (*EN* 1178b1–79a33). Here I am following Amelie Rorty in gesturing towards another possible answer: the life of the social virtues makes available a special sort of contemplation that differs from the divine sort in that it is inextricably dependent upon other people. See Amelie Rorty, "The Place of Contemplation in Aristotle's *Nicomachean Ethics*" in A. O. Rorty, ed., *Essays on Aristotle's Ethics* (Berkeley and Los Angeles: University of California Press, 1980), 377–94.

[18] See for instance Jacquette, "Aristotle on the Value of Friendship," 380–1 and 383.

[19] *EN* 1156b7–26; also 1157a18–20 and *EE* 1237a10–12.

[20] A convincing argument for this claim is found in Cooper, *Reason and Emotion*, 320.

[21] *EN* 1158b12–1159a2; *EE* 1238b15–1239a10. Dean Cocking and Jeanette Kennett read Aristotle as denying that character friendship can obtain among those who are unequal in virtue. However, the passage they cite in defense of this view (*EN* 1165b14–35) arises in the context of Aristotle's argument to the effect that we ought not to create or sustain friendships with those who have become "incurably vicious." Read in its proper context, this passage does not contradict Aristotle's very clear allowance for the possibility of character friendships between parents and children or other parties unequal in virtue. Cocking and Kennett's view is found in "Friendship and the Self," *Ethics* 108, no. 3 (April 1998), 502–27, especially 506.

[22] *EN* 1155a12–16; 1170a11–12; 1172a10–14.   [23] Cooper, *Reason and Emotion*, 320.

static and complacent mutual admiration society, and to portray it instead as an evolving relation within which friends draw each other out and participate in the fine-toothed articulation of each other's character. This interpretation provides us with a revealing way to understand the wide array of personal, familial, and political relations that Aristotle counts as character friendships. In particular, it permits us to see such relationships as lifelong sources of an ethical education that tends towards outcomes that are both *eudaimonistic* and recognizably moral.

FRIENDSHIP AND SELF-AFFIRMING EVALUATIVE OUTLOOKS

Let us use the phrase 'evaluative outlook' to refer to a person's characteristic sense of the evaluative features of actual or possible human doings. With respect to any given evaluative outlook, we can ask whether the outlook is able to affirm or approve of itself without what would count by its own standards as error. This question admits of many interpretations. To specify a particular interpretation, we can begin by distinguishing subjective, intersubjective, and universal self-affirmability. An outlook passes the test of subjective self-affirmability if, when it brings its own verdicts or other manifestations into view, it is invariably able to approve of them. An outlook is intersubjectively self-affirmable if it is capable of affirming at least one instantiation of the same outlook in another person. An outlook is universally self-affirmable if it affirms all possible embodiments of the same outlook, whether in its possessor or in others.

To say that two outlooks are the *same*, in the sense relevant here, is to say—speaking metaphorically for a moment—that they are mirror images of each other. It is not to say that they will generate identical substantive answers to questions about which particular states of affairs are worth bringing about, or which actions are good. They may not. Irreducible indexicals in the verdicts of one outlook will show up as corresponding indexicals in the verdicts of the other outlook. For instance, if A counts as good whatever satisfies A's desires, and if B's outlook is the same as A's, then we can infer that B counts as good whatever satisfies B's desires, but not that B counts as good whatever satisfies A's desires.

In order to articulate a clear standard of self-affirmability, we must say what exactly it means to *affirm* an outlook, for this can be done in different ways. First, one can affirm an outlook *on the whole*, or *unreservedly*. One affirms an outlook on the whole if one counts it as a good sort of outlook to have, while one affirms an outlook unreservedly if one agrees with each and every verdict emanating from the outlook. Second, one can affirm the manifestations of an outlook *conditionally*, under some restricted set of circumstances, or across increasingly more ample sets of counterfactual circumstances, up to and including all possible circumstances. For instance, one might affirm an unyieldingly aggressive outlook in times of unavoidable strife but not unconditionally, whereas one might extend unconditional affirmation to a flexible outlook that is suitably aggressive in times of unavoidable strife but capable of cultivating chances for avoiding strife. When the affirmation of an outlook extends to all possible circumstances, it is *unconditional*.

I am interested for the moment in the sort of self-affirmability that is intersubjective, unreserved, and unconditional. An outlook meets this standard of self-affirmability if it is able to affirm each and every one of its manifestations in at least one other person with the same outlook, across the entire range of possible activities or circumstances. When I speak of self-affirmability *simpliciter*, this is what I will mean. What I hope to show in the remaining sections of the paper is that: (1) the standard of self-affirmability excludes egoistic and malicious evaluative outlooks, hence it has a recognizably moral content (though it may not exhaust our distinctively moral concerns);[24] (2) Aristotelian character friendship is a character-forming (and reforming) relationship that tends over time to bring friends ever closer to fulfilling the standard of self-affirmability; (3) if the demands associated with self-affirmability cannot be systematized in a tractable set of principles, then participation in Aristotelian character friendship might well be the *only* reliable way to approach self-affirmability; and (4) there is a recognizable sense of 'happiness' under which it is true that approaching self-affirmability through friendship conduces to one's happiness.

Let us begin by considering an evaluative outlook that would clearly flunk the test of self-affirmability I've specified, yet might well be subjectively self-affirmable. On the outlook in question, what is good is a strict function of one's own motivational states, or—broadly speaking—one's desires. It is good to satisfy one's own desires so conceived, and whatever promises to bring about such satisfaction is for that reason instrumentally good. It is bad for one's desires to be frustrated, and whatever promises to rule out or diminish the satisfaction of one's desires is for that reason bad. This outlook arguably passes the test of *subjective* self-affirmability, since having the outlook would arguably optimize one's capacity to satisfy one's desires (though perhaps it would not, since it might be possible to satisfy more of one's desires by some other, less direct route). Yet the outlook clearly is not self-affirmable in the sense I've specified.

To see this, consider that any two people who had this outlook and who regularly interacted with each other could and probably would come to have

---

[24] The comparison is complicated, but I believe that the test of self-affirmability is stronger than the test of reasonable acceptability to all that is sometimes associated with John Rawls, yet weaker than T.M. Scanlon's test of reasonable non-rejectability. As Scanlon has pointed out, an ascetic altruist cannot be deemed unreasonable simply in virtue of having accepted heavy personal costs imposed by the predations of an unadulterated egoist, hence even rather extreme forms of egoism seem to be reasonably acceptable to all. I hope to show that such outlooks fail the test of self-affirmability. However, even if an outlook can affirm itself, this hardly shows that no other sort of outlook could give rise to a reasonable rejection against it, hence Scanlon's test would presumably rule out many practical judgments issued by outlooks that would pass the test I've outlined.

conflicting desires, either because the states of affairs they desire to bring about are not jointly possible, or because the most efficient means to the fulfillment of one person's desires would hinder fulfillment of the other's desires. They would then reject each other's assessments of the value of possible states of affairs and of possible actions open to each of them. Of course, two such people *could* conceivably cooperate with each other indefinitely without any such conflict. However, even if this somewhat improbable harmony were to obtain, this would not mean that their outlooks pass the test of self-affirmability, since this test extends to *counterfactual* circumstances.

We can see, then, that the most familiar prudential conceptions of what it is good to do, or what there is reason to do, are not self-affirmable. This is true of those conceptions that ground the good in the satisfaction of one's own desires or preferences, whether actual or informed, and also of pleasure-based conceptions of prudential rationality. Many other morally problematic outlooks, including for instance those straightforwardly malicious outlooks that count the suffering of others itself as good, will also clearly fail the test of self-affirmability. Indeed, the test of self-affirmability would almost certainly not be met by any conception of the good that ties the good for each individual to what might be called an *atomistic* notion of flourishing, where this means a notion of flourishing that can convincingly be elaborated without considering the compossibility of flourishing so conceived with the like flourishing of others. It would be surprising if any such notion of flourishing happened to have, magically built into it, the sorts of recognizably moral limitations demanded by the test of self-affirmability.

Aristotle considers two atomistic conceptions of the good that would surely fail the test of self-affirmability. The first such conception locates the good of each person in that person's pleasure and, by extension, in whatever gives rise to such pleasure. Pleasure is here understood, in what Aristotle takes to be a popular yet incomplete and potentially misleading sense, as an introspectible sensation that can be caused by a variety of activities but that is conceptually separable from engagement in these activities. The second conception locates the good of each person in whatever would be useful for fulfilling that individual's contingent ends or purposes. Aristotle does not say much about how these contingent ends or purposes are to be specified, but I think we can safely take contemporary desire-satisfaction and preference-satisfaction theories of welfare to be instances of the conception of the good that Aristotle has in mind here.

Interestingly, Aristotle's fullest critique of these two atomistic conceptions of the good appears in the midst of his discussion of friendship. He argues that those who value other people only insofar as they are useful or pleasant will not be capable of the best sort of friendship, but only of ontologically derivative and far less valuable forms of friendship. Aristotle's most frequently repeated criticism of pleasure- and utility-based friendships is that they are unstable, lasting only as long as the contingent overlap in what happens to be pleasurable or useful to both friends.[25] This, however, cannot be the sole problem or even the most important problem with such friendships. Aristotle's view is not that friendships of all sorts are of roughly equal value while they last, and that friendships of pleasure or utility are defective only in that they tend not to last. He quite rightly views these friendships as inferior to character friendships even while they last, and even if they happen to last a lifetime.

The fundamental shortcoming of such friendships is that the parties to them are not in a position to affirm each other's evaluative outlooks unreservedly and unconditionally. This makes such relationships fragile, but the real problem with these relationships is that they offer participants an unsatisfying picture of their own value. It will not be possible to attain a proper view of this problem until the end of this chapter. For now, it will perhaps help to note that if such friends imaginatively occupy the external perspective occupied by their friend, they themselves do not show up as valuable in themselves but only as *instrumentally* valuable. From that perspective, their own value, and by extension the value of their own pleasures or desired pursuits, appear to be conditioned upon their contingent tendency to serve the needs or interests of another person. Yet they ordinarily understand their pleasures or the satisfaction of their desires as unconditionally valuable and as the condition of the value of anything else. If the arguments of the last chapter are correct, this disagreement cannot coherently be overcome by introducing a perspective-relative distinction between what is good for each friend, and holding that the pleasure or satisfaction of each friend is correctly seen as intrinsically good from the perspective of that friend but as only instrumentally good from the perspective of the other friend. A cultural propensity to make such distinctions is a sign that interpersonal relationships are in ill health, not a sign of progress beyond simple monistic conceptions of the good.

There is considerable scholarly debate about whether Aristotle believed friendships based on mutual pleasure or utility to require mutual goodwill (*eunoia*), hence to have the same essential structure as character friendships. Aristotle seems to contradict himself on this point. At one point, he seems to say that friendship can involve mutual and mutually known *eunoia* arising either from pleasure, usefulness, or appreciation of virtuous character.[26] However, this claim arises in the context of Aristotle's attempt to illuminate *the common belief* that friendship is reciprocated *eunoia*. Aristotle goes on to reject some elements of this common belief. One element that he explicitly rejects is the notion that friendships grounded in pleasure or usefulness arise from, or tend to engender, *eunoia*.[27] Such friends, he says, do not in fact have *eunoia* towards *each other*, since they seek to benefit each other only because, and insofar as, they expect a reciprocal benefit for themselves. On the contrary, they appear to have *eunoia* only towards

[25] *EN* 1156a19–b3, 1157a7–16, 1158b8–11. [26] *EN* 1156a5–6.
[27] *EN* 1167a13–18.

themselves (though Aristotle goes on to deny even this appearance),[28] since they seek another's benefit only to the extent that this will conduce to their own benefit. Indeed, Aristotle suggests that friends of pleasure or utility do not really love people at all. Rather, they see their "friends" as an extension of the world of things, to be used for personal benefit.[29]

If we are thinking of pure rather than mixed cases of these kinds of deficient friendships (and there may be very few pure cases), this seems like exactly the right thing to say. It would also seem right to point out, as Aristotle does, that such friends can never *really* agree about what is good or worthwhile, but at best can *seem* to agree.[30] They seem to agree upon the goodness of the shared activities that constitute their friendship, but on inspection each traces the real point of these activities to the perceived goodness of different sets of expected effects. A relation can be grounded in genuine agreement about the good only if the parties to it seek to discern and act in the name of objective goods. For Aristotle, this implies that genuine agreement is possible only for the virtuous, since it is the mark of virtue to act in the name of the fine rather than in the name of subjective ends set by one's own desires and pleasures.[31] Hence genuine agreement is available only to good persons, and such agreement should itself be counted as ethically good.[32] Since character friendship involves such agreement, the implication is that it too is good.

---

[28] *EN* 1166b17–29.

[29] *EE* 1237b31–4. This same claim—i.e. that friends from pleasure or utility lack *eunoia* towards each other—surfaces in several other passages (e.g. *EN* 1164a10–12, 1157a14–16, and 1165b3–4), and it is presented throughout as Aristotle's own view rather than as an account of what people commonly say about friendship. Given this, it seems best to take these claims at face value, rather than to embrace John Cooper's ingenious and influential attempt to defuse them. (See Cooper, *Reason and Emotion*, 315–19.) To his credit, Cooper does note (316n) that the main textual evidence for his interpretation arises in the context of Aristotle's elaboration of common beliefs about friendship. Cooper is unimpressed by this fact because Aristotle goes on to rely upon many of the things commonly said about friendship in developing his own account, hence must be construed as affirming the common account. This strikes me as a *non-sequitur*. Aristotle's routine method is to place provisional trust in common beliefs, and to salvage as many as possible while explaining the appeal of those he cannot salvage upon philosophical reflection. The fact that he ends up affirming most of the common beliefs about friendship in no way indicates that we must read him as affirming all of them. Further, Aristotle's position yields a perfectly good explanation of the common belief that (on my reading) he rejects. On Aristotle's view, all friends are motivated to pursue certain things that they believe their friend to need for his/her own good. The difference is that in the best sort of friendship this is done out of appreciation of the friend's intrinsic goodness (i.e. out of *eunoia*), while in other friendships it is done for instrumental reasons, in hopes of securing egoistic benefits. It is not surprising that common beliefs fail to provide a clear register of a motivational difference that lies so far from overt behavior. It is especially unsurprising given that most actual friendships are unlikely to be clear and unalloyed cases of just one of the three forms of friendship that Aristotle distinguishes for his analytical purposes.

[30] *EE* 1241a23–8. Compare to *EN* 1167a33–b16, where Aristotle says that vicious people cannot be expected to agree about matters of distributive justice. They can agree in one sense (they might all want for themselves just what all others want), but not in another sense (except under very rare and fragile circumstances, they will not agree about who is to get what).

[31] *EE* 1236b36–1237a2 and *MM* 1207b31–3.   [32] *EE* 1241a21–3.

On the interpretative approach that I have taken, what is essential to character friendship is that participants are drawn to each other out of appreciation of the intrinsic value of each other's character, where *character* is understood to include, if not to be exhausted by, what I have called an evaluative outlook. Now, Aristotle is sometimes thought to have held that only one sort of character could properly be counted as good in itself, hence that the parties to an ideal character friendship would necessarily have the same type of character. If so, they would clearly have a self-affirmable character, since they unconditionally approve of a friend who shares their character type. However, if we balk at the thought that objectively affirmable human goods are unitary rather than plural (as I think we should), we can question whether participation in an ideal character friendship really requires a self-affirming evaluative outlook. Why, after all, can't there be friends who unconditionally affirm *each other's* differing outlooks, even though at least one of them cannot fully affirm any external instantiation of *his own* (type of) outlook?

If friend A has a non-self-affirming outlook, then he could not affirm certain manifestations of his own type of evaluative outlook if it were instantiated in someone else. Yet friend B could be joined with A in a perfect character friendship only if he could affirm all manifestations of A's type of evaluative outlook when instantiated in someone other than himself (namely, in A). Given this, A cannot be in a perfect character friendship with B, because A cannot agree with B's assessment of actual or possible persons other than A who have the same outlook as A. The inference here does not rely on the questionable principle that when we cannot affirm the goodness or propriety of something, we also cannot affirm another's affirmation of the goodness or value of that thing. The argument goes through because B regards outlooks of A's type as unconditionally affirmable, yet A must maintain that there are conditions on the affirmability of the outlook, since he takes his own circumstances to rule out affirmation of the outlook when instantiated in anyone but himself. Unless friend A modifies his evaluative outlook so as to overcome any obstacles to affirming his outlook in another, he cannot be in a perfect character friendship. The implication is that as character friendship approaches its constitutive ideal, the parties to it must simultaneously approach the standard of self-affirmability.

In the ideal friendship, each friend is able to affirm every evaluation issued by the other. Since this affirmation is unconditional, it would be maintained from the standpoint of any relation that either friend could enter into with the other. The range of relevant relations here is not limited to those that friends *qua friends* could have towards one another; it includes all relations that friends *qua human beings* can have to one another. This is because an ideal friendship of this sort is *constituted* by unconditional mutual approval, and hence cannot itself be called upon to establish or explain the possibility of such approval. What this means is that perfect character friendship has a stronger consequence than mere intersubjective self-affirmability. The parties to such a friendship must be able to affirm an external instantiation of their own outlook unconditionally. But this means that they must be able to affirm any external instantiation of their own outlook, since they impose no conditions on their affirmation of this sort of outlook. Engagement in an ideal character friendship, then, somewhat surprisingly implies attainment of the standard of universal self-affirmability.[33] It requires, in other words, that one be able to affirm all manifestations of one's own outlook as objectively good.

If Aristotle were right to suppose that all vice springs from a tendency to choose in the name of the pleasurable or useful rather than in the name of the fine, then engagement in an ideal character friendship would imply the attainment of perfect virtue. My own view is that Aristotle's diagnosis captures most but not all cases of vice. It seems to me, for instance, that there is a rare though perfectly possible mode of martial self-assertion that unequivocally affirms its mirror images, hence can celebrate the character of a victorious foe even as he raises his sword for the final blow. The Homeric hero seems to answer to this description, as does the possessor of what Nietzsche calls a noble mode of valuation.[34] It seems, then, that we must either count such figures as virtuous, or reject Aristotle's claim that the genuine agreement cultivated by character friendship is available only to the virtuous. It is not easy to say whether we here run up against a fundamental evaluative disagreement with Aristotle or an oversight in his discussion of vice. Still, the consonance between Aristotle's ethical concerns and contemporary moral concerns is at least as impressive as any dissonance that might be thought to emerge here. It may be true that the sort of agreement that accompanies Aristotelian character friendship, and that Aristotle took to be a sure sign of virtue, does not rule out all those forms of character that we moderns would call morally vicious. Still, it does rule out the most common forms of vice, and it lets in only those rare and assiduously self-consistent varieties for which we are likely to have at least a grudging admiration.[35]

---

[33] Put another way, it entails a capacity to affirm oneself from what Thomas Nagel calls the impersonal point of view. I side with Jennifer Whiting, and against the explicit or implicit views of most other commentators, in taking Aristotelian friendship to have an impartial and recognizably moral upshot closely analogous to Nagel-style impersonal reasoning. I would only add (in what I believe to be an Aristotelian vein) that Nagel's view of practical reasoning gives too prominent a role to the formulation and assessment of principles of action. It seems to me that it will very rarely be possible to summarize central elements of one's mode of practical evaluation in terms of principles whose adequacy one could check by monological attempts at impersonal reasoning. My suggestion is that friendship can help to reshape one's outlook so as to make it impersonally affirmable without relying upon such a possibility. See Whiting, "Impersonal Friends," *Monist* 74 (1991), 3–29, especially 21. See also Thomas Nagel, *The Possibility of Altruism* (Princeton: Princeton University Press, 1970). For explicit denials that character friendship requires an entirely impersonal or impartial mode of reasoning, see Nancy Sherman, "Aristotle on Friendship and the Shared Life," 592 and John Benson, "Making Friends: Aristotle's Doctrine of the Friend as Another Oneself," in Andros Loizou and Harry Lesser, eds., *Polis and Politics: Essays in Greek Moral and Political Philosophy* (Brookfield, Hong Kong, Singapore, and Sydney: Avebury Press, 1990), 50–68, especially 62.

[34] Friedrich Nietzsche, *On the Genealogy of Morals*, First Essay, Sections 2–11.

[35] It might well be possible to fill in the gap between what shareability rules out and what morality requires by invoking a broadly Aristotelian conception of human needs. One very

I argued in Chapters 4 and 6 that there is reason to act on our desires or to pursue all but the simplest of what we call our pleasures only if these courses of action have some value that is independent of our desires or pleasures. I also argued that there is no distinctive category of person-relative goodness, and that the burgeoning cottage industry of philosophical analyses of this sort of goodness is the sophisticated philosophical expression of a pervasive illusion about the good—one whose precursors were considered and rejected by both Plato and Aristotle. If this conclusion is right, then one common way of specifying the subject matter of moral theory must be rejected. It is often thought that the moral domain consists in a set of objective and impersonal limits on what can permissibly be done in pursuit of what is good for oneself, or good prudentially. On this view, it can be morally bad, hence bad in an impersonal sense, to act in ways that enhance one's own good, just as it can be morally good, hence good in an impersonal sense, to act in ways that compromise one's own good. Morality, on this view, must have a motivational source quite different from prudential reasoning or egoistic advantage.

If we reject the dualism of practical reason, as I have urged that we should, we must find an alternative way of understanding the nature and source of our moral concerns. Aristotelian virtue ethics can provide such an alternative. The idea that our own good lies in vicious action can be regarded as a tempting illusion, grounded in a reflectively unstable conception of the good. The name of the illusion just is the duality of practical reason, or, in more extreme forms, the egoistic univocity of practical reason. The illusion is grounded in an uncritical acceptance of the picture of value embedded in our desires and/or our pleasures. If we were wholly to overcome this illusion (something that would require a great deal more than the acceptance of a philosophical argument), we would thereby strip away a great deal of the appeal of those actions and lives that we commonly regard as immoral. But we would not strip away all of it. The Nietzschean and Homeric conceptions of virtue might still protrude as viable, objectively affirmable conceptions of how it is best to be and to live (whether this is how Nietzsche thought of the value of supra-moral virtues is another matter). If these conceptions involve an error, it is an error of a very different kind: not a retreat into an incoherently introverted conception of the good, but an affirmation of a coherent yet mistaken conception of the sort of human goodness that merits universal approval. Here we arrive at what really ought to be the center of gravity of the argument over morality's normative authority. This argument ought not to center on the question whether moral reasons have practical authority even when they require us to do what is contrary to our own good, since this question is framed by a misguided dualism about the good. It ought to center, instead,

---

interesting exploration of this possibility can be found in Martha Nussbaum's "Non-Relative Virtues: An Aristotelian Approach," in Nussbaum and Amartya Sen, eds., *The Quality of Life* (Oxford: Oxford University Press, 1993), 242–69.

on the question whether those virtues we call moral really are necessary and/or sufficient for an objectively good human life.

When the center of gravity of debate is altered in this way, one result is to cast light on the vast and interesting disagreements that emerge when we try to say with any degree of specificity what the "moral virtues" actually are. As long as debate within ethical theory centers on the question whether there really is reason to be virtuous rather than assiduously self-interested, these disagreements are swept under the carpet. But if our task is to try to show that a life of activity expressive of the virtues really is an ideally good human life, these disagreements must be confronted. We must ask, for instance, whether the term 'prudence' has shifted its meaning over the years so that it no longer provides a fit translation for Aristotle's '*phronesis*' but has instead come to name something Aristotle would find wholly misguided: the self-interested component of a production-oriented commitment to the good. We must ask whether industry and acquisitiveness ought to be counted as virtues, as Benjamin Franklin thought, or as the internalized impetus for frittering away life in fits of getting and spending. We must ask whether patriotism is a laudable sort of loyalty towards those with whom one shares a fate, or an ideological bulwark for stabilizing political subservience. Or we might ask how prudence, industry, and patriotism must be reconceived if they are to pass muster as genuinely virtuous dispositions. When the discussion unfolds in this way, we abandon stark discussion of opposition between moral demands and preservation of "life and limb" in favor of nuanced discussion of what sort of character merits our admiration. Put another way, we refine our everyday sense of the admirable rather than preparing hortatory speeches for self-sacrifice in emergency occasions that very rarely arise.

FRIENDSHIP AND THE CULTIVATION OF VIRTUE

If the concrete implications of the standard of universal self-affirmability could be captured in some tractable set of principles for evaluating actions or ends, it might be possible to approach this standard outside of friendship, through isolated "monological" reflection. Aristotle, however, seems to have held both that there is such a thing as objective excellence in practical reasoning and that standards of correctness cannot be codified in any tractable set of principles (*EN* 1104a2–11). This "particularist" stance implies that one cannot attain excellence in practical reasoning (i.e. *phronesis*) through monological assessment of practical principles that one has or might seek to adopt. I argued in Chapter 3 that we ought to join Aristotle in his particularism, since a principle-based conception of excellence in practical thinking does not make proper room for the sort of thought by which we carry forward activities that are already underway. Such thought exhibits itself in such activities, but the content of this sort of practical thinking is itself irreducibly evaluative, hence cannot be captured in principles capable of providing guidance to those who do not yet grasp the goods or values exhibited by these activities. Given this, we cannot learn to be good by memorizing and committing ourselves to some list of practical principles. If we are to attain objectively good evaluative outlooks, we will have to do so by some other, less direct route.

Character friendship would seem to provide such a route. Intuitively, it is not hard to see why character friendship might tend over time to make friends more capable of unreservedly and unconditionally affirming each other's evaluative outlooks. After all, such friendships will be marked by conversation about matters of importance to them both, and these conversations will presumably help participants to become more articulate about the best and most laudable patterns of human activity and interactivity, and to correct for idiosyncratic blind spots in their appreciation of these activities.[36] Since such friends admire each other's sense of the good, each will give credence to the other's attempts to put their basic concerns into words. They will, in effect, be partners in the ongoing task of talking their own half-formed evaluative commitments into a full-fledged and determinate stance in the world.[37] Their confidence in each other's outlooks will also lead them to care about each other's approval, and to strive to be worthy of it.[38] This is very different from being moved to self-reform by the mere wish for another's approval. This latter motivation could not yield true virtue, understood as unwavering devotion to the good as such, but only that simulacrum of virtue arising from a sense of shame.[39] Those devoted to the good as such would welcome another's approval only insofar as it indicates that they are good.[40]

The process at issue here is very much like the sort of dialectic described in Chapters 2 and 3, through which we advance our understanding of the goods internal to our own unfolding activities. The difference is that in this case the dialectical apprehension of the value of one's words and actions is offered from an external perspective and filtered through an evaluative outlook that we trust but

---

[36] As Aristotle notes, "We enlist partners in deliberation on large issues when we distrust our own ability to discern [the right answer]" (*EN* 1112b10–12).

[37] My Aristotelian picture of friendship here intersects in part with the conception of friendship set out by Cocking and Kennett, who take friends to engage in the mutual drawing, hence in the partial creation, of each other's characters and self-conceptions. What drops from view, in their picture of friendship, is any good explanation of what we see in our friends in particular that would prompt us to trust them with the elaboration of our character, and of the way in which our special esteem for their audience might inspire us to stretch ourselves towards our own inchoate ideals—i.e. to provide them with more satisfying raw material with which to draw our character. See Dean Cocking and Jeanette Kennett, "Friendship and the Self" and "Friendship and Moral Danger," *Journal of Philosophy* 97 (May 2000), 278–96.

[38] *EN* 1172a8–14. Cf. Martha Nussbaum, *The Fragility of Goodness* (Cambridge: Cambridge University Press, 1986), 363ff; Jacquette, "Aristotle on the Value of Friendship," 379 and 384, and Nancy Sherman, "Aristotle on the Shared Life," in Neera Kapur Badhwar, ed., *Friendship: A Philosophical Reader* (Ithaca, NY: Cornell University Press, 1993), 91–107, especially 92.

[39] *EE* 1230a17–27.   [40] *EN* 1159a18–24.

that is almost sure to be different from our own. This dialectical progression is convincingly described by Aristotle (or possibly one of his followers—authorship is in dispute) in the following passage from *Magna Moralia*:

now we are not able to see what we are from ourselves (and that we cannot do this is plain from the way in which we blame others without being aware that we do the same things ourselves; and this is the effect of favor or passion, and there are many of us who are blinded by these things so that we judge not aright); as when we wish to see our own face, we do so by looking into the mirror, in the same way when we wish to know ourselves we can obtain that knowledge by looking at our friend.[41]

It seems intuitively obvious that we can sometimes gain clearer insight into the value of our own mode of comportment by seeing it exemplified by others. Thus, children (and not only children) who are unable to see what's wrong with their own behavior when they are extremely angry or resentful are rarely inclined to praise or even to defend similar behavior by their siblings or friends. While we might learn about ourselves by watching almost anyone (or by watching movies or reading novels, for that matter), we are particularly able to learn about ourselves by watching our friends in action. There are at least two reasons for this. First, we are better able to understand the characteristic evaluative outlook of those to whom we have devoted prolonged intimate attention. When we see them engaged in some activity whose point remains partially opaque to us, and when they go on to explain to us what they see in it, we are more likely to trust that it has a point and to gain our first glimmer of that point than when we witness a stranger engaged in a similar activity. Second, many of the more idiosyncratic portions of our own evaluative outlooks have been improvised jointly with our intimates. We can assess and refine these elements of our sensibility by dialectical alteration between expressing them in action and conversation, and interpreting the words and actions of our friends as further sources of evaluative insight. At its best, this is a mutual and continuously reiterated process, one that displaces each friend from the confines of his or her existing commitments and concerns, and permits them to discern the outlines of newly evolving concerns in the person of the other. This mutual, dialectical alteration is the process by which a distinctive, shareable sensibility comes to have a determinate and increasingly articulate form.

There are, then, intuitive reasons to suppose that the parties to character friendships will tend increasingly to approximate the standard of self-affirmability. However, Aristotle points the way towards a deeper and philosophically more interesting set of reasons for believing character friendship to have a reformative influence on character. To see these reasons, we will have to grapple first with Aristotle's somewhat obscure thought that each such friend loves the other *as*

----

[41] *MM* 1213a15–22.

another oneself.[42] This thought can easily be misunderstood as an indication of an objectionably narcissistic notion of friendship. I have tried to fend off such a misunderstanding by describing character friendship not as a static mutual admiration society but as a dynamic relation that is typically driven by a certain degree of dissatisfaction with the state of one's own character, or at least by an eagerness to reform that character in such a way as to make it worthy of the admiration of someone admirable. The parties to such friendships become increasingly able to affirm each other's characters without reservation, and they do so through the same process that permits them to affirm their own character without reservation.[43]

This picture of the phenomena rests, to be sure, on a somewhat unfamiliar account of the target of genuine love of self or of others. I have thus far spoken of the proper object of personal love, whether self-directed or other-directed, as a person's characteristic evaluative outlook. In elaborating this view, I believe myself to be adhering closely to Aristotle's claim that the proper object of personal love (whether self-love or love of another) is the person's *nous*—that is, the intelligence or understanding by which the person grasps the *arche* or substantive origins of proper thought in any area of inquiry.[44] Aristotle's picture of the proper object of personal love might seem to be broader than the one I have elaborated, since he understands *nous* to have both a theoretical and practical application, hence to be expressed in one's grasp of the proper starting points for both sorts of thought. In fact it will be broader only if theoretical reflection is properly answerable to a separate *telos* distinct from that of practical reflection—a thesis I challenge in the next chapter. Still, in his discussion of personal love, he focuses primarily on the practical expression of *nous*. On his view, *nous* is loved not as a mere *capacity* for practical reasoning but as an achieved grasp of the proper starting points for such reasoning—an achieved grasp that is the unifying

---

[42] *EN* 1166a32, 1169b6, 1170a3–4, 1170b6–7.

[43] Whiting offers an extremely interesting elaboration and defense of this picture of Aristotelian character friendship in "Impersonal Friends." I follow Whiting in at least two respects: (1) we both understand the sort of love that character friends have towards themselves and others as directed at and justified by the kind of character they exemplify; and (2) we both insist that this obviates the need to choose between justifying concern for others in terms of self-concern or justifying self-concern in terms of concern for others.

[44] *EN* 1140b30–1141a8. As Kahn points out, Aristotle emphasizes this point by mentioning it four times in the brief discussion of the relationship between self-love and love of others found at *EN* 1166a15–33. See Charles H. Kahn, "Aristotle and Altruism," *Mind* 90 (1981), 20–40. I am not entirely persuaded by Kahn's argument that the *nous* Aristotle supposes us capable of loving in ourselves and others is a transpersonal entity. It suffices for my purposes if we love the particular form it takes in certain people, and if we identify these people (or, at least, identify what is loveable in these people) with the basic commitments of their *nous*. This is the reading of Aristotle's view of the self found in Terence Irwin's *Aristotle's First Principles* (Oxford: Oxford University Press, 1988), 345 and 377–8. It has striking resonances with the notion of the practical self, and of "practical identity," found in Lecture III of Christine Korsgaard's *The Sources of Normativity* (Cambridge: Cambridge University Press, 1996).

and properly controlling element of the psyche.[45] The idea is that a grasp of the proper *arche* or origin of practical thinking pulls its possessor together as an unified self, opening the possibility both of full and proper self-love and of undeceived, unreserved, and mutually loving relationships with others.

In the realm of practical reason, the *arche* or origin will be the basic end by reference to which one lives.[46] Stated in very general hence unhelpful terms, this basic end ought to be the fine, or the human good in itself.[47] An individual's *nous* is properly loved only because and to the extent that it constitutes a commitment to the fine or good in itself. This has the important implication that the proper object of interpersonal love is another's evaluative outlook considered as a type—one that could in principle be instantiated in another. (This, however, does not mean that each friend must *have* a determinate representation of the other's outlook considered as a repeatable type. I will return to this crucial point in the next section.) An evaluative outlook is properly loved only because and to the extent that it exemplifies the zeal for adherence to objective truths about the good that is the proper *telos* of the human capacity for practical reason. This is the proper object of the *theôria* that sustains friendships. To love the *nous* of another in itself is to love the other for approximating, or at least striving to approximate, her own proper *telos* as a practical reasoner.

The evaluative outlook of another cannot be loved in itself by those who value only that which conduces to their own contingent pleasures, or only that which satisfies their own desires. Such persons could at best value the evaluative outlook of another as a mere means, affirmable only insofar as its verdicts happen to harmonize with the promotion of their own ends. It is of course possible that a person who values only his own pleasures (an egoist) could encounter another (a servant) whose practical reason is so oriented that he regards as good only that which conduces to the egoist's pleasures. In such a case, the egoist could affirm the verdicts of the servant in all possible circumstances. However, the egoist could not affirm the servant's outlook taken as a type, in abstraction from its contingent relation to himself. After all, the egoist's current outlook would lead him to abhor the prospect of coming himself to have an outlook of the servant's type, and he could not unconditionally affirm that type of outlook when instantiated in someone devoted to a third person whose hedonistic pursuits might conflict with his own. Nor could the egoist unconditionally affirm the generic type of condition that he himself places on the affirmability of the servant's outlook. The egoist would be bound to reject the outlook of another person who stood ready to affirm the egoist's mode of practical reasoning only on condition that the egoist single-mindedly promote that person's pleasure.

The kind of egoist I've sketched is unable to count his own evaluative outlook or that of anyone else (even someone with a servile devotion to his egoistic pursuits) as an intrinsically good type of outlook to have—i.e. as good quite

45 *EN* 1178a3.   46 *EN* 1140b17–19, 1110b10, 1139a32–6.   47 *EN* 1102a1–5.

apart from its contingent relation to himself. This bars him from the proper love of any person, including himself. He cannot love himself in virtue of the character traits that he exemplifies. He can love his character only from a more primitive preference for the more basic, featureless substance in which it is instantiated. Yet this featureless substance has no distinguishing merits that call for, or justify, such love. This helps to bring out the appeal of the claim, made by the author of *Magna Moralia*, that the vicious person can love himself only *qua* self and not *qua* good.[48] When such a person counts his pleasures or desires as guides to the good, this is merely an expression of unmotivated self-preference, and not an expression of his conviction that his substantive life-informing pursuits meet a standard they might conceivably fail. Here we get at the real problem with the subjective pole of the modern dualistic conception of the good. Those caught in its grip cannot direct towards themselves the sort of self-love that might provide a lodestar for their own actions, or that might intelligibly be regarded, even in their own eyes, as a mark of merit or distinction.

Now, Aristotle held that vice just is attentiveness and responsiveness to putative reasons for action that seem to be reasons only because of their relation to one's own contingent desires or pleasures.[49] In other words, vice consists in a tendency to depart from the proper object of choice, the fine, in favor of one of the two other possible objects of choice recognized by Aristotle: the pleasant or the useful. When the vicious deviate from the fine in pursuit of what pleases them or what they desire, they manifest their love of themselves *qua* selves (rather than *qua* good), in the sense that they assign value to their own pleasures or to the satisfaction of their own desires simply in virtue of the fact that these pleasures or desires are their own, and not because they regard pleasure or desire-satisfaction as good in itself (i.e. good wherever it occurs). They are able to affirm and love their evaluative outlook only because it is theirs and not because it is a worthy type of outlook to have. It is because this particular, errant form of self-love is ubiquitous, and because it gives rise to actions whose value cannot be affirmed from all relevant perspectives, that self-love has a bad name.[50] The proper sort of self-love—the sort conditioned on and inspired by the intrinsic goodness of the *form* taken by one's own evaluative outlook—is not only unobjectionable but unreservedly good. As Aristotle puts it, ". . . when everyone competes to achieve what is fine and strains to do the finest actions, everything that is right will be done for the common good, and each person individually will received the greatest of goods, since that is the character of virtue."[51]

Character friendship is the relation within which we engage in the mutual reshaping of our evaluative outlooks so as simultaneously to make possible a proper love of self and a proper love of others. Both sorts of love are directed at practical thought taken not as mere potentiality but as a properly developed

---

[48] *MM* 1212b8–23.   [49] I will argue for this interpretation in the next section.
[50] *EN* 1168a28–35 and 1168b17–28.   [51] *EN* 1169a8–11.

capacity, loveable because it approximates or at least strives to approximate impersonal standards of excellence. Character friendship begins with *eunoia*, understood as spontaneous and still untested approval of another's *nous*, then continuously moves towards greater insight into, investment in and love for that *nous*. As friendship moves in this way towards its constitutive ideal, the friends become increasingly able to love another's form of practical understanding and to love their own. It becomes increasingly true of them that what each does is in a sense done by the other, since their actions often have the same "origin"—that is, they spring from an *arche* or grounding evaluative commitment that is shared by both friends, partly because they have jointly worked out its contours. Perhaps this is why Aristotle claims that "We are ourselves in a way jointly responsible for our states of character, and by having the states of character we have we lay down the sort of end we do."[52]

Self-love, then, cannot be counted upon as a psychological primitive, already in place prior to friendship, that can then be extended to friends insofar as they somehow come to be counted within the boundaries of the self (i.e. as other selves). Rather, the capacity to love ourselves and the capacity to love others arise together, as the result of our struggles to perfect the ubiquitous human relationships that Aristotle calls *philia*—a category broad enough to include friendships, love relationships, parent–child relations, and well-constituted relations among neighbors or fellow citizens.[53] As we deepen and perfect these relationships, we arrive at a picture of the human good whose pursuit and attainment is compossible for all, and we remold our characteristic pleasures and desires so as to orient ourselves towards that picture of the human good. It turns out that we cannot arrive at a fully satisfactory picture of what is good in itself for humans to be or do without simultaneously arriving at a picture of human flourishing that is adequate for entire communities of human beings. Aristotle's discussion of

---

[52] *EN* 1114b23–4. Consider also Aristotle's puzzling claim that ". . . what our friends achieve is, in a way, achieved through our agency, since the origin is in us" (*EN* 1112b28–9) The most obvious reading of this passage is that sometimes our friends do things at our explicit request, and in those cases the origin is in us. But Aristotle might have had in mind the more fundamental idea that I've sketched here.

[53] As Whiting has noted, this departs from the reading of Aristotle favored by many contemporary scholars and theorists, including Terence Irwin and David Brink. It also departs somewhat from Julia Annas' interested account of the matter. Annas rightly points out that Aristotle does not attempt to reduce the concern we have towards a friend to some other sort of concern, such as concern for ourselves in the ordinary sense. She argues that he attempts to avoid this, while retaining the thesis that self-love is the primary human motivation, by conceiving of friendship as an expansion of the bounds of the self as those are ordinarily understood. Where Annas goes wrong, I think, is in attributing to Aristotle the view that in humans, self-love can be regarded as a psychological given. Perhaps this is true of some kind of self-concern, but not of genuine self-love, since Aristotle denies that the vicious are incapable of such self-love (*EN* 1166b2–25). See Julia Annas, *The Morality of Happiness* (New York and Oxford: Oxford University Press, 1993), 254. See also Whiting, "Impersonal Friends," 4–6 and 10; Irwin, *Aristotle's First Principles*, 395 and David O. Brink, "Eudaimonism, Love and Friendship, and Political Community," *Social Philosophy and Policy* (1999), 252–89, especially 255–6.

friendship, then, can be read as a retroactive vindication of his suggestion, at the outset of the *Nicomachean Ethics*, that a proper conception of the human good must be self-sufficient in the sense that it alone suffices for the flourishing for an entire community of humans. His explanation of this sort of self-sufficiency is worth reproducing in full:

> Now what we count as self-sufficient is not what suffices for a solitary person by himself, living an isolated life, but what suffices also for parents, children, wife and in general for friends and fellow citizens, since a human being is a naturally political [animal]. Here, however, we must impose some limit; for if we extend the good to parents' parents and children's children and to friends of friends, we shall go on without limit; but we must examine this another time.[54]

This passage might appear to open up the possibility of conflicts between what promotes the flourishing or happiness of particular individuals, and what it is good for them to do in Aristotle's sense, given his stipulative insistence upon a communal notion of the good. The discussion of friendship can be read as an attempt to show that no such conflict is really possible—that is, that true self-love points us towards goods that are self-sufficient in Aristotle's very ambitious and decidedly moral sense.

THE IRREPLACEABILITY OF CHARACTER FRIENDS

Some have objected to the Aristotelian ideal of friendship on the ground that character friends do not love each other for themselves but only for the excellences of character and thought that they see instantiated in each other.[55] Certainly Aristotle cannot be accused of having adopted the Platonic notion that loving the good in another person is tantamount to loving a separate entity—the Form or Idea of the good—of which the person happens to provide a pale image or reminder.[56] Nor does it seem so bad a thing to be the target of a love inspired by one's own good qualities, as opposed—say—to being loved wholly without regard to one's character, as one among the countless targets of a perfectly universal and indiscriminate love of humankind (e.g. a love of practical reason taken as mere capacity, without regard to its action-guiding commitments). These kinds of love might reflect well on those who feel them, but they imply no particular merit in those at whom they are directed. What we seem to seek in friendship and intimate relationships—including, Aristotle plausibly suggests,

---

[54] *EN* 1097b8–14.

[55] See for instance Gregory Vlastos, "The Individual as an Object of Love in Plato," *Platonic Studies*, 2nd edn (Princeton: Princeton University Press, 1981), 3–42, especially 31–3 and 33n; and Schoeman, "Aristotle on the Good of Friendship," 278.

[56] *EN* 1096a20–b27. Note, though, that Kahn attributes a quasi-Platonic view of this matter to Aristotle in "Aristotle and Altruism."

our self-relationship—is an affirmation inspired and merited by our particular qualities or way of being, even though it is conceptually possible for others to manifest these same qualities or way of being.[57]

On reflection, there is a very strong intuitive case to be made for the Aristotelian view of these matters. If I were asked why I help my friends when they are in need, I might respond simply by saying that after all they are my friends. This, however, should not be taken to mean that friendship provides a basic, non-derivative reason for me to help them. Part of what it *is* for someone to be my friend is for me to assign a very high value to his health and happiness. It can't be, then, that the *reason* I place a high value on the health and happiness of my friends is that they are my friends. To form a friendship is in part to gain a deep appreciation for something whose value pre-dates one's arrival on the scene. If one has good friendships, one feels *lucky* to have arrived on that scene and befriended just those people. To mourn a friend is to give witness to a value that would have been there if fate had not brought one together with that friend. In the absence of the friendship, one might have been wholly untouched by that value, and incapable of imagining it in rich enough detail to admit of a genuine appreciation of it. Still, it must be there and must be seen in any genuinely good friendship.

There is, then, nothing wildly counterintuitive about Aristotle's idea that the best friendships are constituted by mutual admiration of character. Still, Aristotle's view might plausibly be faulted on the ground that it pictures friends as replaceable without loss, since the character we value in them could in principle be instantiated in many strangers, and might be outshone by the character of some others. Aristotle feeds this concern in passages like the following one, where he seems to trace the irreplaceability of friends merely to the *epistemic* difficulty in ascertaining the goodness of strangers:

> Nor should one choose a friend like a garment. Yet in all things it seems the mark of a sensible man to choose the better of two alternatives; and if one has used the worse garment for a long time and not the better, the better is to be chosen, but not in place of an old friend of whom you do not know whether he is better. For a friend is not to be had without trial nor in a single day, but there is need of time . . .[58]

If this is Aristotle's considered account of the irreplaceability of friends, it is inadequate. It is not merely *unlikely* that one could find a replacement for a good friend, nor merely *difficult to verify* that a candidate replacement really does exemplify the valuable character traits of one's friend. It is *absurd* to think that one could *replace* a friend (as opposed, say, to trying to patch the chasm left when

---

[57] I find myself in sympathy with Nussbaum's approving summary of Aristotle's view on these matters: "Aristotle, then, reminds us that deep love, to be deep, must embrace character and value; that the real individuality of another person is not just something ineffable and indescribable; among its most important constituents are excellences that can be shared by another. Aristotle stresses these shared elements, then, not in order to bypass the individuality in love, but in order to give a richer account of what that individuality comes to." See Nussbaum, *The Fragility of Goodness*, 357.

[58] *EE* 1237b36–1238a3.

a friendship comes to a premature end). If one thought that this were possible, one's relationship could be at best a defective friendship and might perhaps be no friendship at all.

Aristotle seems not to have recognized this problem. Still, we might develop a broadly Aristotelian solution by stressing that our grip on the good, like our grip on other universals, is the child and not the parent of our understanding of its instances. We find our way to an articulate conception of the human good by dwelling upon intimates in whom we see intimations of it. As we search for the words to make clear what it is that we think we see in them, we are guided by the people before us and by our apprehension of their goodness. We might perhaps see their goodness more richly and more clearly when we have struggled to find apt words for it, but the words cannot take the place of that which they characterize. Hence we have no independent grasp on the good by reference to which we could find our friends to be less good than strangers. This does not lead to the absurd conclusion that there is no possible way for us to become aware of the shortcomings of our friends. It means only that such awareness is an outgrowth of our first intimations of the goodness of another, more inspiring exemplar.

This stance seems right. Indeed, it seems to pinpoint a crucial feature of the place of exemplars in ethical thought. Their role as lodestones for action is not displaced when we have found apt words for their inspiring qualities, since they enliven our understanding of whatever words we have found. For instance, when the Christian who has long pondered *New Testament* parables is moved to call Jesus a lover of neighbor, this does not provide an independent standard for imitation, or a self-standing and wholly abstract account of the proper target of reverence. Rather, its natural role is to give greater depth and proper focus to the apprehension of that which is worthy of imitation and reverence in the Jesus who comes into view through these parables.[59] Likewise, the reader of Plato's dialogues might give greater articulacy to his sense of what is exemplary about Socrates by coming to see that Socrates' irony is generous and humane, or that Socrates has an integral relation to his own words. But if these formulations are capable of playing a sensible role in one's strivings to be more Socratic, this is because they help one to see the good in Socrates' example, hence to see how to be moved by that example, not because they provide a self-sufficient guideline that captures what is worthy of imitation in Socrates' life and that can be wielded in abstraction from that example.

---

[59] Here I disagree with Kant's claim that no exemplar can reasonably be regarded as a fit guide to action unless the exemplar's actions have been seen to correspond to an antecedently justified practical principle, hence that no exemplar can provide non-redundant practical guidance. My rejection of this position is of a piece with my argument, in Chapters 2 and 3, that our capacity to recognize goodness or value outruns our capacity to articulate the content of that recognition, and provides a fit focal object for our efforts to extend and refine our achieved articulation. Cf. Kant, *Groundwork*, Ak. 408.

In my view, this point is itself sufficient to disarm the challenge at hand. However, if we leave the discussion here, we will have left something crucial to the side. Friends and lovers are irreplaceable in part because friendships and love relationships are essentially historical phenomena. To use the language of Chapter 3, friendships essentially involve temporally extended dialectical activities (or "interactivities"), each of whose moments owes its significance and value to its place in a narrative whole.[60] The irreplaceability of one's friends owes in part to the self-conscious *history* one shares with them, and this is not the sort of thing one could conceivably discover oneself to share with a stranger.

Such a shared history can fundamentally alter present activities. The subjective side of this phenomenon is familiar from many other contexts, including our experience of place. A walk through one's hometown can open a well of especially vivid memories that could not possibly be conjured at will, and that can lend emotional resonance—whether sweet or bitter—to current experience. Likewise, one's subjective experience of long-time companions can be gilded (or stained) by the lingering presence of the past. If we have too atemporal and behaviorist a picture of human activity, we are likely to think that the phenomenon in question is merely subjective, and has no important implications for the objective nature of the activities with which it is associated. This would be a mistake. When a friendship goes well, the parties to it find over and again that they are able to improvise mutually appealing ways of conversing and interacting. When they do, their history of successful improvisations both testifies to, and helps to extend and refine, a shared evaluative sensibility. The rituals and repetitions of friends and lovers are never mere repetitions, because the memory of each prior enactment provides the next enactment with a subjective patina that increases its depth and resonance. Each reenactment is like fresh writing on a half-erased chalkboard: it takes shape among and becomes entangled with its own faded forerunners, some still legible and others nearly gone from view. There is here a

---

[60] Aristotle does occasionally touch on the historical dimension of friendship, as for instance when he asserts that friends can and often do become walking "actualizations" of each other's past activities (See *EN* 1167b34–1168a9). What this passage seems to suggest is that when one has made significant contributions to the character of another, that other comes to be (in a certain limited sense) one's product, and can be loved in part as an external manifestation of one's own being. This point is perhaps most intelligible in the case of the sort of friendship between parents and children, and in that context the thought can easily become pathological. Aristotle extends the point to all character friendships, and this provides one starting point for exploration of the historical dimension of friendship. Still, a full discussion of this topic would take us well beyond Aristotle's text, partly because Aristotle's comments focus too much on what one has contributed to others, and not enough on what both have contributed to currently shared sensibilities and the activities they make possible. One helpful starting point would be Kierkegaard's writings on the "aesthetic validity" of marriage, and in particular on the way in which repeated activities that might be tedious in the telling can provide those who actually live through them with an accumulation of memories that lend resonance and aesthetic richness to their perceptions of each other and to the repeated activities themselves. See Soren Kierkegaard, *Either/Or*, Volume II, edited and translated by Howard and Edna Hong (Princeton: Princeton University Press, 1987), 138, 141–2, and 144.

possibility of limitless accretion of layers of perceived meaning, hence of limitless repetitions in the outward form of shared activities without a single repetition in the inner texture of these same activities.

This progressive enrichment might fruitfully be compared to the sort of aesthetic enrichment one might experience while going through the entire series of a painter's studies of some subject, such as Monet's well-known "series paintings" of the Rouen cathedral or the water lilies in his garden at Giverny. In such series paintings, an artist can pass along a reified exemplar of the human capacity for appreciative return to the familiar. Such an exemplar can amplify our appreciation of the world by helping us to see how to be continuously instructed afresh by what remains unfamiliar in the familiar. These paintings are particularly satisfying when viewed in a series. As one proceeds, one gains an increasingly vivid awareness of the many and varied aspects of the beauty of their subject. The awareness of these aspects lingers in mind, imbuing the paintings with an accumulated resonance that progressively unveils, more and more fully, the splendor of their common subject. This is an effect that no single canvas, viewed in isolation, could possibly have, precisely because no single painting could possibly bring into co-awareness so many different perspectives on its subject.

When things go reasonably well, the self-deepening repetitive interactions of friends can serve to extend and refine a habitable world of shared possibilities that are not open to mere strangers. These possibilities depend upon a shared sense of what is worth doing or saying, what is funny, what deadly serious, what beside the point. With this shared sense in place, subtle forms of humor can be compressed into a few words; rich arrays of proprietary symbols and conceptual associations can be mobilized without fear of losing anyone. A similar referential richness and assurance of mutual understanding attends even the wordless activities of old friends. To engage in such activities is to become momentarily immune to the disturbing doubt that one's thoughts have ever really been understood by another human being—a doubt that perhaps can consistently be sustained in the face of any observable evidence, but whose rise would just be the failure of friendship.

It is possible that one might share a nuanced sense of significance with a stranger, and this would permit forms of coordinated activity that would be impossible with many other strangers. However, it is only with a friend that one can know such a shared sensibility to be a joint product, brought to fruition through a long series of previous interactions.[61] When both parties to a shared activity have joined together in sculpting the shared sensibility that guides and is

---

[61] On the thought that Aristotelian character friends help to make each other what they are, see Elijah Millgram's thought-provoking essay, "Aristotle on Making Other Selves," *Canadian Journal of Philosophy* 17 (June 1987), 361–76.

expressed by the activity, that activity is "theirs" in a particularly strong sense.[62] For example, two newly united lovers might find themselves to have a shared sexual sensibility, and this might be a marvelously pleasant discovery, but their love-making would not be "their" form of intimacy in the same thoroughgoing sense as the love-making of two people who have gradually drawn out and given shape to each other's sexual sensibilities.

The loss of an intimate friend, then, is the loss of a jointly created world of significance and of possible activities—a world that owes its contours to the friends' own past activities rather than to mere serendipity. By emphasizing this historical aspect of friendship, we can disown the Stoic's illusion that friends are replaceable, yet maintain the guiding Aristotelian idea that friendship arises from and is sustained by mutual appreciation of qualities of character.[63] On this approach, the irreplaceability of friends is traced to the fact that these qualities of character are appreciated and loved in part as the historic result of the sort of collaboration that one could not possibly discover oneself to have had with a stranger, and as such they make it possible to engage now in particularly valuable forms of shared activity that one could not possibly engage in with a stranger.

There is something further to be said about these shared activities, something for which it is not easy to find precise or sober words. These sustained patterns of interactivity have the value that they do only because and insofar as they are enlivened by the presence of another human being. Their value is diminished on those occasions when the other's presence is withheld or withdrawn. It is possible for these moments to become the rule rather than the exception, as when two people "go through the motions" of married life without really being present to each other. While we are aware of the possibility of this sort of coordinated somnambulism, and often able to identify it when we see it, it is not easy to say exactly what it is lacking. One wants to say that what is missing are the participants, but perhaps the more precise way to put things is that their appreciative attention is elsewhere (if they are attending to anything at all). They are mindless of whatever value might lie in their interactions, and this eviscerates their interactions of a great deal of the value that they might have had if done mindfully.

This sort of presence is radically particular. One could not appoint a substitute—not even an exactly similar substitute—to muster it for oneself or to supply it to one's partner on one's behalf. It is here, in the context of intimate

---

[62] This phenomenon is an interpersonal and somewhat less tangible correlate of Marx's insight that we elaborate ourselves dialectically, by laboring on the world, finding ourselves confronted by our own thoughts (especially our notions of a world suitable for human habitation) reified in the form of the portion of the world we have worked upon, then critiquing and refining those reified thoughts in preparation for another round of self-e*laboration.* See Karl Marx, "Alienated Labor," the last section of the first manuscript in *The Philosophical and Economic Manuscripts of 1844.*

[63] For a flavor of the Stoic understanding (or *mis*understanding) of these matters, see Epistle IX ("On Philosophy and Friendship") and Epistle LXIII ("On Grief for Lost Friends") of Seneca's *Epistulae Morales.*

relationships, that we gain our most vivid sense of the radically particular sort of value that human beings have, such that the loss of one human being cannot be compensated without remainder by the creation of one who is exactly similar. Hence friendship serves not only as a school of virtue but also as a privileged vantage point for gaining a full appreciation of the mysterious kind of value that human beings have. We would lose track of this value if we attempted to "do" moral philosophy from a maximally impersonal standpoint, abstracting from the merely subjective and parochial perspective that we have on our intimates, in an attempt to gain a detached and objective vantage point on the value of human beings.

SELF-AFFIRMABILITY, OBJECTIVITY, AND ARISTOTELIAN VIRTUES

I have argued that character friendship moves those who participate in it towards the *telos* of universal self-affirmability, and I've suggested that this *telos* has recognizably moral content. One might ask, though, how closely this goal tracks the goal of coming to exemplify the Aristotelian virtues. I think there are good grounds for maintaining that the two goals coincide. If this is true, it suggests that the best sorts of human relationships will depend for their health, and for their capacity to exercise a welcome influence on the character of participants, on the availability of a vital tradition of thought about the virtues and vices. It also suggests an appealing virtue-centric aspiration for ethical philosophy: the aspiration of articulating the importance of the virtue concepts, and shedding light on the concrete differences between virtue and vice, in a way that helps to sustain and deepen those human relationships through which participants become virtuous.

From the beginning of the *Nicomachean Ethics*, Aristotle makes clear that his guiding concern is to identify the *complete* good for humans—i.e. that which is choiceworthy in itself, without condition or qualification.[64] His answer is that what is unconditionally good for humans is a complete and active life expressive of the virtues. When one's actions express the virtues, they emerge from *orthos logos* or right reason, and in the practical sphere this means reason that never comes loose from what is fine or good in itself.[65] Human doings show up as manifestations of a nameable virtue, however, not merely because they are (and are chosen as) good in themselves, but also because they represent the proper navigation of potential distortions in practical reasoning to which humans are characteristically susceptible. Humans are prone to deviate from what is good

---

[64] *EN* 1097a26–35.

[65] On the first of these claims, see *EN* 1103b33, 1105a30–5, 1107a1–3. On the second, see *EN* 1105a32, 1144a17–20; *MM* 1183b37–1184a3.

in itself when in the grip of certain emotions, feelings, or desires, including anger, fear, appetitive pleasures, desire for wealth, and desire for honor or public esteem. As suggested in earlier chapters, such affects are partly constituted by a subjective outlook on the good—an impression that some end or course of action is a good one—and this subjective outlook can come loose from what is genuinely or objectively good. If one is to come to have the Aristotelian virtues of character, one's characteristic affects must be reshaped so that the apparent goods they bring to subjective awareness really are genuine, objectively affirmable goods, and so that the objective goods we most need to notice are salient in our experience. Only in this way can we become fully aware of and responsive to the goods in play in our lives.

The Aristotelian virtues, then, can be thought of as valuable in large part because they are immunities to common forms of distortion in practical reasoning, arising from characteristically human desires, emotions, or feelings.[66] To be courageous is to have the capacity to keep one's eye unwaveringly on goods that matter and to act in their name even when this involves considerable danger. To be temperate is to cleave to projects and commitments that matter even when one might get more sensory pleasure by deviating from them. To be mild is to be immune from the well-known practical distortions associated with run-away anger. To be just is to be capable of seeing what is fair and doing it even when one could secure greater wealth or power by being unfair. Generosity too requires a capacity to see and respond to the needs of others even when this requires a sacrifice of time and material resources. Those who are properly immune to the temptations of public acclaim are able to avoid boastfulness and to lift themselves to magnanimity. It must be said, though, that not all of these virtues can be equated with a single, isolatable immunity from distortion in one's practical thinking. One can be unjust or ungenerous in order to secure public honor and acclaim. One might boast in pursuit of money rather than honor. These possibilities might provide the starting points for vindicating Aristotle's claim that the virtues are unified in the sense that it is impossible to have one virtue in the fullest degree if one lacks any other. But the general drift of the argument would remain unchanged. The Aristotelian virtues are justified because they conduce to the clear apprehension of the good, and they figure in ethical thinking because the good, being itself uncodifiable, is best grasped indirectly by clarifying the traits of character that permit us to see it.

It is worth noting, in passing, that the Aristotelian virtues involve immunity from distortions introduced by the prospect of those goods that are external to our activities, not those goods that are internal to our activities. The doctrine of the mean is supposed to characterize a proper orientation towards goods such as

---

[66] When Aristotle first provides an overview of the virtues of character at *EN* 1107a34–1108a31, he follows precisely this scheme of categorization, grouping them in accordance with the affect to whose attendant distortions the virtue immunizes us.

wealth, health, sensory pleasure, and public esteem that figure in one's immediate doings as their intended product. While one is engaged in an activity, one need not worry about excess in appreciation of and responsiveness to the goods that are internal to that activity. While it might arguably be important to hit a mean when it comes to how much *time* one allots to any given activity, this capacity need not be internalized in one's immediate pre-reflective outlook on life, in the way that the Aristotelian virtues must be.

Some readers will perhaps have concluded that my version of Aristotelianism is not really virtue-theoretic, since it assigns to the virtues only epistemic and not conceptual primacy over excellence in action. It is true that the view I've elaborated does deviate from the conceptual framework found in the work of those contemporary virtue ethicists who claim that what it is for an action to be good is for it to be the sort of action that a virtuous person would voluntarily choose. It is a purely terminological matter whether the phrase 'virtue ethics' is to be limited to these latter views. If it is, I believe that Aristotle was not a virtue ethicist and that virtue ethics is not a plausible view. It would be highly implausible to suppose that what it is for something to be good is for it to be the sort of thing that the virtuous person would do. On the contrary, the virtuous person's doings count as virtuous only because and insofar as they track the human good. After all, it would be absurd to suppose that the person who knows himself to be virtuous makes choices by determining what would be done by someone like himself. Still, while the idea of a virtuous character does not have conceptual primacy over goodness in action, it does have epistemic primacy. If we hope to shed light on how best to live, it is no help whatsoever to remind ourselves that we ought always to do what is in fact good. It is far more helpful to remind ourselves that when faced with certain kinds of temptations or gripped by certain kinds of sentiments, human beings are prone to act in ways that will be regarded as misguided by others who occupy a more dispassionate stance—and perhaps also by themselves, later, as they look back with regret. The language of the virtues, and especially the language of the vices, can be invoked as an accumulated set of insights about which common circumstances and sentiments are particularly likely to lend an appearance of goodness to activities that would seem bad from a more dispassionate standpoint, and that will seem bad in retrospect. This language can be helpful, then, in providing us with guidance concerning what it would be good to do.

This picture of the virtues has the benefit of accounting for a basic asymmetry in the way that virtue and vice terms figure in explicit practical deliberation: virtue terms rarely have an appropriate foreground role in deliberation, but vice terms often do. For instance, it would generally be slightly priggish to choose to help because one would thereby manifest the virtue of generosity, rather than because someone is in need. Likewise, choosing in the name of the courageous, rather than in the name of the person or cause or communal good that stirs one to courageous action, would generally indicate an overweening sense of the figure one cuts in life. By contrast, there is nothing priggish nor disturbingly self-referential about avoiding actions because they strike one as selfish, miserly, vain, boastful, or cowardly. On the approach that I've taken, the asymmetry can be explained as the natural result of trying to see and act in the name of the goods or reasons presented by one's circumstances. Virtue, on this approach, is unclouded moral vision and deliberation. When one's evaluative outlook is unclouded, one acts in the name of those goods or reasons that one clearly sees, and not in the name of the self-constitution that permits one to see them clearly. However, the vice terms provide us with names for distortions in practical deliberation to which humans are characteristically prone, and we can invoke them to identify and correct for these distortions. Put another way, they pick out ways of acting that are likely to show up in one's practical thinking with a specious air of goodness. We can make use of the vice concepts to alert ourselves to such courses of action in prospect, so as to trigger careful scrutiny of those elements of our evaluative outlook that make them seem worthwhile.

By Aristotle's lights, the virtuous person reliably chooses actions that are good in themselves, and chooses them as fine or good in themselves rather than as desired or pleasurable.[67] Aristotle goes on to claim that distortions in our understanding of the proper end of action (i.e. our understanding of the fine or good in itself) can be traced almost entirely to the indulgence of errant pleasures.[68] This diagnosis of practical error is perhaps too simple, but it does seem to explain many of the most common and banal human vices. We can grant this without committing ourselves to the self-alienating and puritanical claim that characteristic pleasures and desires must not be permitted to play any role in practical deliberation. We can avoid this implication if we adopt the Aristotelian view, defended in Chapters 1 and 4, that the affects are the form taken in humans by vivid subjective appearances of value. It is this conception of the affects that lies behind Aristotle's insistence that the virtuous person must have the right desires and pleasures.[69] On this view, full virtue implies a perfect harmony between the subjective appearances of goodness embedded in one's characteristic desires and pleasures, and what it would be objectively good for one to do or be.[70] The nearer one approaches to such a harmony, the more one's pleasures and desires can be relied upon as fitting guides to action.

The philosopher is not in a position to give a direct substantive account of the good life for human beings, partly for lack of any claim to special expertise about these matters and partly because this sort of excellence is not codifiable in a language that would be of help to those who do not yet grasp it. Nor can one hope to make progress, along these lines, through quickly drawn philosophical

---

[67] *EN* 1105a30–5, 1115b13–14, and 1144a14–20.

[68] *EN* 1104b31–5, 1113a35–b2, 1140b12–20. As Aristotle says in *De Anima*, the soul "makes a quasi-affirmation" to that which it finds pleasant (431a9).

[69] *EN* 1104b4–10.   [70] *EN* 1102b14–22; *EE* 1236b33–1237a9; *MM* 1207b31–3.

cases or abstract philosophical discussion. One needs to work with concrete exemplars of goodness in action, with an eye to passing along the art of seeing such exemplars well—that is, in such a way as to understand their goodness. The process can fruitfully be compared to learning to see the excellence of works of art, since this skill is equally resistant to codification. In both cases, the learning proceeds best in the presence of a common exemplar. In the case of excellence in acting and in living, one does best with a living exemplar or the sort of literary exemplar who has been brought to life by a gifted writer.

There is, however, an indirect mode of substantive philosophical inquiry into the human good. We can inquire into the vices in hopes of increasing our articulacy about the sentiments and circumstances that induce us to drift into unshareable outlooks on the good—outlooks that cannot regard their own external instantiations as unconditionally trustworthy. This will cut no ice, of course, with those who believe that (practical) goodness is irreducibly person-relative. But if the arguments of the last chapter hold water, then we ought to disown that conception of the good. Once we do, we will have established a proper conceptual backdrop for retrieving a recognizably Aristotelian conception of the virtues and vices—not merely in an antiquarian spirit but as a source of guidance in our struggle to see the good and to live in light of that vision.

Aristotle's view, at least on Myles Burnyeat's compelling reconstruction, is that properly formed pleasures are fledgling grasps of the good, and are necessary precursors to philosophical insight into the nature of the good.[71] Only those who have been raised so as to become lovers of what is "fine and good"—that is, what is good in itself, quite apart from their subjective outlook on it—can attain such insight.[72] Those whose passions have been misshapen by a bad upbringing are unable to take pleasure in actions that are good in themselves, hence they "have not even a conception of what is noble and truly pleasant, since they have never tasted it."[73]

To be raised well is to be habituated from the beginning to perform and eventually to love those actions that are loveable in themselves. Aristotle seems to have thought that the most optimal arrangement would be to have one's characteristic affects, hence one's pre-reflective outlook on the good, shaped within the context of a properly constituted civic *philia* between ruler and ruled.[74] If we doubt or despair of this possibility, we might still hope to foster such love within smaller and more intimate circles of *philia*, including relations between parents and children, among close-knit neighbors, or within what we moderns would call friendships.[75] The fundamental and quite plausible idea here is that love of the good is fostered and refined only insofar as one's socialization

---

[71] See Myles Burnyeat, "Aristotle on Learning to be Good," in Rorty, ed., *Essays on Aristotle's Ethics*, 69–92.

[72] *EN* 1179b5–18.   [73] *EN* 1179b15–16, W. D. Ross translation.

[74] *EN* 1180a6–33, 1161a10–15.   [75] *EN* 1180a29–33.

is guided by one or more intimates who have themselves attained at least an intimation of the human good.[76] Within such relationships, youths are exposed to what might be called an "anticipatory" love—that is, a love directed at, and suited to encourage, the inchoate stirrings in them of a love of what is good in itself. Such relationships provide a context within which we are able to find loveable in another that other's commitment to what is good in itself. Since what is good in itself is affirmable as good from all standpoints, this goes hand-in-hand with the development of a first-personal (rather than merely spectatorial) attachment to what is good in itself. Virtue, understood as a love of the fine that shows up in the concrete form of consistently good actions, arises in us and is strengthened to the extent that our relationships approximate the proper *telos* of character friendships. These relationships can provide the sort of external, objectivity-tracking formative and corrective mechanism for our characteristic affects that isolated practical reflection alone is unable to provide.[77]

When these unequal or anticipatory friendships go well, they secure the possibility for equal character friendships later in life. Yet these relationships would seem to be subject to the same forms of degeneration that Aristotle discerns in friendships between equals. For instance, parenting will tend to go badly if the parent caters to the child's desires, or if the parent's main goal is to exact pleasing flattery from the child, or to enhance her own reputation by trumpeting the child's achievements. Such interactions prepare children for misunderstanding the good as an unshareable pursuit over which one can expect a contest of wills, rather than as a joint quest for clarity about an objective end that can be affirmed from all relevant social perspectives.

This picture of socialization might perhaps help to explain Aristotle's tentative reliance, in elaborating his account of the virtues, on received beliefs about which kinds of actions are good and fine. Such beliefs are valuable starting points precisely because they have proven capable of gaining the stable affirmation of generations of people facing different circumstances and occupying a wide variety of social standpoints. Given this, they encapsulate concrete findings about what humans need to meet their basic needs, and how their projects and pleasures might conceivably be shaped in the course of socialization to render their effective pursuit compossible with the like pursuits of others. If the approach I've elaborated has the resources to explain the shortcomings of Nietzschean and Homeric conceptions of the virtues, it lies in the rather plausible supposition that widespread adoption of such conceptions would tend to frustrate these basic needs, and that long historical experience with this deficiency has marked our

---

[76] *EN* 1180a17–18.

[77] As Aristotle obscurely remarks, in the context of a discussion of the sort of perception that character friends have of each other: ". . . the perceiver becomes perceived in that way and in that respect in which he first perceives, and according to the way in which and the object which he perceives; and the knower becomes known in the same way" (*EE* 1245a5–9).

culture in ways that bequeath to us a deep-seated intuition that they are not entirely admirable.

Still, our inherited stock of intuitive beliefs can yield at best a sketchy and tentative account of the substantive content of the virtues, and at worst a deeply misguided one. Received beliefs about the virtues and vices might be distorted in ways that reflect the interests of those in power—a possibility hardly unknown to Aristotle, who must be supposed to have considered Thrasymachus's radical denunciation of the so-called "virtues" of the weak and submissive.[78] For instance, patriotism might be called a virtue and all but the most polite dissent might be termed unpatriotic. Prevailing beliefs about the virtues and vices might also be distorted in ways that reflect, and serve to stabilize, the basic economic and political structures of a polity. If these institutional structures are geared towards the efficient production of ends determined by a class of managers or political leaders, this will not provide a hospitable climate for encouraging and reproducing virtues whose value lies in their contribution to unimpeded engagement in intrinsically valuable activities. There will be little social occasion for such engagement, and little chance to "make a living" by it. In such a climate, we can expect public praise to be extended to enterprise, self-assertiveness and ambition, and we can expect a widespread acceptance—if not a genuine admiration—even of material acquisitiveness. Nor should we expect the language of the virtues to flourish in societies characterized by a proliferation of fragmented social roles, each demanding a different set of character traits, especially if the same selves are pressed into many different roles of this sort, sometimes in the space of a single day. Yet as MacIntyre has argued, our society is marked by this sort of serial role-specialization, and there are few if any character traits that suit us to excel in all of them.[79]

Given these significant cultural impediments to attaining a proper understanding of the virtues, those who wish to hone their capacity to distinguish virtue from vice can do no better than to grapple with this question in practice, by throwing themselves into intimate interactions with others and seeing what range of people they are capable of befriending, and how unreservedly and unconditionally it is possible to befriend them. This is the only way we might sensibly attempt to find the Aristotelian *phronimos* whose judgments are the standard of virtue—by finding someone loveable in herself and attempting to make ourselves loveable in her eyes, thereby struggling to do our part in the development of two *phronimoi*. This is the surest way to develop that range of virtues that pare away distortions in one's outlook on the good. It is perhaps also the most promising way to cultivate a different array of virtues—an array that accentuates one's capacity for a vivid and continuous apprehension of the value of one's running activities. When the

---

[78] Plato, *Republic*, Book I.
[79] See MacIntyre, "Moral Philosophy and Contemporary Social Practice," in *The Tasks of Philosophy*, 117.

apprehension of these values and the apt responsiveness to them becomes a joint endeavor, it is also likely to be a more engrossing and cheerful endeavor—one marked by the virtues of hope and good cheer rather than the nearly forgotten vice of *acedia*. The notion of *acedia* is not at all easy to retrieve. It is sometimes rendered with the English terms 'sloth' or 'laziness,' but neither translation really does it justice. At its core, *acedia* is a refusal to recognize and rise to whatever goods might lie within one's reach. Aquinas thought of *acedia* as a protean quality, one that might just as easily manifest itself in torpor as in restlessness or in frenzied pursuit of material goods or bodily pleasures.[80] These latter pursuits count as *acedia* when they are strategies for redirecting one's attention away from one's proper calling and towards inferior goods. *Acedia* has traditionally been regarded by Catholics as one of the seven deadly sins, partly because it constitutes an ungrateful and irreverent refusal of a divine gift or calling. Yet it can protrude as a vice even without a theistic backdrop. It does, for instance, if one follows Aristotle in thinking of the human *telos* as appreciative engagement in the best human activities.

Character friendship, then, can be regarded as the proper form of the active human search for apprehension of and responsiveness to the good. I have stressed throughout this book that our prospects for making headway in this task are greatly enhanced if we engage in the slow and difficult work of estranging ourselves from the prejudices of our times concerning the good life for human beings, and seek to retrieve prior understandings of our status as agents, the point of our activities and lives, and the proper aspirations of our practical thought and our relations with other human beings. There is, however, one particular Aristotelian belief that I think we would do best to discard. The belief in question is that the human good exhaustively determines almost every detail of a truly laudable character. This thought appears to be implicit in Aristotle's claim that in the ideal case, friends would perfectly mirror each other's character, and that each would be in a position to celebrate the other as a duplicate of the self.[81] Perhaps this claim is not to be read too literally, or perhaps it reveals that Aristotle's conception of admirable character is implausibly constricted. Either way, there is no reason in principle why a broadly Aristotelian inquiry into the virtues cannot make room for a pluralistic conception of the good life, or why friends could not exemplify different possibilities for fully self-affirmable evaluative outlooks and unreservedly good human lives. The objective good for humans might well specify invariant answers to some questions about the human good while leaving elbow room for idiosyncrasy with respect to other questions. Indeed, given the limited capacities of humans for focused evaluative

---

[80] Thomas Aquinas, *Summa Theologica*, Second Part of Second Part, 35, 4.

[81] Aristotle writes: "Equality and similarity, and above all the similarity of those who are similar in being virtuous, is friendship" (*NE* 1159b3–5; see also 1156b7–22). He also repeatedly claims that a friend is "another oneself" and celebrated as such (1166a30–3; 1169b5–7; 1170a2–4 and b6–8).

attention, and the multifarious needs and interests of humans, a "division of labor" in evaluative outlooks might well be desirable. For instance, it may be impossible for one person to be fully attentive to the needs of the poor and to the resolution of the most stubborn puzzles in theoretical physics. In that case, interpersonal love might properly be directed at forms of excellence in friends that do not mirror one's own but depart from them in many areas where variation is not only acceptable but intrinsically valuable and properly welcomed.[82] These open possibilities seem to me to remove some of the most troubling obstacles to acceptance of Aristotle's conception of friendship (and, more broadly, of ethics).

RETRIEVING A NON-ABSURD REALISM

I have argued that those who possess the Aristotelian virtues will consistently act in ways that can be affirmed as good or valuable in themselves, and that Aristotelian friendship is one way, if not the only way, of coming to have such virtues. This helps to show why character friendship ought to be welcomed by those who are already committed to becoming virtuous (though, as noted above, character friendship must arise from spontaneous mutual *eunoia*, hence cannot be attained by those who are drawn to each other merely in order to become virtuous). But why, if at all, should the absence of character friendship be lamented by those who are not antecedently committed to attaining a virtuous evaluative outlook?

In Chapter 5, I argued that we pay a steep price in the metric of evaluative articulacy if we take our practical thinking to ground out in the apprehension of reasons rather than goods or values, and I attempted to defang the ontological worries that might prompt us to think this price worth paying. In Chapter 6, I argued against the existence of a special class of person-relative goods, and for the thesis that we ought to deliberate and act under the idea that there are objective goods that provide reasons "external" to our subjective motivational states. Together, these arguments suggest that we ought to strive in our practical thinking to track objective goods or values. If this suggestion is accepted, then clearly we ought to hold our evaluative outlooks to the standard of universal self-affirmability, hence the changes wrought upon these outlooks by character friendship would properly be welcomed. After all, an objective good or value is one that can and ought to be affirmed as good or valuable from all possible standpoints, and an outlook that fails the test of universal self-affirmability yields verdicts from some standpoints that it would itself reject if it happened to occupy some other standpoint. Hence, if a person with such an outlook considered

---

[82] Aristotle suggests that the friendship between a husband and wife can be of this sort, since he takes the proper virtues of each to be different (*EN* 1162a25–7).

matters carefully, he would have to regard his own outlook as an unreliable guide to objective goods. In the case of the two non-self-affirming forms of egoism explicitly considered by Aristotle, the unreliability in question would be entirely pervasive. Each instance of such an outlook will count as unconditionally valuable a set of ends (e.g. the pleasures of its possessor, or the satisfaction of its possessor's desires) that no other instance of the same outlook would count as unconditionally valuable. Those who have such outlooks cannot give credence to the substantive verdicts reached by others with the same kind of outlook without being driven to the nihilistic conclusion that nothing whatever is worth doing. If character friendship is a reliable route to avoiding such a conclusion, then it ought to be welcomed when it arises (though, once again, it cannot be attained if pursued for this reason).[83]

This conclusion is premised on value realism, and for this reason will no doubt be met by a certain measure of philosophical resistance. Such resistance, however, is often sustained by a distorted conception of what the realist must claim. On this conception, the realist thinks that we discover how to live when, in the course of our efforts to take a full inventory of the "furniture of the universe," we make the unanticipated and perplexing discovery that in addition to such things as protons and electrons, the universe contains objective values or categorical requirements. Yet the task of practical thinking is clearly not to ascertain the mere *existence* of entities that happen to be normative. The task is to come to an understanding of how best to live and to live in the light of that understanding. Only the most unappealing sort of realism would propose that we vindicate the plausibility or authority of claims about what to do or how to live by taking an inventory of what there is. The immediate problem with this sort of realism is that it leaves us with nothing to say by way of justification for our moral opinions except that we have intuited the existence of certain requirements. The more fundamental problem is that unquestioned obedience to bald intuitions of this sort would be at odds with any minimally appealing interpretation of the *telos*, or proper actualization, of our capacity for reasoned self-direction. It would be incurious, passive, and servile to heed certain objectively existing mandates simply because one takes oneself to have intuited the bald, unexplained fact of their existence. In short, it would be a genuinely bad way to live, something that we have a real reason to avoid. But if its badness is the most fundamental objection to it, we can safely conclude that its error does not consist in the positing of goodness and badness.

---

[83] Since constructivists join realists in affirming the importance of objectivity in practical reasoning, this might possibly open the way for a constructivist version of Aristotelian virtue theory. I doubt, however, that such an approach could really make good sense of the thesis of uncodifiability that looms large in this book. This thesis makes best sense on realist grounds. It fits ill with the thought that ethics is a human contrivance for the free and fair regulation of social life, for a constructed ethics would seem deficient, and reasonably rejectable, if it were not articulable to all those subject to it in a determinate and comprehensible form.

This might seem like insistence upon one bald evaluative intuition rather than another. But the evaluative claim at hand is not a *bald* intuition; it fits in a mutually supporting relation with an entire arborescence of appealing thoughts concerning the nature and point of human life. We arrive at this assessment in the way that we arrive at all judgments concerning the intrinsic value of activities—by throwing ourselves into the activity in question, on the strength of at least a sketchy sense of what it involves or requires, and seeking on the fly to attain a more articulate grasp of what counts as a full and proper engagement in it. Practical thinking about the proper form of intrinsically valuable activities does not change its structure when we turn to the master activity of making use of our capacity for practical thinking in the unshirkable task of leading a life. (I say "unshirkable" because doing nothing or opting for suicide are not ways of shirking the task but alternative and highly dubious ways of discharging it.) Our inquiry remains dialectical here as elsewhere. The difference is that this particular practical dialectic is both maximally inclusive and highly abstract. Its point is to clarify the sort of practical thinking that is fit to serve as the central constituent of a good human life. When we arrive at an appealing clarification, we arrive at a claim that implies the existence of certain objective norms or values. This is the only tenable way to vindicate such claims.

A central aim of Chapter 4 was to elicit a recognition that no activity arising solely from the brute recognition of a norm's existence could be accompanied and completed by appreciation of its own point or value, rather than of its bare requiredness, hence that no such activity could be the full and proper actualization of the human capacity for self-directed activity. A key aim of Chapter 5 (and to a lesser extent of Chapter 3) was to show that no activity emanating from this stunted sort of "understanding" could manifest a full appreciation of the intrinsic value of other human beings. What we care about when we care about morality is not merely that certain behavioral standards are reliably met but that the inherent dignity or value of persons is expressed in the form and motivational wellsprings of our interactions. These interactions take on a new and deeper value because they are rooted in recognition of this value, and an even deeper value when marked by mutual awareness that they have this motivational source. Given this, moral thinking cannot possibly stop short with the brute recognition that there are categorical reasons to act in certain ways. It must bring value to light.

This is a rather abstract structural feature of good practical thinking, one that would usually remain unarticulated. But there is nothing particularly esoteric or narrowly philosophical about clarifying one's sense of excellence in practical thinking while that sort of thinking is underway. This is a daily and familiar activity. It is what we are doing in everyday conversation and reflection when we attempt to deepen our understanding of the difference between the tactless and the candid, the tactful and the dishonest, the kind and the over-indulgent, the generous and the profligate, the magnanimous and the pompous, the deeply felt and the maudlin or sappy, the self-confident and the conceited, the self-respecting and the self-indulgent, the prudent and the cowardly or spineless, the brave and the rash, the accommodating and the servile. In all of these cases we are trying to clarify particular contour-lines that distinguish good and bad ways of living and acting, while also attempting to refine and strengthen our inoculation to certain simulacra of goodness to which practical thinking is susceptible. For instance, if we are to sharpen our sense of the distinction between the tactless and the candid, we must gain greater clarity about the nature and limits of the human need for access to the viewpoints of others so that we can see when information might play a role in self-correction and when it can conduce to nothing but hurt feelings. We must simultaneously sharpen our sense of what it means in practice for one's psychological propensities to be in the sort of relation to each other that conduces to good practical thinking. For instance, we need to sharpen our capacity to identify and resist those desires to be "candid" with another that wear the guise of concern for another but that spring in fact from petty resentment or insecurity.

The "thick" or "specialized" evaluative concepts invoked in the last paragraph are just the sort of concepts that the Aristotelian virtue ethicist regards as central to our practical thinking. These concepts are sometimes pictured as "bridging" the divide between description and evaluation. There are two ways of understanding this metaphor. On the one hand, we might retain the thought that there is a well-defined distinction between description and evaluation, and hold that thick concepts bridge the divide in the sense that they are amalgams of two semantic components, one descriptive and the other evaluative. On the other hand, we might hold that thick concepts are both descriptive and evaluative but that they cannot be analyzed into two semantic components, one descriptive and the other evaluative. I argued for this latter view in Chapter 5. On this view, thick concepts bridge the description–evaluation divide in the sense of calling into question those versions of the division according to which any exercise of thought is ultimately divisible into purely descriptive and purely evaluative components.

This picture of evaluative thought opens the door to an appealing sort of value realism. Realism would look like a servile doctrine, unfit for human beings, if it posited the brute existence of "thin" evaluative facts or categorical requirements, protruding inexplicably from an otherwise disenchanted field of forces and arrangements of matter in motion. This air of servility is erased when the quarry of evaluative thought is grasped through the thick concepts to which we owe whatever articulacy we have attained in our reflections on the point or value of our activities. A credible realism must posit the sort of value-infused order whose contours and practical significance admit not merely of being known to exist but of being understood or appreciated in depth. This is the sort of order that comes into view when we put the virtue-concepts to use in attempting to make sense of our lives and how best to lead them. Nor is there reason to avoid whatever "ontological baggage" might be associated with making serious use of these simultaneously descriptive and evaluative concepts. As I will argue in the next chapter, one must make serious use of them even in order to make full sense of the proper aspirations of theoretical reasoning—that is, the sort of reasoning that might claim an independent authority to pronounce upon the acceptability of this or that cargo of ontological baggage.

CHARACTER FRIENDSHIP, VIRTUE, AND HAPPINESS

No doubt some will be unpersuaded by these realist grounds for welcoming character friendship when it arises. These readers might perhaps be persuaded by a seemingly quite different sort of argument—one that portrays both self-affirmability and the sort of friendship that conduces to it as necessary elements of a fully happy human life. If this argument can be developed in a persuasive fashion, it will have an additional benefit even for those who do find the realist argument convincing. It will show that it is not after all a category mistake to read Aristotle as having articulated an ideal that has recognizably moral content and that is essential to the enjoyment of a good that might plausibly be called happiness.

To bring this argument into view, we can begin by noting that there are forms of unhappiness, recognizable as such to the virtuous and vicious alike, that are very likely to accompany departures from the standard of self-affirmability. The problem is that those who cannot affirm the substantive verdicts of another self's evaluative outlook, even when that evaluative outlook is a mirror image of their own, are also likely to find themselves at odds with the verdicts of that same kind of evaluative outlook as instantiated in their own past and future selves. Consider, for instance, those who value their own actions only insofar as these actions satisfy their desires. Such people might find that their desires change over time, and when they do, they might condemn their own past actions as poor preparations for the satisfaction of their current desires, and might often spend time preparing for future courses of action that they themselves will later regard as worthless when the time comes for them.[84] They might even find themselves partially at odds with their own current actions, due to the running presence of overruled yet not entirely dissipated desires.[85] This permits us to see one reason why Aristotle regarded the core of the self as *nous*: there is a sense in which the self becomes fully itself—that is, comes to be a genuinely unified self—only insofar as its capacity for rationality comes to answer to its own constitutive ideal by devoting itself to what is fine in itself rather than conforming its verdicts to purely subjective and unreasoned desires or pleasures.[86]

---

[84] *EE* 1239b5–25 and 1240b20–5.   [85] *EN* 1166b2–26.

[86] For an interesting discussion of this topic, and one that I find largely congenial, see Suzanne Stern-Gillet, *Aristotle's Philosophy of Friendship* (Albany, NY: State University of New York Press,

Those who lack self-affirming evaluative outlooks are also likely to suffer from a tendency to give some credence to the evaluations that others make of their actions. It seems, as a matter of psychological fact, that humans are generally disposed to listen and give provisional credence to the evaluations of them made by other persons, and particularly by those persons with whom their lives and daily routines are most closely entwined. Indeed, this is arguably one of the basic psychological mechanisms by which we gain a grasp of the distinction between how things seem and how they are, and come to appreciate the correct deployment of any concepts we manage to grasp, so it might be called a precondition of human reasoning (as opposed to what is sometimes called mere attitudinizing). If someone is subject to this common psychological tendency, yet also has an evaluative outlook that leaves him unable to give credence to the evaluations of others, his condition will be one of continually fighting a sense of the meaninglessness of his own basic pursuits. He will be subject to frequent doubts about the *arche* of his evaluative outlook, which will typically involve an insistence that there is something especially valuable about those pleasures or satisfactions that happen to arise in the space of his own psyche rather than in the psyche of another. These doubts will arise from the simple fact that no one else acknowledges this particular *arche*, even if many acknowledge its mirror image. There will be a corresponding instability in friendships of pleasure or usefulness, since the parties to them will relish the more far-reaching sort of mutual approval that is the defining *telos* of character friendship, hence will experience their own friendships at some level as disappointing. There is a sense, then, in which the defining *telos* of character friendships will be the *telos* of all friendships, even if its applicability is sometimes acknowledged only in the currency of inarticulate disappointment.

Those who exemplify the Aristotelian virtues—hence value and choose actions as fine or good in themselves—will reap corresponding benefits, and the worth of these benefits is recognizable even by those who do not already value the life of virtue. The evaluative outlooks of the virtuous will permit them to survey their own past actions without regret, and to plan for future courses of action without fear that they will appear in their own eyes as worthless when the time for them arrives. Further, the virtuous will be able to give full credence to the evaluative outlooks of others who share their taste for actions good in themselves, and they will be suited for intimate friendships with such people. These benefits of virtue seem to fall within the ambit of what we English-speakers call happiness, and their availability begins to remove the sting of paradox from the notion that the moral virtues conduce to the happiness of their possessor.

One might object, however, that the alleged unhappiness of the vicious owes entirely to two purely contingent features of their psyches: the unsteadiness of

1995), chapter 1, and especially 29, where she calls the Aristotelian notion of self "an evaluative, commendatory notion" and "an achievement word."

their desires and the incompleteness of their egoism. It seems that a vicious person could avoid both of these sources of unhappiness by becoming more focused and insular in his vice—for instance, by unifying his projects around a single master desire and ceasing to give any credence whatever to the evaluations of others. Hence, the objection concludes, it is not vice itself but only incomplete vice—i.e. half-hearted and guilt-ridden vice—that leads to unhappiness.

There are two things to be said about this objection. First, it is hard to see what *reason* a vicious person could have to unify his life around a single master desire unless he thought that it was objectively good to be psychologically unified, or objectively good to devote one's life to pursuing the object of that particular desire. If such a person sought unity simply on the subjective ground that unity happens to please him, or that he happens to desire it, then the reasons for unity will be reasons of the same kind as the reasons for disunity—that is, reasons grounded in contingent pleasures or desires. If unity is achieved at all, its achievement will be a purely contingent and unreasoned happenstance. Yet if the vicious person regards it as good in itself to attain psychological unity, or to engage in the unified pursuit of a single end, then this claim will be subject to those standards of reasoning that govern inquiry into any putatively objective realm, hence it can hardly be regarded as a matter of indifference if others are unable to see the objective good he purports to see in psychological unity per se, or in unification around the particular end that he embraces.

The second thing to be said about the objection at hand is that even if it were accepted, it would show only that some vicious persons might be immune from the psychological debilities and consequent unhappiness that attend vice. It would not show that the vicious could enjoy the distinctive pleasures of character friendship, and Aristotle plausibly argues that these pleasures are indispensable elements of a fully happy human life. What the vicious person cannot do is to affirm his own outlook as a generic form that evaluative outlooks are capable of taking—a form whose verdicts are affirmable no matter where instantiated. Such a person cannot have for himself or for others the sort of *eunoia* that gives rise to proper personal love, since such love is directed towards the distinctive practical understanding of how to live that is one's proper self. As noted above, such a person can love himself only *qua* self, not *qua* good, hence his self-love cannot intelligibly be regarded as a mark of anything especially meritorious.

When Aristotle holds that the vicious are not capable either of friendly feeling or love towards themselves, he has in mind this sort of potentially meritorious *eunoia* and love.[87] On some readings of the *Nicomachean Ethics*, this claim can seem like a bit of empty moralizing—an isolated vestige of Platonism torn loose from its proper metaphysical moorings. On the interpretation under discussion, Aristotle offers a cogent argument for this claim. I suggested above that the argument has a more limited reach than Aristotle supposes: it covers most but

[87] *EN* 1166b3–29.

not all cases of vice. Still, it supports the striking conclusion that the most familiar kinds of vicious people cannot affirm their own activities as good in themselves (i.e. good quite apart from their contingent tendency to give him pleasure or satisfy his desires), and cannot do so even if they are quite single-minded in their vice.

Such people will be unable to enjoy the most satisfying sort of pleasure open to humans—a form of pleasure that cannot effectively be aimed at directly, but can be obtained only by those who become absorbed in their activities under the guise of the intrinsically good.[88] As I argued in Chapter 4, these are the pleasures that Aristotle has in mind when he speaks of pleasures that are conceptually inseparable from the activities that give rise to them. Such pleasures cannot be secured if aimed at directly; they can only be enjoyed by those who choose an activity and becoming thoroughly absorbed in it under the guise of the intrinsically good. To the extent that pleasure friendships are motivated by the self-conscious pursuit of pleasure itself, they cannot conduce to this sort of pleasure, but only to the sort of pleasure yielded by the satisfaction of an appetite—the sort towards which Aristotle thinks moderation is the proper posture.[89] Character friendship, by contrast, yields pleasures of the sort associated with activities one finds intrinsically worthwhile, and moderation is no virtue when it comes to these pleasures.[90]

It is true in one sense, but false in another, that character friendship yields all of the benefits associated with the lesser sorts of friendship, together with

---

[88] There is an interpretive problem here, arising from the fact that Aristotle maintains that each person finds his own actions and actions of that kind pleasant (*EN* 1156b16–18). This would seem to suggest that the friendship of the vicious could after all be stable and could be a source of activity-completing pleasure. Yet this is not Aristotle's view. If we do not wish to dismiss this passage as an aberration, we might read Aristotle as holding that the actions of the vicious person are never unequivocally his own. Having a self, hence being capable of having actions that are genuinely one's own, would then be regarded as a contingent human achievement, arising from a capacity for unconditional affirmation of the commitments of one's own *nous*, hence affirmation of the origins of the behavior engaged in by one's body. This means, however, that full ownership of an action is not necessary for responsibility, since the vicious person can be responsible for what are in some sense his actions. (Here we require two senses of the possessive personal pronouns, one weak and the other full-throated.) It also seems to mean that ownership of an action is not sufficient for responsibility, since the actions of our friends are our own but presumably not our responsibility (at least not in the strongest sense). Something like this reading of Aristotle is favored by Stern-Gillet, who claims that for Aristotle, "Humans are so constituted that they require others actually to become what they essentially are," and that the vicious do not in fact become what they essentially are. See Stern-Gillet, *Aristotle's Philosophy of Friendship*, 141.

[89] At *EN* 1156a32–b6 and 1157a5–10, Aristotle seems to suggest that the pleasure behind such friendships will often be sexual. Whatever Aristotle might have thought of the matter, though, it would be a mistake to hold that sexual pleasures are mere effects of certain activities, unaffected by the way in which one sees the value of those activities. As the etymology of the word 'caress' hints, to enjoy a caress is not to feel some brute sensation produced by another's touch but to enjoy a touch under the aspect of a gesture of love or expression of care.

[90] Aristotle recognizes this at *EN* 1156b16–18, where he attributes the pleasure associated with character friendship to the tendency of virtuous persons to take pleasure in their own actions taken as a type—i.e. their tendency to find their own actions intrinsically good or worthwhile.

distinctive benefits of its own. Character friendship is useful, but it conduces to one's *objective* needs and interests, whereas friendships of mutual utility often contribute to merely subjective and illusory "needs." Character friendship is also pleasant, but mostly because it opens the way for the sort of pleasure that accompanies and completes those activities that can stably be seen as valuable in themselves. Friendships of pleasure offer an abundance of the other kind of pleasures—the kind that are conceptually independent of whatever activities might give rise to them, and that can be secured via activities that are valueless or deeply objectionable. Character friendship can also promote this kind of pleasure, but as it approaches its constitutive ideal it increasingly rules out pleasures arising from objectionable actions.

Character friendship opens the way for activity- and life-completing pleasures in three closely related ways. First, it tends over time to remake the character of those who participate in it so that they have a clear view of what is good in itself, hence are capable of choosing and engaging in such activities with the pleasurable unreservedness born of a running appreciation (or Aristotelian *theorein*) of the activities' intrinsic value. Second, since the capacity to see and affirm the value of one's own characteristic activities goes hand-in-hand with a similar capacity to affirm the value of the characteristic activities of friends, character friendship expands the range of activities that one is in a position to complete with a running appreciation of their objective value. The activities of one's character friends will fall into this category as well. Hence one's life will be completed by pleasurable contemplation (or *theorein*) not only of one's own activities but of those of another.[91] Third, character friendship opens up the possibility of a range of shared activities of a sort that could not be engaged in with non-friends. These activities are most valuable when they can be accompanied and completed by a running appreciation (again, *theorein*) of the words and acts emanating from the two jointly produced sensibilities whose ongoing collaboration makes these activities possible.

All three of these kinds of pleasure involve the immediate appreciative perception of value. In this sense, they are of a piece with the sort of pleasure we might take in a good musical composition.[92] However, the practical pleasures under discussion involve an appreciative grasp of goods that provide proper guides for one's evolving activities. This explains why virtuous activity is pleasurable to those with a vivid understanding of its value. Yet we can have this sort of pleasure whenever we contemplate proper practical understanding (or *nous*) in action. Hence this sort of pleasure can accompany and complete our individual activities, our essentially shared activities, and our active contemplation of the words and actions of others. If the possibility of such pleasure is tied to the pursuit of a somewhat alien ideal of human interaction, and to the concomitant development of an equally unfamiliar ideal of human character and action, this

---

[91] *EN* 1169b34–5.   [92] *EN* 1170a9–11 and 1175a30–b7.

alone seems sufficient to recommend these unfamiliar ideals to our attention, and to prompt us to welcome them in those cultural nooks where they still survive, while casting a critical gaze upon social prejudices or practices that are inhospitable to them.

CONCLUDING REMARKS ON ARISTOTELIAN *EUDAIMONISM* AND MODERN MORAL THEORY

Those familiar with Kantian strands of modern moral philosophy will perhaps have noticed a similarity between the role played by friendship in the version of Aristotelian ethics set out above, and the pivotal role played by the universalizability test in Kantian ethics. Both are supposed to ensure a form of practical thinking that can be affirmed as acceptable (or, as some prefer to put it, that cannot reasonably be rejected) from the vantage point of any human being. This similarity is striking, and might perhaps be surprising to those who have come to think of Aristotle as a champion of a parochial Athenian conception of human excellence. Still there are important disanalogies between the way that Aristotelian friendship operates on evaluative outlooks and the way that Kantian universalizability has generally been thought to operate. By focusing on these disanalogies, we might hope to clarify some of the basic aspects of the "misalignment" one feels when attempting to fit Aristotle's views on the virtues into the array of theoretical possibilities that characterize modern moral philosophy.

To begin with, Kant's universalizability test—at least as it has traditionally been understood—differs from Aristotelian friendship in the *object* on which it operates. Friendship places a limit on characteristic modes of evaluative attention and practical thinking, while universalizability places a limit on maxims, or subjective principles of practical judgment. The Kantian view runs into immediate trouble when we attempt to identify the maxims of unreflective actions and omissions. A great deal of what we do is done without anything remotely like the invocation of a principle. A great deal of what we leave undone never even crosses our mind as a possible course of action, hence does not seem offhand to be omitted due to the application of a subjective principle. Yet if there is no maxim, then by Kantian lights there is no agency and no practical thinking of the sort that could be found morally laudable or wanting, hence no occasion for praise or blame. The Kantian must either find a way to assign maxims of action to unreflective actions and omissions, or impose an extremely implausible constriction on the scope of the morally assessable.[93] But even if the former could be done, the problem would not be solved, since a great deal

93 I have argued previously that the maxims of unreflective actions might be read off of the phenomenological focus of the desires that prompt us to engage in them. This position looks

of our morally significant practical thinking cannot be captured in the form of principles that establish justificatory connections between circumstances and action types—or so I argued in Chapter 3. The Kantian, then, works with too constricted a conception of the nature of moral thinking, hence has too constricted a conception of the proprieties of moral thought that constitute the subject matter of ethical theory. To retrieve Aristotelianism in a way that does not leave the jaw out of alignment would require that we widen our conception of the morally relevant sort of practical thinking beyond the realm of principles that connect circumstances to action types, sweeping in the half-articulate ideas of goodness or value that often inspire us to throw ourselves into particular kinds of activities or relationships and to carry forward with these activities or relationships in the way we do. This means that our theoretical inquiry cannot hope to yield an exhaustive specification of how we ought to live, nor to articulate a substantive conception of the good life whose content might be understood by someone who has no prior intimation of it.

A second key disanalogy between friendship and Kantian universalizability concerns what might be called their *modes of deployment*. Kant's universalizability criterion is generally regarded as a monological procedure for determining the moral permissibility of consciously formulated maxims of action. Aristotelian friendship, by contrast, is clearly unsuited to serve as a guideline for the sort of explicit monological deliberation that sometimes precedes particular actions.[94] Perhaps it would help, in such cases, to imagine how some proposed action would look to one's friend, or what one might say to a friend by way of explaining why one did it. But friendship is a mode of shared activity and conversation that we must actually engage in over time, and strive to perfect, if we are to refine our evaluative outlook, some of whose elements we might well be unable to bring before our mind for direct assessment, so as to make its verdicts shareable by all. This again places a limit on what it might make sense to seek to do by way of moral theorizing. The philosophical reflections on friendship set out in this chapter cannot possibly be a substitute for the sort of life experience, and

---

plausible if one holds—as Scanlon does and as I did at the time—that desires are appearances of reasons for action. As emerged in Chapters 1 and 2 of this book, I have come to think that desires often involve appearances of goodness or value that cannot be reduced to appearances of reasons, hence I no longer think that their representational content can be captured in the form of a Kantian maxim. My prior view is set out in "Maxims and Virtues," *Philosophical Review* 3 (2002), 539–72.

[94] On the other hand, I'm not at all sure that we should understand the Kantian concern for universalizability along the lines of this traditional interpretation. Allen Wood has argued quite forcefully that Kantian universalizability does not and was never intended to provide an independent decision procedure for determining which maxims we must adopt, hence what we ought morally to do. On Wood's reading of Kant, this question cannot be answered without determining what set of maxims are jointly affirmable by the members of a free and equal association of practical reasoners (a kingdom of ends). If we understand Kantian universalizability in this way, then Aristotelian friendship might well be the most practicable means of determining what is required by the standard of universal acceptability. On this matter, see Allen Wood, *Kant's Ethical Thought* (Cambridge: Cambridge University Press, 1999).

sustained interpersonal interaction, by which under the best of circumstances we can hope to deepen and extend our practical wisdom. Nor is there any particular reason to suppose that academic philosophers will be in a better position than others to see what ought and ought not to be done. Moral theory cannot replace life experience as a source of moral insight or wisdom. The wisdom of philosophers will be as dependent upon the quality of their human interactions, and their attention to and investment in those interactions, as will anyone else's. If they have the good fortune to spend their days in active engagement with the likes of Socrates, then perhaps their philosophical reflections will have deepened their wisdom. But it goes without saying that not every academic philosopher is a Socrates, and that no graduate program in philosophy has perfected the art of inspiring students to live Socratic lives. To the extent that academic moral philosophy has presented itself as a route to expertise about matters moral—for instance, to expertise in medical ethics, or business ethics, or environmental ethics—we ought to be skeptical of its pretensions. Yet we can readily admit the rather obvious point that philosophical reflection on ethics does not provide a sure route to wisdom while still reasonably insisting that it is an extremely valuable life activity—one that can at its best deepen and extend one's efforts to engage with others in the mutual shaping of mindful and decent ways of living and acting. We will have to disown the notion that the proper task of philosophical ethics is to capture moral standards of practical thinking in a codification that can be applied by any conscientious person who has a clear sense of the non-evaluative features of her circumstances. But we can happily disown this chimera without being forced to conclude that there is no point in sustained and disciplined thought about the significance of moral decency and about its place in the good life for human beings.

A third and related disanalogy is that the limits placed on evaluative outlooks by friendship are not *a priori* limits valid for all rational beings, but depend upon and record contingent facts about what human beings have actually been able to affirm together. This is partly a matter of what particular friends are actually able to affirm together. Yet since friends find the language for sculpting their shared outlooks from the linguistic inheritance they receive from the similar struggles of past generations, it is also a matter of what human beings are able to affirm together, as captured in their stock of specialized evaluative concepts. That these concepts are not beyond criticism is obvious enough. Many of us have simply ceased to use such terms as 'ladylike' or 'uppity,' presumably because we think that their appeal owed to the benefits that their use conferred upon some particular ascendant social group—on men in the first case, or aristocrats in the second case. It seems overwhelmingly likely that our use of other evaluative concepts has also been shaped by unjust relations of social power, and that these concepts are therefore unsuited to the task of helping to structure genuinely shareable evaluative outlooks. For my part, I accept the broadly Marxist notion that prevailing understandings of our basic political and economic rights are calculated to give a pleasing veneer of egalitarianism to a legal bulwark of social privilege, and I find prevailing notions of patriotism suspiciously convenient for those who depend upon a compliant citizenry to make effective use of political power. But this is the crooked conceptual timber that we have on hand to cobble together a workable and minimally articulate sense of how best to live. We must work with it if we are to undertake this work at all. Of course, working with it can mean using our critical capacities to bring its reflective unshareability into clearer view, partly by dialectical interaction with others who might have a different sense of how best to fashion it into a shape worthy of affirmation. One reason that the philosopher cannot hope to conduct this task alone is that it requires a grasp of social power and its effects on language that is not conferred by the typical training in philosophy. This means that the search for "reflective equilibrium" in substantive philosophical ethics and political theory ought to take place in conversation with historians and political economists and sociologists, not in isolation from them as it typically does in the contemporary academy.

8

The Virtues in Theory and Practice

Perhaps the openness of a human being in his entirety is a condition of philosophical truth. If this is so, contraction and rigidity and deadness of spirit would mark the moments of our philosophical failing as surely as our flagrant contradictions.

(Henry Bugbee)[1]

THE POSSIBILITY OF A RADICAL VIRTUE EPISTEMOLOGY

The guiding idea of this book has been that contemporary understandings of ethics can be enlivened by a retrieval of Ancient conceptions of the virtues. I have tried to show, however, that we cannot attain a full understanding of the virtue concepts unless we widen our inquiry beyond narrowly moral concerns to include ethics in the broadest sense, examining the role of the virtues in the full array of intrinsically valuable activities that compose a good human life. If this suggestion is right, then we might expect the retrieval of the virtue concepts to shed light not only on excellence in practical thought but also on excellence in theoretical thought, since it can hardly be doubted that theoretical reflection is a crucial part of a flourishing human life. As it happens, the florescence of new literature on virtue ethics that has emerged over the past twenty-five years has been paralleled by a somewhat more modest movement within epistemology towards virtue-theoretic inquiries into the proper ends and governing norms of theoretical reasoning.

Can we turn to this recent work in virtue epistemology, then, to supplement our inquiry into the virtues of practical thought with corollary insights into the virtues of theoretical reflection? Unfortunately we cannot. Contemporary virtue ethics and virtue epistemology have been organized around fundamentally dissimilar conceptual templates. This dissimilarity has prevented the return of the language of the virtues from having the sort of salutary influence on the field of epistemology that the best work in virtue ethics has begun to have on

---

[1] Henry Bugbee, *The Inward Morning: A Philosophical Exploration in Journal Form* (New York: Collier Books, 1958), 49.

ethics. More specifically, it has for the most part impeded any truly fundamental reconsideration of epistemology's self-understanding, its idea of what exactly it is supposed to be about. As a consequence, it has encouraged an exaggerated sense of the difference between ethical and epistemic virtues, and more generally of the difference between the proper aspirations of practical and theoretical reasoning. This in turn has fed the temptation to adopt an anti-realist conception of practical norms or values, if only by encouraging the thought that there is a clearly demarcated line at which such skepticism might stop so as to leave intact the norms of theoretical reason.

The most prominent positions in virtue epistemology have deviated in two basic ways from the most prominent work in virtue ethics. The first difference concerns the relation between the virtues and the proper *telos* of deliberation. Virtue epistemologists have generally sought to identify the epistemic virtues by reference to a prior and conceptually independent conception of the proper end of theoretical reasoning—for instance, the end of attaining true beliefs while avoiding false ones. On this approach, the intellectual virtues enter the picture as states that either tend to produce, or manifest an intention to produce, this independent good. By contrast, contemporary virtue ethicists have generally held that we cannot attain a concrete understanding of the proper end(s) of practical reflection without clarifying our conception of the virtues.

The second difference concerns the ontology of the final end of deliberation. Virtue ethicists have tended to follow Aristotle in thinking of the *telos* of practical deliberation as a characteristic *activity* in which the virtues are actualized. The notion of activity has not always been developed in an entirely illuminating way, and one of my main ambitions in this book has been to set out a conception of activity against which the value of the virtues can be appreciated more fully. Still, virtue ethicists have generally understood that the value of the virtues must lie in some form or another of human activity. Virtue epistemologists, by contrast, have generally conceived of the *telos* of theoretical deliberation as a future state to which the virtues conduce, or at which the virtuous person is disposed to aim. There is disagreement among virtue epistemologists about whether the state in question is true belief, or justified true belief, or knowledge, or understanding. But there is wide agreement that whatever the *telos* may be, it is the sort of fixed achievement or attained capacity that can properly be attributed to people even in moments of mental inactivity.

What should we make of these basic differences between the two fields? One hypothesis is that both fields are in good order, and that these fundamental differences in their conceptual structures reflect equally fundamental differences between theoretical and practical thought. On reflection, this hypothesis is dubious. One hint that virtue epistemology is on the wrong track is that the goal with respect to which many virtue epistemologists have sought to specify the virtues—the attainment of true beliefs and the avoidance of false beliefs—is not invariably good or worthwhile. The successful pursuit of trivial truths can be an unmitigated waste of time. It is hard to see how a trait can be certified as a virtue simply because it tends to produce true beliefs, since the true beliefs to which it leads might well be uniformly trivial. Nor does it seem plausible to suppose that the value of theoretical reflection lies in its extrinsic relation to other human concerns, such as the satisfaction of our desires or the attainment of our practical ends. No such view could comfortably be accepted by anyone who counts active and continuously deepening theoretical reflection itself as an intrinsically valuable and potentially focal life activity. That is to say, no such view could comfortably be accepted by a philosopher.

A second hint that virtue epistemology is on the wrong track lies in the inaptness of locating the final end of any human activity in an achieved state. Such a view puts the cart before the horse. It is essential to the sort of being we call human that it unfolds in the living of a life. We lose track of this basic fact if we locate the final ends of human beings in mere dispositional states or potentialities rather than in the life-constituting activities made possible by these dispositions or potentialities.

These considerations point towards serious objections to the views of many virtue epistemologists. However, they hardly amount to a fatal objection to the very idea of a virtue-centric approach to epistemology. It remains possible that the best-known practitioners of virtue epistemology have thus far been insufficiently radical, and that the real promise of the approach lies not in resolving puzzles that already preoccupy epistemologists but in inducing the sort of fundamental shift in the scope, ambitions, and agenda of epistemology that a genuine retrieval of Aristotelian thought spells for ethics. The aim of this chapter is to develop and lend credence to this possibility. The guiding thought is that if we are to locate a *telos* of theoretical reflection with reference to which we can identify a comprehensive account of virtuous intellectual dispositions or capacities, we should look not towards true belief or propositional knowledge but towards the sort of *active appreciation* of the world that both actualizes and typically serves to deepen one's achieved *understanding* of the world.

This conception of the *telos* of theoretical reflection helps to bring out the common source and the harmony of the proper norms and ideals of theoretical and practical reasoning. This, in turn, greatly reduces the appeal of non-cognitivism about practical normativity, since the most persuasive sort of non-cognitivism is the sort that limits its reach to the practical. In a methodological vein, this approach turns on the thought that the prevailing practice of drawing a sharp disciplinary boundary between ethics and epistemology fails to carve the normative world at its true joints, and serves to impede rather than to promote insight into the goods realizable in a human life. Some of the most important of these goods (e.g. understanding or contemplation) do not fall within the bounds of any contemporary specialization, hence rarely receive more than passing philosophical attention. Epistemologists tend to restrict their attention to knowledge rather than understanding or active contemplation. Ethicists, for their part, tend to inquire into the difference between justified and unjustified action rather than on the difference between activities performed with full evaluative understanding and activities performed without such understanding. Even those ethicists who are otherwise friendly to Aristotle's ideas tend to see it as a puzzling anomaly, and not a path to fresh insight into the unity of theoretical and practical reason, that the *Nicomachean Ethics* ends with a discussion of contemplation. Other important goods (e.g. true belief and knowledge) receive a great deal of attention, yet their value cannot adequately be understood without transcending the boundaries of the specializations to which their study is assigned.

Among the more ironic effects of this pattern of specialization is to discourage philosophers from becoming fully articulate about the nature and value of the activity to which they have devoted their lives. There is no recognized specialization within which the understanding of the value of philosophy itself might fruitfully be pursued. If Socrates was right to regard the Delphic oracle's exhortation "Know thyself" as an apt expression of the philosopher's true calling, then contemporary philosophy is admirably suited to deafen its inductees to their proper calling.

VIRTUE EPISTEMOLOGY AND TRUE BELIEF

What distinguishes virtue ethics from other approaches to ethics is not that virtue ethics offers an account of the virtues of character while other approaches do not. Almost any ethical theory will have something to say about which characteristic modes of perception, deliberation, motivation, and action are properly counted as good or bad. Hence almost any ethical theory will purport to offer insights into the virtues. What is distinctive about virtue ethics is its claim that insight into the nature and value of the virtues cannot successfully be derived from a prior grasp of other ethical norms, and that the virtues must be understood if one is to gain anything more than the most abstract understanding of excellence in practical thought and action.

With a few notable exceptions, the nascent field of virtue epistemology has been modeled on a very different conceptual template. Contemporary discussion of virtue epistemology is generally dated to Ernest Sosa's seminal paper "The Raft and the Pyramid."[2] In that essay and several subsequent publications, Sosa seeks to shed light on traditional epistemological puzzles

---

[2] Ernest Sosa, "The Raft and the Pyramid: Coherence Versus Foundations in the Theory of Knowledge," in Peter French, Theodore Uehling, Jr., and Howard Wettstein, eds., *Midwest Studies in Philosophy, Volume V: Studies in Epistemology* (Minneapolis: University of Minnesota Press, 1980), 3–25.

concerning the nature of justification and knowledge by directing attention away from formal inferential relations among beliefs and towards the mental processes by which we generate beliefs. To this end, Sosa proposes that "An intellectual virtue is a quality bound to help maximize one's surplus of truth over intellectual error."[3]

After characterizing the epistemic virtues in terms of true beliefs, Sosa goes on to claim that a belief cannot be called justified, nor counted as knowledge, unless it originates in dispositions of mind that reliably produce true beliefs. Since this claim puts a conception of the epistemic virtues to work in analyzing other epistemic goods, some interpreters purport to see a close analogy between Sosa's epistemology and Aristotelian virtue ethics.[4] In fact the analogy is quite loose. Sosa begins by presupposing the value of true belief. He then counts mental attributes as virtuous to the extent that they reliably bring about true beliefs. It is true that he goes on to suggest that justified belief or knowledge must arise from epistemic virtues, but this talk of virtues is straightforwardly eliminable, since it means nothing more than that justified belief and knowledge must arise from dispositions that reliably produce true beliefs. We gain no further insight into the value of these dispositions when we label them virtues, nor does this re-labeling yield additional insight into the value of justification or knowledge. As Linda Zagzebski has pointed out, the mere fact that a justified belief has been produced by a process that reliably produces true beliefs cannot plausibly be thought to add to the intrinsic value of the belief. To think otherwise would be somewhat like thinking that a tasty cup of coffee produced by a reliable coffee maker is better than an otherwise identical cup produced by an unreliable coffee maker.[5] Thus, whether or not Sosa has found a way to use virtue-talk to produce an apt analysis of justified belief or of propositional knowledge, his talk of intellectual virtue seems unsuited to the task of illuminating the *value* of justification or knowledge.[6]

---

[3] Ernest Sosa, "Knowledge and Intellectual Virtue," in *Knowledge in Perspective: Selected Essays in Epistemology* (Cambridge: Cambridge University Press, 1991), 225. This same recognizably reliabilist conception of intellectual virtue can be discerned in "The Raft and the Pyramid," 23.

[4] See John Greco, "Virtue Epistemology," in *Stanford Encyclopedia of Philosophy*, http://plato. stanford.edu/entries/epistemology-virtue, Section 2. Sosa, by contrast, explicitly develops his view not by analogy with Aristotelianism but with the sort of consequentialism that regards ethical virtues as embodied rules that maximize the likelihood of bringing about good consequences. See "The Raft and the Pyramid," 23.

[5] Linda Zagzebski, "From Reliabilism to Virtue Epistemology," in Guy Axtell, ed., *Knowledge, Belief and Character: Readings in Virtue Epistemology* (Lanham, Maryland: Rowman and Littlefield Publishers, Inc., 2000), 113–22. The coffee-maker example is borrowed from Zagzebski (114).

[6] Sosa has sometimes suggested that this problem can be eased by citing the extra value inhering in achieved ends (including true beliefs) when they have been produced by an exercise of skill. If skill is nothing more than a reliable capacity to produce true beliefs, this suggestion gets us no farther along. If however it is a capacity that has been honed by dint of its possessor's determination to perfect it, then it will add value to its progeny only if this effort has itself been worthwhile. I will go on to argue that we must specify a narrower conception of the proper quarry of theoretical

Many other epistemologists have followed Sosa in identifying true belief and the avoidance of false belief as the proper goals of theoretical reflection, and as the touchstone for determining which traits count as virtues.[7] However, an important disagreement has emerged among virtue epistemologists concerning how a trait must be related to the production of true beliefs if it is to count as a virtue. As noted above, Sosa conceives of the relation in reliabilist terms.[8] For Sosa, intellectual virtues are always relativized to an environment, and consist in innate abilities or acquired habits that reliably dispose their possessors to form true beliefs within that environment.[9] Other virtue epistemologists have thought of the requisite relation as intentional rather than causal. That is, they have held that the mark of epistemic virtue is a standing motivation, or a conscious and determined effort, to arrive at true beliefs and to avoid false beliefs.[10]

---

reflection if we are to locate a skill that is worth trying to hone, and that might plausibly be counted as a credit to those who have taken the time to hone it.

[7] To name a few: John Greco, Alvin Goldman, James Montmarquet, Robert Audi, Keith Lehrer, and Richard Foley. Some of Linda Zagzebski's writings seems to fit this description as well, since she has argued in various places that love of true belief is the central epistemic virtue, and that *phronesis* can resolve conflicts between the pursuit of truth and the avoidance of falsehood without relying upon any third basic epistemic value. She goes on to explain that the desire for truth must be supplemented by other character traits such as perseverance, humility, fairness, and courage that are needed in order to overcome obstacles that block us from attaining true beliefs. See John Greco, "Virtues and Rules in Epistemology," in Linda Zagzebski and Abrol Fairweather, eds., *Virtue Epistemology: Essays on Epistemic Virtue and Responsibility* (Oxford: Oxford University Press, 2001), 137–8; Alvin Goldman, "The Unity of the Epistemic Virtues," in Zagzebski and Fairweather, *Virtue Epistemology*, 30–48; Robert Audi, "Epistemic Virtue and Justified Belief," in Zagzebski and Fairweather, *Virtue Epistemology*, 82–97, especially 87; Keith Lehrer, "The Virtue of Knowledge," in Zagzebski and Fairweather, *Virtue Epistemology*, 200–13, especially 203; Richard Foley, "The Foundational Role of Epistemology in a General Theory of Rationality, in Zagzebski and Fairweather, *Virtue Epistemology*, 214–30, especially 224; and Linda Zagzebski, "Intellectual Motivation and the Good of Truth," in Linda Zagzebski and Michael DePaul, eds., *Intellectual Virtue: Perspectives from Ethics and Epistemology* (Oxford: Oxford University Press, 2003), 135–54, especially 149–50 and 153–4.

[8] Goldman stakes out a view of this sort in "The Unity of the Epistemic Virtues," 31. Foley also takes this view of the epistemic virtues (but not of all intellectual virtues) in "The Foundational Role," 224.

[9] Ernest Sosa, *Knowledge in Perspective: Selected Essays in Epistemology* (Cambridge: Cambridge University Press, 1991), 138–40, 225–9, 284–5.

[10] For instance, John Greco thinks of virtues as stable and reliable dispositions that are manifested when one's thinking is motivated by the attempt to get at the truth. (See Greco, "Virtue Epistemology," Section 5.) Linda Zagzebski holds that intellectual virtues "include motive dispositions connected with the motive to get truth" and are generally reliable in arriving at the truth. (Zagzebski and Fairweather, *Virtue Epistemology*, 5; see also Zagzebski, "Intellectual Motivation," 153–4.) Abrol Fairweather thinks of intellectual virtue as involving a motivating desire for truth. (See Fairweather, "Epistemic Motivation," in Zagzebski and Fairweather, 63–81.) Keith Lehrer thinks of intellectual virtue as involving the adoption of "the purpose of obtaining truth and avoiding error in a reliably successful way." (See Lehrer, "The Virtue of Knowledge," 203.) James Montmarquet counts the desire to attain truth and avoid error as "the fundamental epistemic virtue." (See James A. Montmarquet, *Epistemic Virtue and Doxastic Responsibility* (Lanham, Maryland: Rowman and Littlefield Publishers, Inc., 1993), viii.)

This latter approach to virtue epistemology is sometimes called "responsibilism" because it conceives of epistemic virtue as a matter of consciously assuming responsibility for the truth of what one believes. The responsibilist approach to virtue epistemology has two distinct advantages over the reliabilism of Sosa and Goldman. The first advantage is that it makes better sense of the thought that attributions of virtue and vice are appraisals of *people* and not appraisals of attributes for which people can neither be credited nor faulted. For example, the reliabilist must count such attributes as native calculating capacity and visual acuity as epistemic virtues, since they reliably conduce to true beliefs. The responsibilist would reject this somewhat dubious conclusion, since these attributes do not themselves manifest a commitment to get at the truth (though their deliberate cultivation or careful deployment might do so), and hence do not seem to count to the credit of those who possess them.

A second, closely related advantage is that responsibilism immunizes epistemic virtue from certain dubious form of luck in epistemic circumstances. For example, Sosa's view seems to imply that what we might call intellectual conscientiousness—i.e. a readiness to make a conscientious effort to check up on the truth of one's beliefs and to avoid false beliefs—would not be virtuous in a world in which striving to get at the truth leads systematically to error while intellectual carelessness reliably leads to true beliefs. (Here it is standard fare to imagine an "evil demon" who systematically ensures that intellectual effort leads to false beliefs and intellectual carelessness to true ones.) It counts in favor of responsibilism that it would count intellectual conscientiousness as an epistemic virtue even in those epistemically inhospitable worlds where this trait consistently leads to error.[11]

For present purposes, though, the disagreement between the responsibilist and reliabilist branches of virtue epistemology matters less than their agreement. Many of the best-known proponents of these two approaches agree that the intellectual virtues can be identified by reference to the antecedently specified goal of attaining true beliefs and avoiding false ones. They agree that excellence in thought is to be characterized in terms of its intended product or its efficacy as a means of production, and that its proper product is true belief. They disagree

---

[11] James Montmarquet makes this point, but he does so by means of an argument that quickly lands him in incoherence. He considers the possibility that we might discover that the traits we have previously considered to be intellectual virtues are not truth-conducive. We might discover, for instance, that one tracks the truth only if one is careless, hasty, close-minded, and in general indifferent about the truth of one's beliefs. Such a discovery is not a coherent possibility. It supposes that we can see the superiority of a picture of how the world is that would be believed by an intellectually vicious person, but that would be rejected by a virtuous person. If the allegedly better picture of the world can be seen as better through the lens of our virtuous outlook, then there is no reason to reject our virtues after all. But if the allegedly better picture of the world can only be seen as superior by thinking in ways that we regard as vicious, then we have no reason to accept that it is in fact a better picture of how the world is, and that our virtues have led us astray. It would be reasonable for us to draw this conclusion only if it stood up to what is, by our lights, the most intellectually virtuous inquiry of which we are capable. But by hypothesis it would not.

only on the question whether the virtues get their value because they are causally efficacious in producing true beliefs or because they manifest a firm intention to produce them.

To be sure, this view of the proper goal of theoretical reasoning has not attracted a perfect consensus. There are a handful of dissenters, some of whom will be discussed below. Still, it is clearly the predominant view. Because its conceptual frame is so strikingly different from the pattern of thought that structures most work in virtue ethics, it tends to leap out at those who approach the study of virtue epistemology with a background in ethics. Simon Blackburn is one of several such philosophers who have noted the difference and speculated on the prospects for a more purely virtue-theoretic epistemology.[12] In Blackburn's view, the key to such a virtue epistemology would be a virtue-theoretic account of truth. True belief, that is, might be analyzed as the sort of belief that a virtuous person would have in standard circumstances. Blackburn plausibly suggests that this might work for beliefs about secondary properties and other properties lying at the intersection of our human sensibilities and the world.[13] It seems, however, that there is little hope for a more comprehensive virtue-theoretic analysis of truth. If Blackburn were right that the prospects of pure virtue epistemology depend upon the tenability of a virtue-theoretic account of truth, this would cast grave doubt on the appeal of pure virtue epistemology.

What Blackburn's suggestion presupposes is that true belief is in fact the proper *telos* of theoretical reflection. This seems mistaken. The attainment of true beliefs and avoidance of false beliefs is not a proper *telos* for theoretical reflection. It is at once too specific and too inclusive: it omits a good deal of what the good thinker properly aspires to, and it includes many things that the good thinker would find totally valueless. This is not to suggest that we ought not to care if our beliefs are true, or that we ought sometimes to believe falsehoods. The point at hand rests on the more modest claims that some matters are so trivial that forming true beliefs about them has no value, and that the formation of beliefs is not the sole end of theoretical deliberation. If these two claims can be substantiated, this will show that the attainment of true belief and the avoidance of false belief does not constitute the sort of *telos* with respect to which a fully adequate picture of the intellectual virtues can be elaborated.

It should be clear, to begin with, that the avoidance of false beliefs is a radically incomplete goal for theoretical reflection. After all, this goal could in principle be attained by an assiduous refusal to assent to any proposition, no matter how evident. Contemporary virtue epistemologists have shown little if any sympathy for the sort of radical Pyhrronism that would count such a refusal as virtuous. So even if avoidance of error is invariably good, it does not provide an adequate

---

[12] Simon Blackburn, "Reason, Virtue and Knowledge," in Linda Zagzebski and Abrol Fairweather, eds., *Virtue Epistemology*, 15–29.

[13] *Ibid.*, 24–6.

telos for theoretical reflection, nor a fit starting point for a truth-centric account of the epistemic virtues.

The basic intuition shared by reliabilists and many responsibilists is that theoretical reflection ought to be responsive to two ends — the attainment of true beliefs and the avoidance of false beliefs — and that epistemic excellence consists in striking a proper balance between these ends. Indeed, this intuition plays a foundational role in contemporary epistemology, providing the standard stage-setting for virtue-theoretic and non-virtue-theoretic work in the field.[14] The basic idea here is that our cognitive faculties or strategies should generate fresh beliefs, or at least aim to do so, whenever the risk of error is tolerably low. The trouble with this idea is that it is not always good to generate true beliefs even if one can do so with little risk of error. This is not to deny that true beliefs are always good qua beliefs, the way that sharp knives are good qua knives. But from the fact that sharp knives are good qua knives and that true beliefs are good qua beliefs, it does not follow that the world is better or that anyone is better off when more sharp knives or true beliefs come into existence.

What's wrong with claiming that the attainment of true beliefs is always good? Suppose I am intent upon efficiently increasing my stock of true beliefs. I might do so by going around with a ruler and making a mental catalogue of things that are clearly less than a foot tall. If having more true beliefs were invariably good, the pay-off of this exercise would be remarkable. After all, if I know that something is less than a foot tall, I also know that it is less than two feet tall, that it is less than three feet tall, and so on. In other words, I come into possession of an infinite number of new true beliefs, one corresponding to each positive integer. What could it mean to say that each of these beliefs is good? Certainly it can't be supposed that each member of this infinite series of beliefs makes me or my life one whit better. Without some further story, securing such beliefs would be a thorough waste of time even though they are true and seem indeed to count as propositional knowledge. We don't have here a good, knowledge, whose pursuit is ill-advised because it requires us to forego other, weightier goods. Without some special story, we have here a pursuit that has nothing to be said for it, even though it would produce a great quantity of knowledge.

On further reflection, then, it seems that we ought to qualify Linda Zagzebski's claim that any adequate epistemology must explain why knowledge is more valuable than mere true belief.[15] This so-called "value problem" needs to be sharpened, since it is not true that knowledge always has more intrinsic value than true belief. There is valuable knowledge and there is valueless knowledge,

---

[14] To take but one example, Laurence BonJour frames the theoretical discussion of his most influential work in epistemology with the following bald assertion: "What makes us cognitive beings at all is our capacity for belief, and the goal of our distinctively cognitive endeavors is *truth*: we want our beliefs to correctly and accurately depict the world." See BonJour, *The Structure of Empirical Knowledge* (Cambridge: Harvard University Press, 1985), 7.

[15] Zagzebski, "From Reliabilism to Virtue Epistemology," 114–15.

just as there is valuable and valueless true belief, and valuable and valueless justified belief. There is no general feature of knowledge that distinguishes it from mere true belief and that always brings some measure of intrinsic value with it. If the "value problem" supposes that there must be, then the problem cannot be solved. We see this in Zagzebski's own proposed solution, which traces the special value of knowledge to the fact that it originates in the knower's motive to get at the truth. As noted above, this motive is simply too general to confer praiseworthiness on all of its progeny. We must look beyond beliefs that are true, or justified, or that qualify as knowledge, if we are to locate a genuine intrinsic good around which a self-standing normative epistemology might be constructed.[16]

Another way to see that true belief is not intrinsically good is to notice that one can often convert someone else's false belief into a true belief simply by rearranging the world so as to correspond to that belief, yet it hardly seems true that one always thereby confers some benefit upon the person in question. Again, this is easiest to see in the case of trivial beliefs. Suppose that I have taken an unaccountable interest in filling vials with sand and counting the grains in each vial, and I tell my son before he leaves for school in the morning that there are 1124 grains in vial number three. I spend the morning recounting the grains and realize that in fact there are 1125. I could then bring it about that my son has one fewer false beliefs, and one more true belief, by removing a grain of sand from vial three. Without some special story, it is hard to believe that I would thereby make the world, or my son, or my son's life, one whit better. There is no value in true belief *per se*.

It seems, then, that we should reject the following thesis, which Blackburn proposes as a suitable starting point for normative epistemology: "It is good that, if *p*, I believe that *p*, and if I believe that *p*, then *p*."[17] Likewise, we should reject Linda Zagzebski's blanket insistence that "true belief is good."[18] At most we can defend the weaker thesis that *if* one is intent upon forming a belief about some matter, *then* one must recognize that there is a reason to believe what is true and not what is false.[19] This thesis is hard to deny. Since believing something just is counting it as true, one cannot coherently regard oneself as attempting to form a belief unless one regards one's efforts as answerable to evidence concerning how things actually are. But this weaker thesis imposes only a conditional requirement

---

[16] Wayne Riggs makes this same point in "Understanding 'Virtue' and the Virtue of Understanding," in Zagzebski and DePaul, *Intellectual Virtue*, 203–26, especially 213.

[17] Blackburn, "Reason, Virtue and Knowledge," 23.

[18] Zagzebski, "Intellectual Motivation," 137. Later in the same essay Zagzebski writes: "Ever since the ancient Greeks Western thinkers have admired those who are relentless in the pursuit of truth. Such people are thought to be noble, certainly beyond the ordinary" (153). This again is far too sweeping. The relentless memorizer of baseball statistics is not generally admired or thought particularly noble.

[19] Ernest Sosa suggests such a retreat in "The Place of Truth in Epistemology," in Zagzebski and DePaul, *Intellectual Virtue*, 155–79, especially 157 and 160.

on us—one that could in principle be met by assiduously refraining from belief formation. For this reason it cannot provide a plausible truth-centric *telos* around which to build an exhaustive account of the epistemic virtues.

The examples I've offered suggest that true beliefs must be *important* if they are to be proper ends of theoretical reflection—ends whose reliable attainment is plausibly regarded as virtuous. A theorist who wishes to deny any ultimate epistemic value other than truth might try to distinguish between important and trivial true beliefs in terms of the *number* of true beliefs that they generate or imply. This won't work. As noted above, the true belief that a certain object is less than a foot tall turns out to be a tremendously fecund source of true beliefs. The problem with the belief is not that it does not imply many other true beliefs, but that the truths that can be inferred from it are without exception unimportant. In the absence of some special story, even an infinite number of them do not add up to anything worth pursuing. We must look beyond true belief to other epistemic values if we are to locate a proper end of theoretical reflection.

These ruminations yield serious objections to Sosa and others who favor a reliabilist form of virtue epistemology.[20] One objection is that there are dispositions of mind that reliably produce true beliefs yet cannot plausibly be counted as epistemic virtues. An example is the disposition to make repetitive use of the above-sketched method to reliably generate infinite sets of true beliefs. A second objection is that the reliabilist approach mistakenly implies that a reliably truth-tracking disposition to form beliefs about trivial matters is more virtuous than a slightly less reliable disposition to form beliefs about more important matters. Indeed, a reliabilist theory is arguably obliged to count the disposition to engage in philosophical reflection as vicious, since such reflection hardly provides a reliable recipe for attaining true beliefs. (Those who reject the rest of my argument might for this very reason be persuaded to grant me at least this last point!) Perhaps this reliabilist version of "virtue epistemology" can still succeed in offering tenable analyses of justification or propositional knowledge, but it must disown the more ambitious agenda of offering a comprehensive account of the virtues of theoretical reflection, and must simultaneously disown the analogy with Aristotelian virtue ethics that informs this ambition.[21]

These same ruminations also present problems for responsibilists like Montmarquet, Greco, and Fairweather (and Zagzebski in her recent work) who regard the epistemic virtues as traits that one would have or want to have insofar as one is determined to generate true beliefs and avoid false ones. They too are committed to the thought that dispositions to generate reliably true but trivial

---

[20] In more recent work, Sosa has recognized that true beliefs are not always valuable, yet to my knowledge he has not recognized how serious a difficulty this poses for his approach to virtue epistemology. See Sosa, "The Place of Truth in Epistemology," 157–60; and Sosa, "For the Love of Truth?" in Zagzebski and Fairweather, *Virtue Epistemology*, 49–62.

[21] See for instance Sosa, "The Place of Truth in Epistemology," 155 and 179n.

beliefs are markers of virtue, since those who are dedicated to the pursuit of truth would have reason to cultivate such dispositions.[22] What this case suggests is that one can voluntarily refuse to pursue the truth about a particular topic, or set no value on trying to attain certain infinite sets of true beliefs, without showing a lack of epistemic virtue. One would show a lack of the undifferentiated zeal for truth, but that just shows that the undifferentiated zeal for truth cannot be counted as virtuous, and indeed can manifest itself in minor vices—for instance, the vice of distracting fascination with triviality, something that can be part of a larger aversion to, or flight from, the struggle to understand the world and one's place in it.

TRUE BELIEF VS. UNDERSTANDING

Suppose we accept the point that some true beliefs are too trivial to merit our pursuit. Can we still hold to the idea that the proper *telos* of theoretical reflection is the attainment of true beliefs and the avoidance of error, so long as we add that the true beliefs in question must meet some as-yet-unspecified standard of importance? I don't think so. The problem is that one can have any number of important and true beliefs about some subject matter but still lack full understanding of that subject matter. Understanding seems to be a required element of the sort of perspicuous grasp of the world to which theoretical reflection properly aspires, yet understanding does not seem to be composed exhaustively of true beliefs.

The claim that understanding is the proper *telos* of theoretical reflection has surfaced in the works of several virtue epistemologists who have broken with the truth-centric conceptual framework discussed above.[23] These theorists differ subtly in their conceptions of what it is to understand something, some emphasizing that it consists in a grasp of the unity of some array of facts and others emphasizing that it involves a grasp of what explains why

---

[22] Zagzebski tries to resolve the problem by maintaining that the wise person—i.e. the person with *phronesis*—will be able to see when it is worth risking falsehood to pursue truth. (See "Intellectual Motivation," 149–50.) But this understates the problem in two ways. First, wisdom cannot here boil down to grasping the proper trade-offs between these two aims. Falsehood is not the only risk one can run in pursuing true beliefs. One can run little risk of falsehood but great risk of wasting one's time and, in the long run, of misspending one's life. Only a more comprehensive sort of *phronesis* can make the needed discriminations. Second, Zagzebski's solution retains the initial notion that true beliefs are always good, yet this initial idea is itself mistaken.

[23] See especially Wayne Riggs, "Understanding 'Virtue'." See also Jonathan Kvanvig, *The Value of Knowledge and the Pursuit of Understanding* (Cambridge: Cambridge University Press, 2003), 185–203. Earlier hints of this approach can be found in Montmarquet, *Epistemic Virtue*, 33; in Lorraine Code, *Epistemic Responsibility* (Hanover, New Hampshire: University Press of New England, 1987), 59 and 149; and in Linda Zagzebski, *Virtues of the Mind: An Inquiry into the Nature of Virtue and the Ethical Foundations of Knowledge* (Cambridge: Cambridge University Press, 1996), 43–50.

certain facts are as they are. They converge, however, on the crucial point that understanding involves an insight into some array of facts that does not consist solely in coming to believe a longer list of true propositions. This step represents a genuine and vital contribution to a fully adequate virtue epistemology. In my view, however, these thinkers have not made adequately clear *why* understanding must involve something more than propositional beliefs, and they have erred in thinking of understanding as an achieved state rather than an activity.

Wayne Riggs, for instance, argues that understanding must be non-propositional because it consists in a grasp of why certain bodies of facts are as they are. To use his examples, the car mechanic who understands engines will be able to say why an engine is behaving as it is and how its behavior might be altered by various interventions; likewise the historian who understands a particular epoch will have a clear grasp of why events unfolded as they did, hence of what might have happened if certain historical contingencies had been otherwise.[24] The problem is that these examples and Riggs' ensuing discussion do not show why understanding cannot be purely propositional—that is, why it cannot consist entirely in affirmations of true propositions concerning why certain things are as they are. Why can't the car mechanic's diagnostic expertise consist solely in a set of true beliefs about the signs and causes of various engine problems? Why can't the historian's expertise consist solely in a list of true beliefs about why certain historical events unfolded as they did? Riggs' examples certainly suggest answers to these questions, but he does not make these answers explicit.

Jonathan Kvanvig also suggests that understanding is the proper end of theoretical reflection, and the proper touchstone for an account of the intellectual virtues. Kvanvig takes understanding to involve a grasp of the explanatory, logical, and probabilistic interrelations among propositions that form a common body of information.[25] He makes clear that he does not think of understanding as simply a matter of affirming some larger set of propositions that characterize these explanatory, logical, and probabilistic interrelations.[26] But like Riggs he doesn't manage to explain why it cannot be purely propositional.

A more illuminating approach to the understanding of understanding can be found in Julius Moravcsik's work on the Ancient Greek notion of *episteme*.[27] Moravcsik argues quite convincingly that what Plato and Aristotle meant by the Greek term '*episteme*' is better captured by the English term 'understanding' than by the term's more common translation, 'knowledge.' To set the stage for this argument, Moravcsik distinguishes between propositional knowledge

[24] Riggs, "Understanding 'Virtue'," 220–1.   [25] Kvanvig, *The Value of Knowledge*, 192–3.
[26] *Ibid.*, 202.
[27] Julius Moravcsik, "Understanding and Knowledge in Plato's Philosophy," in *Neue Hefte Für Philosophie* 15/16 (1979), 53–69.

of the sort that interests most contemporary epistemologists, and the sort of understanding involved in understanding a proof or a language or an epoch of history. By Moravcsik's lights, this sort of understanding is not entirely propositional because it requires the internalization of rules expressing proprieties of thought. We have internalized a rule in the relevant sense when an attachment to the rule is implicit in our characteristic sense of how best to think—for instance, in our sense of what counts as a proof or an apt use of a word or a correct calculation. It is possible to internalize a rule in this sense without being able to articulate it. When an internalized rule manifests itself in our characteristic sense of some propriety of thought, we are sometimes able to articulate the rule, and we can generally formulate many of its deliverances in propositional form—as for instance when we say that some comment is illuminating or irrelevant. Still, as Moravscik convincingly argues, our understanding of these proprieties of thought explains such propositional affirmations and is not reducible to them.

We can see Moravscik's point quite clearly in the case of proprieties of logical inference. As Lewis Carroll saw, if understanding the proprieties of inference were just a matter of sincerely affirming propositions that specify them, then the proprieties of inference would add indefinitely to the premises of arguments without ever yielding a conclusion.[28] Understanding what implies what, and when an inference is a good one, involves something more than being able to formulate general truths about what follows from what and sincerely affirm that these rules are authoritative. It requires a facility in putting such rules to use. Nor would we attribute understanding to someone who put these rules to use mechanically, without seeing the point of using them, like a child who has just learned the technique of long division but doesn't yet understand what exactly he is doing. If a rule of inference does not structure one's intuitive sense of which lines of argument are convincing and which are unconvincing, and of what it makes sense to affirm on the strength of certain classes of premises, then one has not yet attained a full understanding of the rule *qua* propriety of thought or of the lines of thought governed by the rule. For example, one cannot master *modus tollens* simply by memorizing the following sentence from what one believes to be an authoritative logic text: If one proposition implies a second and the second is false, then the first is false. One has not grasped *modus tollens* unless and until one characteristically thinks in accordance with it and balks at accepting lines of reasoning that deviate from it.

These observations can be amplified to cover the understanding of any domain of thought. Scientists, for instance, must learn to recognize certain phenomena—e.g. symptoms of diseases, species of plants, traces on computer screens that signify the presence of charged particles, etc.—and these recognitional capacities can no more be reduced to propositional beliefs than the recognitional

---

[28] Lewis Carroll, "What the Tortoise Said to Achilles," *Mind* 4 (1895), 278–80.

capacities we display when we pick a friend's face out of a crowd. (After all, any propositional belief that purported to capture the conditions for truly identifying a particular face as that of one's friend would itself require, for its judicious application, a capacity to recognize these identifying conditions.) Scientists must also develop a feel for what counts as an apt explanation, how to go about assessing proposed explanations and devising others that might be better, how best to interpret experimental results, and how to incorporate anomalous data into an evolving picture of the phenomena. All of these things can be done well or badly. Those who are able to do them well have a more piercing understanding of science than those who do them badly. Nor can this extra measure of understanding be regarded as a mere lengthening of the list of propositions one sincerely believes. It is notoriously difficult to capture these proprieties of scientific thought in propositional form. If these proprieties cannot be expressed in the form of tractable propositions, then it is clear why coming to have them is not simply a matter of coming to have certain beliefs. But even if they could be captured in tractable propositions, mastering them would require something more than simply memorizing and sincerely affirming the relevant propositions, since one could do this without attaining a reliable capacity to follow the rule and to apprehend the authority of the rule's dictates (e.g. to see what is unconvincing about an invalid argument).[29]

What holds for the sciences holds even more obviously for many other commonly recognized disciplines of thought. It is exceedingly dubious that one could codify the proprieties of thought that make for excellence in history or anthropology, much less in critical reflection on films or poems. Such thought is like philosophy in that excellence emerges from a concerted effort to stretch one's evolving thoughts towards intimations of insight that are not yet wholly articulate, and that lie at the horizon of one's understanding. The problem is not to figure out how to go on from what one can clearly see; it is to bring what one dimly sees into clearer view. If there were rules or principles of proper thought, they might perhaps help with the first sort of problem but not with the second. The understanding of historical epochs, human cultures, philosophical arguments, or literary texts cannot be reduced to the acquisition of true beliefs concerning how best to think about them. It requires a vivid and reliable sense of the difference between fruitful or illuminating thoughts and distractions or trivialities, and between charitable and forced interpretations of texts.

It seems, then, that there is good reason to accept Moravscik's general claim that understanding a field of thought involves internalizing the proprieties of thought that govern thinking in that field. It would be a mistake, however, to follow

---

[29] It is solely for the sake of argument that I speak here as if a rule could be expressed in the form of propositions about how one ought to think. This must be assumed by those who regard the internalization of rules as nothing more than the attainment of a further set of propositional beliefs. One might plausibly insist that rules are better expressed in imperatival rather than propositional form (or as declared commitments to think and act in certain ways).

Moravscik in thinking of understanding entirely in terms of the internalization and tacit application of *rules* of thought. The problem is not just that it is hard to imagine invariant rules for crucial tasks such as striking upon fruitful questions or well-formulated problems with which to initiate fresh lines of philosophical reflection or scientific research. This might be chalked up to lack of imagination. The more fundamental problem is that we would fall into vicious regress if we claimed that all of the competencies associated with understanding the world can be explained as tacit applications of internalized rules. A rule of thought tells us what it makes sense to think in some array of conditions, and to do this it must include a description of its own triggering conditions. The application of a rule, then, presupposes a tacit or explicit judgment to the effect that the world meets these triggering conditions. But this requires a prior conceptualization of the world that must itself manifest some degree of understanding if it is to set the stage for correct application of the rule. We cannot exhaustively explain our capacity to understand the world, all the way down, by reference to internalized rules, since any such rule presupposes a prior conceptualization that must itself manifest understanding if it is to set the stage for applying the rule with full understanding.

Understanding is hardly the exclusive provenance of academics. It can be attained in many different aspects or walks of life. One can understand people and their relationships, ways of life, social situations, cultures, words, languages, conversations and their subtexts, poems and parables, not to mention such things as chess, baseball, the game of politics, and the world of advertising. When we reflect on this list of possible objects of understanding, it becomes quite obvious that not everything that can be understood can be believed or known (at least in the propositional sense of 'belief' and 'knowledge' to which epistemologists tend to limit their attention). Of the items on this list, it seems that only people can be believed, but here 'believed' means *taken to be truthful and reliable* rather than *taken to be true*. And while one can certainly know such things as ways of life, languages, poems, parables, and people, the kind of knowledge in question is not straightforwardly reducible to the propositional knowledge to which epistemologists tend to limit their attention.

Just as many things can be understood but not believed or known, so too many things can be believed or known but do not admit of being understood. Some facts are simply *shallow* in the sense of being dissociated from any deeper order or underlying explanation that one might understand or fail to understand. It is possible not only to believe and to know but also to understand that the area of an isosceles right triangle is one fourth of the area of a square whose sides are the length of the triangle's hypotenuse. By contrast, it's hard to see what might be meant by saying that one not only believes and knows but also understands that the fourth number listed in the current edition of the local phone book is '252-4983', or that there are 1125 grains of sand in a certain vial. It is of course possible to understand or fail to understand the words that pick out these facts, but without further explanation it does not seem that the facts themselves admit of being understood. It is worth recalling that understanding is the sort of thing that comes in degrees and can be clear or hazy, partial or complete. It is not clear what it might mean to say that one has a partial or hazy understanding of the facts now under discussion.

It seems to be an ontological question as to whether a fact is a possible object of understanding. Moravcsik suggests that Plato was developing precisely this insight when he held that all genuine *episteme* must be directed at the Forms, since only the Forms are such as to admit of being understood. On this reading, we entirely miss the point of Plato's insightful discussion if we think of *episteme* as propositional knowledge, and interpret Plato as having denied that one can know such things as that one has two hands.[30] Myles Burnyeat makes a similar claim about Aristotle's discussion of *episteme* in the *Posterior Analytics*.[31]

I argued above that true belief and the avoidance of falsehood cannot be an adequate *telos* of theoretical reflection, since some true beliefs are entirely worthless. Call this the importance problem. As it happens, the clearest examples of true beliefs that have no intrinsic value are beliefs about matters that do not admit of being understood. The cases of trivial knowledge-acquisition discussed above are all cases of gains in knowledge without any gain in understanding. The same would seem to hold for the entire stock of philosophical examples of worthless epistemic pursuits, from memorizing phonebooks to counting blades of grass.[32] It seems plausible, then, that we can alleviate and perhaps entirely resolve the importance problem by identifying the *telos* of theoretical reflection as understanding rather than true belief.[33] Understanding always involves insight into why things are as they are, or how they cohere in larger patterns of order or coherence, and arguably such insight always has some intrinsic value.

If this is right, then centering normative epistemology on the understanding of understanding is perhaps not a matter simply of abandoning the traditional

---

[30] Moravcsik, "Understanding and Knowledge in Plato's Philosophy," 59–66.

[31] According to Burnyeat, if we construe *episteme* as understanding, we can see the plausibility of Aristotle's claim that we have *episteme* of a thing only if we see what explains it and why it must be as it is. If we accept the standard translation of *episteme* as 'knowledge,' Aristotle will seem to have held a highly dubious sort of skepticism about contingent empirical facts. See M. F. Burnyeat, "Aristotle on Understanding Knowledge," in Enrico Berti, ed., *Aristotle on Science: The "Posterior Analytics"* (Padova: Editrice Antenore, 1981), 97–139.

[32] The latter example is from John Rawls, *A Theory of Justice* (Cambridge: Harvard University Press, 1971), 432–3.

[33] This point is prefigured by Kvanvig, who claims that understanding "tracks what is important in a body of information, so that failure to grasp what is important in that body of information renders a person lacking in understanding. It is only when information is less important within that body of information that one can be credited with understanding in spite of such a failure of perfect understanding." See Kvanvig, *The Value of Knowledge*, 203. Kvanvig does not explain or develop this thought. Riggs, by contrast, does not seem to think that locating the *telos* of practical reflection in understanding can resolve what I have called the importance problem. He holds that the proper *telos* of theoretical reflection is wisdom, where wisdom consists in understanding of that which is important. See Riggs, "Understanding 'Virtue'," 219.

epistemological concern with true belief, justification, and knowledge, but of providing those concerns with a more illuminating context. As noted above, we cannot fully understand a domain of thought unless we have many true beliefs about it. When we gain understanding of the subject matter, we will be able to say a great deal about why these beliefs are true, and about how they hold together in a coherent and unified picture of the subject matter. Hence our beliefs will be well justified, and many of them are likely to qualify as knowledge. When we contextualize truth, justification, and knowledge within a broader theory of understanding, we can see more clearly when true beliefs and propositional knowledge are intrinsically valuable, and why they have the value they do. They are intrinsically valuable when, and because, they extend or deepen our understanding of the world.

This does not mean that we will be able to provide straightforward virtue-theoretic analyses of knowledge and justification if we conceive of the virtues as states that contribute to understanding. We should avoid the compromise position adopted by Zagzebski, who shows sympathies for the sort of virtue epistemology that fundamentally alters our conception of what epistemic excellence amounts to, but who nonetheless hopes to use her conception of the intellectual virtues to resolve the traditional problems of contemporary epistemology by offering analyses of propositional knowledge and justified belief. These twin aims cause Zagzebski to oscillate between two very different conceptions of the intellectual virtues. On the one hand, she sometimes seems to affirm a truly radical conception of the intellectual virtues, oriented around the self-standing and intrinsically valuable *telos* of cognitive contact with reality, and especially that sort of "high-quality" contact that expresses and deepens one's understanding of the world.[34] On the other hand, she sometimes seems to affirm a more standard responsibilist conception of the virtues, oriented around the conventional truth-centric *telos*.[35] Only the second of these conceptions provides a straightforward and plausible building block for analyses of propositional knowledge or justified belief. Zagzebski does not seem to be aware of this tension in her work, since within the space of a single work she expresses enthusiasm for the first and more radical view of the virtues of mind, then proceeds to analyze knowledge as true belief arising from acts of intellectual virtue.[36] This analysis might hold water on the second, truth-centric conception of intellectual virtue. But if the intellectual virtues are dispositions of thought that conduce optimally to understanding, or to high-quality contact with reality, then this analysis fails. One can know many things that are not worth knowing and that would neither be believed nor disbelieved by those whose motivations and capacities optimally

---

[34] See Zagzebski, *Virtues of the Mind*, 43–50, 167–8.
[35] See Zagzebski, "Intellectual Motivation and the Good of Truth," 149–50 and 153–4.
[36] Zagzebski, *Virtues of the Mind*, 270–1. Similar analyses are found in "Intellectual Motivation and the Good of Truth," 153.

suit them for attaining high-quality cognitive contact with reality. Zagzebski also analyzes justification of belief by reference to the intellectual virtues, on analogy with right action in ethics.[37] This too could not possibly work unless Zagzebski were either to abandon the more radical elements of her conception of the virtues, or radicalize her notion of justified belief (e.g. by affirming that beliefs are not justified if they are not worth having, even if they are known to be true).

By centering normative epistemology on understanding, we can shed light on why certain epistemological debates have proven so intractable. It has been suggested, for instance, that coherentism makes best sense as a view about understanding rather than knowledge, since we can come to know things we've seen or heard from experts well before we manage to weave them into a maximally coherent body of beliefs, and since coherence and understanding both come in degrees while knowledge does not. Likewise, the best diagnosis of the stand-off between internalists and externalists might be that there is no real conflict between the two, since internalists are theorizing about the preconditions for full understanding while externalists are theorizing about the necessary conditions for bare knowledge. It seems, after all, that the testimony of a known expert (or a benevolent deity) can confer all the warrant one could possibly want for most beliefs, including many that one does not fully understand. While it seems like a genuinely valuable cognitive achievement to have internal access to a justification for one's beliefs, this achievement seems to be a precondition for understanding and not for knowledge. If the internalist were right to put forward the internalized grasp of a justification as a constituent of knowledge, it would be hard to avoid the implication that knowledge comes in degrees. Yet we do not generally speak of ourselves as knowing that q a little bit or a lot.[38] We do, however, recognize that understanding comes in degrees. If this is right, then perhaps one need not return to the Ancients to find attempts to shed light on understanding. Such attempts may well be continuing in contemporary philosophy, albeit under a mistaken self-conception—one encouraged by an overly constricted idea of the subject matter of epistemology, and one that impedes insight and engenders needless controversy.[39]

---

[37] See Zagzebski, *Virtues of the Mind*, 241; see also Zagzebski and Fairweather, *Virtue Epistemology*, 5.

[38] Lorraine Code would deny this claim. As Code points out, we do speak of knowing things well or less well (Code, *Epistemic Responsibility*, 11). I think, however, that such talk normally pertains to non-propositional knowledge. For instance, I might be said to know a person less well than her best friend. It is less clear to me that I can be said to know that it rained yesterday, or that the earth has an elliptical orbit, but not to know these things very well. At any rate, Code goes on to spell out the difference between knowing well and less well in terms of varying levels of understanding, so it seems that any disagreement here is merely terminological.

[39] Inquiry under mistaken identity has its pitfalls. One of today's leading internalists, Laurence BonJour, maintains that the basic role of the quest for internalist justification is the production of true beliefs. He probably would not be tempted to say this, and at any rate would clearly be wrong

ACTIVE UNDERSTANDING AS THE *TELOS* OF THEORETICAL REFLECTION

I hope to have shown that the handful of virtue epistemologists who have identified understanding as the *telos* of theoretical reflection and the proper lodestar for specifying the intellectual virtues have taken a crucial step in the right direction. Still, I do not think it quite right to say that understanding is the *telos* of theoretical reflection—at least not if understanding is conceived of as something one *has* rather than as something one *does*. Understanding so conceived could in principle be possessed by someone who is asleep or otherwise mentally inactive. It is a mere capacity or potentiality. The final end of theoretical reflection cannot plausibly be thought to lie in a mere capacity to apprehend the world. The value of such a capacity must surely lie in the active thought that is its full actualization.

As argued in earlier chapters, human beings are not the sorts of things whose good can plausibly be located in punctual properties. The human good lies in the actualization of the capacity for self-directed activity, and not a disconnected series of actions but sustained activities and relationships that build upon each other, attaining progressively greater depth and maturity over time and lending direction and unity to a life.[40] If we set out in search of final human ends or goods—that is, goods whose value is not explained by their relation to other,

to say this, if he were engaged in an explicit attempt to make sense of understanding. (See BonJour, *The Structure of Empirical Knowledge*, 7.)

[40] Cf. Aristotle, *Nicomachean Ethics*, Book I, chapter 8, paragraph 2. Interestingly, Sosa opens his essay "The Place of Truth in Epistemology" by quoting this passage, which makes the point that the final ends of human beings are to be found in activities rather than in the mental states that make them possible. Sosa also quotes two other passages from the *Nicomachean Ethics*, including Aristotle's claim (Book VI, chapter 2) that the good state of the theoretical intellect is truth and the bad state falsity. In a footnote, Sosa remarks that his essay "may amount to little more than a partial reading" of the three quoted passages. While he adds that the reading may be partial "in more than one sense," still it comes as a bit of a surprise that at the close of the essay Sosa takes himself to be in agreement with Aristotle's picture of the goods realizable through theoretical reflection (178). Sosa believes the good in question to be true beliefs that originate in our skillful mental exertions. This is hard to square with Aristotle's suggestion that the chief goods of human beings lie not in states but in activities. There are signs, though, that Sosa may be attempting to accommodate this point by departing from his earlier reliabilism and thinking of the chief good as the actualization of true belief rather than merely as true believing conceived as a disposition. The clearest sign comes at the foot of 178, where Sosa says that what matters is not the true proposition in splendid isolation but "your *having* the truth" or "your grasping the truth attributably to your intellectual virtues." This is on the right track, but Sosa then goes on to say that his claims are perfectly consistent with a familiarly reliabilist conception of virtue epistemology sketched earlier in the essay (163), according to which intellectual virtues are psychological traits that reliably give rise to true beliefs. On due consideration, then, I don't think that Sosa has fully incorporated the insight contained in the passage on which he is commenting. It is noteworthy, in this vein, that Sosa does not mention Aristotle's prolonged argument (*Nicomachean Ethics*, Book X) that the highest human good is the contemplative appreciation of invariant truths.

more final or ultimate goods—it would be a recipe for confusion to direct our search at properties or states that a human being could have or be in during moments of inactivity. Such states or properties are ontologically unsuited to be final ends for human beings, and can at best be propensities or potentialities for engaging in the activities that compose the best human life. Hence contemporary epistemology looks in precisely the wrong place to the extent that it seeks the final end of theoretical reasoning in the *possession* of such things as true beliefs, propositional knowledge, or understanding.[41] Responsibilism can be seen as arising from a correct apprehension that the activity of the knower has dropped through the cracks of contemporary epistemology's conceptual framework, but as mistakenly locating the knower's most valuable activity in the responsible production of an inactive state of affairs. To put the point in the terminology of this book, they misconceive of theoretical reasoning as a technique of world-making—an error that is not canceled or overcome by the fact that the worlds being made are characterized in terms of the future psychological states of the world-maker.

Some might be tempted to accept the point that static properties or states cannot be final ends for human beings, yet to insist that theoretical reasoning does not have a self-standing *telos*, and that its value lies solely in its instrumental contribution to the production of conceptually independent ends such as pleasure, the satisfaction of desires, or the reliable performance of virtuous actions. Such a conclusion would harmonize with the all-too-familiar ideas that the value of science lies in the advance of technology, and that the value of philosophy lies in the sharpening of analytical skills for other, more practical applications. It is perhaps not surprising that a philosopher would find this alternative badly misguided. It would be best to oppose this outlook with something more substantial than mere insistence upon the intrinsic value of reflection. Yet this is a delicate matter. If theoretical reflection is a final end, then its vindication cannot consist in bringing out its relation to some other more fundamental value, but can only consist in a portrayal that illuminates its intrinsic appeal and its ineliminable place in a good human life. In the remainder of this chapter I attempt to offer such a portrayal.

Suppose we accept the suggestion that the *telos* of theoretical reflection must be a characteristic and continuous activity rather than a state or possession. What could the activity in question possibly be? I believe that we have already found the answer, and that the answer is understanding, but that we arrive at a

---

[41] Zagzebski begins to break loose from the idea that the goal of thought lies in a state or possession, e.g. knowledge, when she suggests that beliefs are at least analogous to acts, and when she calls knowledge an act of intellectual virtue. (Zagzebski, "Intellectual Motivation," 137 and 153.) But she does not elaborate on the analogy between beliefs and acts, saying merely that it is suggested by the fact that we are responsible for both acts and beliefs. In particular, she does not explain how a belief could be dispositional rather than occurrent, yet still be closely analogous to an act.

correct interpretation of this answer only when we take seriously the gerundival form of the term 'understanding.' Just as the value of possessing hearing lies in this capacity's actualization in hearing (for instance, in hearing music or in hearing another human being), so too the value of possessing understanding lies its actualization in understanding or appreciating various things (for instance, in understanding a book one is reading or appreciating a natural phenomenon to which one is attending). The final value of understanding comes to light only when we conceive of understanding not as an achieved state that can be attributed to people while they are mentally inactive, but as a complete or unimpeded actualization of that achieved state in active appreciation of the world in which our lives unfold.[42]

To get hold of the operative idea of active appreciation, we can begin by noting the degree to which the world is conceptually organized in our continuous and immediate apprehensions of it. Even the simplest perceptions are perceptions of things that show up in ways that involve—or, at least, prepare things for—the application of sortal concepts. Michael Polanyi puts the point nicely in the following passage:

When I move my hand before my eyes, it would keep changing its colour, its shape and its size, but for the fact that I take into account a host of rapidly changing clues, some in the field of vision, some in my eye muscles and some deeper still in my body, as in the labyrinth of the inner ear. My powers of perceiving coherence make me see these thousand varied and changing clues jointly as one single unchanging object . . .[43]

As we learn to make sense of the world, our immediate apprehension of things becomes more refined and more revealing. A child might gain insight into the way hands function by learning to see the fingers as distinguishable parts with functional roles in the holding and manipulating of things. A child might also learn to see certain movements of things adjacent to hands as manipulations of things by hands. Then the child is in a position to apprehend a hand holding a ball or a finger pulling a trigger. It seems natural to say that the child can then see hands as pulling triggers, and does not need to judge that they do so, just as it seems natural to say that we see moving flesh-colored splotches as hands, and do not judge that they are. But however we choose to speak, what is clear is that we cannot explain the imposition of order as

---

[42] Riggs speaks at one point of the "life of wisdom"—that is, by his lights, the life of understanding of important things—as the proper *telos* of thought. (Riggs, "Understanding 'Virtue'," 215.) This seems right to me. However, he does not stick with this formulation, but moves back and forth within the space of a single argument between wisdom (premises 1 and 3) and the life of wisdom (premises 2 and 4), and he speaks elsewhere of understanding, hence of wisdom, as something one has—i.e. a possession or attribute. Code also expresses enthusiasm for the idea that the *telos* of reflection is a cognitive activity (see *Epistemic Responsibility*, 52–4), but curiously she goes on (56–7) to insist that her conception of the virtues is closely analogous to Sosa's, and differs only in that she thinks of epistemic virtue as a matter of taking responsibility for the pursuit of true beliefs rather than simply as a matter of having faculties that help to produce true beliefs.

[43] Michael Polanyi, *Knowing and Being* (Chicago: The University of Chicago Press, 1969), 139.

"judgment all the way down," since the order-conferring judgments will need to begin their work with entities already fit to serve as subjects of judgment. Even our most ordinary perceptions actualize a rudimentary understanding of the world.

When someone with botanical understanding perceives a new kind of flower, there is generally no need for her to *conclude* such things as that a protrusion with this shape and color, in this location, must be the pistil. The pistil shows forth as pistil to the botanist's eye. Implicit in this immediate apprehension is an understanding of the functional role of flowers and their parts in the lives of plants. If the botanist in question is interested in gaining a deeper understanding of the process by which flowers receive pollen, then puzzling or anomalous features of a particular pistil's stigma will tend to show forth immediately as surprising or puzzling. That is, they will come to the botanist's attention and "call out" for further explanation. If the botanist understood less, she would be oblivious to the presence of such puzzles and to the pathways towards deeper understanding that they mark. Her subsequent discursive thought can be said to manifest botanical understanding partly because it takes its orientation from a prior apprehension that itself manifests understanding. It will also display botanical understanding insofar as it displays the sort of intuitive feel for the proprieties of scientific thought mentioned in the previous section—e.g. a feel for what counts as a likely explanation, or for how to assess and refine proposed explanations. If this episode of discursive thought goes well, its results will be actualized in still more illuminating apprehensions of the functional organization of flowers—apprehensions that will give rise to further puzzles and further lines of potentially fruitful inquiry that the botanist is not yet capable of discerning. This is actualized understanding, fueling its own dialectical advance.

It will not do to think of this actualized understanding, and the active pursuit of its own deepening that it sparks, as valuable only because and insofar as they help to justify the botanist's propositional beliefs. This would get things backwards. The value of inquiring into the natural world and deepening one's understanding of it cannot be thought to lie, ultimately, in adding to one's stock of *static* dispositional beliefs, nor in bolstering one's *capacity* to offer persuasive vindications of these beliefs. These static beliefs and justificatory capacities might in principle never be actualized, and it seems deeply counterintuitive to suppose that their mere existence makes the world, or one's life, better than it would otherwise have been. It is of course true that achieved states of this sort can have a great deal of extrinsic value. But if we are to find intrinsic value within the domain of theoretical reflection, it seems most plausible to locate it in reflective activity itself. The real value of understanding seems to lie in the running actualization of that understanding itself, both in one's own life and in the lives of others whose view of nature is deepened and extended by one's inquiries. Its value lies in active and self-deepening apprehension of the elegant order of the world in which one's life unfolds, and perhaps also in appreciative awareness of the world's surprising hospitability to human thought.

Scientific discovery is not ordinarily a matter of applying a rule to data but rather a matter of slowly coming to see how the data fit together in a coherent whole. Here again we can take our cue from Polanyi, who was not only a philosopher but also an accomplished scientist. Polanyi calls this process "tacit integration" and describes it as follows:

> Discovery comes in stages, and at the beginning the scientist has but a vague and subtle intimation of its prospects. Yet these anticipations, which alert his solitary mind, are the precious gifts of his originality. They contain a deepened sense of the nature of things and an awareness of the facts that might serve as clues to a suspected coherence in nature. Such expectations are decisive for inquiry, yet their content is elusive, and the process by which they are reached often cannot be specified.[44]

The scientist's achieved understanding of a domain of inquiry is here presented as involving a capacity for bringing into view those lines of further inquiry that are likely to be most fruitful in deepening and extending that understanding. This highlights a similarity between actualized scientific understanding and the sort of practical understanding that accompanies and completes other intrinsically valuable activities. Both are autotelic in the sense that they involve the sort of appreciation that draws one's attention to its object and that, under propitious conditions, deepens one's understanding of it. And both are valuable not merely as reliable causes of valuable effects but also as essential constituents of the activities in which they are actualized. These activities would be different and far less valuable activities if they answered to the norms applicable to them by accident rather than by dint of an achieved appreciation of these proprieties.

Once we see that understanding *qua* potentiality is valuable because of the intrinsic value of the activities in which it is expressed or actualized, we simultaneously gain insight into why the capacity for understanding some things is more important than the capacity for understanding other things, and why there might be a great deal of interpersonal variation in what it makes most sense to seek to understand. The value of the state of understanding some field of phenomena will vary in accordance with the centrality in one's life of the actualization of that understanding. It is particularly valuable, for instance, to understand the natural and social environments in which we spend most of our lives. To lack an understanding of these things is to be consigned to spending most of one's life moving through an opaque and disorienting world. It is less bad to lack an understanding of natural, cultural, or political environments that one rarely experiences first-hand or has little occasion to think about, though no doubt there is some value in possessing such an understanding—partly

---

[44] Polanyi, *Knowing and Being*, 143.

because this is intrinsically worthwhile and partly because it tends to deepen and extend one's understanding of one's more immediate environment. It also makes sense to consult one's contingent enthusiasms and interests when deciding what to invest effort in trying to understand. This is not a tacit concession that understanding derives its value from our contingent interests or desires. We can explain why we should follow our idiosyncratic interests simply by noting that the value of understanding lies in its actualization in a vivid running apprehension of that which is understood, and that we are most likely to be able to sustain and delight in such active understanding if we sculpt it around our enthusiasms.

It is neither a common nor a popular view that the *telos* of theoretical reflection lies in an activity rather than in an achieved state. The explanation for this, I suspect, is that theoretical reflection itself seems to involve, and indeed to be propelled forward by, a quest for an imagined future attainment. It might seem confused to assign intrinsic value to an activity that cannot be done well without continuously pressing for some further attainment.

One way to respond to this line of objection would be to think of the consummation of theoretical reflection in Aristotelian terms, as a kind of continuous and unchanging apprehension of truths already wholly understood. This answer seems at first blush ill-suited to vindicating the intrinsic value of most human reflection. As Aristotle notes, full and complete understanding is more properly godlike than human.[45] For human beings, theoretical reflection generally takes a discursive form, and while one might hope that it will move towards complete and perfect understanding, it cannot sensibly be expected to arrive at this end. An alternative response to the objection at hand, then, would be to seek to vindicate the intrinsic value of this sort of discursive movement towards understanding. One might attempt to do this in one or both of two ways. One approach would be to try to show that certain activities that are guided by the thought of some future attainment nonetheless have intrinsic value at each moment, and that the discursive movement towards understanding is such an activity. A second approach would be to distinguish two elements of active understanding—an attained apprehension of the world and a discursive movement towards a deeper apprehension—and to argue for the intrinsic value of the first element. I will take these up in order.

As I argued in Chapter 4, it is because of a mistaken elaboration of the difference between activities and processes that Aristotle comes to the conclusion that the highest human good must be a static and unchanging activity. What drops from view in Aristotle's discussion is that a future consummation can confer value on present doings in two very different ways. Our present doings can be valuable solely as efficient means for producing the future consummation, and in that case these doings will lack intrinsic value. However, a future

---

[45] Aristotle, *Nicomachean Ethics*, 1177b26–33.

consummation can also confer value on present doings by situating them in an unfolding narrative without reference to which these present doings would be neither fully intelligible nor choice worthy. Intuitively, it seems plausible that many cases of discursive theoretical reasoning depend for their intelligibility on an orientation towards a future attainment—for instance, a deepening of understanding—yet are properly seen as valuable in themselves, quite apart from the actual arrival of this attainment. The person who reflects on her immediate experience, and attempts to see more deeply into it, is living well precisely because she is refusing self-satisfaction with her immediate apprehensions of the world and making responsible, self-formative use of her capacity for critical reflection about these apprehensions. Such reasoning seems to fall within the expanded category of Aristotelian activity, hence seems to be a candidate final end.

Discursive thought might aptly be conceived of as unfolding on a moving horizon between an achieved understanding that is actualized in one's current apprehension of the subject matter at hand, and a further stretch of understanding whose prospect continuously motivates and guides one's discursive reflection. When it goes well, this discursive reflection accounts for the horizon's motion, since it continually casts fresh light on the details of a possible understanding that had previously been grasped only in the dim or sketchy form of a question to be answered, a hunch to be followed, or a puzzle to be resolved. Such thought is carried forward, then, precisely because it involves intimations of a better way of thinking whose content we are not yet able to formulate precisely because it lies at the horizon of our achieved understanding. The sort of thinking that carries reflection forward, then, does not differ in its fundamental nature from the sort that carries forward other dialectical activities. Such thinking proceeds by way of a dialectical interaction between one's intimations of how best to carry forward with the activity, and a series of reifications of these intimations in the form of stretches of activity inspired by them, each stretch providing further opportunity for sharpening one's grasp of how best to carry forward with the activity. Theoretical reflection, then, turns out to be a special case of the sort of dialectical activity described in Chapter 3.

The Ancients thought of the highest sort of theoretical inquiry, philosophy, as the expression of a kind of love (*philia*), and here we can begin to see the appeal of the idea that there is at least a close analogy between actualized understanding and interpersonal love. When love arises in the form of appreciative apprehension of another person, this incites the sort of attention to that other person that tends to extend and deepen this selfsame appreciative apprehension. We might speak here of a *fit* between one's evaluative sensibility and the words, gestures, expressions, and actions of the person one loves—a fit whose continuous uncovering incites a wish to see more. Similarly, when the reflective mind attains some measure of understanding of the world, it grasps an order that is fitted to the human faculty of understanding, and this incites the sort of attention that tends toward a deeper and more extensive understanding of the world. A life of active and continuously deepening understanding is a life that unfolds in a world whose order admits of being apprehended, rather than in a world that remains opaque or absurd.

The idea that finding the world to be absurd is the same as finding it to be impenetrable to understanding is eloquently developed in the pivotal passage of Sartre's *Nausea* where Roquentin confronts the bare existence, and (he believes) the impenetrability to understanding, of the roots of the chestnut tree under which he sits:

A movement, an event in the tiny coloured world of men is only relatively absurd: by relation to the accompanying circumstances. A madman's ravings, for example, are absurd in relation to the situation in which he finds himself, but not in relation to his delirium. But a little while ago I made an experiment with the absolute or the absurd. This root—there was nothing in relation to which it was absurd. Oh, how can I put it in words? Absurd: in relation to the stones, the tufts of yellow grass, the dry mud, the tree, the sky, the green benches. Absurd, irreducible; nothing—not even a profound, secret upheaval of nature—could explain it. Evidently I did not know everything, I had not seen the seeds sprout, or the tree grow. But faced with this great wrinkled paw, neither ignorance nor knowledge was important: the world of explanations and reasons is not the world of existence. A circle is not absurd, it is clearly explained by the rotation of a straight segment around one of its extremities. But neither does a circle exist. This root, on the other hand, existed in such a way that I could not explain it. Knotty, inert, nameless, it fascinated me, filled my eyes, brought me back unceasingly to its own existence. In vain to repeat: "This is a root"—it didn't work any more. I saw clearly that you could not pass from its function as a root, as a breathing pump, *to that*, to this hard and compact skin of a sea lion, to this oily, callous, headstrong look. The function explained nothing: it allowed you to understand generally that it was a root, but not *that one* at all. This root, with its colour, shape, its congealed movement, was . . . below all explanation.

It is worth noting that Roquentin regards this reverie as a moment in which he extends his understanding by seeing through his own tendency to project a false veneer of order upon an orderless world, and by reckoning with the fact that the world of existing things is inhospitable to understanding. Roquentin might well be wrong about this, but if so his mistake concerns the sort of world in which he finds himself, and not what it would be to understand a world of that sort. This brings out an important feature of understanding: by its nature it cannot come loose from the truth. One could in principle come to understand that the world admits of no (further) understanding. Such an understanding would not lose its intrinsic value simply on grounds of its painfulness, but it would amount to the discovery of the world's inhospitability to (further) theoretical reflection, hence of the world's shortcomings as a fit habitation for beings who are inexorably drawn to theoretical reflection about themselves and their world (i.e. to human beings). Then again, the world might not prove wholly recalcitrant to the quest for understanding. The activity of understanding might instead be drawn into an unending dialectical extension of itself. If it were, this would provide a suitable grounding for a working confidence in, and enjoyment of, a more comprehensive at-homeness in the world.[46]

UNDERSTANDING AND THE VIRTUES OF THOUGHT

Those few virtue epistemologists who have proposed that the proper *telos* of theoretical reflection is understanding rather than true belief have generally proceeded as if understanding could itself be understood without invoking the language of the virtues. They have then sought to analyze the virtues in terms of the *telos* of understanding, usually along responsibilist lines. That is, they have viewed the virtues as essential elements of a character-defining commitment to the pursuit of understanding. This production-oriented conception of the intellectual virtues can seem inevitable if one thinks of understanding as a state to be achieved or attained. I have suggested, by contrast, that if it is to play the role of a final end for theoretical reflection, understanding ought to be conceived not as an achieved state but as an activity in which the virtues of theoretical reflection are actualized. If this is right, it suggests a distinctively virtue-theoretic approach to the understanding of understanding. Just as Aristotle was able to shed light on the best sort of human activity (*eudaimonia*) by seeking to characterize the practical virtues, so too we might hope to shed light on understanding by seeking to characterize the vices that undermine it and the virtues that gain their proper actualization in it.

It is an instructive fact that when virtue epistemologists attempt to enumerate the states of character that conduce to excellence in thought, they invariably end up mentioning many of the same states of character that conduce to excellence in action. Excellence in theoretical reflection requires courage, perseverance, carefulness, impartiality, unflinching honesty, and openness to the views and criticisms of others. Our grasp of the world can go astray in the face of the same kinds of temptations that can induce us to act viciously. For instance,

---

[46] There is, then, no guarantee that all advances in understanding will be accompanied by a pleasing sense of the world's fitness for one's habitation. This point also comes to light, though in a somewhat different way, when we consider the understanding of painful truths—for instance, truths concerning the psychology of human evil. This sort of understanding is hardly autotelic. On the contrary, the more one sees of the human capacity for evil, the more one wants to turn one's eyes. Yet this understanding would seem to have intrinsic value. This suggests that the value of understanding cannot be grounded in a conceptually distinct feeling that it tends to cause—a feeling of pleasure or contentment or at-homeness in the world. As noted above, we cannot ground the value of understanding in something else without thereby losing hold of the thesis that it is a final end. Active understanding has a value of its own, consisting in living with a continuous and vivid apprehension of the world in which one's life unfolds. This sort of life is intrinsically good even if wishful thinking or projected fantasies would be more comforting.

we might be tempted to form a distorted understanding of the world because a more illuminating apprehension would be unpopular, or unpublishable, or unwelcome in those who aspire to positions of public prominence and honor, or unappealing to potential employers and patrons. We might be tempted to maintain an inflated picture of the plausibility of our own views because being proven wrong would be publicly humiliating or would carry heavy reputational costs. We might be overly hasty in accepting an ill-reasoned and unconvincing picture of the world because we lack the fortitude to bear up under prolonged and disorienting confusion about the world, or to live with doubts about whether the world has a fully intelligible order. We might be tempted to formulate our thoughts in jargon not in order to gain precision and clarity but in order to provide our views with a semblance of authority or expertise—both in the eyes of others and even in our own self-deceived eyes.

In the last chapter, I argued that the Aristotelian virtues of character are laudable because they are immunities against common distortions in practical thought. When we are in the grip of these distortions, we are prone to issue verdicts that we ourselves would be unable to affirm if we occupied some other possible perspective. Given that the world does not itself change with changes in our perspective, it is not entirely surprising that the same states of character that immunize us against perspective-relative practical thoughts might also conduce to a proper understanding of the world. It is especially unsurprising when we consider the indistinctness, or permeability, of the boundary between theoretical and practical reflection. It is widely recognized that distortions in our ethical thinking can require, as a condition of their own stabilization, that we affirm further distortions in our picture of how things are in the world. For instance, if we are gripped by an aversion to entertaining the possibility that our actions or those of our nation are unjust or evil, this might induce us to affirm a misleading or one-sided description of the motivational well-springs or effects of these actions. Similarly, we might be tempted to accept false and defamatory descriptions of the intentions and actions of others in order to lend an air of justifiability to our pre-existing hatred for them, or to our established pattern of violence towards them.

As in ethics, so too here we find an asymmetry between the role of virtue and vice terms in first-personal reflection. When one engages in theoretical reflection, one's thought is generally not turned towards the habits of mind exemplified in one's thoughts but towards those features of the world that one seeks to understand. For example, one's understanding should not be shaped merely by the thought that seeing things in some particular way would display great boldness or originality. This mode of deliberation is a recipe not for virtuous thought but for its simulacrum—e.g. for aping originality and boldness by offering tendentious interpretations of received views then posing as their slayer. Similarly, it would arguably be self-defeating to understand something in a particular way because that would be unsentimental, rather than because things are that way (and hence appear to be that way when one takes an unsentimental look at them). The way to avoid sentimentality is to try to see things as they are, not to aim at thoughts that strike one as unsentimental. The latter strategy is a recipe for *posing* as unsentimental, not for achieving the goods associated with the avoidance of sentimentality. (A novelist who adopted this dubious strategy would run the risk of producing the sort of imitation of Hemingway whose possibility one can already see in Hemingway's own lesser works.) By contrast, it makes perfect sense to reject a way of recalling one's childhood, or of describing the experience of parenthood, as pretentious or as sentimental. To reject a thought as sentimental is to offer a debunking diagnosis of one's tendency to take it seriously, and this can help to dispel the tendency it diagnoses. Nor does it seem even remotely possible that we could get a grip on what it means to avoid sentimentality by accepting some tractable rule that can be formulated without using the term 'sentimentality' or its cognates, so here we seem to have encountered a pair of virtue–vice concepts that play an ineliminable role in any fully adequate grasp of genuine understanding.[47]

The benefits of a virtue-theoretic approach to the understanding of understanding are most obvious when we turn from the question of the nature of active understanding to the question of its quality. To see this, we will need to consider a register of virtues that concern not so much *what* we think as *how* we think it—that is, the quality of our relation to, or investment in, the ongoing activity of thinking. Liveliness of thought is a virtue of this sort, while lethargy and listlessness are corresponding vices. Seriousness of mind is also a virtue of this sort—though perhaps it ceases to be so if one loses a feel for what is comical in the discrepancy between what we reach for and what we are capable of grasping. One perverse simulacrum of the virtue of serious-mindedness is insistence upon precision of thought as a compensatory mask for the triviality of one's preoccupations. A related vice is to permit oneself to be talked out of one's inchoate philosophical questions by embarrassment over their imprecision—a vice that effectively elevates a mere means to intellectual insight into an end in itself, in whose name the most important inquiries can be choked off prematurely.[48] Another virtue in this family is the sort of integrity or authenticity we display when we insist upon finding words adequate to the task of dragging our own half-formed thoughts into full articulacy, rather than letting their nascent shape be compromised by readily found phrases with a familiar or meretricious ring to them.

The virtues in this family are admired not merely because they are conducive to active understanding but also because they manifest a proper grasp of the value

---

[47] See Raimond Gaita, "The Personal in Ethics," in D. Z. Phillips and Peter Winch, eds., *Wittgenstein: Attention to Particulars: Essays in Honour of Rush Rhees (1905–89)* (New York: St. Martin's Press, 1989), 124–50, especially 138.

[48] See Theodor Adorno, *Negative Dialectics* (New York: The Continuum Publishing Company, 1997), 170 and 211.

of active understanding. By dwelling on these virtues, we can gain a richer sense of this value, in something like the way we might get hold of the intrinsic value of loyalty by observing the fidelity of someone with a discerning sense of the value of friendship and other trusting relationships. For example, by dwelling on the sort of integrity involved in trying to speak one's own mind, one can highlight the connection between virtuous thought and the lifelong struggle to escape from mental tutelage or conformism and to make one's thoughts more truly one's own. Indeed, almost all of our life-defining activities and relationships are made better by lively engagement in them and by persistent and serious-minded efforts to attain a deeper and more adequate apprehension of their point or value. Philosophical inquiry into the value of this range of virtues cannot be isolated, then, from a broader inquiry into the human good. To the extent that epistemology manages to shed light on these virtues and the goods allied to them, to that extent epistemology shades into the expansive sort of ethics that concerns itself not merely with moral rightness but more broadly with the good life for human beings.

Virtues are traditionally differentiated from mere skills or talents on the ground that one can voluntarily refuse to make use of one's skills and talents without thereby showing oneself to lack them, but one cannot voluntarily refuse to actualize a genuine virtue without thereby showing that one lacks the virtue.[49] This distinction makes perfect sense if virtues are elements of an evaluative outlook that ensures an appreciative apprehension of goods bearing on human life. If one consistently refuses to act in the name of some such goods, then one thereby shows that one lacks a full appreciation of them. Those virtue epistemologists who extend the name 'virtue' to native capacities like keen memory or eyesight,[50] or to acquired cognitive skills,[51] cannot endorse this straightforward distinction between the virtues and mere skills and talents. One does not show oneself to lack capacities or skills by refusing to make use of them. Nor is it clear why it should redound to one's credit that one has keen memory or eyesight, or that one has cultivated a skill for critical thought that one neglects to use. The capacity of sight is not a virtue, though a disposition to look at various things in various ways might be. By contrast, if we conceive of the virtues

---

[49] See Aristotle, *Nicomachean Ethics*, 1140b22–5; see also Philippa Foot, *Virtues and Vices and Other Essays in Moral Philosophy* (Oxford: Oxford University Press, 2002), 7–8.

[50] For an example, see Ernest Sosa, "Knowledge and Intellectual Virtue," 225–7, 235–6. Sosa recognizes that in this particular he departs from the Aristotelian conception of virtues, but he claims Platonic roots for this broader conception. This claim is grounded in the simple point that Plato took any functionally organized entity to have virtues, but this is an unconvincing basis for claiming that Plato affirmed the position being defended. The question is not whether keenness of vision can be the virtue of something or another, but whether it can be the virtue of a person qua thinker. Breathing and staying nourished are necessary if human beings are reliably to make sound inferences or to keep their promises, but this does not make them intellectual or ethical virtues.

[51] For an example, see John Greco, "Virtue, Skepticism and Context," in Axtell, *Knowledge, Belief and Character*, 55–71, especially 63–7.

as sensitivities to the intrinsic value of those ways of thinking and acting that are intrinsically valuable, we can see why it is not possible to have them yet lack any motivation to use them, and we can see why they are laudable: they manifest a wholehearted appreciation of genuine goodness.[52]

THE INSEPARABILITY OF EPISTEMIC AND ETHICAL VIRTUES

There are striking similarities between the sketch I've offered of the epistemic virtues and the Aristotelian account of the ethical virtues. Aristotle pictures ethical learning as beginning with the development of proper habits of thought and action. If things go reasonably well, the learner gains an increasingly rich appreciation of the goodness of activities in which he has been encouraged to engage and the badness of activities he has been told to avoid. This first-personal ethical understanding provides a more accurate grasp of goodness than could be conveyed by the verbal instructions that initiate it, or indeed by any tractable formulation of the proprieties of action. Attainment of this understanding requires the development of characteristic desires and aversions that continuously draw one's evaluative attention to what ought to be done or avoided. In other words, it requires proper pre-deliberative apprehensions of goods that are latent in one's continuously evolving activities or made available by one's continuously changing circumstances. Those who have attained this sort of pre-deliberative understanding of value are pained when they act badly, while their good activities are completed and rendered enjoyable by a vivid running apprehension of their value.

If we think of the *telos* of theoretical reason as active understanding rather than bare knowledge, then the elements of this Aristotelian picture of ethical maturation can be extended without alteration to the epistemic virtues. Aspiring theoretical reasoners must develop a whole range of habits of mind that make understanding possible, including for instance that complex array of habits of mind that permit us to hear patterns of noise as meaningful speech. They must

[52] This approach seems to me preferable to James Montmarquet's interesting strategy for explaining the assessability of the epistemic virtues. Montmarquet holds that we can be blamed for epistemic vices because we can display the epistemic virtues simply by trying. This seems wrong. If we are not sensitive to the appeal of a valuable line of thought, and if it therefore does not even show up for us as an option, no momentary effort of will can suffice to set our thinking down that valuable path. What we appreciate as good often limits what we are capable of doing at will. To think of the virtues as traits that we can always display at any given moment, by a concerted effort of will, is to lose sight of the fact that they are embedded in an achieved evaluative outlook, or a character. The assessability of the virtues is far more convincingly grounded in the fact that they manifest our ultimate concerns or values than in the implausible notion that we can always display them at will. See James Montmarquet, "An Internalist Conception of Epistemic Virtue," in Axtell, *Knowledge, Belief and Character*, 135–47, especially 137.

take it on the word of others that a great many things are true, then gradually seek to fit these truths together into a coherent whole and to appreciate why they are true. To do this, they must gain a feel for proprieties of thought that cannot be mastered by learning a list of tractable rules, but only by gaining a first-person appreciation of the goodness of lines of thought that are relevant or illuminating, and the badness of lines of thought that are distracting or misguided. This appreciation will consist in vivid pre-reflective awareness of the goods latent in their continuously evolving thoughts and of the thoughts called for by their continuously changing circumstances.

The internalization of this theoretical sensibility involves a conversion in what might aptly be called one's intellectual desires—that is, in the patterns of interest and attention that determine which objects of thought one is motivated to concentrate on, and which lines of thought one is inclined to pursue. Like other temporally extended activities, discursive thought requires continuous selectivity and discrimination, since there are always more available paths for further thought than one can possibly pursue. For a thinker with understanding, fruitful and interesting lines of thought will be accompanied and completed by a vivid running sense of their value or interest—a feeling that might be called intellectual excitement. Misguided or trivial lines of thought usually will not suggest themselves in the first place, and even when they are followed they will often be accompanied by an inarticulate sense that something has gone wrong.

The proper shaping of one's intellectual desires cannot be regarded as an extra-cognitive achievement. It is the form taken in human experience by the apprehension of proprieties of thought, and as such it is the *sine qua non* of understanding. Of course, if it is stipulated that 'cognition' simply refers to the formation and revision of beliefs, then it can harmlessly be admitted that the conversion in question essentially involves something non-cognitive. But this would imply that a complete theoretical understanding of the world essentially involves an achievement that is non-cognitive in the stipulated sense, and would leave open the possibility that a similarly complete understanding of the practical realm would guarantee ethically admirable motivations. Those who favor ethical non-cognitivism generally have in mind a very different view. They hold that what we call ethical insight, or practical wisdom, consists in something other or something more than a full grasp of the goods realizable in our actions and lives. This invidious sort of non-cognitivism will look particularly tempting if we think of true belief as the proper *telos* of theoretical reflection. After all, true beliefs taken in themselves seem to be motivationally inert, no matter what their subject matter. Nor will it help to hold that the *telos* of theoretical reflection is justified true belief. The problem, as suggested above, is that the testimony of an expert or a benevolent deity seems capable of conferring justification on one's beliefs without making them motivationally efficacious. Even if we insist that beliefs are not justified unless their truth is implied by other justified true beliefs that one also has, this will not help, since it seems possible to affirm each of a web of mutually supporting true beliefs without being moved to act in those ways that one believes to be good. By contrast, if we hold that actualized understanding is the proper *telos* of theoretical reflection, the appeal of the invidious sort of non-cognitivism is considerably diminished. An understanding of the human good will shape one's pre-deliberative outlook on one's circumstances, ongoing activities, and possible future activities, with the effect that one will have vivid subject impressions as of the goodness of those things that really are good. If the arguments of Chapters 1 and 2 are correct, such subjective impressions just are desires. This stance accords with common sense, since we would not attribute an actualized understanding of the good to someone who mouths the words of a compelling conception of the good but has no inclination to act in accordance with this conception.

Given the account of the ethical and epistemic virtues set out in this book, it should come as no surprise that there are striking parallels between epistemic and ethical virtues. I have argued that the full actualization of the human capacity for practical thought lies in the actualized understanding with which we complete and carry forward intrinsically valuable human activities, and that it is only by striving to attain the ethical virtues that we can hope to attain such actualized understanding. Theoretical inquiry and reflection is one of the most pervasive and central of these intrinsically valuable human activities. This is not to say that everyone ought to be a theorist. It is, however, to say both that no fully good human life can be wholly bereft of, or even badly deficient in, the sort of thinking by which we attain understanding of the world, and that wholesale devotion to theoretical inquiry is not an alternative to the active life but one among the many alternative ways of being active in life. If theoretical inquiry is an intrinsically valuable human activity, we should expect our engagement in it to be deepened and enhanced by the ethical virtues, since these permit us to answer to the goods internal to such activities when they come into conflict with the production of external goods such as fame or wealth.

Christopher Hookway expresses a commonplace of contemporary philosophy when he writes that "Ethics and epistemology deal with different parts of our normative practice. Each tries to understand our ways of applying normative standards in a different area of life, to conduct and to the search for knowledge."[53] This view must be carefully qualified if it is to withstand scrutiny. On the one hand, theoretical inquiry is an activity, and we can carry forward with it sensibly only by making continuous decisions concerning what to concentrate on, what to observe, what to read, whom to converse with, and so on. On the other hand, our efforts to make good decisions about what to do will be continuously conditioned by our understanding of the world in which we must act. This understanding

---

[53] Christopher Hookway, "How to Be a Virtue Epistemologist," in Zagzebski and DePaul, *Intellectual Virtue*, 183–202.

will largely determine what practical problems we will be in a position to notice, and what lines of action will strike as worthy of serious consideration. The world enters into experience already bearing the marks of our practical concerns. The idea that there are two "areas of life" here cannot be vindicated merely as a bit of common sense. It could be vindicated only by showing the philosophical fruitfulness of isolating these two intertwined aspects of almost all "parts" of our lives and conducting separate investigations of each.

The difficulties in separating these two "areas of life" are particularly acute when we think about the interactions between those of our beliefs that are ordinarily regarded as political, sociological, or historical, and those we count as plainly moral. For example, it makes a great difference to our grasp of the practical possibilities open to us, and of the lines of action that might possibly be justified, if we think of social classes in terms of relations to the means of production rather than in terms of income levels, or if we deploy categories such as "ladylike" or "manly" in describing people and their actions. Likewise, when we make judgments about which weapons are properly categorized as "weapons of mass destruction," which violent acts are properly categorized as "terrorism," and which uses of military force are properly counted as "preemptive self-defense" (to mention just a few of the categories that play a pivotal role today in the public understanding of world events), we have deployed categories that both describe the world and give an initial shape to our thoughts about what it makes most sense to do, or about which agents deserves praise and which agents deserve condemnation. Such judgments cannot easily be categorized as simply theoretical or simply practical.

I argued in Chapter 3 that when we attempt to bring our own unfolding activities into view in such a way as to see how best to carry forward with them, we must try to discern what is good or valuable about them. Excellence in this sort of thinking requires an understanding of value that is both truth-tracking and motivationally efficacious, hence that both spans and calls into question the traditional division between theoretical and practical thinking. In Chapter 5, I argued that articulacy in this sort of thinking requires that we deploy "thick" evaluative concepts such as cruelty and kindness, vanity and modesty, friendship and betrayal, and that these concepts cannot be decomposed into descriptive and evaluative semantic components. When we engage articulately in this sort of thought, our thinking spans the theory/practice divide, and cannot be broken down into components that fall cleanly on one side or another of the divide. Such thinking is a counterexample to those philosophical schemes that insist upon a strict division between theoretical and practical reasoning, and that suppose it possible to engage in distinct inquiries into the nature of each sort of thinking and the preconditions for excellence in it.

We might illustrate this point by dwelling on the lifelong reflections by which we might hope to deepen our understanding of the value of other human beings. The moral education of a child typically requires frequent reminders of the fact that there are other people in the house, or the family, or the classroom, or the world—people whose inner lives and needs and interests are just as real as the child's own. Moral decency requires that we remain continuously mindful of these basic truths. Our failings in this vicinity cannot fruitfully be sorted into those involving a theoretical failure to affirm these truths and those involving a practical failure to act in accordance with them. When we say that these facts are hard to keep in mind, and easy to forget, surely we are not saying that we are prone to deny or disbelieve these facts. The sort of forgetting in question is not a matter of ceasing to believe that there are other people, equally real; it is a matter of losing hold of a vivid understanding of what we are in the presence of when we are in the presence of another human being. As I argued in Chapter 5, one cannot attain a full understanding of the value of other human beings simply by coming sincerely to believe some list of propositions about other human beings and their value. One must become susceptible to a mature array of the sentiments that constitute a full recognition of this value—sentiments such as love, friendly affection, loneliness, and grief. One cannot understand what exactly these attitudes are unless one has some understanding of how other human beings look when one is in their grip, and one cannot understand how other human beings look when their presence is fully and vividly understood unless one has some sense of how they look when viewed with love or remembered in grief. Such understanding comes in degrees, and further experience might always reveal one's prior understanding to have been lacking.

The difficulties with the philosophical separation of theoretical inquiry and conduct are compounded by the fact that the errors we count as theoretical and those we count as practical can often be traced to the same character flaws—e.g. to ambition, defensiveness, greed, conformism, failure to consider how things look from other vantage points, the desire for public esteem, or the desire to think well of oneself. It would take an objectionably expansionist conception of morality to insist that errors with these sources are always at heart immoral, even when they have no effect on one's actions and do not harm anyone. It seems more apt to say that the vices under discussion are distortions in one's outlook that typically involve a disturbing inversion in one's relation to certain normative standards. That is, they typically involve a tendency to interpret standards or proprieties so as to vindicate the propriety of what one wants, for independent reasons, to do or to think. This inverted relation to proprieties of thought can lead to misapprehensions of how things are and of what it would be best to do. Sometimes the progeny of these vices can be criticized as falsehoods or misunderstandings, while in other cases they can occasion moral blame. Yet these two kinds of criticisms do not pick out two wholly different kinds of character flaws to which the distortions in our thinking might be traced; they pick out different kinds of goods that can hang on errors arising from the same basic character flaws.

None of these ruminations are meant to suggest that the intellectual and ethical virtues are unified in the Aristotelian sense that one cannot have any single intellectual or ethical virtue without having all of them. No doubt there are people who are evil yet exceedingly clever. But the Aristotelian doctrine of the unity of the virtues is implausible even in the restricted domain of plainly ethical virtues. Indeed, to accept the doctrine in its strictest form is to lose hold of one key advantage of the virtue terms—their thickness—since it would imply that no act can exemplify any virtue unless it is, all things considered, the best thing to do in the circumstances. On this view, it would never be possible to use virtue terms as provisional guides to all-things-considered judgments concerning what it would be best to do, since their correct application presupposes such judgments. Given this, it would be a mistake to expect unity in the broader domain of intellectual and ethical virtues. We can reject the thesis of the unity of the virtues while still insisting that these two categories of virtues are closely intertwined, and that certain character traits (e.g. patience, open-mindedness, unpretentiousness, and courage) fall into both categories.

I believe that this latter point would be unsurprising to most non-philosophers, supposing they stopped to think about it. If it is philosophically surprising, this is because we philosophers have been operating with overly constricted conceptions both of the scope of ethical concern and of what counts as genuinely good theoretical reflection. We have tended to think of the ethical virtues solely as states of character that incline us to fulfill interpersonal obligations, and to measure excellence in theoretical inquiry by the justified true beliefs and other conferrable insights produced by that inquiry. It would clearly be false to hold that only those who are stably inclined to fulfill their interpersonal obligations can excel in producing these latter deliverables. A key theme of this book has been that we gain a more illuminating sense of the value of the ethical virtues if we widen the field of ethics so that it includes not only our interpersonal obligations but also our flourishing as human beings. I have also argued that we ought to think of excellence in various activities in terms of the intrinsic quality of our engagement in them rather than in terms of what we produce or promote by engaging in them. This point can convincingly be carried over to theoretical thinking, which can have intrinsic value when directed towards truly important matters and conducted in the right spirit. The vices that are ordinarily categorized as ethical will tend in certain circumstances to interrupt that spirit by riveting one's evaluative attention on the extra-theoretical rewards of one's reflections rather than on whatever is of value in those unfolding reflections themselves.

It is widely believed that epistemology and ethics pertain to areas of life that are distinct enough that their normative dimensions can be investigated and theorized in isolation. If we affirm genuinely virtue-centric approaches to ethics and epistemology, we cannot hold fast to this pattern of specialization. A virtue-centric epistemology requires the identification of a *telos* of theoretical reflection with respect to which we can identify traits that are genuinely good, and this in turn requires wider reflection on the place of theoretical reflection in the good life for human beings. That is, it falls squarely into the expansive field of inquiry into the good life for human beings that virtue ethicists favor for the field of ethics.

CONCLUDING REMARKS ON PHILOSOPHICAL OVER-SPECIALIZATION

Because virtue ethics assigns conceptual primacy to the virtues, it opens the possibility of arriving at notions of the good life, or ideals of human action, that depart significantly from received cultural and philosophical notions of the moral or the ethical domain. The rise of virtue ethics has led some philosophers to conclude that we cannot grasp the value of the disposition to answer to the norms we call moral without seeing how this disposition fits together with other dispositions in a comprehensively well-composed character—that is, a character optimally suited for a flourishing life. Virtue ethics, then, has arisen hand-in-hand with a growing conviction that the current division of labor in normative philosophy is misguided, and that those who specialize in the norms we moderns call *moral* or in those we call *prudential* are not cleaving the normative realm at its real joints, and will therefore be unable to provide a fully adequate account of the normative phenomena on which they focus.

Virtue epistemologists have for the most part followed a different conceptual pattern. They have not turned to the virtues to identify the proper *telos* of theoretical reflection; rather, they have specified the virtues in terms of one or another antecedently established, and usually quite conventional, conception of the *telos* of theoretical reflection. This approach closes off any possibility for radical re-conception of the proper subject matter of epistemology, hence it is no surprise that the epistemic virtues have thus far been put to use mostly to resolve traditional epistemological puzzles concerning justification and knowledge.[54]

Partly because it follows a more purely virtue-theoretic template, the view sketched in this chapter does involve a far-reaching re-conception of the proper subject matter of epistemology. Just as virtue ethics (at its best) has shifted attention from the narrow topic of what we owe to each other by way of overt actions to the broader perfectionist question what sort of life we ought to live, so too this version of virtue epistemology widens the focus of epistemology from the cognitions that bear most directly on other thinkers (i.e. the propositional

---

[54] For interesting comments on the inherent conservatism of contemporary virtue epistemology, see Hookway, "How to Be a Virtue Epistemologist"; see also David Solomon, "Virtue Ethics: Radical or Routine?" in Zagzebski and DePaul, *Virtue Epistemology*, 57–80.

affirmations that provide the medium of communication among strangers) so as to sweep in those temporally extended activities of inquiry and appreciative thought that help to constitute a good human life. And just as virtue ethics (at its best) draws upon the virtue concepts to give us a richer sense of the nature and point of intrinsically valuable ways of acting, so too this version of virtue epistemology draws upon virtue-theoretic terms like curiosity, creativity, honesty, patience, unsentimentality, and integrity to give us a richer sense of the nature and the value of a life of optimally active thought.

This version of virtue epistemology also follows virtue ethics in highlighting the vital role in a good human life of deeply ingrained patterns of evaluative attention and responsiveness. It raises the possibility that the path to the deepest kinds of understanding must be prepared by living a certain kind of life, one that inculcates a vivid taste for certain kinds of questions and certain ways of thinking about them. It raises the possibility, for instance, that part of what we call intelligence is an appreciation of the point or value of the sort of thought in which that intelligence is displayed, and that what distinguishes the most promising students of philosophy is not merely a kind of raw analytical power but also and perhaps more importantly a keen sense of the intrinsic value of intellectual inquiry. By extension, it raises the possibility that an incapacity for philosophy, or a propensity for a merely superficial or meretricious form of philosophy, could be a culture-wide condition, grounded not in a culturally rooted blindness to the point of theoretical reflection that does not produce some tangible product (e.g. a dissertation, or a publication, or a conveyable piece of propositional knowledge that can be added to the ever-expanding "stock" of human knowledge).

Given that this version of virtue epistemology leads to a radical re-conception of the proper subject matter of epistemology, one might object that it does not advance epistemological understanding but merely changes the subject. This would be too hasty. In the first instance, 'understanding' is arguably a better translation of the Greek *episteme* than is knowledge, and it is hardly foreign to Platonic or Aristotelian thought to hold that the reward of thinking lies in active apprehension of the finest objects of thought rather than in unactualized dispositions or capabilities. So arguably the real question is not "Why change the field's subject matter?" but "Why has the field's subject matter been changed?" More pointedly, why has it been changed in such a way as to organize epistemology around an end that could not possibly be final?

This is a question worthy of another book. While I lack the expertise to write this book, I believe that I can identify some of its main themes. One theme would be the unhealthy preoccupation of contemporary epistemology with Cartesian skepticism.[55] This has tended to focus attention almost exclusively on

---

[55] On this theme, see Richard Rorty, *Philosophy and the Mirror of Nature* (Princeton: Princeton University Press, 1979) and Michael Williams, *Unnatural Doubts* (Princeton: Princeton University Press, 1996).

the vindication of the best cases for propositional knowledge, many of which would fall into the category of the sort of trivial beliefs that I've set aside as valueless and as external to the *telos* of theoretical reasoning properly understood. A second theme would be the loss of confidence that there is a believable philosophical story to be told about the good life for human beings. This loss of confidence has expressed itself politically in the demise of the notion that misguided religious and philosophical views of the good life are to be tolerated, and the rise of the conviction that no such view should be singled out as misguided since all have an equally unsustainable claim to truth. It has expressed itself philosophically in a proliferation of subjectivist, existentialist, and relativist conceptions of value. And it has encouraged normative philosophers to shrink their substantive investigations to abstract domains of value that all humans can be presumed to have reason to care about, whatever else they might wish to think about or to do—that is, to rightness and welfare in action, and to truth and justification in belief.

Even if these historical speculations are on target, they are hardly decisive reasons to reject the prevailing picture of the proper subject matter of epistemology. However, they do serve at least to underline the fact that there are other ways of delimiting epistemology and that the prevailing delimitation requires some vindication. Certainly it cannot be vindicated merely by reference to a common-sense grasp of the domain of epistemic value. Outside of philosophical circles, it is exceedingly rare to hear talk of "epistemic reasons" or "epistemic value." Nor is it possible to derive a compelling vindication of contemporary epistemology's typical boundaries from the common-sense notion of knowledge. An investigation of the ordinary idea of knowledge would take us far beyond a truncated preoccupation with propositional knowledge, sweeping in whatever it is that we have in mind when we speak of knowing such things as botany, Hegelian idealism, French history, some rudimentary Spanish, the Australian Outback, the Arab World, not to mention an old friend, an old friend's face, how to ride a bike, or the difference between right and wrong. For reasons elaborated above, it seems unlikely that our knowledge of any of these things can be reduced to dispositions to avow some series of propositions, and likely that it will involve what I have called understanding.

I do not mean to suggest that contemporary epistemologists should cease and desist from their efforts to produce a defensible analysis of knowledge or of justified belief. I have my doubts about whether this analytical project is tractable, but I do not doubt that its completion would be of value. It seems to me, however, that contemporary epistemologists fall into error to the extent that they frame their theoretical efforts by putting forward propositional knowledge, true belief, and/or justified belief as the focal elements of an account of the proper aims of theoretical inquiry. This common theoretical frame serves to obscure the distinction between worthwhile reflection and trivial intellectual pursuits. Philosophical insight is also impeded by the idea that epistemic ends are states to be produced rather than activities to be engaged in, since this obscures the place of active thinking in a good human life, and leads to an implausibly instrumental conception of the difference between deficient and exemplary modes of engagement in the activity of thought.

More practically, philosophical insight is impeded by the prevailing notion that aspiring epistemologists need to know metaphysics but can safely ignore ethics, while aspiring ethicists can benefit from a bit of political philosophy and applied ethics but can get by with only a cursory exposure to epistemology. Ethics and epistemology both concern norms bearing on individual human lives, and what philosophers refer to as "theoretical" and "practical" reasoning are so thoroughly intertwined that it is hard to see how their constitutive norms can be cleaved apart for isolated philosophical investigation. Intuitively it seems quite obvious that one cannot act well in a world that one does not understand, and that one cannot hope to improve one's understanding of the world without choosing to act in ways that will help one to test and to deepen one's existing picture of it. On inspection it becomes clear that defects in "theoretical" reflection and in action can often be traced to the same character flaws. Yet the prevailing organization of professional philosophy tends to discourage students (and, at least at the more prestigious research universities, professors) from gaining the competence to explore the common ground between these fields.

Academic specialization makes clearest sense in those fields where the point of research is the efficient and reliable production of discrete bits of information that can be grasped and put to use by others without recapitulation of the arduous research by which the findings were first substantiated. In such fields, specialization can serve the cause of efficiency, vastly increasing the number and the reliability of findings available to all practitioners. Medical research is a clear case of a field in which specialization is eminently desirable. This is not to deny that thinking about the working of the human body can be rewarding in its own right, quite apart from its practical benefits. It is simply to say that there is a powerful instrumental reason to engage in medical research: it promotes health and reduces suffering. This reason supports the sort of research that produces a maximally ample array of specialized findings so that future researchers can efficiently resolve specialized problems of their own.

The point of philosophy would seem to lie in large part in the intrinsic value of living a life shaped by a frequently actualized and continuously extended understanding of oneself, one's world, and how best to live in that world. Given this, it would be a betrayal of the philosophical calling to splinter professional philosophy into a large number of isolated areas of "research" with their own proprietary jargons, journals, and conferences. This would be suited to a mode of thinking whose point is the reliable production of true beliefs or consumable information, but it makes little sense in philosophy, since its *telos* is philosophical thought itself, continuously deepened and extended. Interestingly, then, the truth-centric conception of excellence in theoretical reflection provides a rationalization for the sort of over-specialization that tends to blind philosophers to its inadequacy. It impedes understanding of the value of understanding, and also of the shortcomings of the division of philosophical labor in which it has taken root and come to seem all but inevitable. This blind spot leaves philosophy unable to make full sense of the value of those incipient philosophical moments that punctuate the everyday musings of almost any mentally active and curious person, and that represent something of a continuous opening to philosophical thought, an inchoate grasp of its value.

Bibliography

Adams, Robert M., *Finite and Infinite Goods: A Framework for Ethics* (Oxford: Oxford University Press, 1999).

Adorno, Theodor, *Negative Dialectics* (New York: The Continuum Publishing Company, 1997).

Alston, William, "Pleasure," in Paul Edwards, ed., *The Encyclopedia of Philosophy* (New York: Macmillan Publishing, 1967), Volume 6, 341–7.

Anderson, Elizabeth, *Values in Ethics and Economics* (Cambridge, MA: Harvard University Press, 1993).

Annas, Julia, *The Morality of Happiness* (New York and Oxford: Oxford University Press, 1993).

Anscombe, Elizabeth, "Modern Moral Philosophy," in *The Collected Philosophical Papers of G.E.M. Anscombe, Volume Three: Ethics, Religion and Politics* (Oxford: Basil Blackwell, 1981).

—— *Intention* (Cambridge, MA: Harvard University Press, 2000; first published by Basil Blackwell in 1957).

Aquinas, *Summa Theologica*, translated by English Dominican Fathers (New York: Benziger Brothers, 1948).

Aristotle, *De Anima*.

—— *Eudemian Ethics*, translated by J. Solomon under the editorship of W. D. Ross (Oxford: Clarendon Press of Oxford University Press, 1915).

—— *Metaphysics*.

—— (or possibly a follower of Aristotle), *Minima Moralia*, translated by St. George Stock under the editorship of W. D. Ross (Oxford: Clarendon Press of Oxford University Press, 1915).

—— *Nicomachean Ethics*, translated by Terence Irwin (Indianapolis: Hackett Publishing Company, 1985).

Audi, Robert, "Epistemic Virtue and Justified Belief," in Zagzebski and Fairweather, eds., *Virtue Epistemology: Essays on Epistemic Virtue and Responsibility* (Oxford: Oxford University Press, 2001), 82–97.

—— "Intending, Intentional Action and Desire," in Joel Marks, ed., *The Ways of Desire* (Chicago: Precedent Publishing, 1986), 17–38.

—— "Moral Judgments and Reasons for Action," in Garrett Cullitty and Berys Gaut, eds., *Ethics and Practical Reason* (Oxford: Oxford University Press, 1997), 125–60.

Augustine, *Confessions*.

Axtell, Guy, ed., *Knowledge, Belief and Character: Readings in Virtue Epistemology* (Lanham, Maryland: Rowman and Littlefield Publishers, Inc., 2000).

Balthasar, Hans Urs von, *Prayer* (San Francisco: Ignatius Press, 1986).

—— *Seeing the Form*, Volume I of *The Glory of the Lord: A Theological Aesthetics* (Edinburgh: T&T Clark, 1982).

Benson, John, "Making Friends: Aristotle's Doctrine of the Friend as Another Oneself," in Andros Loizou and Harry Lesser, eds., *Polis and Politics: Essays in Greek Moral and*

Political Philosophy (Brookfield, Hong Kong, Singapore, and Sydney: Avebury Press, 1990), 50–68.

Bergmann, Frithjof, "The Experience of Values," *Inquiry* 16 (1973), 247–79.

Blackburn, Simon, "How To Be an Ethical Antirealist," in Stephen Darwall, Allan Gibbard, and Peter Railton, eds., *Moral Discourse and Practice: Some Philosophical Approaches* (Oxford: Oxford University Press, 1996), 167–78.

—— "Reason, Virtue and Knowledge," in Zagzebski and Fairweather, eds., *Virtue Epistemology: Essays on Epistemic Virtue and Responsibility* (Oxford: Oxford University Press, 2001), 15–29.

—— "Through Thick and Thin," *Proceedings of the Aristotelian Society*, Supplementary Volume 66 (1992), 285–99.

BonJour, Laurence, *The Structure of Empirical Knowledge* (Cambridge, MA: Harvard University Press, 1985).

Bostock, David, "Pleasure and Activity in Aristotle's Ethics," *Phronesis* 33 (1988), 251–72.

Brandom, Robert, *Making It Explicit* (Cambridge, MA: Harvard University Press, 1994).

Brandt, Richard, *Ethical Theory: The Problems of Normative and Critical Ethics* (Englewood Cliffs: Prentice-Hall Inc., 1959).

Bratman, Michael, *Intention, Plans and Practical Reason* (Cambridge, MA: Harvard University Press, 1987).

—— *Structures of Agency* (Oxford: Oxford University Press, 2007).

Brewer, Talbot, "The Character of Temptation: Towards a More Plausible Kantian Moral Psychology," *Pacific Philosophical Quarterly* 83 (2002), 103–30.

—— "Maxims and Virtues," *Philosophical Review* 3 (2002), 539–72.

—— "The Real Problem with Internalism about Reasons," *Canadian Journal of Philosophy* 42 (2002), 443–73.

—— "Savoring Time: Desire, Pleasure and Wholehearted Activity," *Ethical Theory and Moral Practice* 6 (2003), 143–60.

—— "Three Dogmas of Desire," in Timothy Chappell, ed., *Values and Virtues* (Oxford: Oxford University Press, 2007), 257–84.

—— "Two Kinds of Commitments (And Two Kinds of Social Groups)," *Philosophy and Phenomenological Research* 66 (2003), 554–83.

—— "Virtues We Can Share: A Reading of Aristotle's Ethics," *Ethics* 115 (2005), 721–58.

Brink, David O., "Eudaimonism, Love and Friendship, and Political Community," *Social Philosophy and Policy* (1999), 252–89.

—— "Kantian Rationalism: Inescapability, Authority and Supremacy," in Cullitty and Gaut, *Ethics and Practical Reason* (Oxford: Oxford University Press, 1997), 255–92.

Bugbee, Henry, *The Inward Morning: A Philosophical Exploration in Journal Form* (New York: Collier Books, 1958).

—— "The Moment of Obligation in Experience," *Journal of Religion* 33 (1953), 1–15.

Burnyeat, Myles, "Aristotle on Learning to be Good," in Amelie Rorty, ed., *Essays on Aristotle's Ethics* (Berkeley: University of California Press, 1981), 69–92.

—— "Aristotle on Understanding Knowledge," in Enrico Berti, ed., *Aristotle on Science: The "Posterior Analytics"* (Padova: Editrice Antenore, 1981), 97–139.

Carroll, Lewis, "What the Tortoise Said to Achilles," *Mind* 4 (1895), 278–80.

Castaneda, Hector-Neri, *Thinking and Doing: The Philosophical Foundations of Institutions* (Dordrecht and Boston: D. Reidel Publishing Company, 1975).

Cocking, Dean and Jeanette Kennett, "Friendship and Moral Danger," *Journal of Philosophy* 97 (2000), 278–96.

—— "Friendship and the Self," *Ethics* 108, no. 3 (April 1998), 502–27.

Code, Lorraine, *Epistemic Responsibility* (Hanover, New Hampshire: University Press of New England, 1987).

Cooper, John, *Reason and Emotion* (Princeton: Princeton University Press, 1998).

Crisp, Roger and Michael Slote, eds., *Virtue Ethics* (Oxford: Oxford University Press, 1997).

Cullitty, Garrett and Berys Gaut, eds., *Ethics and Practical Reason* (Oxford: Oxford University Press, 1997).

D'Arms, Justin and Daniel Jacobson, "Sentiment and Value," *Ethics* 110 (2000), 722–48.

Dancy, Jonathan, "In Defense of Thick Concepts," in Peter A. French, Theodore E. Uehling Jr., and Howard K. Wettstein, eds., *Midwest Studies in Philosophy, Volume XX: Moral Concepts* (Notre Dame: University of Notre Dame Press, 1995), 263–79.

—— *Ethics without Principles* (Oxford: Oxford University Press, 2004).

—— *Moral Reasons* (Oxford: Blackwell Publishers, 1993).

Darwall, Stephen, *Impartial Reason* (Ithaca, NY: Cornell University Press, 1983).

—— *Welfare and Rational Care* (Princeton: Princeton University Press, 2002).

—— *The Second-Personal Standpoint* (Cambridge, MA: Harvard University Press, 2006).

Davidson, Donald, *Essays on Actions and Events* (Oxford: Oxford University Press, 1980).

Dennett, Daniel C., *The Intentional Stance* (Cambridge, MA: MIT Press, 1987).

—— *Kinds of Minds: Toward an Understanding of Consciousness* (New York: Basic Books, 1996).

Dewey, John, "The Reflex Arc Concept in Psychology," *Psychological Review* 3 (1896), 357–70.

Diamond, Cora, "Missing the Adventure: Reply to Martha Nussbaum," in *The Realistic Spirit* (Cambridge, MA: MIT Press, 1991), 309–18.

—— " 'We Are Perpetually Moralists': Iris Murdoch, Fact, and Value," in Maria Antonaccio and William Schweiker, eds., *Iris Murdoch and the Search for Human Goodness* (Chicago: University of Chicago Press, 1996), 79–109.

Dreier, Jamie, "The Structure of Normative Theories," *Monist* 76 (1993), 22–40.

Dretske, Fred, *Explaining Behavior: Reasons in a World of Causes* (Cambridge, MA: MIT Press, 1988).

Emerson, Ralph Waldo, "Friendship," reprinted in Michael Pakaluk, ed., *Other Selves: Philosophers on Friendship* (Indianapolis: Hackett Publishing Company, Inc., 1991), 218–32.

Engstrom, Stephen and Jennifer Whiting, eds., *Aristotle, Kant and the Stoics: Rethinking Happiness and Virtue* (Cambridge: Cambridge University Press, 1996).

Ewing, A. C., *The Definition of Good* (London: Macmillan, 1947).

Falk, W. D., *Oughts, Reasons and Morality* (Ithaca, NY: Cornell University Press, 1986).

Feldman, Fred, *Utilitarianism, Hedonism and Desert: Essays in Moral Philosophy* (Cambridge: Cambridge University Press, 1997).

Foley, Richard, "The Foundational Role of Epistemology in a General Theory of Rationality," in Zagzebski and Fairweather, eds., *Virtue Epistemology: Essays on Epistemic Virtue and Responsibility* (Oxford: Oxford University Press, 2001), 214–30.

Foot, Philippa, *Natural Goodness* (Oxford: Oxford University Press, 2001).

—— *Virtues and Vices and Other Essays in Moral Philosophy* (Oxford: Oxford University Press, 2002; first published by Blackwell, 1978).

Frankena, William, *Ethics*, 2nd edn (New York: Prentice Hall, 1973 and 1963).

Frankfurt, Harry G., *The Importance of What We Care About* (Cambridge: Cambridge University Press, 1988).

—— *Necessity, Volition and Love* (Cambridge; Cambridge University Press: 1999).

Frede, Dorothea, "The Cognitive Role of *Phantasia* in Aristotle," in *Essays on Aristotle's De Anima*, Martha Nussbaum and Amelie Rorty, eds. (Oxford: Clarendon Press, 1992), 279–96.

Frede, Michael and Striker, Gisela, eds., *Rationality in Greek Thought* (Oxford: Oxford University Press, 1996).

Gaita, Raimond, "Narrative, Identity and Moral Philosophy," *Philosophical Papers* 32 (2003), 261–77.

—— "The Personal in Ethics," in D. Z. Phillips and Peter Winch, eds., *Wittgenstein: Attention to Particulars: Essays in Honour of Rush Rhees (1905–89)* (New York: St. Martin's Press, 1989), 124–50.

—— *Good and Evil: An Absolute Conception*, 2nd edn (London: Routledge, 1991 and 2004).

Gallie, W. B., "Pleasure," *Proceedings of the Aristotelian Society*, Supplementary Volume (1954).

Gibbard, Allan, *Wise Choices, Apt Feelings* (Cambridge, MA: Harvard University Press, 1990).

Goldberg, S. L., *Agents and Lives* (Cambridge: Cambridge University Press, 1993).

Goldman, Alvin, *A Theory of Human Action* (Princeton: Princeton University Press, 1970).

—— "The Unity of the Epistemic Virtues," in Zagzebski and Fairweather, eds., *Virtue Epistemology: Essays on Epistemic Virtue and Responsibility* (Oxford: Oxford University Press, 2001), 30–48.

—— *A Theory of Human Action* (Princeton: Princeton University Press, 1970).

Goldstein, Irwin, "Pleasure and Pain: Unconditional, Intrinsic Values," *Philosophy and Phenomenological Research* 50 (1989), 255–76.

—— "Why People Prefer Pleasure to Pain," *Philosophy* 55 (1980), 349–62.

Greco, John, "Virtue Epistemology," in *Stanford Encyclopedia of Philosophy* (http://plato.stanford.edu/entries/epistemology-virtue).

—— "Virtue, Skepticism and Context," in Guy Axtell, ed., *Knowledge, Belief and Character*, 55–71.

—— "Virtues and Rules in Epistemology," in Linda Zagzebski and Abrol Fairweather, eds., *Virtue Epistemology: Essays on Epistemic Virtue and Responsibility* (Oxford: Oxford University Press, 2001), 117–41.

Greene, Brian, *The Elegant Universe: Superstrings, Hidden Dimensions, and the Quest for the Ultimate Theory* (New York: Vintage Books, 1999).

Gregory of Nyssa, *Commentary on the Song of Songs*.

—— *The Life of Moses*, translated by Abraham J. Malherbe and Everett Ferguson (New York: Paulist Press, 1978).

Hare, R. M., *Freedom and Reason* (Oxford: Oxford University Press, 1963).

Heathwood, Chris, "The Reduction of Sensory Pleasure to Desire," *Philosophical Studies* 133 (2007), 23–44.

Heidegger, Martin, *Nietzsche: Volumes I and II* (San Francisco: Harper Publishing, 1991).

Herman, Barbara, "Making Room for Character," in Stephen Engstrom and Jennifer Whiting, eds., *Aristotle, Kant and the Stoics: Rethinking Happiness and Virtue* (Cambridge: Cambridge University Press, 1996), 36–60.

—— *The Practice of Moral Judgment* (Cambridge, MA: Harvard University Press, 1993).

Heschel, Abraham, *The Sabbath, Its Meaning for Modern Man* (New York: Farrar, Straus and Giroux, 1977, original copyright 1951).

Hilton, Walter, *The Ladder of Perfection*, translated by Leo Sherley-Price (New York: Penguin, 1957).

Hookway, Christopher, "How to Be a Virtue Epistemologist," in Zagzebski and DePaul, eds., *Intellectual Virtue*, 183–202.

Hume, David, *Enquiries Concerning Human Understanding and Concerning the Principles of Morals*, 3rd edn, L. A. Selby-Bigge and P. H. Nidditch, eds. (New York and Oxford: Oxford University Press, 1975).

Hurka, Thomas, "Moore in the Middle," *Ethics* 113 (2003), 599–628.

Hursthouse, Rosalind, *On Virtue Ethics* (Oxford: Oxford University Press, 1999).

Irwin, Terence, *Aristotle's First Principles* (Oxford: Oxford University Press, 1988).

—— "Prudence and Morality in Greek Ethics," *Ethics* 105 (1995), 284–95.

Jacquette, Dale, "Aristotle on the Value of Friendship as a Motivation for Morality," *Journal of Value Inquiry* 35 (2001), 371–89.

Kagan, Shelly, *The Limits of Morality* (Oxford: Oxford University Press, 1991).

Kahn, Charles H., "Aristotle and Altruism," *Mind* 90 (1981), 20–40.

Kamm, Frances, *Morality, Mortality: Volume I: Death and Whom to Save from It* (Oxford: Oxford University Press, 1998).

Kant, Immanuel Kant, *Groundwork of the Metaphysics of Morals*.

Kierkegaard, Soren, *Either/Or*, edited and translated by Howard and Edna Hong (Princeton: Princeton University Press, 1987).

Korsgaard, Christine, *Creating the Kingdom of Ends* (Cambridge: Cambridge University Press, 1996).

—— *The Sources of Normativity* (Cambridge: Cambridge University Press, 1996).

Kraut, Richard, *What is Good and Why? The Ethics of Well-Being* (Cambridge, MA: Harvard University Press, 2007).

Kvanvig, Jonathan, *The Value of Knowledge and the Pursuit of Understanding* (Cambridge: Cambridge University Press, 2003).

Larson, Richard K., "The Grammar of Intensionality," in G. Preyer and G. Peter, eds., *Logical Form and Language* (Oxford: Clarendon Press, 2000).

Lehrer, Keith, "The Virtue of Knowledge," in Zagzebski and Fairweather, eds., *Virtue Epistemology: Essays on Epistemic Virtue and Responsibility* (Oxford: Oxford University Press, 2001), 200–13.

Levinas, Emmanuel, *Totality and Infinity: An Essay on Exteriority*, tr. Alphonso Lingis (Pittsburgh: Duquesne University Press, 1969).

Locke, John, *An Essay Concerning Human Understanding*.

Louden, Robert, "On Some Vices of Virtue Ethics," first published in *American Philosophical Quarterly* 21 (1984), 227–36.

Lucretius, *The Way of Nature*.

MacIntyre, Alasdair, *After Virtue: A Study in Moral Theory* (Notre Dame: University of Notre Dame Press, 1981).

—— *The Tasks of Philosophy: Selected Essays* (Cambridge: Cambridge University Press, 2006).

Mackie, J. L., *Ethics: Inventing Right and Wrong* (New York: Penguin Books, 1977).

Marks, Joel, ed., *The Ways of Desire* (Chicago: Precedent Publishing, 1986).

Marx, Karl, *The Philosophical and Economic Manuscripts of 1844*.

McDowell, John, "Might There Be External Reasons?" in J. E. J. Altham and Ross Harrison, eds., *World, Mind, and Ethics: Essays on the Ethical Philosophy of Bernard Williams* (Cambridge: Cambridge University Press, 1995).

—— *Mind, Value and Reality* (Cambridge, MA: Harvard University Press, 1998).

McNaughton, David, *Moral Vision: An Introduction to Ethics* (Oxford: Basil Blackwell Ltd, 1998).

Millgram, Elijah, "Aristotle on Making Other Selves," *Canadian Journal of Philosophy* 17 (1987), 361–76.

—— "Pleasure in Practical Reasoning," *Monist* 76 (1993), 394–415.

—— *Ethics Done Right: Practical Reasoning as a Foundation for Moral Theory* (Cambridge: Cambridge University Press, 2005).

Montmarquet, James A., *Epistemic Virtue and Doxastic Responsibility* (Lanham, Maryland: Rowman and Littlefield Publishers, Inc., 1993).

—— "An Internalist Conception of Epistemic Virtue," in Guy Axtell, ed., *Knowledge, Belief and Character*, 135–47.

Moore, G. E., *Principia Ethica* (Cambridge: Cambridge University Press, 1903).

Moran, Richard, "Self-Knowledge: Discovery, Resolution and Undoing," *European Journal of Philosophy* 5(2) (1997), 141–61.

—— "Vision, Choice and Existentialism," *Notizie di Politeia* 12 (2002), 88–101.

Moravcsik, Julius, "Understanding and Knowledge in Plato's Philosophy," *Neue Hefte Für Philosophie* 15/16 (1979), 53–69.

Moya, Carlos J., *The Philosophy of Action: An Introduction* (Oxford: Polity Press, 1990).

Murdoch, Iris, *The Sovereignty of Good* (London: Routledge and Kegan Paul, 1970).

Nagel, Thomas, *The Possibility of Altruism* (Princeton: Princeton University Press, 1970).

—— *The View from Nowhere* (Oxford: Oxford University Press, 1986).

Nietzsche, Friedrich, *The Gay Science*.

—— *On the Genealogy of Morals*, First Essay, Sections 2–11.

Nozick, Robert, *Anarchy, State and Utopia* (New York: Basic Books, 1974).

Nussbaum, Martha, *Aristotle's de Motu Animalium* (Princeton: Princeton University Press, 1978).

—— *The Fragility of Goodness: Luck and Ethics in Greek Tragedy and Philosophy* (Cambridge: Cambridge University Press, 1986).

—— "Non-Relative Virtues: An Aristotelian Approach," in Nussbaum and Amartya Sen, eds., *The Quality of Life* (Oxford: Oxford University Press, 1993).

O'Neill, Onora, "The Power of Example," *Philosophy* 61 (1986), 5–29.

Pakaluk, Michael, ed., *Other Selves: Philosophers on Friendship* (Indianapolis: Hackett Publishing Company, Inc., 1991).

Parfit, Derek, *Manuscript*.

Pascal, Blaise, *Pensées*, translated by W. F. Trotter (New York: E. P. Dutton and Co., Inc., 1931).

Pieper, Josef, *The Silence of St. Thomas: Three Essays*, translated by John Murray and Daniel O'Connor (Chicago: Henry Regnery, 1965; original copyright 1957 by Pantheon Books).

Pincoffs, Edmund L., *Quandaries and Virtues: Against Reductivism in Ethics* (Lawrence, Kansas: University Press of Kansas, 1986).

Plato, *Apology*.

—— *Crito*.

—— *Gorgias*.

—— *Republic*.

Platts, Mark, "Moral Reality and the End of Desire," in *Reference, Truth and Reality* (New York: Routledge and Kegan Paul, 1981).

Plotinus, *The Enneads*, translated by Stephen MacKenna (New York: Penguin Books, 1991).

Polanyi, Michael, *Knowing and Being* (Chicago: University of Chicago Press, 1969).

Quinn, Warren, *Morality and Action* (Cambridge: Cambridge University Press, 1993).

Rabinowicz, Wlodek and Toni Ronnow-Rasmussen, "Buck-Passing and the Right Kind of Reasons," *Philosophical Quarterly* 56 (2006), 114–20.

—— "The Strike of the Demon: On Fitting Pro-Attitudes and Value," *Ethics* 114 (2004), 391–424.

Rawls, John, *John Rawls: Collected Papers* (Cambridge, MA: Harvard University Press, 1999).

—— "Kantian Constructivism in Moral Theory: The Dewey Lectures 1980," *Journal of Philosophy* 77 (1980), 515–72.

—— *A Theory of Justice* (Cambridge: Harvard University Press, 1971).

Raz, Joseph, *Engaging Reason: On the Theory of Value and Action* (Oxford: Oxford University Press, 1999).

Regan, Donald H., "The Value of Rational Nature," *Ethics* 112 (2002), 267–91.

Richardson, Henry S., "Thinking about Conflicts of Desire," in Peter Bauman and Monika Betzler, eds., *Practical Conflicts: New Philosophical Essays* (Cambridge: Cambridge University Press, 2004), 92–117.

Riggs, Wayne, "Understanding 'Virtue' and the Virtue of Understanding," in Zagzebski and DePaul, eds., *Intellectual Virtue*, 203–26.

Rorty, Amelie O., ed., *Essays on Aristotle's Ethics* (Berkeley and Los Angeles: University of California Press, 1980).

—— "The Place of Contemplation in Aristotle's *Nicomachean Ethics*," in A. O. Rorty, ed., *Essays on Aristotle's Ethics* (Berkeley and Los Angeles: University of California Press, 1980), 377–94.

Rorty, Richard, *Philosophy and the Mirror of Nature* (Princeton: Princeton University Press, 1979).

Ross, W. D., *Foundations of Ethics* (Oxford: Oxford University Press, 1939).

Rousseau, Jean-Jacques, *Emile: Or On Education*, translated and introduced by Allan Bloom (New York: Basic Books, 1979).

Rushkoff, Douglas, *Coercion: Why We Listen to What "They" Say* (New York: Riverhead Books, 1999).

Ryle, Gilbert, "Pleasure," in *Collected Papers, Volume 2: Collected Essays 1929–1968* (New York: Barnes and Noble Inc., 1971), 326–35.

—— *The Concept of Mind* (Chicago: University of Chicago Press, 1949).

Scanlon, Thomas M., "Reasons, Responsibility and Reliance: Replies to Wallace, Dworkin, and Deigh," *Ethics* 112 (2002), 507–28.

—— *What We Owe to Each Other* (Cambridge, MA: Harvard University Press, 1998).

Scheffler, Samuel, *Human Morality* (Oxford: Oxford University Press, 1992).

Schoeman, Ferdinand, "Aristotle on the Good of Friendship," *Australasian Journal of Philosophy* 63 (1985).

Schroeder, Mark, "Not So Promising After All: Evaluator-Relative Teleology and Common-Sense Morality," *Pacific Philosophical Quarterly* 87 (2006), 348–56.

—— "Teleology, Agent-Relative Value, and 'Good,'" *Ethics* 117 (2007), 265–95.

Schueler, G. F., *Desire: Its Role in Practical Reason and the Explanation of Action* (Cambridge, MA: MIT Press, 1995).

Searle, John, *Intentionality: An Essay in the Philosophy of Mind* (Cambridge: Cambridge University Press, 1983).

Sherman, Nancy, "Aristotle on Friendship and the Shared Life," *Philosophy and Phenomenological Research* 47 (June 1987), 589–613.

—— "Aristotle on the Shared Life," in Neera Kapur Badhwar, ed., *Friendship: A Philosophical Reader* (Ithaca, NY: Cornell University Press, 1993), 91–107.

—— "Character, Planning and Choice in Aristotle," *Review of Metaphysics* 34 (1985), 83–106.

—— *Making a Necessity of Virtue: Aristotle and Kant on Virtue* (Cambridge: Cambridge University Press, 1997).

Shusterman, Richard, "The End of Aesthetic Experience," *Journal of Aesthetics and Art Criticism* 55 (1997), 29–41.

Sidgwick, Henry, *The Methods of Ethics*, 7th edn (Indianapolis: Hackett Publishing Company, 1981; first published 1907).

—— *Outlines of the History of Ethics*, 6th edn (London: MacMillan and Company Limited, 1931; 1st edn 1886).

Simons, Daniel J. and Christopher F. Chabris, "Gorillas in Our Midst: Sustained Inattentional Blindness for Dynamic Events," *Perception* 28 (1999), 1059–74.

Singer, Marcus George, *Generalization in Ethics* (New York: Atheneum, 1961 and 1971).

Slote, Michael, "Agent-Based Virtue Ethics," in Roger Crisp and Michael Slote, *Virtue Ethics* (Oxford: Oxford University Press, 1997).

Smith, Bruce, *The World, the Flesh and Father Smith* (Boston: Houghton Mifflin Co., 1945).

Smith, Michael, *The Moral Problem* (Oxford: Blackwell Publishing Company, 1994).

—— "Neutral and Relative Value after Moore," *Ethics* 113 (2003), 576–98.

—— and Philip Pettit, "Backgrounding Desire," *Philosophical Review* 99 (1990), 565–92.

Sobel, David, "Subjective Accounts of Reasons for Action," *Ethics* 111 (2001), 461–92.

Solomon, David, "Virtue Ethics: Radical or Routine?" in Zagzebski and DePaul, eds., *Virtue Epistemology*, 57–80.

Solomon, Robert C., *The Passions* (New York: Doubleday, 1976).

Sosa, Ernest, "For the Love of Truth?" in Zagzebski and Fairweather, eds., *Virtue Epistemology*, 49–62.

—— "The Place of Truth in Epistemology," in Zagzebski and DePaul, eds., *Intellectual Virtue*, 155–79.

—— "The Raft and the Pyramid: Coherence Versus Foundations in the Theory of Knowledge," in Peter French, Theodore Uehling, Jr., and Howard Wettstein, eds., *Midwest*

Studies in Philosophy, Volume V: Studies in Epistemology (Minneapolis: University of Minnesota Press, 1980), 3–25.

Sosa, Ernest, *Knowledge in Perspective: Selected Essays in Epistemology* (Cambridge: Cambridge University Press, 1991).

Stampe, Dennis, "The Authority of Desire," *Philosophical Review* 96/2 (1987), 335–82.

Statman, Daniel, ed., *Virtue Ethics: A Critical Reader* (Washington DC: Georgetown University Press, 1997 and Edinburgh: University of Edinburgh Press, 1997).

Stern-Gillet, Suzanne, *Aristotle's Philosophy of Friendship* (Albany, NY: State University of New York Press, 1995).

Stratton-Lake, Philip, "How to Deal with Evil Demons: Comment on Rabinowicz and Ronnow-Rasmussen," *Ethics* 115 (2005), 788–98.

Sumner, L. W., *Welfare, Happiness and Ethics* (Oxford: Oxford University Press, 1996).

Taylor, C. C. W., "Pleasure," *Analysis,* Supplementary Volume (1962), 2–19.

Taylor, Charles, "Responsibility for Self," in Gary Watson, ed., *Free Will* (Oxford: Oxford University Press, 1982), 111–26.

Thomson, Judith Jarvis, "Killing, Letting Die and the Trolley Problem," *Monist* 59 (1976), 204–17.

—— "The Trolley Problem," *Yale Law Journal* 94 (1985), 1395–1415.

—— "The Right and the Good," *Journal of Philosophy* 94 (1997), 273–98.

Trianosky, Gregory, "What Is Virtue Ethics All About?" *American Philosophical Quarterly* 27 (October 1990), 335–44.

Van Riel, Gerd, "Does a Perfect Activity Necessarily Yield Pleasure? An Evaluation of the Relation between Pleasure and Activity in Aristotle, *Nichomachean Ethics* VII and X," *International Journal of Philosophical Studies* 7 (1999), 212.

Velleman, David, *The Possibility of Practical Reason* (Oxford: Oxford University Press, 2000).

Vlastos, Gregory, "The Individual as an Object of Love in Plato," in *Platonic Studies*, 2nd edn (Princeton: Princeton University Press, 1981), 3–42.

Vogler, Candace, *Reasonably Vicious* (Cambridge, MA: Harvard University Press, 2002).

Wallace, R. Jay, "Scanlon's Contractualism," *Ethics* 112 (2002), 429–70.

Watson, Gary, "On the Primacy of Character," in *Identity, Character and Morality*, Owen Flanagan and Amelie Rorty, eds. (Cambridge, MA: The MIT Press, 1990), 449–69.

Whiting, Jennifer, "Impersonal Friends," *Monist* 74 (1991), 3–29.

Wiggins, David, *Needs, Values, Truth: Essays in the Philosophy of Value* (Oxford: Blackwell, 1987).

Williams, Bernard, "A Critique of Utilitarianism," in Williams and J. J. C. Smart, *Utilitarianism: For and Against* (Cambridge: Cambridge University Press, 1973).

—— *Ethics and the Limits of Philosophy* (Cambridge, MA: Harvard University Press, 1985).

—— *Making Sense of Humanity and Other Philosophical Papers, 1982–1993* (Cambridge: Cambridge University Press, 1995).

—— *Moral Luck: Philosophical Papers, 1973–1980* (Cambridge: Cambridge University Press, 1981).

Williams, Michael, *Unnatural Doubts* (Princeton: Princeton University Press, 1996).

Wittgenstein, Ludwig, *Philosophical Investigations* (3rd edn), translated by G. E. M. Anscombe (New York: Macmillan Publishing Company, Inc., 1958).

Wood, Allen W., *Kant's Ethical Thought* (Cambridge: Cambridge University Press, 1999).

Zagzebski, Linda, *Virtues of the Mind: An Inquiry into the Nature of Virtue and the Ethical Foundations of Knowledge* (Cambridge: Cambridge University Press, 1996).

—— "From Reliabilism to Virtue Epistemology," in Guy Axtell, ed., *Knowledge, Belief and Character: Readings in Virtue Epistemology* (Lanham, Maryland: Rowman and Littlefield Publishers, Inc., 2000), 113–22.

—— "Intellectual Motivation and the Good of Truth," in Linda Zagzebski and Michael DePaul, eds., *Intellectual Virtue: Perspectives from Ethics and Epistemology* (Oxford: Oxford University Press, 2003), 135–54.

—— and Abrol Fairweather, eds., *Virtue Epistemology: Essays on Epistemic Virtue and Responsibility* (Oxford: Oxford University Press, 2001).

—— and Michael DePaul, eds., *Intellectual Virtue: Perspectives from Ethics and Epistemology* (Oxford: Oxford University Press, 2003).

Index